CREATIVE UNION

CREATIVE UNION

The Professional Organization
of Soviet Composers, 1939–1953

Kiril Tomoff

CORNELL UNIVERSITY PRESS   *Ithaca and London*

First published 2006 by Cornell University Press

Printed in the United States of America

Library of Congress Cataloging-in-Publication Data

Tomoff, Kiril.
  Creative union : the professional organization of Soviet composers, 1939–1953 / Kiril Tomoff.
    p. cm.
  Includes bibliographical references and index.
  ISBN-13: 978-0-8014-4411-1 (cloth : alk. paper)
  ISBN-10: 0-8014-4411-X (cloth : alk. paper)
  1. Soiuz kompozitorov SSSR—History. 2. Music and state—Soviet Union—History. 3. Musicians—Labor unions—Soviet Union—History.
4. Music—Soviet Union—History and criticism. I. Title.
  ML3917.S65T66 2006
  780.6′047—dc22   2006001749

Cornell University Press strives to use environmentally responsible suppliers and materials to the fullest extent possible in the publishing of its books. Such materials include vegetable-based, low-VOC inks and acid-free papers that are recycled, totally chlorine-free, or partly composed of nonwood fibers. For further information, visit our website at www.cornellpress.cornell.edu.

Cloth printing   10   9   8   7   6   5   4   3   2   1

FOR LISA

Contents

Acknowledgments

This book has been a long time in the making. My interest in the place of music in Soviet society was sparked by my first visit to the then collapsing Soviet Union in the summer of 1990 under the auspices of a language instruction exchange between the University of Arizona and Leningrad State University. As I took advantage of what to me were shockingly low ticket prices for world-class orchestral and operatic performances night after night, I was struck by the prominent and important place that such music held for the large, multigenerational audiences in attendance, night after night. I wasn't in Arizona anymore. A few years later, when I had the good fortune to enter the History Department at the University of Chicago, I had the opportunity to investigate that phenomenon more systematically. This study of the Soviet music profession is the end result.

In the years since, I have accumulated many debts of gratitude. Intellectually, academically, and professionally, I am most indebted to the incomparable Sheila Fitzpatrick, whose critical but unflagging support for me and the project has meant the world to me. Her scholarship stands on its own, but her legacy includes the astonishing breadth of her selfless mentorship. The intellectual diversity and rigorous intensity of her community of students is inspiring, and I count myself lucky to have been part of it. My work and my approach to Russian history also benefited immeasurably from the attention, criticism, support, and varying points of view provided by Ron Suny, Richard Hellie, and Larry Zbikowski, to whom I am very grateful. My time in Chicago was also enriched by my friendship with Barbara Schubert, to whom I am thankful for always keeping music on the front burner.

This project gestated in the fertile environment at the University of Chicago created by Sheila Fitzpatrick, Richard Hellie, and Ron Suny at the Russian Studies Workshop. Chicago's workshop system provided the forum for presentations of many chapters of this book, and the people at those workshops provided many examples of accomplishment and pushed me to improve my work. The cohort that was finishing when I arrived first intimidated and then inspired me, and their tales of Soviet archival successes and frustrations served as guides for my own experiences later on. The cohort with whom I went through the Chicago program continued to challenge me while providing the friendship that helped sustain me through the process. Informal discussions over beer after workshops helped form my approach as a historian. So thank you to the Chicago crowd, in particular Terry Martin, Matthew Payne, Julie Hessler, James Harris, Golfo Alexopoulos, Matthew Lenoe, Steven Richmond, Jonathan Bone, Joshua Sanborn, Julie Gilmour, Christopher Burton, Stephen Bittner, the late Jenifer Stenfors, whose memory lives on in the hearts of those who knew her, Michael David, Steven Harris, Charles Hachten, Mark Edele, Christine Haynes, James Bjork, Wendy Norris, Melissa Feinberg, Paul Hanebrink, and especially Alison Smith.

I was also fortunate to spend research trips in Russia with an amazingly gifted, supportive, and tight-knit group of scholars. Exploring Moscow, the archives, and the contours of Russian history together was a joy and privilege. On a weekly basis, over donuts, they encouraged me to continue thinking about the big picture while I was working with the minutiae of archival sources. I extend my appreciation to all of them, but I must single out Frank Grüner and Ethan Pollock, with whom I grappled with postwar Stalinism, and my roommates at the Sportivnaia place, with whom I shared not just my apartment but my excitement, frustrations, and sometimes arguments about daily life in the archives: Brian Kassof, Steven Harris, James Harris, and especially Michael David. That daily life was made immeasurably more comfortable and productive by the tireless efforts of the archival staff in each of the archives in which I worked. Their professionalism under always adverse circumstances is inspirational, but I extend particular appreciation to the reading room staff at the Russian State Archive of Literature and Art: Elena Ermilovna Gafner, Irina Iur'evna Zelenina, and Irina Vadimovna Upadysheva. Many thanks also to Elena Drozdova and Leonid Weintraub, who first provided visa support and have since become friends.

I also thank those composers and Composers' Union administrators (especially Tikhon Nikolaevich Khrennikov, Rodion Konstantinovich Shchedrin, and Alla Semenovna Sedova) who were kind enough to share their experiences with me in personal conversations, sometimes briefly and sometimes over repeated meetings. Memories of my weekly visits to the Moskovskii muzykal'nyi klub will always remind me of the passion with which Muscovites are drawn to their city's rich musical offerings, and I will be forever indebted to its director, Grigorii Samuilovich Frid, a warm, inviting, extremely thoughtful, and all-around wonderful man, for his willingness to extend his hospitality and share his insights about musical life under Stalin.

Funding for the research was provided by a Fulbright-Hays Doctoral Dissertation Abroad Fellowship, for which I will always be thankful, and by the University of Chicago. Dean of Graduate Education Lois Stein's flexibility and understanding proved invaluable. Funding and much appreciated time for writing were provided by the Academic Senate and Center for Ideas and Society at the University of California, Riverside. My colleagues at UCR have provided a most supportive environment for a junior faculty member, for which I am very thankful. Special appreciation is due to Thomas Cogswell and Sharon Salinger.

Earlier drafts of all or parts of chapters 6, 9, and 10 were presented to the Russian Studies Workshop at the University of Chicago. An early version of chapter 3 was presented to the University of Chicago's Modern European History Workshop. A draft of chapter 4 was presented at the conference "Stalin's Last Decade," held in Chicago in March 2000, and a first version of chapter 10 was presented to the PEECS NTNU International Workshop "Patronage under Social-Democracy and State Socialism: A Comparative Study of Academic and Artistic Life in Scandinavia and Eastern Europe," which was held in Trondheim-Brekstad, Norway, in August 1999. It was published as "'Most Respected Comrade . . .': Patrons, Clients, Brokers and Unofficial Networks in the Stalinist Music World," *Contemporary European History* 11, no. 1 (2002): 33–65 (c) 2002 Cambridge University Press, here reprinted with permission. An earlier version of chapter 5 was presented to the Midwest Russian History Workshop meeting in Chicago, October 2000. Finally, two different versions of all or part of chapter 7 were presented at the National Convention of the American Association for the Advancement of Slavic Studies in Boca Raton, Florida, September 1998, and at the Midwest Conference of Modern Russian Historians meeting in Columbus, Ohio, October 1998. I am grateful to all of the participants of these workshops and conferences for their constructive criticism and stimulating discussion. I am particularly indebted to the discussants who spent extra time preparing thought-provoking and challenging comments: Christine Haynes, Michael David-Fox, and György Peteri. I also thank John G. Ackerman at Cornell University Press for his interest in the project, his judiciousness during the acquisitions process, and his insightful editorial suggestions. Thanks also to the anonymous readers for the Press for their encouraging praise, perceptive critiques, and useful recommendations. Their efforts significantly improved the manuscript.

Finally, my family has always been extremely supportive, patient, and understanding throughout the long process that began with instilling a love of academic pursuits (modeled by my parents' ongoing intellectual curiosity and engagement) and forming and fostering interests in history (sparked on those childhood trips with my grandparents) and music (nurtured by my parents through countless music lessons). They supported me emotionally and sometimes financially through years of graduate study, always understanding why it was so important to me to spend so many years in such seemingly arcane pursuits. They visited me in Russia, and they cheered me as this book took shape. So thank you to Joan and Carl Tomoff, William C. and Ruth Skibbe, Alyssa Tomoff and Andrew Gagne, Gareth and Denny Geering. Most of all, thanks to Lisa Geering Tomoff for her encouragement, support, patience, musicality, and love. She has made my otherwise preoccupied life complete. It is to her that I dedicate this book.

Abbreviations

Frequently Cited Organizations

ASM	Asotsiatsiia sovremennoi muzyki, Association of Contemporary Music
DTK	Dom tvorchestva kompozitorov, House of Creativity of Composers, creative resort
GOMETs	Gosudarstvennoe ob″edinenie muzykal′nykh, estradnykh i tsirkovykh predpriiatii, State Association of Music, Estrada and Circus Enterprises
GUMT	Glavnoe upravlenie muzykal′nykh teatrov, Chief Musical Theater Administration (of the VKI)
GUMU	Glavnoe upravlenie muzykal′nykh uchrezhdenii, Chief Musical Institution Administration (of the VKI)
KSP	Komitet po Stalinskim premiiam, Stalin Prize Committee
KDI, KDI RSFSR	Komitet po delam iskusstv RSFSR, Committee on Artistic Affairs of the Russian republic (republican division of VKI)
LSSK	Leningradskii soiuz sovetskikh kompozitorov, Leningrad composers' union (1932–39), Leningrad chapter of the Composers' Union (1939–)
Mossovet	Moskovskii gorodskoi Sovet deputatov, Moscow City Council of Deputies
MSSK	Moskovskii soiuz sovetskikh kompozitorov, Moscow composers' union (1932–39), Moscow chapter of the Composers' Union (1939–).
Muzfond	Muzykal′nyi fond SSSR, Musical fund of the USSR
Muzgiz	Gosudarstvennoe muzykal′noe izdatel′stvo, State Musical Publisher
Narkom	Narodnyi komissar, People's Commissar
Narkomfin	Narodnyi komissariat finansov, People's Commissariat of Finance
Narkompros	Narodnyi komissariat prosveshcheniia, People's Commissariat of Enlightenment
OKhLI	Otdel khudozhestvennoi literatury i iskusstv pri TsK VKP(b), Department of Literature and the Arts of the Central Committee of All-USSR Communist Party (Bolsheviks), Literature and Arts Department (1950–53)
ONK	Otdel nauki i kul′tury TsK KPSS, Department of Science and Culture of the Central Committee of the Communist Party of the Soviet Union, Science and Culture Department (1953)
OPA	Otdel propagandy i agitatsii pri TsK VKP(b), Department of Propaganda and Agitation of the Central Committee of the All-USSR Communist Party (Bolsheviks), Agitprop (1948–53)
Orgkom	Organizatsionnyi komitet, Organizational committee
Rabis	Profsoiuz rabotnikov iskusstv, Trade Union of Arts Workers

RAPM	Rossiiskaia asotsiatsiia proletarskikh muzykantov, Russian Association of Proletarian Musicians
RAPP	Rossiiskaia asotsiatsiia proletarskikh pisatelei, Russian Association of Proletarian Writers
Sovnarkom (SNK)	Sovet narodnykh komissarov, Council of People's Commissars
Sovmin (SM)	Sovet ministrov, Council of Ministers
SSK SSSR (or SSK)	Soiuz sovetskikh kompozitorov SSSR, Union of Soviet Composers of the USSR, all-USSR Composers' Union (1939–), Composers' Union
TsK	Tsentral'nyi komitet VKP(b), Central Committee of the Communist Party
UDI	Upravlenie po delam iskusstv, Administration on Artistic Affairs (local division of VKI)
UPA	Upravlenie propagandy i agitatsii pri TsK VKP(b), Agency of Propaganda and Agitation of the Central Committee of the All-USSR Communist Party (Bolsheviks), Agitprop (1938–48)
VGKO	Vsesoiuznoe gastrol'no-kontsertnoe ob"edineniia, All-USSR Concert Tour Association
VKI	Vsesoiuznyi komitet po delam iskusstv, All-USSR Committee on Artistic Affairs, Committee on Artistic Affairs
VKP(b)	Vsesoiuznaia kommunisticheskaia partiia (bolshevikov), Communist Party, Bolsheviks
VOKS	Vsesoiuznoe obshchestvo kul'turnykh sviazei s zagranitsei, All-USSR Society for Cultural Ties Abroad
VRK	Vsesoiuznyi radio komitet, All-USSR Radio Committee
Vserosskomdram	Vserossiiskoe obshchestvo kompozitorov i dramaticheskikh pisatelei, All-Russian Society of Composers and Dramatists
VTO	Vserossiiskoe teatral'noe obshchestvo, All-Russian Theater Society
VUOAP	Vsesoiuznoe upravlenie dlia okhraneniia avtorskikh prav, All-USSR Administration for the Preservation of Authors' Rights, Copyright Administration

Archives

GARF	Gosudarstvennyi arkhiv Rossiiskoi Federatsii, State Archive of the Russian Federation
RGALI	Rossiiskii gosudarstvennyi arkhiv literatury i iskusstv, Russian State Archive of Literature and the Arts
RGANI	Rossiiskii gosudarstvennyi arkhiv noveishei istorii, Russian State Archive of Contemporary History
RGASPI	Rossiiskii gosudarstvennyi arkhiv sotsial'no-politicheskoi istorii, Russian State Archive of Socio-Political History
TsMAM	Tsentral'nyi munitsipial'nyi arkhiv gorod Moskvy, Central Municipal Archive of the City of Moscow

Terms for Citation of Archival Sources, Published Laws, and Musical Scores

f.	fond (holding)
op.	opis' (register)
d.	delo (file)
dd.	dela (files)
l.	list (sheet/page)
ll.	listy (sheets/pages)
ob.	oborot (reverse)
pt.	point
pts.	points
mm.	measure numbers
st.	stat'ia (article)

Introduction

When we read about the arts in Stalin's Soviet Union, we often encounter individual tales of artistic geniuses struggling against a capricious Soviet bureaucracy and Stalin's brutally repressive, arbitrary, and incompetent interventions. The 1936 denunciation of Dmitrii Shostakovich's opera *Lady Macbeth of Mtsensk* on the pages of *Pravda,* the brutal murders of theater greats Vsevolod Meyerhold and Solomon Mikhoels, the relentless hounding of poets Anna Akhmatova and Boris Pasternak, and Andrei Zhdanov's coarse browbeating of composers and musicians in 1948 are just a few of the most famous examples of the dangers that confronted artists in Stalin's Soviet Union.

But coupled with many of these stories are equally striking tales of artistic achievement. The gales of applause that greeted Shostakovich's Fifth Symphony in 1937, his first major public performance after the *Lady Macbeth* affair, the runaway popular success of the Stalinist musicals of the 1930s, and the nearly mythical power of Soviet wartime songs and of Shostakovich's Seventh Symphony, the *Leningrad,* all bear witness to the profound significance of music in that same Stalinist Soviet Union. What accounts for this seeming paradox of spectacular artistic achievement in the face of fierce repression? Though the phenomenon has been noted in the past, earlier studies have tended to focus on the often heroic struggle of the lone artist against the repressive system.[1] This focus on individual cases fails to explain the prominence in Soviet society not only of music itself but also of its performers and composers.

In the pages that follow, I attempt to provide a more complete explanation by shifting primary focus from the individual artist to the Soviet music profession as a whole and especially to the Union of Soviet Composers, the institution that came to dominate musical production in the Soviet Union. The Union

---

1. For the paradox, see N. G. Shakhnazarova, *Paradoksy sovetskoi muzykal'noi kul'tury 30-e gody* (Moscow: Gosudarstvennyi institut iskusstvoznaniia, Izdatel'stvo Indrik, 2001). The focus on the lone artist was initiated by Max Eastman's paradigmatically titled *Artists in Uniform: A Study of Literature and Bureaucratism* (New York: Knopf, 1934).

of Soviet Composers was one of four institutions which were known in Soviet parlance as "creative unions." Each creative union dominated artistic production in its respective area of expertise, the Composers' Union in music, the Writers' Union in literature, the Architects' Union in architecture, and the Artists' Union in the visual arts. It is impossible to understand Soviet culture without ascertaining the nature of these creative unions and their role in the Stalinist system. I analyze the Composers' Union in institutional, cultural, social, and economic terms in order to show that in the Soviet cultural world, artistic expertise mattered. It afforded professional musicians the agency to construct a musical culture that appealed to audiences at home and abroad.

Even a cursory list of prominent Soviet composers demonstrates the acclaim generated by those who fell under the purview of the Soviet music system. Besides the twentieth-century greats Dmitrii Shostakovich and Sergei Prokofiev, the list includes Aram Khachaturian, Reinhold Glier, Nikolai Miaskovskii, and Dmitrii Kabalevskii, as well as prominent post-Stalin-era composers such as Alfred Schnittke, Arvo Pärt, Giya Kancheli, and Rodion Shchedrin. Popular music also thrilled listeners during the Stalin years. Songwriters like the film and musical composer Isaak Dunaevskii attained fame that surpassed even that of the performers who sang their songs. Perhaps most remarkable, composers of all kinds came to occupy a particularly elite position in Soviet society. Their success *as a profession* is a central theme of this book, one that sheds new light on the nature of the Stalinist system.

Sources declassified after the collapse of the Soviet Union enable us to describe the system in which these artists worked. In the pages that follow, I analyze how composers and musicologists interacted with powerful political leaders and the government bureaucracy, and how their Composers' Union competed with other cultural institutions to define and create Soviet music. I examine the Composers' Union not as a government oversight body or a trade union, but as a professional organization whose control function was contained within a bureaucratic structure designed and populated entirely by professionals. The Composers' Union gathered the Soviet Union's musical experts into one institution and eventually used the expertise that it embodied to dominate Soviet musical production.

This argument helps to explain how the Soviet cultural elite was formed and how it operated. It hinges on three closely related concepts: *expertise, authority,* and *agency.* I define "expertise" as mastery of technical knowledge that requires advanced educational training. In the music profession, that expertise was the ability to use theoretical understandings of music either in discussions about music (musicologists) or in the production of new music (composers). This definition does not include technical mastery of a musical instrument (performing musicians), though I certainly do not wish to minimize the skill that such mastery requires. This distinction not only follows a common, characteristically modern division between so-called head and hand work but also conforms to the organizational principles of the Soviet music world itself.

I define "authority" as power conferred on individuals or institutions by other groups of individuals. To accrue authority, an individual must have an audience, and often a knowledgeable one.[2] Authority is closely related to several other mutually reinforcing concepts, including prestige, respect, and privilege. Though increasing authority generally also enhanced one's prestige, respect, and privilege, the relationship between the four is not necessarily predictable, since different kinds of audiences conferred different kinds of authority. The interplay between prestige, respect, privilege, and the various possible audiences before whom Soviet music professionals performed (musically and otherwise) thus makes authority an extremely complicated concept. Consequently, I devote a great deal of attention to untangling and analyzing several different audiences and the authority they granted.

Finally, I define "agency" as the ability to act within a complicated system of restraints. Whereas many early studies of professions stress a profession's *autonomy* from the state, I suggest that it is much more useful to inquire into how structures constrain or enable professionals' actions. "Agency" as I have defined it here is *not* synonymous with "autonomy," a more absolute concept. The Composers' Union was decidedly not an autonomous institution. Party leaders always could and sometimes did intervene in the music world. Nevertheless, the Union's eventual monopoly of musical expertise allowed music professionals to maneuver within the system. "Agency" thus captures the vast gray area between the two poles of autonomy and subjugation and enables analysis of the breadth of music professionals' experience in the Stalinist system.[3] Understanding the real possibilities of action that agency suggests can help explain both the productivity of Soviet composers during the Stalin period and their attainment of elite status within the Soviet Union.

This definition of "agency" and the related argument that the Composers' Union is best understood as a professional organization suggest the emergence in the Soviet Union of a profoundly modern social category, the professional, in a field—music—that would be unexpected in more typically studied Anglo-American and continental European contexts.[4] For the Composers' Union was indeed a professional organization. It was an elite, organized occupational

2. In her study of the Romanian intelligentsia, Katherine Verdery calls such knowledgeable audiences "cognizant publics," a concept derived from her reading of Pierre Bourdieu. See Katherine Verdery, *National Ideology under Socialism: Identity and Cultural Politics in Ceausescu's Romania* (Berkeley and Los Angeles: University of California Press, 1991).

3. William H. Sewell, Jr., provides an excellent analysis of a long-term debate about the relative explanatory power of individual agency and determinant structure in William H. Sewell, Jr., "A Theory of Structure: Duality, Agency, and Transformation," *American Journal of Sociology* 98, no. 1 (Jul 1992): 1–29. My understanding of agency lies between the two explanatory poles that he describes. That is, actors' "agency" cannot be understood without an analysis of the structural restrictions placed on their activity—and vice versa.

4. From their original focus on the Anglo-American "free professions," these studies gradually became more inclusive and descriptive, extending and modifying the Anglo-American model to fit similar high-status occupational groups in continental Europe and developing complex but disputed lists of traits that qualified specific groups as professions. For a concise description of the consensus on the historiography of professions, see Ivan Waddington, "Professions," in *The Social Science Encyclopedia*, ed. A. Kuper and J. Kuper, 2d ed. (London: Routledge, 1996), 677–78.

group defined by its creative or intellectual authority. That collective authority eventually earned it state-sanctioned control over a specific type of socially useful labor, the production and interpretation of Soviet music. Practicing this labor required a high level of expertise and educational accomplishment, typical preconditions of professionalization in other contexts. Like professions elsewhere, the professional organization of Soviet composers controlled its members. It set the terms for admission and decided the success of each potential applicant, and its leadership set the standards of appropriate professional behavior and disciplined members who did not follow those standards.[5]

To understand the Composers' Union as a professional organization is to recognize the structural similarities between the Composers' Union in the Soviet system and professions in other modern European societies. In the Soviet Union, as elsewhere, understanding how discrete professions take shape requires examining their successful struggles against other occupational groups with claims to similar socially useful labor.[6] Because Soviet society was embedded in an immense bureaucracy, however, professions took shape in the course of competitions between institutions rather than occupations. Because they shared a cultural field, performers might seem to be the natural professional rivals of composers and musicologists. But they often formed close personal and artistic collaborations rather than competing with one another. Instead, competition for priority within the music field played out in the institutional struggles between the Composers' Union and the Committee on Artistic Affairs, the government organization that oversaw the activities of musicians. In the end, the Composers' Union consolidated its jurisdiction in the music field by marginalizing the Committee on Artistic Affairs.[7]

One of the most distinctive features of the Soviet music profession is the socially useful labor that professionals offered society. Members of the Soviet music profession created and interpreted Soviet music. From at least the middle of the nineteenth century, music had always been an important component of Russian national culture. The Soviets inherited a broad commitment to musical culture, but music became, if anything, even more significant in the Soviet period. Even in the 1930s, the success of the Soviet system internationally was trumpeted through the exploits of Soviet musicians at international competitions, and musicians were held up alongside pilots and polar explorers as exemplary heroes for new generations of Soviet citizens. In fact, all the arts were extremely important to the Soviet system, which conceived of artists as indispensable

---

5. Whatever their disagreements, most who write about professions agree that these characteristics define a professional group.

6. Andrew Abbott, *The System of Professions: An Essay on the Division of Expert Labor* (Chicago: University of Chicago Press, 1988).

7. For another study of the institutional struggles of the Committee on Artistic Affairs, see Leonid Maksimenkov, *Sumbur vmesto muzyki: Stalinskaia kul'turnaia revoliutsiia, 1936–1938* (Moscow: Iuridicheskaia kniga, 1997).

agents of enlightenment and ideological education. According to the oft-quoted quip, they were engineers of human souls. And they performed this task well enough to warrant the elite status afforded them.

But among the arts, music was especially difficult for politicians and bureaucrats to control because of its inherently abstract nature. Composers and musicologists could use their privileged access to the interpretation of this abstract art form to ensure that they always had some maneuverability, that they preserved their agency. In this sense, they were more like practitioners of abstract sciences, such as physics and mathematics, than their closer counterparts, the writers. After all, members of the party elite were confident of their ability to interpret written texts, see through the veils of Aesopian language, and intervene when they thought writers, poets, or playwrights had gotten out of control. They did not have that confidence with respect to musical scores. Considering the importance of music in the Russian heritage and its phenomenal success in the Soviet system, it is striking, but perhaps not surprising, that music professionals would come to occupy such an elite status in Soviet society.

This study of the Soviet music profession also speaks directly to the nature of the Stalinist system and its evolution, particularly in the postwar years. I contend that postwar Stalinist society was not a mere resumption of the structures established before the war, but that despite many strong continuities, the war did indeed change things.[8] The history of the Composers' Union sheds light on many of those changes, including the reconfiguration of the Stalinist social, cultural, and material elite; the increasing importance of expertise in Soviet governance; the party leadership's efforts to engage in ideological dialogues rather than endless purges; and the rise of official anti-Semitism.

Finally, in the pages that follow, I dispense with "the state" as a useful explanatory concept in the Soviet context, instead disaggregating it into various component parts, including the party, the government, and such officially dubbed "social organizations" as the creative unions. As far as is practicable, each of these still vast entities is further disaggregated into specific actors. I treat the "state" only as an arena for interactions that are analogous to many of the processes that students of modern Western societies have observed in bureaucracies, courts, markets, and public spheres. By simultaneously shifting the analytical terrain regarding the arts from autonomy and subjugation to the more sophisticated maneuverability and agency, I hope to demonstrate that technical expertise gave individuals and groups in the Stalinist Soviet Union real possibilities of creative power.

Of course, no book about the Soviet music system can proceed without noting the controversy in Shostakovich studies that has been raging since 1979, when

---

8. The most forcefully articulated argument about the transformative power of the war to date is Amir Weiner, *Making Sense of War: The Second World War and the Fate of the Bolshevik Revolution* (Princeton: Princeton University Press, 2001).

Solomon Volkov published what he claimed were Shostakovich's memoirs.[9] When the authenticity of the memoirs was challenged and defended, the terms of this debate were set: was Shostakovich a loyal Soviet composer or a tortured dissident? Though I do not seek to participate in this controversy because I do not think the terms of the debate capture the complexity of the historical context, I offer an outsider's comment by way of explaining my own limited use of Volkov's *Testimony*.

This furor is in essence the clash of two views, an analytic scholarly view typically espoused by musicologists and music historians using the tools of their trade to analyze Shostakovich and his music, and a view typically advanced or inspired by emigré Soviet intellectuals who employ some of the most potent tropes of Russian culture to interpret Shostakovich—what I will call here the metaphorical view. Those who take the analytic view insist on scholarly standards of source evaluation and music analysis and typically push for a reading of Shostakovich's career and music that seeks an appreciation of the multiple interpretations possible in our approach to musical texts. This view has been most thoroughly expounded by Laurel Fay, who has written the definitive scholarly biography of Shostakovich and whose systematic and convincing refutations of the authenticity of *Testimony* put her at the center of the controversy. It can also be found in Richard Taruskin's sophisticated reading of the meaning of Shostakovich.[10]

Those who take the metaphorical view, on the other hand, seek to understand Shostakovich as an unambiguously dissident figure whose music spoke the truth to Stalin just as the traditional Russian literary figure, the Holy Fool or *iurodivyi*, spoke the truth to the imperial Russian tsar, a theme central to the national Russian literary canon and one held dear by many Russian artists and intellectuals. At its worst, this "*iurodivyi* thesis" imposes clumsy literary codes on Shostakovich's musical tropes.[11] At its best, it provides evidence of how Shostakovich's music was received and thus helps to explain its power among the Soviet intelligentsia from as early as the mid-1930s.[12]

From outside the musicological and journalistic circles in which this dispute has raged, the bitterness appears, at least in part, to result from a clash of discourses, modes of understanding, and evidentiary standards.[13] In *Shostakovich*

9. Solomon Volkov, *Testimony: The Memoirs of Dmitry Shostakovich as Related to and Edited by Solomon Volkov*, trans. A. W. Bouis (New York: Harper and Row, 1979).

10. Laurel Fay, *Shostakovich: A Life* (Oxford: Oxford University Press, 2000); idem, "Shostakovich versus Volkov: Whose *Testimony*?" *Russian Review* 39, no. 4 (1980): 484–93; idem, "Volkov's *Testimony* Reconsidered," in *A Shostakovich Casebook*, ed. Malcolm Hamrick Brown (Bloomington: Indiana University Press, 2004), 22–66. Richard Taruskin, *Defining Russia Musically: Historical and Hermeneutical Essays* (Princeton: Princeton University Press, 1997), 468–510. Brown's collection is a convenient summary of this position.

11. Ian MacDonald, *The New Shostakovich* (London: Fourth Estate, 1990).

12. Solomon Volkov, *Shostakovich and Stalin: The Extraordinary Relationship between the Great Composer and the Brutal Dictator* (New York: Knopf, 2004).

13. The contours of the debate were sharpened again in 2004 by Malcolm Hamrick Brown's

and Stalin, Volkov illustrates strikingly clearly the discursive clash as he repeatedly makes vague reference to the dynamics of the Russian intelligentsia, its political engagement, the conditions of friendship within it, and so forth. His metaphorical understanding of Shostakovich's career seeks to capture the essence rather than the mundane facts of the composer's relationship with the regime.[14] Volkov reduces that relationship to a personal struggle between two great personalities, Shostakovich and Stalin. His picture contains interesting insights, not into Shostakovich personally (though in general his sarcastic voice of the 1970s may have been partially captured in *Testimony*), but into views held by some members of the creative intelligentsia that surrounded him. It is for those insights that I utilize *Testimony* in this study, and for those reasons that I cite the book under Volkov's name, not Shostakovich's.

I seek in this book to move beyond debates focused on individuals to a study of the professional music system. In taking this approach, I hope to explain both the paradox with which this introduction began and the views of those who perceived systemic, institutionalized relationships in personal terms and thought about them through familiar cultural metaphors. Such a reading was understandable given the personalized power relations at the top of the system and the personalized networks that permeated the rest of it, and I analyze these networks in the book's final chapter.

This book has three parts. Part I describes the formation and basic activities of the All-USSR Union of Soviet Composers and its municipal and republican predecessors of the 1930s. Though some examples of typical activities are unavoidably taken from the postwar period, I have attempted to concentrate on the period through the end of World War II, by which time the Composers' Union had become a full-blown professional organization. The emergence of a professional organization was the result of a nearly decade-long process during which an institutional infrastructure was constructed, came to be directed exclusively by professional composers and musicologists, and proved its utility to society during the cataclysmic upheaval of World War II. During the war, composers and musicologists were left to their own devices more than at any other time during the years covered by this study. Like so many others in Soviet society, their interests and those of the regime coincided more closely than before or after, while they both fought to survive the brutal Nazi invasion and occupation. Soviet musicians served in many capacities during the war, but the vast

---

edited collection, *A Shostakovich Casebook,* which reprints Laurel Fay's articles and accompanies them with a systematic and overwhelming refutation of the literal authenticity of the *Testimony* document and by Volkov's effort, in *Shostakovich and Stalin,* to lay out the *iurodivyi* thesis systematically and more thoroughly than he had previously.

14. What is implicit in Volkov's work is made explicit in another emigré intellectual's memoirs: Rostislav Dubinsky, *Stormy Applause: Making Music in a Worker's State* (1989; repr., Boston: Northeastern University Press, 1992). In an unpaginated introductory note, Dubinsky notes exactly this goal: to reproduce the essence, not the precise facts, of his experiences as an elite performing musician.

majority energetically directed their intellectual and creative powers to the war effort, writing the songs and symphonies that even today are emblematic of that titanic struggle.

Part II concentrates on the sometimes traumatic interaction between music professionals, the Composers' Union, and the government and party bureaucrats who administered the cultural bureaucracy during Andrei Zhdanov's ideological campaigns (the Zhdanovshchina, 1946–48) and the anticosmopolitanism campaigns at the end of Stalin's life (1949–53). This period witnessed the disintegration of the theoretical congruence between the priorities of professionals and party ideologues, which had peaked during the war. After 1945, the party elite set about reasserting ideological discipline, first within the party and then within the creative intelligentsia, those all-important agents of ideological production and enlightenment.[15] Though the Composers' Union was not a direct target of the early phases of the Zhdanovshchina, professional leaders' ability to set their own professional agenda, so strong during the war, came under assault. As chapter 4 demonstrates, they responded with a revealing two-part effort, first to preserve distinct professional and political spheres and then to use their control over the professional sphere to fulfill the tasks assigned to them according to the party's agenda. This effort shows the importance of agency in understanding how the profession operated. The professional leadership *worked* to keep political and professional spheres intact, but they did so as loyal party members.

Chapter 5 explains the genesis and results of the party's most dramatic intervention into professional music life. There could be no clearer evidence that the Soviet music profession was not and could not be autonomous than the public browbeating and humiliation meted out to the leading Soviet composers in the early months of 1948, and the wholesale change in leadership that accompanied it in the Composers' Union, the government's Committee on Artistic Affairs, and at the prestigious Bol'shoi Theater. Still, it was in the context of this intervention that the Composers' Union realized its decisive moment of professional success, gaining initial input even into music performance and more decisively marginalizing its institutional competitors. The new leadership could bide its time before starting off on the same path as its predecessors, maintaining a distinct professional realm based on an institutional monopolization of expertise.

That the new professional leadership maintained this agency became clear during the next general party campaign in the cultural world, the struggle against so-called cosmopolitans in cultural and intellectual life. If the Zhdanovshchina had primarily been a campaign for stricter ideological discipline, anticosmopolitanism constituted an effort to mold Soviet institutions through a

---

15. For an interesting study of the relationship between the academic intellectual elite and Soviet ideology formation after the war, see Ethan Pollock, "The Politics of Knowledge: Party Ideology and Soviet Science, 1945–1953" (Ph.D. diss., University of California, Berkeley, 2000).

personnel policy biased in favor of Russians and against Jews. Chapter 6 traces these efforts from 1949 until the end of the Stalin period. It demonstrates the surprising fact that it was the leaders of the Composers' Union who defined the operative terms of anticosmopolitanism within the broader, unavoidable framework established by the party leadership. Despite the overtly anti-Semitic elements of the official campaign and the presence of a large and often resented group of successful popular song composers who happened to be Jewish, the Composers' Union largely managed to avoid the disastrous results of official anti-Semitism that struck other Soviet institutions. In chapter 7, I examine the effects of party intervention on the internal operations of the Composers' Union over the entire postwar period, including the configuration of its creative apparatus, its concentration of expertise within the profession, and its preservation of a professional realm for theoretical discussion and music composition. Chapters 6 and 7 thus finish tracing the trajectory of the professional organization of Soviet composers from its rather humble origins to its status as a full-fledged cultural elite, and they show the importance of that elite in setting the terms of common, official ideology, through the meanings that it created within its institutional context and through its decisive control of expertise.

In Part III, I examine different aspects of the other concept that is key to understanding Soviet creative professions and Stalinist cultural elite formation more generally: intellectual or artistic authority. Chapter 8 describes the basic system of material support available to composers and musicologists, especially funding from the professional organization and the incredibly uneven distribution of royalties. Since Composers' Union leaders maintained virtually unmonitored control over the Union's funding apparatus, the leadership's priorities, creative preferences, and personal connections determined which professionals received grants, loans, subsidized working vacations, and the other perquisites of Composers' Union membership. As is the case with any royalties system, composers whose work was popular with general audiences were rewarded most generously. Indeed, some composers were able to amass stunning fortunes, though such lavish incomes were viewed as tainted with illegitimacy. Chapter 9 analyzes the extraordinary rewards that simultaneously reflected a composer's authority with elite audiences and, by conferring official prestige, molded that authority and shaped the audience's tastes. Honorary titles and Stalin Prizes made and marked the pinnacle of the Soviet cultural elite. Taken together, professional authority, prestige, official status, and unofficial recognition constituted composers' intellectual or creative authority, both individually and as an elite group in Stalinist society. Enshrined in the Stalin Prize Committee, the most authoritative members of that elite also formed one of the crucial interfaces between the political leadership and the intelligentsia.

In Chapter 10, I address another of those crucial interfaces, the ubiquitous unofficial networks, primarily of patronage, that permeated the official bureaucracy. It argues that the official bureaucracy and related resource allocation institutions could not fulfill their respective tasks. On a case-by-case basis, individuals could and did utilize unofficial networks to facilitate their negotiations through the official bureaucracy. At the same time, the existence of unofficial networks was a continual source of suspicion for those outside each one. The entire music system cannot be understood without coming to grips with the significance of these informal networks.

By virtue of its institutional monopolization of theoretical expertise and through its members' informal relationships and real professional agency, the Composers' Union dominated musical production in the Soviet Union. It determined the hierarchies of prestige and privilege in the music world, controlled many of the resources allocated to the music field, took responsibility for setting and policing the boundaries of appropriate professional behavior, and defined the nature of Soviet music.

Part I

THE PROFESSIONAL
ORGANIZATION
OF SOVIET COMPOSERS

Whether they examine the "free professions" characteristic of Anglo-American capitalist parliamentary democratic societies or the more state-regulated professional groups of continental Europe, most scholars of professions agree that a profession is an elite occupational group defined by its state-protected monopoly on a specific type of socially valuable, expertise-based work. The All-USSR Union of Soviet Composers (SSK) was a professional organization analogous to more familiar professions of modern societies that emerged contemporaneously with the Soviet Union. After a nearly decade-long formation process, the Composers' Union exhibited almost all of these defining characteristics. The rest were achieved in the cauldron of World War II, when the Composers' Union consolidated its institutional structure and its members demonstrated the extreme importance—the social significance—of their creative work.

The Soviet Union shared with its contemporary modern societies the phenomenon of the profession. However, the Soviet Union was also a peculiar modern phenomenon, governed as it was by a state with ambitions of nearly complete control of its population. It would be extremely surprising to find that its professional groups were more or less exact replicas of professional groups elsewhere. They were not. Part I of this study begins to examine that Soviet exceptionalism. By introducing the relationship between the municipal and all-USSR composers' unions and other Stalinist institutions—especially the government's arts watchdog, the Committee on Artistic Affairs—it also sets the stage for one of the great conflicts that marked the professional organization's most significant postwar successes. Just as professions elsewhere emerged through conflict with other groups that claimed solutions to similar socially relevant problems, so the Composers' Union emerged in the midst of tension with the Committee on Artistic Affairs. Part I traces that tension from its early seeds in the mid-1930s through World War II. It describes the emerging membership contours of a professional organization that united otherwise potentially disparate groups of professionals, conservatory-trained composers, musicologists, and popular song writers, but not performers. And it analyzes the first phases of the centralization of authority that characterized the professional organization throughout the Stalin period.

Part I begins by examining the details of the Composers' Union's institutional growth from theoretically related but distinct municipal and republican composers' unions in the early 1930s to a single all-USSR Composers' Union with developed institutional forms, hierarchical decision-making structures, control over membership, and responsibility for professional behavior and work. This bureaucratic history helps us to understand the institutional constraints placed on composers and musicologists, the institutional context in which they lived and worked, and the formal development of an important Stalinist cultural profession. In a society so deeply embedded in bureaucracy, we must understand the bureaucracy to understand the society.

CHAPTER 1

The Formation of the Composers' Union, 1932–41

Organized music professionalism in Russia can be dated to the formation of the Imperial Russian Musical Society in 1859 and its music conservatories in St. Petersburg (1862) and Moscow (1866).[1] Through these conservatories and its system of secondary music schools, the Imperial Russian Musical Society formed the main center of music professionalism that bequeathed a rich but incompletely solidified professional music heritage to the fledgling Soviet state after the Revolution. In the 1920s, that heritage became a flash point of contention between new associations that sought to organize and dominate the musical culture of the revolutionary society.[2] The most famous of these feuding associations were the Russian Association of Proletarian Musicians (RAPM) and the Association of Contemporary Music (ASM). Their often vitriolic disputes culminated in the temporary ascendance of RAPM in the late 1920s and early 1930s before the whole system of the 1920s was swept away in a landmark 1932 Central Committee resolution that called for the creation of new artistic organizations, the creative unions.

The Composers' Union was the music field's creative union. It emerged from humble origins in the 1930s to dominate the Soviet music world by the end of the 1940s.

Creative unions were designed to be different sorts of Stalinist institutions. The Composers' Union formed gradually, from the advent of creative unions in 1932 to the foundation of the all-USSR Organizational Committee of the Union of Soviet Composers in 1939 and to the expanded reach of the all-USSR

---

1. The Russian Musical Society became the Imperial Russian Musical Society in 1873, four years after it began receiving limited state funding, but it was always patronized by members of the royal family. Lynn Sargeant, "A New Class of People: The Conservatoire and Musical Professionalization in Russia, 1861–1917," *Music and Letters* 85, no. 1 (2004): 41–61; and idem, "*Kashchei the Immortal:* Liberal Politics, Cultural Memory, and the Rimsky-Korsakov Scandal of 1905," *Russian Review* 64, no. 1 (2005): 22–43.

2. See Amy Nelson, *Music for the Revolution: Musicians and Power in Early Soviet Russia* (University Park: Pennsylvania State University Press, 2004).

Composers' Union beyond the cultural capitals just before the Second World War. Though it was always subject to outside ideological monitoring, the Composers' Union became a bureaucratic institution juridically distinct from both government oversight committees and the Communist Party. Thus the bureaucracy that most closely touched the lives of composers and musicologists was formed primarily according to the demands of Composers' Union leaders, all of whom were, by the beginning of the war, professional composers and musicologists.

Prehistory: Russian Music Professionalism and Revolutionary Cultural Politics

The vaunted Russian school of music was initially created by art critics whose nationalist ideology exhorted and exalted the diverse works of aristocratic dilettante composers, especially the famed Mighty Five: Milyi Balakirev, Aleksandr Borodin, Cesar Cui, Modest Musorgsky, and Nikolai Rimsky-Korsakov. The most powerful voice at the creation of this Russian nationalist school was Vladimir Stasov, whose forceful writings and longevity shaped the history of Russian music for more than a century.[3] From the 1860s on, the most powerful competitor to Stasov's emerging nationalist conception—and the target of his critical reviews—was the Imperial Russian Music Society (IRMO) and its leaders, Anton and Nikolai Rubinstein. The brothers Rubinstein considered that Russian music would be best served through the professionalization provided by Western European–style conservatory education.

In the 1860s the IRMO opened conservatories in St. Petersburg and Moscow and began creating a large system of secondary music schools. It also pressured the Russian state to confer legal status and privileges on its conservatory graduates and provide pension rights to its conservatory professors. This long and difficult struggle was mostly accomplished before the 1905 revolution, and by the beginning of World War I the IRMO could legitimately claim to have created a class of professional musicians whose status was codified in Russian law.[4] Prerevolutionary music professionalism thus hinged primarily on the legal provisions afforded those who successfully completed advanced conservatory education.

But the prominent role of aristocratic dilettantes in nineteenth-century musical culture and the practices of conservatory enrollment limited and conditioned this conservatory professionalism, preventing it from flowering into a profession according to the technical definition I use here.[5] Important though

---

3. On the dangers of following Stasov's definition of Russian music and for an alternative, see Richard Taruskin, *Defining Russia Musically: Historical and Hermeneutical Essays* (Princeton: Princeton University Press, 1997).

4. Sargeant, "A New Class," 43–48, 60.

5. I distinguish between the general sense of "professional musician," as someone who makes a living in music, and the technical definition of a profession outlined in the introduction.

a conservatory graduation credential had become, one could make a living as a musician without it, and many students only completed part of the program before embarking on music teaching careers. Some peculiarities of prerevolutionary conservatory education policies and practice left strong imprints on the development of the music profession after the Revolution. Class and gender biases in the selection of disciplines within the conservatory attached long-lasting associations to musicians trained there. These biases endowed composers and a few select instrumentalists (especially violinists and cellists) with the most prestige, while other orchestral musicians (usually recruited from lower estates) had far less. Women matriculated in especially high numbers in the piano department but completed their degrees far less frequently than men, as they left the conservatories for teaching careers or marriages.[6] With certain exceptions, the biases created by these patterns would continue after the Revolution. Outside of opera and ballet, women would be strikingly underrepresented among Soviet musicians, and precious few would enter the Stalinist professional music organization, which was dominated by musicologists and especially composers.

Because of the odd relationship between the conservatories, the IRMO, and the Imperial Russian state, the conservatories afforded one of the few paths of even limited upward mobility for the Russian empire's large, oppressed Jewish population. Though rampant anti-Semitism posed serious problems for Jewish students and their conservatories before the Revolution,[7] their access to advanced musical education and its legal status helped make Jews particularly prominent in the Soviet music profession.

The heritage of this conservatory professionalism was carried into the Soviet period by professors who reproduced the training they received from such figures as Rimsky-Korsakov, Anatol Liadov, Sergei Taneev, Anton Arenskii, and Mikhail Ippolitov-Ivanov. Among the most influential such professors were Reinhold Glier, Mikhail Gnesin, and especially Nikolai Miaskovskii. Glier, the eventual head of the Composers' Union, was a professor at the Moscow Conservatory for twenty years. From 1925 to 1951 Gnesin held various professorial posts at the Moscow and Leningrad conservatories and at the top music education school in the Soviet Union, the Gnesin Institute for Musical Education, which was founded by his sisters Evgeniia, Mariia, and Elena Gnesina, the last of whom ably directed it throughout the Stalin period. His students included both of the Composers' Union's most powerful leaders, Aram Khachaturian and Tikhon Khrennikov. Miaskovskii's nearly thirty-year tenure at the Moscow Conservatory from 1921 until his death in 1950 allowed him to instill rigorous ideals of technical mastery and intellectual musical construction in generations of composers, including Khachaturian. In addition to his conservatory post and his leadership positions in the Composers' Union, Miaskovskii's extensive work as a consultant on publishing and programming made him one of the most influential Soviet musicians, whose opinion helped determine

6. Sargeant, "A New Class," 48–54.
7. Ibid., 55–60.

what was published and performed. Contemporaries and students alike stressed Miaskovskii's wide-ranging musical interests, his remarkable musical memory, and his openness to diverse musical styles, provided they were professionally executed.[8] A solid, advanced education in musical theory and classical compositional techniques would prove to be important to Composers' Union leaders throughout the Stalin period.

The first fifteen years after the Revolution were turbulent ones for Soviet musicians. Groups of composers, musicologists, and performers organized music associations to promote their conceptions about the place music should occupy in revolutionary society. Amy Nelson has identified three musical agendas that found organizational expression in the 1920s: Russian traditionalists, modernists, and advocates of "proletarian" culture. These three found rough representation respectively among the conservatory professorate, the ASM, and a series of groups who spoke for proletarian music, including RAPM.[9] Representatives of the ASM and the proletarian music groups waged vitriolic press campaigns throughout the 1920s before their sparring came to a head during the Cultural Revolution that accompanied crash industrialization and agricultural collectivization from 1928 to 1932.

Attempting to capitalize on the class war spirit of the Cultural Revolution and follow the lead of its literary namesake, RAPP (Russian Association of Proletarian Writers), RAPM sought to dominate musical production, browbeating its modernist and popular opponents, supporting preferential admissions for proletarian applicants to the conservatories, calling for a unified state music policy beneficial to RAPM, and trying to write proletarian music. Though all of these efforts were partly successful, by 1932 the energies of the Cultural Revolution were spent, and RAPM was dissolved in a call for more catholic creative unions.

Even after the wrangling between them in the 1920s came to an end, all three creative positions continued to exert an influence on the development of the Stalinist professional organization, the Composers' Union. Though they remained largely outside the fray in the 1920s, the professorate emerged from the upheavals of the late 1920s and early 1930s relatively unscathed, and their work training new composers and musicologists meant that they had a profound influence shaping the artistic outlooks of the Stalinist music profession's younger generation.

The ASM was a large and diverse group that most famously included such radical modernists as Nikolai Roslavets, who devised a twelve-tone compositional technique independently and contemporaneously with Arnold Schoen-

8. Vissarion Shebalin, "Iz vospominanii o Nikolae Iakovleviche Miaskovskom," in *N. Ia. Miaskovskii: Sobranie materialov v dvukh tomakh*, 2nd ed., ed. S. Shlifshtein (Moscow: Muzyka, 1964), 1:276–98, here 295; A. B. Gol'denveizer, "O Miaskovskom—cheloveke," in ibid., 254–55; Dmitrii Kabalevskii, "O N. Ia. Miaskovskom," in ibid., 307–33, here 309, 315, 317; Vladimir Vlasov, "Nikolai Iakovlevich Miaskovskii slushaet muzyku," in ibid., 351–55.

9. Nelson, *Music for the Revolution*, 42–43.

berg. Roslavets was a fiery polemicist in the 1920s who thought that the political and social revolution called for new, revolutionary innovations in composition. Roslavets and those who shared similar visions fancied themselves the musical avant-garde, but most members were considerably more conservative and included conservatory professors and young talents like Dmitrii Shostakovich. By the early 1930s, radical modernism was expunged from the sphere of appropriate Soviet music, but a significant proportion of Composers' Union members subscribed to the ASM's general interest in new musical experiments. Looking back nearly five decades later, Khachaturian noted that despite its shortcomings, the ASM provided a crucial forum for the development of new music and laid the groundwork for later achievements.[10] Its positions were later associated not only with such members as Miaskovskii, the young and talented Gavriil Popov and Lev Knipper, and the influential Vissarion Shebalin, but also Sergei Prokofiev (who spent the 1920s in emigration) and sometimes Shostakovich. A crucial Leningrad organizer of the ASM was the musicologist and composer Boris Asaf'ev. Before his death in 1949, Asaf'ev would become one of the single most authoritative members of the Stalinist professional organization, respected by all factions as a composer of ballets, a music theorist, and a powerful critic.

Though RAPM is the most famous of the proletarian groups, for most of the 1920s its members were exclusively musicologists and music critics, who polemicized about music and exhorted composers to write music that would be accessible to the masses. Later known for advocating mass songs for large amateur performance, RAPM members did not actually write any such music until RAPM absorbed composers from other groups during the Cultural Revolution.[11]

More influential for the later development of the Stalinist music profession was a group of Moscow conservatory students who formed a collective devoted to cooperative composition and the ideals of proletarian music. This collective was called Prokoll.[12] In 1929 Prokoll folded itself into RAPM, providing the latter with much-needed composers, and after the dissolution of RAPM some of its members ascended to prominent leadership positions in the Composers' Union. Though Aleksandr Davidenko's mass songs were most noteworthy at the time, the influence of Prokoll in the Stalin period was exerted more prominently by Dmitrii Kabalevskii, Nikolai Chemberdzhi, and especially Viktor Belyi.

A founding member of Prokoll, Belyi studied at the Moscow Conservatory with Miaskovskii, graduating in 1929. He taught composition in various capacities at the Moscow Conservatory from 1925 until 1948 and at the conser-

10. A. I. Khachaturian, "Muzyka i narod," in *Aram Khachaturian: Stat'i i vospominaniia*, ed. I. E. Popova (Moscow: Sovetskii kompozitor, 1980), 9–30, here 14.

11. On RAPM and some of its lesser-known competitors, see Nelson, *Music for the Revolution*, 68–83, 213–31.

12. On Prokoll, see ibid., 83–89.

vatory in Minsk after that. But he was most influential as a top Composers' Union official from 1939 to 1948 and as a trusted unofficial advisor to the Composers' Union leadership thereafter. Aside from his considerable organizational skills, he was known for his intellectually constructed song suites.

These associations bequeathed not only members to the professional organization of Soviet composers but also competing visions of appropriate Soviet music that would remain resonant for those members long after the associations were dissolved. Like the composers' unions that replaced them in the 1930s, they organized artistic links and points of view, but otherwise they were very different. First, associational membership in the 1920s was supposedly based on a single, shared musical vision, especially among proletarian culture groups. The Composers' Union united a surprisingly broad range of musical vision under one bureaucratic umbrella. Second, the associations of the 1920s did not as a general rule fund composers. For instance, the ASM organized performances and publicized the achievements of its members, but it did not give commissions. The Composers' Union did. Third, the organizations of the 1920s were advocacy groups devoted to a particular type of music. Try though they might, they did not exert any direct control over the creative process or the musical product. The Composers' Union did. The type of institutional agency characteristic of these early associations was very different and much less potent than that which would eventually accrue to the Composers' Union.

Finally, it was ideas that united members in the 1920s; in the Composers' Union, it was instead an expertise-based professionalism. This professionalism was related to the conservatory professionalism adopted by some of those who ascribed to the three prominent musical visions of the 1920s. But the Composers' Union should not be considered a direct heir to prerevolutionary conservatory professionalism because of two other key differences. The Composers' Union never admitted the music teachers who were so prominent in the IRMO before the Revolution, and by the end of World War II the Composers' Union closed its doors to performers, limiting the professional organization to composers and musicologists. Furthermore, the Composers' Union always found room within its ranks for composers of popular songs, consistent targets of almost all players in the 1920s. Excluding conservatory-trained violinists and pianists while including these *melodisty* (tunesmiths) made for a distinct professional organization.

From Municipal Composers' Unions
to an All-USSR Union

The impetus to form creative unions came from a resolution of the Central Committee of the Communist Party dated 23 April 1932. This resolution banned all existing societies of professional artists, particularly singling out the tendentious Russian Association of Proletarian Writers (RAPP), and called for the creation of an umbrella literary organization—the Union of Soviet Writers. The Writers' Union was to unify all Soviet writers in the same organization and orient them to the production of constructive, socialist literature. The resolution also demanded the creation of analogous institutions in other artistic fields.[13]

Members of the Communist Party apparatus oversaw even minor decisions about personnel, institutional structure, and content while they sought to bring contentious groups of writers into this umbrella organization.[14] The process was completed in August 1934, when the First All-USSR Congress of Soviet Writers convened in Moscow.[15]

Though the 23 April 1932 resolution called for analogous creative unions in other spheres, no other group in the early 1930s organized as effectively or thoroughly as the writers, driven as they were by Central Committee attention. Still, other groups did begin to organize, only sometimes under the watchful eye of the party leadership. Architects began to attract attention at the highest level shortly after writers, beginning in 1934.[16] Party leaders focused early deliberations on artists, too, though they did not take as active an interest in organizational matters.[17] Amidst this clamor for the creation of creative unions, the issue of what to do in the music sphere attracted virtually no attention at the highest levels. In fact, at the same meeting that questions relating to architects and artists were actively considered, the party leadership declined to make any suggestions about music.[18]

Groups of musicians in the Soviet Union's main cultural capitals nevertheless began forming their own municipal composers' unions. By the fall of 1932 the Moscow composers' union was established with the participation of Rabis, the trade union for arts workers, and the Arts Sector of the Peoples' Commissariat of Enlightenment (Narkompros), the revolutionary equivalent of the Russian republic's education ministry. On 19 September 1932 the new creative union

13. RGASPI, f. 17, op. 3, d. 881, l. 21, pt. 21 (23 Apr 1932), a follow-up to RGASPI, f. 17, op. 3, d. 875, l. 10, pt. 50/18 (8 Mar 1932), repr. in *Schast'e literatury: Gosudarstvo i pisateli, 1925–1938. Dokumenty,* ed. D. L. Babichenko (Moscow: ROSSPEN, 1997), 130–31.

14. Some decisions set personnel: RGASPI, f. 17, op. 114, d. 298, l. 8, pt. 15g. (15 May 1932); d. 305, ll. 5–6, 124–25, pt. 14 (22 Jun 1932); d. 307, l. 15, pt. 54g. (15 Jul 1932); d. 310, l. 8, pt. 1g. (29 Jul 1932). Others set journal editorial boards or mediated conflicts: d. 305, ll. 5, 111–23, pt. 13 (22 Jun 1932); d. 348, ll. 95–97, pt. 12 (15 May 1933). For reprints of some of these decisions and many others relating to writers in this period, see Babichenko, *Schast'e literatury,* esp. 130–78.

15. *Pervyi vsesoiuznyi s'ezd sovetskiskh pisatelei, 1934: Stenograficheskii otchet* (Moscow: Gosizdat Khudozhestvennaia literatura, 1934). For planning the congress see RGASPI, f. 17, op. 114, d. 341, l. 4, pt. 4 (22 Mar 1933).

16. RGASPI, f. 17, op. 114, d. 573, l. 20, pt. 105g. (11 Nov 1934); d. 584, l. 23, pt. 145g. (23 May 1935); d. 588, l. 4, pt. 12 (9 Jul 1935).

17. Ibid., d. 292, ll. 3, 132–33ob., pt. 7 (17 Apr 1932); d. 305, ll. 5, 108–10, pt. 12 (22 Jun 1932).

18. Ibid., d. 300, l. 5, pts. 15–16 (5 Jun 1932). The Secretariat declined to make a final decision regarding architects on their own: RGASPI, f. 17, op. 114, d. 302, l. 4, pt. 10 (15 Jun 1932).

met, elected a governing board, and set about drawing up a charter.[19] The Presidium of the governing board was comprised of I. P. Arkad'ev, Viktor Gorodinskii, Aleksandr Gol'denveizer, Nikolai Miaskovskii, Vissarion Shebalin, and Aleksandr Krein.[20] Though this leadership group was comprised entirely of professional musicians and musicologists, that would shortly change, when leadership of the new creative union was assumed by the lawyer and career administrator Nikolai Cheliapov.[21]

The Moscow composers' union immediately formed three main departments: an organizational planning department, a department charged with educational outreach and other "mass enlightenment" work, and a creative production department that funded commission contracts. The Creative Department was further divided into a series of groups and sections which were headed up by a creative leadership of approximately forty musicians, including such influential and authoritative composers as conservatory professors Miaskovskii, Glier, and Aleksandr Gedike.[22]

A Leningrad municipal composers' union also began to operate in the fall of 1932. It was founded by a group of prominent musicologists, performers, and composers who thought that their creative work allied them with the Soviet project. These founding members formed a Creative Commission to examine concrete creative materials and admit new members. By 1934 the Leningrad composers' union had 122 members, 85 percent of whom were composers, 10 percent musicologists, and 5 percent performers.[23]

This Creative Commission and its successor, the Creative Department, remained an essential early center for the practical creative activities of the Leningrad organization. Most importantly, the Creative Department discussed and funded new compositions. When compared to its predecessor, the music section of the All-Russian Society of Composers and Dramatists (Vserosskomdram), the Leningrad chapter increased composers' commissions sevenfold

19. Ia. B., "V soiuze sovetskikh kompozitorov," *Sovetskaia muzyka,* 1933, no. 1:140–41, here 140.

20. Gorodinskii was a Moscow-based musicologist, and Miaskovskii and Shebalin were two of the most-respected composition professors at the Moscow Conservatory. Gol'denveizer was most respected as a pianist, Moscow Conservatory professor, and music administrator; he was assistant director of the conservatory, 1932–34, and its director, 1939–42. Krein was trained at the Moscow Conservatory (cello) and in private composition lessons with the influential Boleslav Iavorskii; he had been active in government music administration from the revolution until 1927. I. P. Arkad'ev was a conductor and composer who lived in Leningrad; this may not have been the Arkad'ev on the Moscow composers' union board, but I was unable to identify another likely candidate. The Presidium's numbers were also augmented by an organizational secretary, one Shargorodskii (who does not appear to be the conductor, violist, composer, and eventual Kazakh Conservatory professor L. M. Shargorodskii).

21. Sheila Fitzpatrick, "The Lady Macbeth Affair: Shostakovich and the Soviet Puritans," in *The Cultural Front: Power and Culture in Revolutionary Russia* (Ithaca: Cornell University Press, 1992), 196; Amy Nelson, *Music for the Revolution,* 288n30.

22. Ia. B., "V soiuze," 140–41.

23. A. Ashkenazi, "Leningradskii soiuz sovetskikh kompozitorov," *Sovetskaia muzyka,* 1934, no. 6:61–65, here 61.

in just two and a half years.[24] Most of this money was spent on commissions for symphonic compositions, despite the Leningrad union's expressed efforts to attract composers of all types of music, including the oft-maligned "light genres."[25]

Moscow and Leningrad had the largest municipal composers' unions, and starting in 1933 their activities were most widely publicized by the professional journal *Sovetskaia muzyka,* but they were not alone. In the 1930s, composers' unions formed in Armenia (1932), Georgia (1932), Ukraine (1932), Azerbaidzhan (1934), Belorussia (1938), and Uzbekistan (1938).[26] Some combined multiple municipal composers' unions in one overarching republican organization. For example, by the end of the decade there were chapters of the Ukrainian composers' union in the cities of Kharkov, Kiev, and Odessa. The Odessa chapter even had an affiliated union of Moldavian composers, which would later become the Moldavian chapter of the all-USSR Composers' Union.[27] Others had much less developed institutional forms. The Belorussian composers' union spent six years (1932–38) as a subsection of the Belorussian Writers' Union, and by 1938, the Uzbek composers' union had only formed an organizational committee.[28] Other Central Asian republics would not form composers' unions until after the creation of the all-USSR Composers' Union in 1939.

At first, these composers' unions attracted very little attention from government and party institutions. Then, in early January 1936, the Soviet government formed a new, powerful arts oversight body called the Committee on Artistic Affairs (eventually, Vsesoiuznyi komitet po delam iskusstv pri SNK SSSR, or VKI).[29] The first head of the new committee, P. M. Kerzhentsev, was an ideologically tough-minded and able administrator with experience in the party cultural apparatus dating back to the late 1920s. Kerzhentsev and his Committee on Artistic Affairs received a broad mandate to overhaul the entire Soviet arts establishment and bring it under unified supervision.[30] The municipal composers' unions were no exception, and the new committee eventually gave impetus to unite the far-flung composers' unions into a single all-USSR organization.

24. Ibid., 61–62; Nelson, *Music for the Revolution,* 226 (on Vserosskomdram). This new funding brought Leningrad in line with Moscow, for which see Ia. B., "V soiuze," 140–41.

25. Ashkenazi, "Leningradskii soiuz sovetskikh kompozitorov," 61–62; for attacks on "light genres" in the period of cultural revolution that immediately preceded the formation of creative unions, see Nelson, *Music for the Revolution,* 220–28.

26. *Muzykal'naia entsiklopediia* (Moscow: Sovetskaia entsiklopediia, 1973–82), 1:66, 215, 387; 2:88; 5:688, 711.

27. Iu. V. Keldysh, *Istoriia muzyki narodov SSSR, Tom II (1932–1941)* (Moscow: Sovetskii kompozitor, 1970), 281, 338; *Muzykal'naia entsiklopediia,* 3:634.

28. *Muzykal'naia entsiklopediia,* 1:387, 5:688.

29. Leonid Maksimenkov, *Sumbur vmesto muzyki: Stalinskaia kul'turnaia revoliutsiia, 1936–1938* (Moscow: Iuridicheskaia kniga, 1997), 54.

30. For the reorganization of the Bol'shoi Theater, see RGASPI, f. 17, op. 163, d. 1103, ll. 144–46 (Kerzhentsev to Stalin and Malenkov, 3 Apr 1936); and RGASPI, f. 17, op. 3, d. 976, l. 56, pt. 243 (20 Apr 1936). See also Maksimenkov, *Sumbur vmesto muzyki.*

The formation of the Committee on Artistic Affairs also coincided with the first of the two major interventions into the music world during the Stalin period—the denunciation of Dmitrii Shostakovich's critically acclaimed opera *Lady Macbeth of Mtsensk* and his ballet *The Limpid Stream,* which appeared in quick succession in prominent editorials published by *Pravda,* the Communist Party daily newspaper.[31] These two editorials and the new committee shaped the general environment in which composers and musicologists operated from 1936 until 1939. The Committee on Artistic Affairs dominated musical production through its oversight of performance institutions and publications while composers and musicologists struggled to decipher and respond to the vague directions suggested in the *Pravda* articles.[32]

The municipal composers' unions in Moscow and Leningrad provided one of the main forums for composers and musicologists to react to the *Pravda* intervention. In the cultural capitals, composers' union members flocked to meetings sponsored by the Committee on Artistic Affairs and the local composers' union.[33] They took turns browbeating the denounced Shostakovich and castigating the experimental and stormy music of the previously acclaimed *Lady Macbeth.* Some composers also took to the factories to renew their connection with the workers as an antidote to the academicism that some thought was responsible for the music at the center of the *Pravda* attacks.[34]

The cornerstone of a general campaign against formalism in all of the arts, this intervention established a pole beyond which musical production dared not far stray for the rest of the Stalin period.[35] Already a staple in cultural debates before 1936, "formalism" became the primary derogatory charge leveled at unfavorably reviewed symphonic and chamber music at least until 1949, when "cosmopolitanism" was added to the arsenal of attack vocabulary. Though assigning musical content to the term was always very slippery, "formalism" was often applied to music that was atonal or even just dissonant and was always associated with Western modernist influence. "Formalism" remained a chief

---

31. "Sumbur vmesto muzyki," *Pravda,* 28 Jan 1936, 3; and "Baletnaia fal'sh'," *Pravda,* 6 Feb 1936, 3. This event has drawn significant attention in the West: Boris Schwarz, *Music and Musical Life in Soviet Russia, 1917–1970* (Bloomington: Indiana University Press, 1972), 119–132, 141–142; Fitzpatrick, "Lady Macbeth Affair"; Royal S. Brown, "The Three Faces of Lady Macbeth," in *Russian and Soviet Music: Essays for Boris Schwartz,* ed. M. H. Brown (Ann Arbor: UMI Research Press, 1984), 245–252; and Fay, *Shostakovich,* 84–105. Soviet treatments typically ignore *Lady Macbeth*'s successful early years. See the anthology of Stalin-period writings on "Soviet opera" in *Sovetskaia opera: sbornik kriticheskikh statei,* ed. M. Grinberg and N. Poliakova (Moscow: Gosudarstvennoe muzykal'noe izdatel'stvo, 1953), which begins with "Sumbur vmesto muzyki."

32. For VKI control of music publishing and arts press, see RGASPI, f. 17, op. 114, d. 644, l. 26, pt. 119g. (10 Apr 1938); d. 637, l. 9, pt. 4g. (1 Jan 1938).

33. *Sovetskaia muzyka,* 1936, no. 5.

34. "V Kharkovskom orgkomitete SSK," *Sovetskaia muzyka,* 1936, no. 6:77.

35. Sheila Fitzpatrick convincingly contextualizes this attack as a major blow in what was a much larger campaign against formalism, with Meyerhold as its ultimate target, in "Lady Macbeth Affair," 183–215.

bugaboo of Stalinist cultural administrators and concern of those most prominent and authoritative composers like Shostakovich and Prokofiev who pushed
the boundaries of creative acceptability.

The already tense atmosphere of early 1936 intensified considerably during
the horrifying days of the Great Terror, with its Moscow show trials of Old Bolsheviks, its roundups of social marginals, its executions, and its swelling prison
camp population. Prominent cultural leaders, from the talented poet Osip Man-
delstam to the influential theater director Vsevolod Meyerhold, disappeared,
later to be executed or die in prison camps.

Yet from this truly terrifying period, the Stalinist music world emerged trau-
matized but relatively unscathed. The Terror in the music world initially consisted of an attack on former members of RAPM. When one of the principal
patrons of Soviet musicians, Marshall Mikhail Tukhachevskii, was arrested and
shot in 1937, his clients, including Shostakovich, fell under increased suspicion.[36] The director of the Moscow Philharmonic and the musicologist Nikolai Zhiliaev were arrested (and the latter was shot) for their association with
Tukhachevskii.[37] The increased tension created by the Great Terror caused less
serious changes as well. For example, on the eve of its premier, Shostakovich
was forced to withdraw his Fourth Symphony as simply too risky.[38]

But the brunt of the Terror did not fall on rank-and-file composers' union
members or even on composers and musicologists in leadership positions. Instead, the nonprofessional bureaucratic leadership of the arts world was scape-
goated, fired, and sometimes arrested and shot. Moscow composers' union
head Cheliapov was removed and probably executed in 1937, and Committee
on Artistic Affairs chief Kerzhentsev was relieved of his post in early 1938. With
the disappearance of Cheliapov, the composers' union was never again to be led
by a nonprofessional.[39] During these terrifying years, the composers' unions
came a step closer to emerging as professional organizations.

Both before and in the midst of this uproar, the municipal and republican
composers' unions attempted to cooperate, and communication between composers' unions was facilitated by monthly publication of *Sovetskaia muzyka*.
But some local chapters were suspicious of interference from Moscow. As time
went on, the dynamics of the relationship between the central leadership and
chapters in cities and national republics would change, depending on whether
local chapters sought less interference or more resources from the center. In any
case, cooperating required overcoming tension about the fear that the Moscow
composers' union was positing itself as a coordinating body for all of them. Be-

---

36. Fay, *Shostakovich*, 27, 92, 99; Caroline Brooke, "Soviet Musicians and the Great Terror,"
Europe-Asia Studies 54, no. 3, (2002): 407.

37. Brooke, "Soviet Musicians," 407–8.

38. The exact proximate cause of the withdrawal is still murky, but for the definitive discussion,
see Fay, *Shostakovich*, 96–97.

39. Brooke, "Soviet Musicians," 397–413.

fore the creation of the all-USSR Composers' Union, the Moscow union acted as a de facto coordinating body, but inefficiently and only on an ad hoc basis.[40]

At least in part because of this suspicion and inefficiency, real institutional and practical integration did not begin until the creation of an all-USSR Organizational Committee (Orgkom) of the Composers' Union in 1939. Though preparations to form an all-USSR Composers' Union started in 1938,[41] the final push really began the following March. On 4 March 1939 the new head of the Committee on Artistic Affairs, A. I. Nazarov, wrote to Viacheslav Molotov and Andrei Andreev, high-ranking government and party officials. Nazarov noted that he was responding to an earlier request from the Soviet Union's central government, the Council of Peoples' Commissars (Sovnarkom SSSR), to investigate forming an all-USSR Composers' Union and temporary Orgkom. Nazarov sent a brief proposal and a draft Orgkom membership, which included those whom he considered the greatest composers in Russia and the national republics augmented with representatives from the oldest generation of Soviet composers and some young and talented composers.[42]

During the second week of March, this proposal circulated among top government leaders until one of them was instructed to look into a very tersely worded proposal: "With the goal of an exchange of creative experience, we request the formation of a Union of Soviet Composers of the USSR. To manage preparatory work for the convening of a congress of composers, we request the foundation of an Organizational Committee according to the enclosed list of members. The proposed composition of the Organizational Committee includes the twenty-four most outstanding composers of the RSFSR and national republics."[43] The motivation for creating an all-USSR Composers' Union was thus to promote the "exchange of creative experience" at a level impossible or as yet impractical for local unions and to concentrate in one institution the Soviet Union's reserve of musical expertise, embodied in a diverse group of composers.

The proposed membership of the Orgkom prefigured the eventual diversity of the Composers' Union. Of the twenty-four composers suggested by Nazarov, fifteen lived in one of Russia's two creative centers (eight in Moscow and seven in Leningrad), but nine more hailed from the national republics. There was creative diversity as well. Of the twenty-four, nineteen were primarily known for

40. RGALI, f. 962, op. 3, d. 107 (VKI stenogram on MSSK composers, 21 Dec 1936); op. 10s, d. 28, ll. 34–35 (MSSK and VKI to SNK SSR and TsK VKP(b), 8 Mar 1938).

41. Ibid., op. 10s, d. 28, ll. 36–38, 45 (on forming the OK SSK SSSR, Apr–Nov 1938).

42. GARF, f. 5446, op. 23, d. 1836, l. 4 (Nazarov to Molotov and Andreev, 4 Mar 1939). Nazarov's proposal also included a draft resolution and a list of candidates (l. 3): Glier, A. V. Aleksandrov, Miaskovskii, Dunaevskii, Uzeir Gadzhibekov, D. Ia. Pokrass, Asaf'ev, L. N. Revutskii, B. I. Liatoshinskii, Aro Stepanian, I. I. Dzerzhinskii, Khachaturian, Shostakovich, Kabalevskii, Belyi, A. V. Bogatyrev, L. I. Arakashvili, Vano Gakieli, Talib Sadykov, Abdylas Maldybaev, Iu. A. Shaporin, M. O. Shteinberg, Kh. S. Kushnarev, and V. I. Muradeli.

43. GARF, f. 5446, op. 23, d. 1836, l. 6 (excerpt sent to Mikoian, 7–8 Mar 1939). Marginalia indicate that the request originated with the Committee on Artistic Affairs.

their symphonic, ballet, or opera music, and five were famous for their popular songs. This skew toward "serious" music, but inclusion of popular song composers, was to become typical for the rest of the Stalin period. Typical also was the variety of artistic orientation within the nineteen symphonic or serious theater composers. They ranged from Shostakovich, who had already been disciplined and rehabilitated, to Glier, a direct creative descendant of the late-nineteenth-century greats, to Ivan Dzerzhinskii, whose tuneful opera *Tikhii Don* had taken the mantle of Soviet opera from Shostakovich's *Lady Macbeth* in 1936.[44]

For almost two months, no action was taken.[45] Then, on 4 May 1939, Sovnarkom passed Nazarov's draft unchanged.[46] Glier was the new head of the Composers' Union, and he was to be assisted by Aram Khachaturian, an extremely talented Moscow-based Armenian composer primarily known for his catchy ballet music, and Isaak Dunaevskii, the Leningrad-based superstar composer of popular songs, musical scores, and film music. The creative diversity of the leadership was maintained even at the highest levels. In practical terms, Khachaturian quickly and energetically came to dominate the Composers' Union leadership, and he remained the de facto head of the Composers' Union until 1948.

The other significant provision of the resolution that established the all-USSR Orgkom called on the Committee on Artistic Affairs to draft a resolution creating another crucial institution—the funding organization operated by the Composers' Union, Muzykal'nyi fond SSSR (Muzfond).[47] This provision was one example of a phenomenon that repeated in the first years of the Composers' Union. Even after the formation of the all-USSR Composers' Union, the Committee on Artistic Affairs was supposed to oversee its activities.[48] This state of affairs prevailed despite the fact that the Committee on Artistic Affairs was too busy with performance institutions to pay much attention to the Composers' Union, especially after the beginning of the war. Nevertheless, this oversight provision provided the background for the struggle of the Composers' Union to dominate musical production, which forms one of the central stories of this book. This is not to suggest that the composers and musicologists who pushed for the creation of an all-USSR Composers' Union did so *in order to* compete

44. Ibid., ll. 1–2 (final Orgkom membership list, 5 May 1939). The exact same individuals are listed in Nazarov's March proposal; ibid., l. 3.

45. With existing sources, it is impossible to determine what happened to the proposal between the time Mikoian was asked to look into it in early March and the time Sovnarkom finally acted on it two months later. However, the initial addressees of Nazarov's memo provide a good clue. His proposal had to clear both the governmental apparatus and the Communist Party's arts oversight body, agit-prop. Unfortunately, the prewar agit-prop archives are not extant. Luckily, in this case, nothing of substance changed during the intervening months.

46. GARF, f. 5446, op. 23, d. 1836, l. 7 (4 May 1939); RGALI, f. 2077, op. 1, d. 21, l. 1 (identical, SSK copy).

47. Ibid., pt. 3.

48. GARF, f. 5446, op. 23, d. 1811, l. 22 (VKI to Vyshinskii, 21 Dec 1939).

with the Committee on Artistic Affairs. This was not their explicit intent, and even if it had been, they would not have been able to articulate it publicly. Rather, the Composers' Union's monopolization of technical musical expertise and its juridical separation from the Committee on Artistic Affairs meant that competition between the two was an important characteristic of the Composers' Union's future activities. Successful advancement of the importance of expertise during this competition was one of the most salient features of postwar Stalinism that this study elucidates.

Despite the formation of the Orgkom in 1939, the Composers' Union did not achieve a full juridical existence for almost another decade, since its official status hinged on the convocation of an all-USSR Congress of Soviet Composers and the subsequent adoption of a charter. The 1939 decision instructed the Orgkom to begin organizing that congress. For the next nine years, the Composers' Union was officially and legally still in the process of formation. But by the end of 1939 the municipal and republican composers' unions had been superseded by, and united into, the all-USSR Composers' Union that would constitute them as a profession.

Institutional Infrastructure and Membership

The new Orgkom immediately got to work, expanding the institutional and material reach of the all-USSR Composers' Union beyond the Russian cultural capitals and adding large blocks of new members. The primary purpose of the Composers' Union was to unite composers in one institution in order to produce ideologically sound music that would speak to all of the peoples of the USSR. In grandiose statements of purpose, there was always an underlying assumption about the latent importance of fostering creativity and eventually unleashing the creative potential of the socialist population.[49] To paraphrase Stalin's oft-quoted quip about writers, artists were expected to engineer human souls.[50] This abstract value was demonstrated to be very real during the war.

Within this overriding task, there lurked more practical functions as well. First and foremost, the Composers' Union was to coordinate the production and interpretation of new music by uniting in one organization those with the requisite expertise to take on such a task.[51] It was also to take responsibility for the ideological education of those experts, and then use them to popularize

49. See the following charters: RGALI, f. 2077, op. 1, d. 1, ll. 1–13 (All-Russian Voluntary Society SSK, 23 Feb 1934); f. 2075, op. 9, d. 8, ll. 2–12 (Leningrad SSK, 7 Jan 1939); f. 2085, op. 1, d. 1209, ll. 72–76 (draft, SSK SSSR, 24 Apr 1948); RGASPI, f. 17, op. 121, d. 723, ll. 49–57 (SSK SSSR, [20 Sep 1948]).

50. Stalin made the remark to writers at Maksim Gorkii's apartment on 26 October 1932: I. V. Stalin, *Sochineniia* (Moscow: Gosizdat Politicheskoi literatury, 1951), 13:410.

51. RGALI, f. 2077, op. 1, d. 1, ll. 1–2, pt. I.b, I.v, I.e, I.i; f. 2075, op. 9, d. 8, ll. 2, 4, pt. I, II.5; f. 2085, op. 1, d. 1209, l. 73ob., pt. II.1, II.3.

Soviet music at home and abroad.[52] Finally, the Composers' Union was meant to help provide material and professional support—funding—to its members.[53] In practice composers and musicologists almost always held other professional positions in conservatories and research institutes or as consultants to theaters, performance ensembles, and government institutions in order to earn regular salaries; but Composers' Union membership became a necessary credential for such positions, and Muzfond provided other material support services that dramatically improved its members' creative working conditions.

As soon as the Orgkom was established in 1939, it began expanding its institutional reach. Composers' Union chapters were set up in the Central Asian republics of Turkmenistan, Kirgizia, Kazakhstan, and Tadzhikistan.[54] In late 1939 the Orgkom took control of the construction and staffing of working resorts that eventually provided one of the most coveted incentives for composers and musicologists throughout the Stalin period.[55] In 1940 the Orgkom opened a new building in Moscow, the Central House of Composers (Tsentral'nyi dom kompozitorov), that became the center of the professional organization's activities over the next several years. The Central House of Composers was a personal and professional center, providing housing, performance venues, and meeting spaces for Composers' Union members.[56] The Orgkom also established two small printing houses, one in Moscow and one in Leningrad, that published performance parts and scores from composers' handwritten originals. This incredibly valuable, time-saving service had existed in less systematic form before 1939, but the Orgkom transformed earlier hand-copying services into new presses.[57] The Orgkom also sponsored creative discussions on issues as diverse as national musical culture in the Caucasus, the development of young composers, and the state of musical genres from opera to popular song.[58]

52. Ibid., f. 2077, op. 1, d. 1, ll. 1–2, pt. I.g, I.z, I.k; f. 2075, op. 9, d. 8, l. 2, 4, pt. I, II.4, II.5, II.7; f. 2085, op. 1, d. 1209, l. 74, pt. II.6, II.7; RGASPI, f. 17, op. 121, d. 723, l. 51, pt. II.8.

53. RGALI, f. 2077, op. 1, d. 1, ll. 1–3, pt. I.zh, II.a–v, d–z, n; f. 2075, op. 9, d. 8, l. 4, pt. II.2–3; f. 2085, op. 1, d. 1209, l. 74, pt. II.9.

54. *Muzykal'naia entsiklopediia*, 5:650; 2:799, 643; 5:378.

55. RGALI, f. 2077, op. 1, d. 22, l. 15 (Prikaz #32, 8 Aug 1939); l. 17 (Prikaz #34, 19 Aug 1939), pt. 4.

56. Ibid., d. 26, ll. 1–5 (29 Dec 1940).

57. Regulations for the new institution were approved in September 1940 for the Moscow press and in October for the Leningrad one: RGALI, f. 2077, op. 1, d. 27, ll. 1–3 (Moscow, 10 Sep 1940) and ll. 4–7 (Leningrad, Oct 1940). See also d. 34, l. 1 (introductory letter, 1940). The letter explains that the publishing service only received its own funds in October 1940; before that it had been funded by the Moscow chapter of Muzfond. For evidence concerning the minutiae of the 1940 transition, see RGALI, f. 2077, op. 1, d. 29 (1940). For evidence of analogous activities under the auspices of the municipal composers' unions see "Sovetskaia orkestroteka," *Sovetskaia muzyka*, 1935, no. 12:90–91; and "Rezoliutsiia [Upravleniia kinofikatsii pri SNK SSSR] po voprosu o khudozhestvenno-muzykal'noi rabote v kino" (9 May 1935), pt. 13, *Sovetskaia muzyka*, 1935, no. 6:79.

58. See the following Orgkom resolutions: RGALI, f. 2077, op. 1, d. 30, ll. 1–14 (23 Oct 1944), on the state of Soviet music; ll. 15–18 [Oct 1940], on the state of Georgian music; and ll. 19–24 (15 Nov 1940), a joint meeting with the Moscow chapter and the Central House of Composers. For additional creative activities, see *Sovetskaia muzyka*, 1939–40.

But institutional expansion primarily meant establishing Muzfond chapters throughout the Soviet Union and distributing to them the new resources that Muzfond controlled. In its first year of operations, Muzfond formed chapters, funded them, and experimented with administrative forms. In 1940 Muzfond created chapters or affiliated institutions in nineteen cities: Moscow, Ruza (a retreat for Moscow-based members), Ol'gino (a retreat for Leningrad-based members), Kiev (with additional representatives stationed in L'vov, Kharkov, and Odessa), Minsk (with an additional representative in Belostok), Tbilisi, Baku, Erevan, Tashkent, Alma-Ata, Frunze, Stalinabad, Ashkhabad, Kazan, Rostov-on-Don, Simferopol, Voronezh, Petrozavodsk, and Sverdlovsk.[59] Controlled entirely by the Composers' Union leadership, the expansion of Muzfond constituted the first steps taken by the emerging professional organization to integrate across the Soviet Union.

With administrative expansion came a significant distribution of financial resources. In February and March 1940, Muzfond received representatives from all over the Soviet Union as the central Muzfond leadership allocated nearly 5.6 million rubles, a staggering sum when compared to the few hundred thousand rubles that the municipal composers' unions had controlled just five years earlier.[60]

Of these total appropriations, 3.3 million rubles (59 percent) were allocated to general operational expenses, and just under 2 million rubles (36 percent) were allocated to capital investment in the physical infrastructure of Composers' Union chapters throughout the Soviet Union. Of the 3.3 million rubles devoted to general, ongoing expenses, almost exactly one-third was devoted to each of Muzfond's two main charges, creative support (33 percent) and material assistance (34 percent). The vast majority (24 percent) of the rest of these operating funds was fingered for administrative expenses, including the salaries of support staff. Ideological education and mass outreach programs (2 percent) and various capital acquisitions (5 percent), like pianos and dachas, comprised the rest. The other 5 percent of the total allocation went to general loan funds, and during most allocation meetings it was made clear that the fund was a maximum that the local leadership could loan to its members. This loan fund brings the total proportion of allocated funds devoted to direct support of Muzfond members' creative activities, material assistance, and loans to 45 percent, or 2.5 million rubles. Capital acquisitions and major capital investments amounted to 39 percent, or 2.1 million rubles, and administration (14 percent) and outreach (1 percent) accounted for the rest.

The expansion of Muzfond also entailed setting up Composers' Union chapters where they had not existed before, like Central Asia. The newly formed Central Asian chapters required a disproportionate infusion of resources in or-

59. RGALI, f. 2077, op. 1, d. 33, ll. 1–14 (Muzfond accounting report, [Feb 1941]), here l. 1.
60. Ibid., d. 28 (Muzfond protocols, Jan–Mar 1940), ll. 5–7 (#2, 5–10 Feb); ll. 8–8ob. (#3, 10 Feb); ll. 9–10ob. (#4, 16 Feb); ll. 11–12 (#5, 26 Feb); ll. 14–16ob. (#6, 7 Mar); ll. 19ob.–21 (#7, 13 Mar); ll. 22–23ob. (#8, 25 Mar).

der to build the infrastructure that was started in Moscow, Leningrad, and Ukraine in the 1930s. Conditional language attached to capital fund allocations for Armenia and throughout Central Asia reveals the importance of this first allocation to building new physical infrastructure. When the Uzbek chapter received 75,000 rubles for its capital fund, the allocation was contingent upon the Uzbek leadership getting local approval to build a House of Composers. On the other hand, the large 500,000-ruble capital investment in Armenia was not modified by such a qualifier and spread over two years, presumably because the Armenian Composers' Union had already gotten the approval to begin to acquire a House of Composers. The relatively underfunded Azerbaidzhani chapter was told to begin looking into acquiring a building, or at least apartments, for its members.[61] Investment outside of Moscow dramatically expanded the all-USSR Composers' Union's reach following the 1939 formation of the Orgkom and Muzfond. This expansion happened so quickly in Central Asia that the Muzfond leadership utilized a distinct organizational form for work there, naming plenipotentiaries in the Central Asian chapters to coordinate membership approval and resource disbursement.[62]

Once monies were disbursed, the professional leadership began to confirm the members of the Composers' Union and Muzfond in these far flung locales. Starting in April, there were eight major membership accessions in 1940. On 16 April, fifty-five Moscow members and eighteen Leningrad members were admitted to Muzfond. On 4 July, there was a massive influx of two hundred new members, including fifty from Leningrad, ninety-eight from Ukraine, forty-three from Georgia, and nine from Azerbaidzhan. The largest single influx took place on 8 August, when 344 new members were approved, including 210 from Moscow and Leningrad, 31 from elsewhere in Russia, and 90 from the Caucasus, Central Asia, and Belorussia. After these major summertime decisions, eighty-six more members were admitted, almost entirely from existing chapters or new, small Composers' Union chapters in the cities of the RSFSR. All told, 703 members were officially admitted to Muzfond in 1940 and approved by the Orgkom on 19 January 1941.[63] In almost exactly one year, Muzfond had undergone a massive expansion of its material and administrative reach, disbursed millions of rubles, and confirmed the basic prewar membership of the professional organization and its material support infrastructure.

Not surprisingly, this rapid administrative expansion did not go without a hitch. Most problematically, the 703 new members constituted a substantial 367-member shortfall from the estimates on which the February and March disbursements were based. The original overestimation caused Muzfond's administrative structure and relationship with the Composers' Union leadership that

---

61. Ibid., ll. 8–8ob. (Protokol #3, 10 Feb); ll. 11–12 (Protokol #5, 26 Feb); ll. 15ob. (Protokol #6, 7 Mar).

62. RGALI, f. 2077, op. 1, d. 28, ll. 22, 23ob. (Protokol #8, 25 Mar).

63. Ibid., d. 33, l. 35 (Report on Muzfond membership, [Feb 1941]); l. 3 (1941).

controlled it to change within the year. The organizational structure envisioned at the beginning of 1940 included providing Muzfond with a full-fledged administrative apparatus, crowned with a governing board in Moscow and including local boards wherever there was a Composers' Union chapter. The governing board was headed by Vano Muradeli, a young composer whose unsuccessful opera would provide the occasion for the 1948 party intervention analyzed in chapter 5. He was joined by six others: the musicologist Petr Zimin, who carried much of the administrative load in these early months; the musicologist Mikhail Pekelis; the former Prokoll composer Nikolai Chemberdzhi, who had chaired the Moscow municipal composers' union from 1936 to 1937; the composer and organ professor Aleksandr Gedike; the young Tikhon Khrennikov, who would take the leadership reigns of the professional organization in 1948; and the composer Aleksandr Krein.[64] From the very beginning, this leadership group was consistently assisted by the composer, orchestrator, and experienced music administrator Levon Atovm'ian. Atovm'ian was appointed to lead Muzfond's creative section in early March 1940, and he would be a crucial mainstay in the Muzfond leadership through the war.[65] This central leadership received representatives from local Muzfond chapters, each of which was tied to a Composers' Union chapter.[66]

By the end of the year, this plan was judged to be unworkable and inefficient because in small chapters, local Muzfond and Composers' Union leadership duplicated one another. Muzfond chapters that had been formed early in 1940 were shut down, and the professional leadership attempted a different sort of institutional organization. On 1 October 1940, Muzfond liquidated twelve chapters that had fewer than fifteen members, including four of the newly-created Central Asian chapters (Kazakh, Turkmen, Tadzhik, and Kirgiz), chapters in three autonomous republics in the RSFSR (Karelian-Finnish, Crimean, and Tatar), and five municipal chapters in Russia and Ukraine (Rostov, Sverdlovsk, Voronezh, Odessa, and Kharkov). The local Composers' Union leadership boards were instructed to designate one of their number as liaison to the central Muzfond leadership, which would control resource allocation from afar.[67] This administrative reform at least partly reversed the earlier focus on the non-Russian republics.

So who were all of these Composers' Union members, newly confirmed by early 1941? Determining their identity was central to the task of uniting musical experts from across the Soviet Union. Whether in its early municipal man-

---

64. This is a complete list of everyone identified as a member of the Muzfond governing board at their meetings in the first quarter of 1940. Most active were Zimin, who handled most internal matters, and Muradeli, who communicated with the Orgkom. RGALI, f. 2077, op. 1, d. 28, and passim. The first Muzfond meeting was presided over by Khachaturian (ibid., 1).

65. Ibid., ll. 14, 17 (Protokol #6, 7 Mar).

66. This organizational structure has been deduced from the practices represented in RGALI, f. 2077, op. 1, d. 28.

67. Ibid., d. 33, l. 2 (1941).

ifestations or as a full-fledged all-USSR professional organization, the Composers' Union always reserved the right to define its own membership, within vague guidelines.[68] This tendentious process is detailed in the next five chapters. However, one category of expert is worth highlighting here, the performer. The 1930s municipal unions allowed particularly highly qualified performers to gain membership, which created a porous and relatively unelaborated boundary for membership.[69] In fact, some performers, like the pianist Aleksandr Gol'denveizer in Moscow, occupied key leadership positions. In Ukraine, performers were so clearly considered a part of the new creative union that when it first formed in Kharkov, it was called the Union of Soviet Musicians of Ukraine.[70] After becoming well established in the 1930s, however, this inclusive definition of the professional body would be rejected, porous boundary solidified, and performers permanently excluded.

Excluding performers was the most significant institutional consolidation that the Composers' Union enacted during the war years and is worthy of explanation here. This process began in June 1943 when a group of extremely prominent performers attempted to dissolve the Composers' Union into a new Musicians' Union. This attempt was led by violinist David Oistrakh and cellist Vladimir Sofronitskii, both Stalin Prize laureates, by Gol'denveizer, and by the pianists Iakov Flier and Grigorii Ginzburg, both international prize winners. Along with seven of their colleagues, this high-powered group of performers wrote a collective letter to a patron favored among performers, Stalin's close advisor Viacheslav Molotov.

They pointed out that the USSR contained several creative unions which brought together all of the components that comprised a particular artistic profession. The Writers' Union, Architects' Union, Artists' Union, and All-Russian Theater Society, they argued, were all such organizations. However, in music there was only a Composers' Union, which contained just a few performers and musicologists and was dominated by composers despite the relatively small role that composers had in the large field of music and despite the small percentage of total musicians that they comprised. Their remedy was to propose a Musicians' Union that would absorb the Composers' Union as just one of many sections. This move would give musicians the same rights as "members of other creative collectives and would play a great role in the matter of livening up creative musical activities in the USSR."[71]

This letter was very craftily constructed, appealing as it did to senses of consistency between art professions, and seeking to exploit a personal relationship between famous musicians and their highly placed patron. Perhaps most important in explaining its failure, however, is the way it elided several crucial dis-

68. RGALI, f. 2077, op. 1, d. 1, l. 5, pt. II.9; f. 2075, op. 9, d. 8, l. 8, pt. III.2; f. 2085, op. 1, d. 1209, l. 74ob., pt. III.2; RGASPI, f. 17, op. 121, d. 723, l. 52, pt. III.2.

69. RGALI, f. 2077, op. 1, d. 1, l. 4, pt. II.1.a; f. 2075, op. 9, d. 8, ll. 7–8, pt. III.1.v.

70. D. P., "Muzykal'naia zhizn' v Khar'kove," *Sovetskaia muzyka,* 1933, no. 3:156–58.

71. RGASPI, f. 17, op. 125, d. 216, l. 68 (to V. M. Molotov, 3 Jun 1943).

tinctions between types of arts organizations by lumping the All-Russian The-ater Society (VTO) with the creative unions. As Oistrakh and company doubt-less knew, the VTO was a very different beast from the creative unions; it alone of these institutions was comprised of performers whose primary creative ac-tivity took place under the auspices of other arts organizations. Actors, ac-tresses, and theater directors, like music performers and ballet dancers, had well-established systems of employment, material support, and hierarchy that operated primarily through the theaters and performance institutions that em-ployed them. They were so distinct from the institutions that governed the lives of composers, artists, architects, writers, and playwrights that they lie almost entirely outside the bounds of this study.[72] Despite the fact that Composers' Union members typically earned regular salaries from positions in education or research and worked as consultants to performance or government institutions, from the point of view of both a theoretical division of labor in the arts and a practical allocation of resources, performers were treated differently than com-posers and musicologists.[73]

In retrospect, it is easy to see why this attempt to absorb the Composers' Union into a larger Musicians' Union failed. At the time, however, the theoret-ical boundaries between performers on the one hand and composers and mu-sicologists on the other were not yet so clearly drawn. In fact, the performers' proposal received serious attention, passing from Molotov down to the Com-mittee on Artistic Affairs and back up again to the Central Committee before being decided once and for all by the Composers' Union itself a year later.[74]

The Composers' Union came very close to formalizing the position of per-formers as Union members rather than excluding them. A proposed "Position on Membership of the Most Outstanding Performers in the SSK" was circu-lated before the 1944 vote. This draft preserved the distinctness of the Com-

72. For a Central Committee reiteration of this argument at a much later date, see RGASPI, f. 17, op. 133, d. 323, ll. 220–21 (Kruzhkov and Bespalov to Malenkov, 11 Aug 1951), a negative reaction to a later group of performers' attempt to form an analogous "Performers Fund." The *ap-paratchiki* chastised the performers for failing to recognize the difference between their own posi-tions, which included regular salaries and performance payments, and the union-based artists' irregular income and need for the additional subsidies that Muzfond, Litfond, Khudfond, etc. provided.

73. The distinction between composers and musicologists, on the one hand, and performers, on the other, has clear analogs in the West. In the United States, for example, composers and musi-cologists are professionalized through the academy while professional performers are de-profes-sionalized through an often elite labor union. For professionalization of European musicians through the academy, see Andrew Abbott, *System of Professions,* 54. Unlike Abbott, Howard Becker uses a less technical definition of "professional" to connote anyone who makes a living in art, including performers. However, he still notes a similar distinction between the two groups: see Howard S. Becker, *Art Worlds* (Berkeley and Los Angeles: University of California Press, 1985), 10 (differentiation of training at American conservatories), 292 (performers as "craftsmen").

74. See RGASPI, f. 17, op. 125, d. 216, l. 67 (Khrapchenko to Shcherbakov, 22 Jun 1943) for the immediate fate. It is not clear what happened to this request in the intervening eleven months, but no further discussion of the issue has been preserved in the available archives of the UPA TsK, Sekretariat, Orgbiuro, Politburo, or Molotov's personal party archive.

posers' Union and its status as an exclusive professional body, a repository of theoretical expertise. But it also rather creatively sought to carve out a place for performers within that theoretical structure. It argued that performers had no independent center for discussing the problems inherent in performing Soviet music and suggested that creating a special section within the Composers' Union would "unite Soviet performers around the most important questions of Soviet musical performance." Furthermore, it could work with the Union's other sections to popularize music by Soviet composers, much as performers in the municipal composers' unions had done in the 1930s.[75] In order to accomplish these goals, however, the Composers' Union would have to invite as members "the most outstanding performers who systematically and successfully work on Soviet musical pieces."[76]

Unfortunately for the performers who sought access to the Composers' Union, this draft was never enacted. The top leadership of the all-USSR Composers' Union debated the issue on 5 June 1944, but they could not come to a consensus on the issue and finally put it to a vote, a somewhat extraordinary occurrence. The vote itself was no less extraordinary. Of the eight members present, three abstained, two voted in favor of allowing performers in, and three voted against them. The measure was narrowly defeated, and performers were left out of the Stalinist professional music organization for good.[77]

Composers and performers maintained close personal ties and working relationships before and after this decision, and a few composers and musicologists also performed publicly. Composers, musicologists, and performers considered themselves members of the Soviet artistic intelligentsia, and all remained in the Soviet cultural and material elite. Excluding performers from the Composers' Union marked a break from prerevolutionary conservatory professionalism and institutionalized a distinction between intellectual and technical labor within the music world. Perhaps by analogy with the paradigmatic Writers' Union, composers, musicologists, and critics formed one group, and performers, who had no real analog in the literary world, formed another.[78] The resulting professional organization mapped oddly onto the Soviet musical landscape, reifying a rarely articulated distinction between head- and handwork while eliding a much more frequently expressed division between high and low culture evident in campaigns against popular songs and dance music. Composers of such music were typically admitted to the professional organization. These features made for a peculiar profession.

75. Multiple examples are listed in "V Len. soiuze sov. kompozitorov," *Sovetskaia muzyka,* 1935, no. 11:96.

76. RGALI, f. 2085, op. 1, d. 1209, l. 45. This draft was undated, but it circulated with a provisional agenda for an Orgkomitet SSK SSSR meeting to take place on 7 June 1944 (ibid., l. 46).

77. RGALI, f. 2077, op. 1, d. 96, l. 57 (Orgkom Protokol #9, 5 Jun 1944), pt. 1.

78. The analog would be actors, but since works for stage figured so much less prominently than prose and poetry in the Soviet literary imagination, the distinction in literature was not so peculiar. The petitioning musicians discussed above articulated this logic by suggesting that the SSP and VTO represented separate fields.

Another peculiarity of this professional organization was its hierarchical leadership structure. Formally, the most powerful leadership body of the Moscow composers' union in 1934 was the Board (Pravlenie), which was elected by the body's combined membership at a congress convened for the purpose. The Board's activities were open for audit by an elected Inspection Commission (Revizionnaia komissiia).[79] Finally, any changes in this structure were formally subject to the approval of Narkompros, the Peoples' Commissariat of Enlightenment, the revolutionary equivalent of an education ministry.[80] The Leningrad union had a similar structure, but it added a Presidium to the Board and subjugated the equivalent of the Inspection Commission to the Board, thus centralizing the auditing function and, crucially, cutting the even more powerful government control institution, the Committee on Artistic Affairs, out of the equation.[81]

After 1939 leadership authority was concentrated in the twenty-four member Orgkom and especially Aram Khachaturian. The young and energetic Khachaturian quickly took practical control of the institution, no doubt with the support of the much older official head, Glier, and Khachaturian's fellow assistant head, the distant Dunaevskii, who still lived in Leningrad. Until 1948, whatever Orgkom members were present at the meetings in Moscow decided virtually every question of importance relating to musical life in the Composers' Union. The one constant presence was Khachaturian.

Khachaturian was an Armenian composer who had grown up in the Georgian capital of Tbilisi. After receiving basic education at a school for aspiring merchants in prerevolutionary Tbilisi, Khachaturian moved to Moscow as an eighteen-year-old in 1921. A year later, he enrolled at the Gnesin Institute as a composition student of the renowned pedagog and composer Mikhail Gnesin. After graduating in 1929, he continued his studies with Nikolai Miaskovskii at the Moscow Conservatory. He finished one degree in 1934 and completed his graduate work in 1936. After he was appointed assistant head of the Composers' Union Orgkom in 1939, he joined the Communist Party in 1943.[82]

Khachaturian's own musical style reflected his background. He was highly skilled and well trained in the Russian classical tradition, and he frequently utilized the rich folk music traditions of the Caucasus in his original compositions, especially for the ballet. In fact, it is for his ballet music that he was and remains best known both in the Soviet Union and in the West. Besides maintaining an active creative schedule, Khachaturian also appeared to relish his administrative position atop the Composers' Union.[83] Throughout the early and mid-1940s, Khachaturian used that position to help shape Soviet music, always stressing accessible but technically masterful composition. In fact, in his mem-

79. RGALI, f. 2077, op. 1, d. 1, ll. 6–9, pt. III.16–30.
80. Ibid., l. 13, pt. VI.51.
81. RGALI, f. 2075, op. 9, d. 8, ll. 10–11, pts. IV–V.
82. "Khachaturian Aram Il'ich," in *Muzykal'naia entsiklopediia*, 5:1044–52.
83. G. S. Frid, personal communication, 7 May 1999.

oirs he reported pride about leading an institution that organized creative work in many musical genres and especially in all Soviet republics, but he singled out symphonic traditions for his lengthiest discussions and pointed to the role of the Composers' Union in organizing *professional* composers in republics that did not have prerevolutionary professional music traditions.[84]

The Central Committee dramatically intervened into the music world in 1948, completely disrupting the Composers' Union leadership, but some leadership structures remained the same. As before, Composers' Union members were to gather in a congress and elect a Board and Inspection Commission.[85] Some innovations, however, codified the experience of the previous decade. De facto power was concentrated in a six-person Secretariat, which was formally appointed by the Board and run by a general secretary.[86] From the time he was named general secretary in 1948, Tikhon Khrennikov remained in charge of the Composers' Union until the collapse of the Soviet Union. The other innovation of 1948 reflected the increased authority of the Composers' Union with respect to other institutions. All power to change its charter or dissolve itself rested with the Composers' Union leadership—not any outside agency.[87]

Despite the formation of the all-USSR Orgkom and Muzfond in 1939, the resources devoted to the Composers' Union were still relatively modest. By the time the Soviet distribution system was disrupted by the war, composers had not approached the levels of material well-being that writers had enjoyed for years.[88] Fittingly, expectations about composers' contributions to the heroic task of building socialism were correspondingly low. When bureaucrats in the Central Committee apparatus reported on shortcomings in Soviet opera near the end of 1940, they considered the Committee on Artistic Affairs more liable than the Orgkom, even for facilitating composers' efforts to construct Soviet opera.[89] Central Committee bureaucrats implied that they did not consider the Composers' Union yet effective enough to be dependable. This would soon change. The Composers' Union would eventually parlay its musical expertise and relatively independent control of ever-increasing material resources into dominance of the music realm by the end of the Stalin period. That process began during the war.

The infrastructure described in this chapter provided the general institutional

84. Khachaturian, "Muzyka i narod," 19–21.

85. RGALI, f. 2085, op. 1, d. 1209, ll. 75–76, pt. IV.2, IV.12; RGASPI, f. 17, op. 121, d. 723, ll. 54–56, pt. IV.2, IV.13.

86. RGALI, f. 2085, op. 1, d. 1209, ll. 75–76, pt. IV.7–11; RGASPI, f. 17, op. 121, d. 723, ll. 55–56, pt. IV.7–10, 12. The second version sets the Secretariat at six instead of five. In practice the Secretariat, like the Orgkom before it, was appointed by the Central Committee and approved by the membership later.

87. RGALI, f. 2085, op. 1, d. 1209, l. 75, pt. IV.2.v; RGASPI, f. 17, op. 121, d. 723, l. 54, pt. IV.2.v.

88. RGALI, f. 2077, op. 1, d. 51, ll. 41–45 (Orgkom Protokol #9, 23 Jul 1942).

89. RGASPI, f. 17, op. 125, d. 11, ll. 30–34 (G. Aleksandrov and D. Polikarpov to A. A. Andreev, A. A. Zhdanov, G. M. Malenkov, 1 Nov 1940), esp. l. 32.

context in which composers and musicologists lived their professional lives. They occupied an anomalous position in the Soviet bureaucracy, not formally and juridically subjugated to any government agency. Though of course subject to ideological direction and constrained by the political realities of Stalinist life, the Composers' Union and its members were a juridically distinct entity, free to create their own professional and material support infrastructure.

CHAPTER 2

Administering the Creative Process

In 1939 and 1940, the new all-USSR Composers' Union paid a great deal of attention to institution-building measures, but the Composers' Union was never just a bureaucracy. Instead, it was primarily an institutional venue for the formation and operation of the Soviet music profession. Throughout its local and all-USSR existence, the Composers' Union had two main functions that are typical of professional organizations in any modern system: providing professional support for and monitoring of its members, and overseeing the conditions that maintain members as an elite group, especially by funding them. By tracing the emergence of those two functions and sketching the basic activities of the Composers' Union institution in its various guises, this chapter shows how the creative unions, and the Composers' Union in particular, differed from other types of Stalinist institutions, including trade unions, conservatories, and government control institutions. By the start of the war, the Composers' Union had acquired most of the distinctive features of a professional organization, though it had not yet solidified its status and its members were still only on the fringes of the Stalinist material elite.

Professional Support: The Creative Apparatus

Professional support meant funding creative work and providing an institutional venue for discussing, evaluating, and controlling the creative process and its musical and theoretical products. Key to this process was the creative apparatus of the Composers' Union, a system of subcommittees devoted to specific types of music, to the organizing of professional personnel, or to training programs. The creative apparatus was part of the Composers' Union bureaucracy. Other parts were devoted to purely administrative tasks, bookkeeping, and legal issues, such as the Leningrad union's Finances and Legal Department.[1] Still

1. A. Ashkenazi, "Leningradskii soiuz sovetskikh kompozitorov," *Sovetskaia muzyka,* 1934, no. 6:64–65.

other parts sought to popularize Soviet music and find performance outlets. The Leningrad municipal union devoted a separate internal division to this task.[2] But most important was the creative apparatus, which was supposed to provide a forum in which composers and musicologists could discuss their work in a specific genre. Over time, the creative sections became a crucial institutional arena for the evaluation of work in progress and the production and operation of internal professional authority that evaluating peers' work necessarily entailed. Tracking changes in the apparatus and the ways in which its tasks were conceptualized helps explain how the Composers' Union administered the creative process and provided institutional support for diverse musical agendas.

From the beginning, the municipal composers' unions of the 1930s were key sites for Soviet music discussions. Both municipal unions in Moscow and Leningrad had Creative Departments with various subsections devoted to musical genres or creative groups that united members with common interests or professional profiles, like the Critics and Theorists Section of the Leningrad composers' union. These sections hosted discussions, the most important of which became prominent when they were publicized in *Sovetskaia muzyka*. For example, the Leningrad composers' union noted that it brought together listeners, performers, administrative leaders of performance institutions, music students, and music theorists so that its discussions could form the basis for new, specifically Soviet musicological work, facilitate the union's efforts to rework composers' world views, and help composers improve their compositions.[3] Once they retreated out of such public forums into a more exclusively professional sphere, discussions like these formed the backbone of the organization's professional life.

When the all-USSR Composers' Union was established in 1939, it inherited from the Moscow municipal composers' union a system of eleven creative sections defined by musical genre: Symphonic, Chamber Music, Vocal, Choral, Opera, Film and Theater, Variety Music (*estradnaia sektsiia*), and Children's Music Sections, a section of Music for Wind and Folk Instruments, a Military Music Section, and a section for Antifascist Music.[4] Over the next decade these were augmented by new sections. Some of them dropped out of existence, reemerged, combined, or underwent other substantial structural changes, but they always spanned a similar creative range.

Appointment to a leadership position of one of these subcommittees depended on composers' authority within the profession. It was a sign that composers' colleagues respected their professional competence in the area covered by the subcommittee, and it provided an opportunity to extend that authority by imparting their musical visions to other professionals. Consequently, these subcommittees formed a reservoir of creative authority within the profession

2. Ibid., 63.
3. Ibid., 61.
4. RGALI, f. 2085, op. 1, d. 1196, l. 67 (9 Jan 1939).

and constituted the institutional arena in which internal professional authority was created and deployed. The organization of professional activity thus depended on the operation of musical expertise.

The 1939 system of categorizing the expertise and activity of Soviet composers was interrupted by war in June 1941. Though creative activity continued virtually unabated, the Composers' Union's creative apparatus was streamlined. By the summer of 1943 after the Orgkom had returned from evacuation, only three sections (some now called commissions) continued to function, the Military Commission, the Children's Music Section, and the Creative Commission (something of an umbrella commission that, like its municipal predecessors in 1932 and 1933, served the function of the earlier sections on symphonic music, chamber music, and other "serious" music genres). Musicologists and critics also met regularly during the war, and in July 1943 they were organized into a fourth active commission, the Musicology Commission.[5] With only one significant change, these four commissions continued to be the only ones that met until the end of the war.[6] How they functioned determined how Composers' Union experts used their internal professional authority in the midst of traumatic wartime conditions.

The Military Commission was an active creative forum for the composers who wrote the popular songs that contributed so much to Soviet citizens' morale during the war.[7] It oversaw every step of the ideal creative process from the inspiration provided by contact with the troops at the front to the discussion of the theoretical problems of writing songs and marches to the dissemination and evaluation of the finished products. A significant amount of creative authority accrued to leaders of the commission, especially regarding the composition of popular music, and they could potentially cash in on the popularity of the results of their leadership both within the profession and without.

In 1943 the Orgkom charged the Military Commission with the task of ensuring that composers who were active in Moscow addressed the daily needs of the soldiers by organizing systematic trips to the front and more lengthy attachments of composers to individual units of the Red Army. Some composers considered these trips and long-term affiliations to be among the most important formative experiences of their creative careers.[8]

The Military Commission was also supposed to provide a forum for addressing questions that pertained particularly to writing music "of a military

5. Ibid., d. 1209, ll. 39–40ob. (Orgkom June schedule, 26 May 1943); RGALI, f. 2077, op. 1, d. 71, l. 34ob. (Protokol #9, 9 Jul 1943).

6. See the following Orgkom monthly schedules: RGALI, f. 2085, op. 1, d. 1209, ll. 49a–49 (Oct 1944), 50a–50 (Jan 1945), 52a–52 (Mar 1945), 53–53a (Apr 1945).

7. For a positive evaluation of the role of popular music in the war effort, see Robert A. Rothstein, "Homeland, Home Town, and Battlefield: The Popular Song," in *Culture and Entertainment in Wartime Russia*, ed. Richard Stites (Bloomington: Indiana University Press, 1995), 77–94.

8. RGALI, f. 2077, op. 1, d. 71, l. 34 (Protokol #9, 20 Jul 1943); Richard Stites, "Frontline Entertainment," in Stites, *Culture and Entertainment*, 126–40; Tikhon Khrennikov, *Tak eto bylo: Tikhon Khrennikov o vremeni i o sebe* (Moscow: Muzyka, 1994), 84–91.

repertoire, in particular construction songs and military marches." In other words, the Military Commission provided the institutional location for creating and using a specific type of professional expertise. The commission also helped disseminate composers' songs to performance institutions and publication outlets, and it held monthly concerts to showcase innovation in songs and marches.[9]

Because of the successes of the Military Commission and a resulting influx of song composers with little professional training into the Composers' Union during the war, the Orgkom began to implement changes in the structure of the creative sections even before the war ended. By the middle of 1944, the professional leadership had created a system of advanced professional training—they called it "consultation"—to operate parallel to the creative sections, which were quickly fading from view. The first step in this process took place at the end of March 1944 when the Orgkom approved the official regulations of a new Consultation Center.[10] Financed by Muzfond, the center was supposed to respond to individual composers' increasing interest in various aspects of professional creative knowledge. It was organized around questions of composition, orchestration, polyphony, and conducting. Twelve of the most prominent specialists in those areas were appointed to the center, and their activities were coordinated by its salaried director, Genrikh Litinskii, a composition professor at the Moscow Conservatory. In 1944 the Orgkom expected forty composers to attend what amounted to private instruction with some of the best music educators in the Soviet Union. Composers who participated were to receive a one-month series of two lessons in each of the areas that they chose.[11]

By creating the Consultation Center, the Orgkom made an institutional excursion into an area on which it had merely exerted indirect influence in the past—professional training. Wartime changes in the Composers' Union's membership rendered its earlier system of creative sections insufficient, and the professional leadership responded by creating what was to blossom into an entire system that operated alongside the creative sections, sometimes even forming an intermediate step between a composer's application for admittance and acceptance into the professional organization.[12]

Just a few months after the creation of the Consultation Center, a new Consultation Commission was formed to replace the old Creative Commission. The immediate impetus for the change was a suggestion that the Orgkom create a new commission to evaluate the work of composers from outside Moscow. Though this proposal was seriously discussed, the Orgkom decided not to divide composers into Muscovites and others. Instead, it created the Consulta-

9. RGALI, f. 2077, op. 1, d. 71, l. 34.

10. Ibid., d. 96, l. 43 (Protokol #6, 28 Mar 1944).

11. Ibid., l. 45 (Polozhenie o Konsul'tatsionnom Tsentre pri Orkomitete SSK SSSR).

12. RGALI, f. 2077, op. 1, d. 96, l. 53 (Protokol #8, 18 May 1944). In this example, an applicant was admitted to Muzfond and directed to the Consultation Center to complete his professional training before being taken into the SSK.

tion Commission, the raison d'être of which was to evaluate Soviet composers' "most interesting and discussed works" and provide help in closed session to any composer who asked.[13]

Since composers of all types of music were expected to turn to the new commission, it formed a parallel to the moribund system of generic sections. However, since only the Military Commission, the Children's Music Section, and the Musicology Commission continued to operate, the shift *in practice* was to a system that focused on teaching skills rather than organizing specialists in different types of music. Just as important, because a single commission held the authority to train all composers regardless of genre, internal professional authority became concentrated in one committee within the creative apparatus for the first time.

This change contributed to an institutional basis for postwar tensions between the highbrow experts of the Consultation Commission and the populist experts of the Military Commission. Creating the Consultation Commission marginalized the Military Commission and undermined the authority of its members by requiring that all composers regardless of generic proclivity seek the assistance of the Consultation Commission rather than rely exclusively on the expertise housed in the sections. Another Orgkom decision later in 1944 underscored this effect by restricting the Military Commission's purview to just "composer-songwriters."[14] Though this limitation of the Military Commission's mandate probably reflected existing practice, it represented a definite— if temporary—official decline in the status of the Military Commission and its resident experts as the front moved ever further from the Soviet border.

By the end of the war the Orgkom had begun to recreate the old genre system and use its creative apparatus to assert intellectual control over the production of Soviet opera, always an extremely high-profile genre. This process began with the creation of a new Opera Commission in April 1945. The Opera Commission operated in three arenas: within the profession, between artistic professions, and outside the profession. Within the Composers' Union, the Orgkom encouraged composers who were writing operas to turn to it instead of the highbrow dominated Consultation Commission or the populist Military Commission. It was charged with typical goals of providing a forum for composers to explore problems of composing operas and to furnish the training they needed to do so. Its leadership was supposed to work with the Musicology Commission to develop lectures and seminars on questions of operatic dramaturgy. In managing relations between artistic professions, the Opera Commission was supposed to commission playwrights to write new librettos. Outside the profession, it was supposed to ensure that the Soviet Union's opera theaters paid attention to the efforts of Soviet composers, appealing to the

13. RGALI, f. 2077, op. 1, d. 96, ll. 51–51ob. (Protokol #7, 9 May 1944); ll. 57–58 (Protokol #9, 5 Jun 1944).
14. Ibid., ll. 62ob. (Protokol #12, 4 Oct 1944).

higher authorities of the Committee on Artistic Affairs or the Central Committee if necessary.[15] By adopting these aggressive goals, the Composers' Union began to try to extend its authority into areas of arts production outside its usual bailiwick of composers, musicologists, and music critics. Its tool was expertise, backed by institutional authority.

After the war, the prewar system of genre-based sections was reinstated alongside the consultation system. The first act of this reorganization was an October 1945 transformation of the Military Commission into its postwar form, the Mass Music Section. The section's responsibilities and authority were expanded beyond that of the Military Commission before its status was diminished in 1944. At the request of Military Commission chairman Isaak Dunaevskii, the Orgkom agreed to assign to the renamed Section of Songs and Mass Musical Genres responsibility for the "organization, direction, and stimulation of the creativity of Soviet composers" in all popular music genres, including mass songs, solo variety show songs (*sol'no-estradnaia pesnia*), folk songs, musical comedies, operetta, and music for military band. Though most of these genres were already in the purview of the Military Commission, when the new Mass Music Section assumed responsibility for musical theater, operetta, and especially folk music, it became the institutional home for composition in all "popular" music genres.[16] This reform sharpened and balanced the institutional expression of two latent camps within the Composers' Union.

This trend continued along with the postwar reorganization of the creative apparatus in October 1946, when the creative commissions were reorganized to reaffirm the parallel system of consultation and genre-based organization.[17] The Orgkom reduced the Consultation Commission's mandate to symphonic and chamber music and returned the Consultation Center to its original purpose—improving credentials of composers judged to be borderline, especially those from non-Russian republics.[18]

The October reform also introduced a new Youth Section. The Youth Section's primary goal was not, as might have been expected in a consultation system, the purely technical education of young composers. Nor was it, as might have been expected in a genre-based system, the coordination of efforts to create a youth-based musical culture like the pop music culture in the West. Rather, its goal was to create conditions for the "ideological-creative perfection of composer youth," an exhortation that combined technical education with ideolog-

---

15. RGALI, f. 2077, op. 1, d. 120, l. 14ob. (Protokol #6, 23 Jun 1945), pts. 2.1–2.4.

16. Ibid., ll. 19ob–20 (Protokol #9, 29 Oct 1945). This section went through a number of name changes. For clarity, it will be referred to by the shorthand "Mass Music Section" in the text. For precision, notes will use its correct title at the given time.

17. RGALI, f. 2077, op. 1, d. 139, l. 60ob. (Protokol #19, 8 Oct 1946).

18. Ibid., l. 61ob. (Protokol #20, 16 Oct 1946), pt. 4. For an example of how the Consultation Center was used after the 1946 reform, see RGALI, f. 2077, op. 1, d. 164, l. 1ob. (Protokol #1, 6 Jan 1947), pt. 3.3, which called several composers from the Buriat-Mongol ASSR to Moscow "for creative consultation," undoubtedly under the auspices of the Consultation Commission.

ical oversight or advice.[19] The Youth Section thus joined the Musicology Commission as an organization defined by membership rather than musical genre.

Though almost always a vehicle for organizing professional work according to the priorities of the Composers' Union leaders, the creative apparatus also occasionally responded to outside pressure. After the Mass Music Section was criticized in June 1947 for not paying sufficient attention to folklore, the Orgkom created a new Folklore Commission to study "problems connected with the utilization of folklore in the works of Soviet composers."[20] The creation of the Folklore Commission partially decreased the authority and purview of the Mass Music Section and created an institution that was directly responsible for something that the party elite considered very important, the manipulation of folklore into new, socialist realist music.

From the end of the war until 1948, the sections and commissions of the creative apparatus operated on a weekly schedule. In addition to discussing work in progress and evaluating completed pieces, the creative apparatus provided a number of support services for Composers' Union members, such as requesting funds for members' compositional work and nominating them for special awards or titles.[21] The resulting system was disrupted by the party intervention of 1948. But as we shall see in chapter 7, intervention was only a temporary interruption in the long-term trend of maintaining a creative apparatus as a venue in which to utilize the most authoritative experts within the Composers' Union to direct creative discussions according to professional norms.

Throughout their existence, these creative sections and commissions were meant to affect the composition process. Whether that effect was considered helpful assistance, exciting creative collaboration, or onerous efforts to control depended on the composer or musicologist in question. For example, Shostakovich was so loath to amend his scores in the face of criticism from colleagues (or, even worse, from nonprofessionals) that he famously and unmistakably inscribed his musical signature as a defiant expression of individuality in the early post-Stalin period.[22] Similarly, the musicologist Aleksei Ogolevets was so dismissive of collective criticism that his obstinance prompted a major discussion about appropriate professional behavior in 1947. On the other hand, some Composers' Union members clearly valued the collaboration and feedback that working in the creative apparatus required. This positive evaluation was most frequently exhibited by members of the sections that produced music inspired

---

19. RGALI, f. 2077, op. 1, d. 139, l. 61ob. (Protokol #20, 16 Oct 1946), pt. 3.

20. Ibid., d. 164, ll. 24–41 (Protokol #10, 16, 19 May 1947, 12 Jun 1947), which includes a transcript of the SSK-wide discussion of song music and the activities of the Commission of Mass Genres; l. 46 (Protokol #11, 20 Jun 1947), pt. 4.

21. Ibid., l. 12ob. (Protokol #4, 21 Feb 1947), pt. 3; l. 52 (Protokol #13, 2 Jul 1947); l. 47 (Protokol #11), pt. "raznoe."

22. First introduced in his Tenth Symphony (1953), the most striking instance of this DSCH musical signature is his autobiographical String Quartet no. 8. Taruskin, *Defining Russia Musically*, 493–95; Fay, *Shostakovich*, 217–18.

or intended for performance by amateur groups, especially in the armed forces. Reports about the activities of this section often contained barely concealed excitement about professional collaboration and section-sponsored trips to visit the troops, factories, or collective farms.[23] Much more common was probably an attitude between these two extremes, an acceptance of the realities of professional life that the creative apparatus engendered, and a willingness to participate in the standard professional peer review process. Such a point of view was often reflected in appreciation of the role that senior, authoritative composers could play in the apparatus.[24]

Varying attitudes of composers based in the capitals about collaborative work with composers from the non-Russian republics are typical. Some made careers out of cross-cultural collaboration, others leant their considerable expertise and clout to close collaborations, and yet others participated in training programs and the perquisites they provided to both instructor and students.[25] However they were experienced by the composers and musicologists who subjected their work to the scrutiny of their colleagues in the creative apparatus, the apparatus remained an essential component of the professional organization's institutional structure and its direction of the creative process.

In fact, participants in a May 1947 discussion about the state of the Soviet popular song demonstrated that it was sometimes difficult for some of them even to conceptualize musical production outside the organizational categories provided by the creative apparatus. At the end of the discussion, judgments of the songs were mixed, but participants agreed that the variety music (*estrada*) produced by Soviet composers in 1946 and 1947 was good. However, they also agreed that certain subgenres, like folklore, were being ignored. To remedy the problem, one composer suggested creating a series of subsections within the commission so that proper attention could be paid to those neglected genres.[26] This suggestion demonstrates the high degree to which the categorization of professional expertise and its institutional codification in the creative apparatus of the Composers' Union affected musical production. Some composers simply felt unable to focus attention on genres that were not explicitly included in the Composers' Union apparatus.

One of the most consistent criticisms of the creative apparatus was that it failed to bring composers and musicologists together successfully enough. Musicologists could have been easily accommodated by the genre-based organiza-

23. N. Chemberdzhi, "V oboronnoi sektsii SSK," *Sovetskaia muzyka*, 1935, no. 12:86.

24. Kabalevskii, "O N. Ia. Miaskovskom," 1:309–10.

25. Examples of these three attitudes are provided by the fertile collaboration between V. A. Vlasov, V. G. Fere, and Abdylas Maldybaev, who coauthored four operas, the Kirgiz national anthem, and a host of other pieces; R. M. Glier's creative relationship with Uzbek composer Talib Sadykov, a student with whom he wrote one of the most oft-performed Uzbek operas; and G. S. Frid's impressions formed as a consultant after the war (G. S. Frid, personal communication, 7 May 1999).

26. RGALI, f. 2077, op. 1, d. 164, l. 15ob. (Protokol #6, 24 Mar 1947); ll. 42–44 (Performance programs, [May 1947]), and esp. ll. 24–38ob. (Protokol #10, 1947), here ll. 26–26ob.

tional system, as in fact they sometimes were in practice.[27] However, these efforts proved insufficient to prevent composers from lambasting their counterparts in rare joint meetings and prompted musicologists to complain about their isolation from the much larger group of composers in the professional organization, blaming that isolation for their perceived lack of productivity.[28] The Musicology Commission thus did not always effectively integrate the two groups of professionals, but better work within the creative apparatus was almost always seen as the solution.

This apparatus operated as the primary location for discussion of creative issues, evaluation of musical products, and assimilation of relatively untrained or underprepared composers to norms of membership set by the professional leadership. The creative apparatus thus accomplished the fundamental task of any professional organization, setting norms of professional output and monitoring professionals' work. The conditions created by the Composers' Union were onerous to some and indispensable to others, but for the profession as a whole, maintaining this sphere was crucial to professional work.

Material Support: From Uneven Attention to Muzfond

Another defining characteristic of professions the world over is their elite status and consequent material privilege. The Composers' Union was crucial to maintaining its members in the material elite, especially after World War II, by providing support during the creative process, maintaining conditions conducive to creative work, and extending exclusive benefits to its members. Though the Composers' Union never provided enough money to be a viable exclusive funding source, the direct funding and indirect services it would eventually provide were measures of its success from the earliest days of the municipal composers' unions until the end of the Soviet period. Whether in the form of direct grants, loans, or supplements to salaries earned in other cultural institutions, Composers' Union support was a crucial and definitive professional function.

In September 1934 Sovnarkom passed a decree that dramatically increased the initially feeble funding of the municipal composers' unions. It called on the

---

27. For example, the Orgkom reported on Koval's opera *Sevastopol'tsy* and decided to ensure that two composers and a musicologist would report on the opera at the next Opera Commission meeting. Ibid., l. 13 (Protokol #5, 12 Mar 1947).

28. See comments made by various musicologists during an Orgkom meeting called to discuss the activities of the Musicology Commission in May 1946. The remarks of Shlifshtein, Martynov, Briusova, and to a lesser extent Asaf'ev's post facto written comment complained about isolation, while those of Tsytovich and Khachaturian (in his summary at the end of the discussion) at least implicitly insisted on the value of maintaining musicologists as a separate group that worked independently of the generic commissions. RGALI, f. 2077, op. 1, d. 139, ll. 21–48 (Protokol #10, 17 May 1946).

Central Committee of Rabis (the trade union for arts workers), Muzgiz (the main musical publisher), and the Radio Committee to join the Composers' Union in establishing a new system of higher royalties rates for composers. Sovnarkom also intervened directly, forming a commission to look into music copyright issues and doling out hefty one-time payments to the two municipal composers' unions in the Russian cultural capitals to help them commission new works and organize concerts of new Soviet music. Sovnarkom called on several top administrators to formulate plans for long-term improvements in the material condition of composers. The top education administrator, the head of international cultural ties, and the head of the Moscow composers' union were to look into how to promote Soviet compositions at home and abroad, and the Moscow city government was told to find buildings to house the Moscow union's administrative headquarters and a composers' union club. Opinions were also solicited about additional requests that had come directly from the municipal unions. Relevant institutions were asked to draft proposals regarding efforts to transfer to personal property instruments that had been on loan to Moscow and Leningrad composers' union members, to improve general provisions to composers, and to build new housing that would be allocated to composers' union members.[29]

This decree laid the groundwork for a significant temporary improvement in the still precarious material lot of municipal composers' union members. In 1935 members of the Leningrad composers' union saw the system of direct funding for creative work change from an earlier contract system to a new one. The Leningrad union paid advances to individual composers on the basis of entire one- or two-year work plans while expanding the range of musical styles that received funding to include popular music for the variety stage and all forms of so-called mass music, thus beginning to realize earlier promises of catholicity.[30]

However, the relatively flush funding envisioned by the 1934 decree quickly withered as "non-copyright" royalties were revoked and composers' unions dropped off government funding lists. In May 1937 the Peoples' Commissariat of Finances (Narkomfin) investigated the governmental body that administered copyright and found "serious doubts" about the rights of the Composers' Union to this main source of funding. From 1934 to May 1937 each municipal composers' union received significant funding from royalties collected from concerts of music of "non-copyrighted" composers, including the Russian composers whose works had been "nationalized" in 1919. Losing these royalties would have been a serious blow alone, but it was made far worse by the fact that the Committee on Artistic Affairs failed to include composers in future budgets. All composers' union chapters combined had received one mil-

---

29. SNK SSSR Decree #2278 (28 Sep 1934), "Ob uluchshenii uslovii tvorchestva sovetskikh kompozitorov," *Sovetskaia muzyka,* 1934, no.12:4.

30. T. Svirina, "V Len. soiuze sov. kompozitorov," *Sovetskaia muzyka,* 1935, no. 11:94.

lion rubles in direct governmental funding in the first half of 1937, but this funding would not be sufficient to last the year. Financial crisis loomed.[31]

The Moscow union's resulting plea for assistance initiated an extensive two-year discussion about the formation of Muzfond, its form, and its institutional home. In July 1937 P. M. Kerzhentsev, the powerful head of the Committee on Artistic Affairs called for the preservation of the funding policies for the scattered composers' unions that had sprung up in many of the Russian republic's leading cities through the end of 1937. He argued that composers' funding should only be reconsidered in 1938.[32]

In August, Narkomfin responded with a criticism of this delay, citing the need to form a comprehensive, united Composers' Union. Narkomfin suggested creating a funding institution that would be controlled by Kerzhentsev's Committee on Artistic Affairs and could provide support for young and talented composers who did not have the funds they needed to support themselves while they worked on large-scale compositions. It would also organize concerts for the evaluation of new compositions by Soviet composers.[33]

Kerzhentsev responded with a detailed plan that entailed creating a Muzfond that would be analogous to the Litfond that had been serving writers since 1934. Kerzhentsev noted that since the inception of Litfond, the formation of Muzfond seemed a matter of course but had been delayed because of the "disorderliness of the organizational forms of composers' creative organizations and especially the lack until the very present of an all-USSR organization." Without an all-USSR Composers' Union, there could be no Muzfond, until the Committee on Artistic Affairs came along to provide the necessary institutional home.[34]

Kerzhentsev followed Narkomfin's lead and joined the effort to place all financial control of composers' unions and their members under the jurisdiction of the Committee on Artistic Affairs. His proposal included an elaborate dis-

---

31. RGALI, f. 962, op. 3, d. 188, ll. 9–9ob. (Cheliapov to Antipov, 14 Jun 1937); see also ll. 10–10ob. (Cheliapov's longer complaint to Narkomfin [Grin′ko] and VKI [Kerzhentsev], 23 Jun 1937). The latter provides a more detailed accounting of MSSK's financial situation, as do the following financial worksheets for the MSSK and LSSK, 1937: RGALI, f. 962, op. 3, d. 188, ll. 19–24. For a reference to Narkomfin's reason to revoke royalties, see l. 11 (Kerzhentsev to SNK SSSR, [Jul 1937]). In 1919 Narkompros "nationalized" the music of many of the most prominent and popular Russian composers, who became known as "the Russian classics" during the Stalin period: Tchaikovsky, Borodin, Balakirev, Cui, Musorgsky, Rimsky-Korsakov, Taneev, Liadov, Arensky, Skriabin, Laroche, A. Rubinstein, Serov, Stasov, Smolenskii, Sakketi, and Kalinnikov. See Postanovlenie Narodnogo Komissariata Prosveshcheniia "O natsionalizatsii muzykal′nykh proizvedenii nekotorykh avtorov," 16 Aug 1919, reprinted in *Avtorskoe pravo SSSR i RSFSR: Sbornik dekretov i rasporiazhenii i tipovoi izdatel′skii dogovor, utverzhdennyi NKProsom i NKTorgom RSFSR, s alfavitno-predmetnym ukazatelem*, ed. B. M. Gan (Moscow: Gosizdat, 1929), 44.

32. RGALI, f. 962, op. 3, d. 188, ll. 26–27 (Kerzhentsev to SNK SSSR, 29 Jul 1937), which includes his draft SNK resolution.

33. Ibid., l. 1 (K. Abolin to SNK SSSR, 14 Aug 1937). Details of the Narkomfin proposal are contained in its draft Postanovlenie SNK SSSR; ibid., l. 2.

34. Ibid., l. 3 (Kerzhentsev to SNK SSSR, 28 Sep 1937).

cussion of the sources of funding that Muzfond could receive: a 10 percent cut of all music-related royalties, a cut of box office grosses from musical performances similar to those paid by theaters to Litfond, 10 percent of the amount paid in royalties by theaters, performance institutions, and movie houses, and all of the royalties collected according to the 1919 nationalization decree. Besides these royalties-based sources, Kerzhentsev asked for a one-time payment of 500,000 rubles from the government budget, and promised that Muzfond would also partially support itself through membership dues.[35] Despite this rather detailed accounting of potential funds for the new institution, Kerzhentsev's proposal included almost no suggestion of what Muzfond would do. That he reserved for a set of draft regulations.[36]

Despite the fact that the Committee on Artistic Affairs was at its strongest, these efforts failed.[37] The existence of a comprehensive funding institution for composers required an all-USSR Composers' Union. Creation of Muzfond quickly followed the formation of the Orgkom in 1939. The Orgkom immediately prepared drafts of a Muzfond charter, and when its proposals got mired in the Committee on Artistic Affairs, it submitted them directly to Sovnarkom.[38]

The Composers' Union's proposal predicted that Muzfond would take in 4.5 million rubles per year from a number of different sources. It suggested that 3.7 percent of all publishing royalties be allocated to Muzfond along with deductions taken directly from theater box office grosses, in accordance with the order that had created Litfond five years earlier. It also suggested that Muzfond receive all of the royalties from music written by "non-copyrighted" and nationalized composers, as established in 1919, reaffirmed in 1932, challenged in 1937, and then reinstated in 1938. This practice included collecting part of the total royalties for concerts that contained "mixed" programming—music composed by Soviet composers and by "non-copyrighted" or nationalized composers. This measure would prevent the enrichment of Soviet composers who were fortunate enough to have their music performed alongside the classics, and it would contribute a significant amount of money to Muzfond.[39]

The Committee on Artistic Affairs countered with its own draft resolution

---

35. Ibid., ll. 4–5 (Kerzhentsev's draft Postanovlenie SNK SSSR, 28 Sep 1937). One of the Sovnarkom readers of the proposal seems to have questioned the 10 percent tax on royalties, though not the 10 percent cuts from theater box offices. See marginal notation, "*Mnogo!*" on l. 4.

36. Ibid., ll. 12–16 (draft resolution on Muzfond).

37. For the 1938 resolution to this 1937 dispute, see GARF, f. 5446, op. 23, d. 1852, l. 13 (VKI Prikaz #342, 5 Jul 1938), which clarifies that the Narkompros order of 1932 was still in effect. VKI had already reaffirmed the state of affairs twice, on 7 December 1937 and again on 1 April 1938.

38. GARF, f. 5446, op. 23, d. 1852, l. 7 (Glier to SNK, 16 Jul 1939). Couched in a defense of a suggestion to reallocate money earmarked for Litfond but more accurately pertaining to music, this statement notes the pressing need to build housing, establish basic improvements in composers' material conditions, and provide basic health care for them; ll. 11–12 (SSK SSSR to Kuznetsov [SNK SSSR], 16 Jul 1939). The memo was signed by the entire leadership: Glier, Khachaturian, Dunaevskii, Dzerzhinskii, Bogatyrev, Liatoshinskii, Belyi, Shaporin, and Muradeli.

39. Ibid., ll. 9–10 (draft resolution on Muzfond), ll. 7–8 (Glier's explanatory note).

and Muzfond charter. M. B. Khrapchenko, the new head of the committee, noted that its proposal was based on existing charters of Litfond and its architecture analog. Specifics had been added in consultation with the Composers' Union.[40] The two proposals differed significantly only on two key issues. First, the Committee on Artistic Affairs suggested that Muzfond should receive not 3.7 percent of publication royalties but 5 percent. Such a measure would take more money from the pockets of publishing composers and put more into the coffers of the professional organization. Second, and much more significant, the Committee on Artistic Affairs named itself instead of the Composers' Union to control Muzfond.[41]

Sovnarkom considered both drafts and submitted them to the financial discipline exerted by Narkomfin.[42] In September 1939, A. G. Zverev, the People's Commissar (Narkom) of Finances, gave his approval to the entire project with one exception. He objected to a practice that remained controversial throughout the Stalin period and was discussed in some detail above. Namely, he did not understand why Muzfond should collect the royalties paid for performances of the classics of Russian music. Uncharacteristically, his complaint was not based on a perceived waste of resources. Without explanation, he just noted that it was not advisable.[43] The Composers' Union responded with a lengthy defense based on precedent, need, and the claim that over the years such revenues would surely fall as music by Soviet composers became more widespread.[44] The defense was persuasive.

Sovnarkom's final resolution officially created Muzfond, accepted the language and funding levels proposed by the Committee on Artistic Affairs, and gave control over it to the Composers' Union Orgkom.[45] Muzfond would receive 5 percent of publication royalties and 2 percent deductions from theater box offices when those theaters put on musical performances like operas, ballets, and operettas. Royalties collected on concerts featuring "non-copyrighted" music would remain a main source of money. Much less significant sources of funding were to come from membership dues and income from Muzfond properties.

The most momentous component of this resolution was the decision to subjugate Muzfond not to the governmental Committee on Artistic Affairs but to the juridically distinct Composers' Union. This decision provided a shield against the fiscal discipline supposedly required of government institutions and opened the door for the personalistic practices that would continually characterize Muzfond's distributions of resources.

40. Ibid., l. 24 (Khrapchenko to SNK SSSR, 17 Jul 1939).
41. Ibid., ll. 22–23 (Proekt Postanovleniia SNK SSSR Ob uchrezhdenii "Muzykal'nogo fonda SSSR").
42. Ibid., l. 25 (undated report signed by Kuznetsov and V. Pakhomov).
43. Ibid., l. 15 (A. Zverev to SNK SSSR, 8 Sep 1939).
44. Ibid., ll. 14–14ob. (Lempert to Pakhomov, 17 Sep 1939).
45. Ibid., ll. 30–31 (SNK SSSR Post. #2522, 20 Sep 1939).

But what was Muzfond supposed to do with these resources? The resolution provided the answer in a Muzfond charter.[46] Muzfond's principal task was to "facilitate its members in the development of their creative activity by improving their everyday cultural services and material state, and also to provide help to developing composer-cadres by creating the necessary material conditions for them." Muzfond could give loans, stipends, and travel grants to support composers and musicologists while they worked on pieces and scholarly works. It could give both temporary and ongoing material assistance to members and their families in times of need, provide medical care and treatments at sanatoria, and help improve their housing conditions.[47]

Such extensive promises required that Muzfond have the power to build housing complexes, dachas, vacation resorts (*doma otdykha*), sanatoria, creative resorts (*doma tvorchestva*), cafeterias, kindergartens, and nurseries. It could also organize public lectures, discussions, and concerts, and it could open libraries and music bookstores.[48] Muzfond was empowered to build the material infrastructure that would help support music professionals and their families in virtually every sphere of their professional and personal lives.

The charter also provided membership guidelines for Muzfond that differed from those laid out for the Composers' Union. Membership in the Composers' Union automatically conferred membership in Muzfond, but Muzfond could also admit individuals who were not Composers' Union members but worked actively and independently in music and music criticism. It could also accept composers and musicologists who could no longer work but who made significant contributions to the field earlier in their lives, and young composers who had not yet achieved the status necessary for admittance to the Composers' Union. Members could be removed from Muzfond if they were thrown out of the Composers' Union or if they failed to pay their monthly dues for three consecutive months.[49]

These membership requirements meant that Muzfond could theoretically take on more members than the Composers' Union, a state of affairs that eventually aggravated the leadership of both organizations. Almost immediately, Muzfond leaders began to struggle against Composers' Union leaders to try to limit Muzfond membership. In one of their discussions, a Muzfond official explained that the number of members far outweighed the resources that were flowing into the new institution; in fact, membership outstripped resources by almost three to one.[50] To solve this financial problem, Muzfond suggested that

46. Ibid., ll. 26–29 and RGALI, f. 2077, op. 1, d. 21, ll. 10–12.

47. RGALI, f. 2077, op. 1, d. 21, l. 10, pts. I.2–3.

48. Ibid., l. 10, pt. I.4.

49. Ibid., l. 10ob., pt. II.8–9. It is extremely doubtful that anyone was ever thrown out for not paying their dues.

50. RGALI, f. 2077, op. 1, d. 31, ll. 1–48, here 17–18 (Muzfond stenogram, 26 May 1940). The main speaker, Zimin, explained that Muzfond received materials based on a membership of 570, but the actual membership was fast approaching 1,500. Even Zimin and Muradeli's target of about 1,100 was much greater than the fully supportable 570. The discussion began when Muz-

the Orgkom of the Composers' Union thoroughly and systematically reevaluate its membership and exclude members that Muzfond could not support, namely, performers who were admitted to local unions before the formation of the all-USSR organization and members in provincial and republican chapters who some Muzfond leaders assumed were not *really* deserving of membership. Realizing the political complexity of such a systematic reevaluation, one speaker actually called for the Central Committee to get involved. Others enthusiastically objected.[51]

Muzfond leaders pressed for a membership size determined by financial rather than professional considerations. In a governmental control organization, such an argument may have worked. As a subsidiary leadership group in a professional organization, however, Muzfond leaders were bound to lose, and they did. The Muzfond charter ensured that the Orgkom would win out because it made the Orgkom of the Composers' Union Muzfond's controlling organization. The Orgkom named the Muzfond leadership board, examined and approved Muzfond financial plans, set dues levels, and decided all basic questions pertaining to Muzfond's operation, including establishing basic rules and instructions governing how Muzfond's grants, stipends, loans, and other means of material support were distributed. Muzfond's leadership board was essentially an administrative body rather than a policy-setting or decision-making institution.[52]

It took time to clarify patterns of professional and material administration as expressed in the relationship between Muzfond, its local chapters, the Composers' Union's central leadership, and the local chapters of the Composers' Union. In 1939 the independence of local Composers' Union chapters was initially maintained. The Orgkom would appoint the leadership boards of local Muzfond chapters, but beyond that the local chapters of the Composers' Union—not the central leadership in Moscow—would control local Muzfond organizations and activities.[53]

This institutional arrangement was clarified and centralized during the war as one of the most important aspects of the Composers' Union's wartime institutional consolidation. The relationship between the Orgkom and Muzfond solidified even as Muzfond's own role changed during the war years, first concentrating primarily on creative support and then, near the end of the war, switching its efforts to more purely material issues like emergency loans, health care payments, and housing assistance.

---

fond submitted a report to the Orgkom with instruction about how to admit members to Muzfond earlier that year: RGALI, f. 2077, op. 1, d. 28, l. 1 (Muzfond Protokol #1, 3 Jan 1940).

51. Zimin called for Central Committee action. RGALI, f. 2077, op. 1, d. 31, ll. 8–10 (Zimin on basic problem), 13–15 (Muradeli's reservations about regional lists), 19–20 (Muradeli on performers). See also ll. 15–17, Shirokov's strong objection to conducting a purge of the Composers' Union ("o chistke rech byt' ne mozhet") and reminder that Muzfond was subsidiary to the Composers' Union.

52. RGALI, f. 2077, op. 1, d. 21, l. 11ob. (Ustav, pt. IV.15–16).

53. Ibid., l. 12 (Ustav, pt. V. 19–24).

Before the war, the question of the institutional relationship between Muzfond and the Orgkom had not been settled. In principle, the Orgkom was the leadership body for the all-USSR Composers' Union, and Muzfond was a subsidiary institution. Thus, in principle, the Orgkom was supposed to direct Muzfond activities. However, there remained to be decided several questions about the division of labor between the two institutions. Who would decide whether composers' creative obligations to Muzfond had been fulfilled? Who would decide housing questions? Who was in charge of the publication and popularization of new compositions or musicological works? Who should have the final say in operational questions pertaining to creative and vacation resorts? And who should decide material support issues in the provinces? All of these questions were raised during the war and finally decided at the beginning of 1944.[54]

These questions boil down to two basic issues: the division of labor between the professional support function of the Composers' Union and its resource allocation function, and a question of regional versus central control in both areas. The first issue was confused during the war because of earlier inconsistencies in the assigned leadership of subsidiary institutions like the composers' housing building in Moscow, the main cafeteria (both controlled by the Orgkom), and the system of vacation resorts, creative getaway spots, sanatoria, and state farms (all controlled by Muzfond). Though almost everyone agreed that the Orgkom should reclaim control over all creative questions, there was some disagreement about the allocation institutions. Some suggested that they should all be given to Muzfond while others argued that the Orgkom should control everything. Some even suggested that all tasks should remain split in case the government decided to shut down one of the two institutions. The final decision affirmed Muzfond's subjugation to the Orgkom but gave it control of all material allocation questions. The Orgkom would set allocation policy, but Muzfond would carry it out.[55] In practice, Muzfond's relatively unmonitored control of resource distribution left it open to charges of favoritism and corruption as it provided heavily disproportionate funding to Composers' Union leaders. The centralization of leadership authority was a defining feature of the professional organization.

The issue of regional versus central control was much less tangled. It hinged on a simple question of who set local Muzfond policy, the local Composers' Union chapter or the central Muzfond leadership. Without much discussion, though with some objections from those who dwelled outside of Moscow, local Muzfond branches were made responsible to the central leadership and not their local chapters. This decision eventually left the central Muzfond open to charges of neglecting the periphery.[56]

The other major change in the operation of Muzfond supported this newly

54. RGALI, f. 2077, op. 1, d. 99 (stenogram, 12–24 Feb 1944).
55. Ibid., ll. 12–13, 16–20ob., 24–26.
56. Ibid., l. 4 (decision), l. 15 (objection from Tashkent representative).

clarified division of labor and underscored a more prosperous time for Composers' Union members. At the beginning of the war, a special fund was established to give financial support to composers while they were engaged in creative work. Through that fund, Muzfond markedly increased its payments to composers for pieces that had not been commissioned by the government or by a performance institution. By the end of the war, Muzfond was pleased with the results; however, the return of arts institutions from evacuation meant new, expanded opportunities for outside commissions. Consequently, Muzfond suggested discontinuing its creative support function (except for the neediest young composers and with isolated temporary exceptions for Orgkom members) and concentrating all of its financial resources on material resource allocation, especially housing. The Orgkom commended Muzfond and approved the proposal. In a separate decision, the Orgkom also recognized that Muzfond's leadership body had long been seriously understaffed (Levon Atovm'ian had been running the show by himself), so they appointed a new, eighteen-member leadership body.[57]

By 1944 the Orgkom had completely solidified its status as the chief decision-making body for professional questions and material allocation issues, and Muzfond gained administrative jurisdiction over all areas of material support, including some that were originally formed within the Orgkom's administrative apparatus. The relationship between Muzfond and the Composers' Union was centralized and flattened out. In fact, some chapters in Central Asia saw their Muzfond organizations completely shut down and replaced with a single central representative until 1947. This division of labor and centralized control was reiterated after the reorganization of the professional body in 1948.[58]

Throughout the rest of the Stalin period, Muzfond actively built, expanded, maintained, and managed the basic infrastructure of material support that the Composers' Union provided its members. One of the most crucial elements of material support was housing, and Muzfond almost immediately began building housing structures in major cities throughout the Soviet Union.[59] In Moscow, Muzfond took on a number of construction projects. At one of its first meetings in 1939, the new Orgkom set a construction schedule for the com-

57. RGALI, f. 2077, op. 1, d. 96, ll. 64–66 (23 Oct 1944); ll. 69–71 (Protokol #14, 23 Oct 1944), pts. 4–5.

58. RGALI, f. 2077, op. 1, d. 33, l. 2 (explanatory note, 1940). For the reversal, see d. 164, l. 51 (Protokol #13, 2 Jul 1947), pt. 2; d. 99; RGASPI, f. 17, op. 121, d. 723, l. 57 (draft Ustav SSK SSSR, 1948); RGALI, f. 2085, op. 1, d. 1209, l. 75 (draft Ustav SSK SSSR, 1948). In both drafts, the first of which was approved, Muzfond was called an "economically independent" institution governed by the leadership of the Composers' Union.

59. These construction projects did not always go smoothly. For complaints about slow progress in Leningrad, Tbilisi, and Erevan, see RGALI, f. 2077, op. 1, d. 99, l. 4 (stenogram on Muzfond, 12 Feb 1944). The war disrupted construction, especially in Leningrad. The report that construction on the planned Erevan building had begun came in the midst of a catalog of other war damage, to creative resorts, etc. The report also noted that construction was about to begin in Tashkent, and there were already apartment buildings in "many" cities.

pletion of the first such building. In 1950 another housing construction cooperative was founded, but housing was available only to those who paid into the construction fund from the beginning.[60] The demand for apartments in these controlled housing complexes far outstripped their availability. In 1944 Composers' Union leaders acknowledged that efforts on this extremely difficult front had been woefully ineffective. Khachaturian partially abdicated responsibility for the matter by noting that he did not think that it was a "creative organization's" responsibility. Nevertheless, he agreed that it was extremely important and both the Orgkom and Muzfond were working on possible solutions.[61] The Composers' Union leadership often had to use personal connections to broker arrangements that sped composers through the lengthy general housing allocation process controlled by the Moscow city government.

Muzfond also provided many more specifically professional support services. After the collapse of the system near the end of the twentieth century, even composers critical of the Soviet regime looked back at many of the elements of this system with fondness, stressing how much they helped alleviate practical difficulties. Chief among these much-appreciated professional services were score copying and access to creative resorts.[62]

The Composers' Union always administered score-copying services through Muzfond.[63] Composers could submit their handwritten draft of a completed score to this service, and professional copyists would convert that often scribbled and barely legible draft into a clean, publishable, playable score.[64] If the piece called for it, the service would also produce individual performance parts. Then, the service would publish a small run of the piece and prepare it to be sent to performance institutions. To a nonspecialist, this service may seem trivial, but it could save composers months of tedious, uncreative labor.

The value and desirability of creative resorts is perhaps more obvious. During the first years of the all-USSR Composers' Union, its system of creative re-

60. RGALI, f. 2085, op. 1, d. 1161, ll. 74–74ob. (Orgkom resolutions, Jun 1939), pt. 6; d. 1209, l. 91 (Dunaevskii and A. Buial'skii [chair and secretary of Zhilishchno-stroitel'nyi kooperativ "Sovetskii kompozitor"] to Glier, [1950]).

61. RGALI, f. 2077, op. 1, d. 99, l. 7ob. The issue was raised in the midst of the division of labor between Muzfond and the Tsentral'nyi Dom Kompozitorov, which was soon to be controlled by Muzfond anyway.

62. G. S. Frid, personal communication, 3 Jul 1999.

63. The Composers' Union took full financial control of the service in 1943; by then it was unable to meet the demand for its services because it operated under a system of self-financing, counting on money from performance institutions who paid for access to the performance parts. To alleviate the tremendous strain on the service, the Composers' Union leadership decided to put it on a monthly financial plan: RGALI, f. 2077, op. 1, d. 71, ll. 21–21ob. (Protokol #6, 28 Apr 1943), pt. 3.

64. Payment rates for copyists were first set by the VKI in 1940, amended in 1943, and then altered in 1949. Original and final product determined the rates, which in 1949 ranged from about 40 kopeks per page to copy an already prepared instrumental part to three rubles per page to transcribe an original score. See RGALI, f. 2077, op. 1, d. 339, l. 81 (Prilozhenie #4 to Protokol #41, 9 Sep 1949).

sorts was modest at best, but it began to expand almost immediately. At one of its first meetings in 1939, the Orgkom approved construction of eight buildings at a new creative resort in Ruza. In 1949 the Ruza location was expanded to accommodate more visitors, and that same year the Composers' Union leadership decided to add another creative resort outside Moscow.[65] This new construction brought the total number of creative resorts around the capital to three, including the central resort in Ivanovo; but one composer who appreciated them remembered several others: Repino (near Leningrad), Sartavala (in Karelia), Druskininkai (in Latvia), Vorozil (in Ukraine), and Firiuza (in the Kirgiz mountains).[66]

The basic task of these creative resorts was laid out in a set of 1945 regulations that governed the central resort in Ivanovo. That goal was "to create pleasant conditions for the creative work of Soviet composers." Composers and musicologists were to be sent by the Orgkom to the resort for a limited period in order to work intensively on a particular piece. Though they were supposed to be self-financing institutions, these resorts survived on the basis of heavy subsidies, in the form of both raw materials allocated by the central government and funds provided by Muzfond.[67]

They worked well, frequently surfacing in memoir accounts as scenes of idyllic work, relaxation, creative exchange, and comfortable professional sociability. When writing from the creative resort in Ivanovo to his closest colleague in 1944 and 1945, Sergei Prokofiev called the creative resort a state farm but noted the fresh, tasty food and comfortable accommodations. After he had stayed for a year, his positive description expanded to include the sounds of children playing and the wonderful air. He also reported significant productivity.[68] Similarly,

65. RGALI, f. 2085, op. 1, d. 1161, ll. 74–74ob. (Orgkom resolutions, Jun 1939), pt. 7; RGALI, f. 2077, op. 1, d. 338, l. 134 (Protokol #28, 17 Jun 1949), pt. 2; l. 12 (Protokol #3, 14 Jan 1949), pt. 2. The new Dom tvorchestva kompozitorov (DTK) would be built on land in Sheremet'evo. The Secretariat also discussed new working profiles of the DTK Ivanovo, DTK Ruza, and the vacation resort in Riga.

66. G. S. Frid, personal communication, 3 Jul 1999. There may have been others, and not all of these may have been operational during the Stalin period, though Frid noted that there were fewer later. The Ivanovo DTK existed at least as early as 1944, when the Orgkom discussed details of food allocations to visitors and workers: RGALI, f. 2077, op. 1, d. 96, l. 42 (26 Mar 1944). It was reorganized into the Tsentral'nyi dom tvorchestva kompozitorov Ivanovo in 1945; d. 120, ll. 10ob. (Protokol #3, 20 Mar 1945), pt. 3.

67. Ibid., d. 119, ll. 1–4 (27 Oct 1945); GARF, f. 5446, op. 46, d. 2430, ll. 77–79 (Orgkom and SNK SSSR correspondence, Mar–Apr 1944); and RGALI, f. 2077, op. 1, d. 163, l. 15 (SM SSSR Rasporiazhenie #8623r, 7 Jul 1947). This last instruction allocated six forested hectares to the Orgkom for the construction of a creative resort and children's medical facility. These are only a few examples of a huge number of such allocations, though not all of them supported creative resorts alone. For one example of a request and response that covered a broad range of raw and manufactured goods, see GARF, f. 5446, op. 46, d. 2431, ll. 62–72 (1944). For an example of one year's Muzfond contributions, see RGALI, f. 2077, op. 1, d. 164, ll. 22–23 (Protokol #9, 15 May 1947), which approved allocations of 900,000 rubles to five DTK (Ivanovo, Ruza, Riga, Sartavala, and Odessa).

68. Prokofiev to Miaskovskii, 10 June 1944 and 19 August 1945, in *S. S. Prokof'ev i N. Ia. Miaskovskii: Perepiska*, ed. D. B. Kabalevskii et al. (Moscow: Sovetskii kompozitor, 1977), 473.

Khachaturian remembered a summer stay in 1943 in which he, Prokofiev, Miaskovskii, Glier, Kabalevskii, Shaporin, and the musicologists Nina Makarova and Grigorii Shneerson spent their free time visiting in their cabins, outfitted with pianos, and exchanging thoughts about works in progress and future creative plans.[69] Throughout his career, Shostakovich frequented the composers' resorts in Repino, Ruza, Ivanovo, and Komarovo, sometimes to work and other times to rest and recover his health.[70]

Creative resorts and the copy service were important aspects of a larger system that provided the most fundamental material support to Composers' Union members. The cornerstones of that system were the Muzfond loans and stipends that composers received while they were working on a composition. Before 1943, support during creative work seems to have been determined on a case-by-case basis as composers presented proposals for funding. In 1943 that ad hoc system was regularized in a set of Orgkom regulations that governed such payments. Any Composers' Union member was eligible to receive creative support given out according to a thematic plan approved by the Orgkom. In exceptional cases, less accomplished composers who were just starting their professional careers could also receive support "to stimulate their creative growth." In either case, grants were given to composers upon presentation of a written agreement that had been examined by a creative consultation committee and approved by the Orgkom. Composers and musicologists from the periphery needed only to submit a proposal signed by their local chapter's chair to receive Orgkom approval. Provision of this material support changed over time, but it never ceased to be a crucial aspect of maintaining professionals in a material elite.

Muzfond's other most basic task was providing material aid in individual cases. Regulations passed in 1948 and 1949 provide the most systematic description of the range of that aid, though it was a constant feature of Muzfond's activities from the first funding meetings in February and March 1940 until the end of the Stalin period. Eligibility was extended to active members and their families, including children under the age of eighteen, the spouse, and dependent parents and children regardless of age. Material assistance fell into the following categories: (1) assistance during creative work; (2) political education (payments for libraries, consultations, and courses on Marxism-Leninism); (3) physical education (payments to use sporting complexes and organization of sports clubs); (4) medical assistance and general health care (Muzfond set up agreements with Ministry of Health organizations and with individual specialists); (5) support during periods when a member could not work due to pregnancy, birth of a child, or for health reasons; (6) support after an accident (including serious illness or death in the family, fire, and other emergencies); (7)

69. Aram Khachaturian, "Master—Grazhdanin—Chelovek," in *Aram Khachaturian: Stat'i i vospominaniia,* ed. I. E. Popov (Moscow: Sovetskii kompozitor, 1980), 189.

70. For an example of convalescing during the Stalin period, see Shostakovich to I. D. Glikman, 4 and 21 July 1951, in *Pis'ma k drugu: Dmitrii Shostakovich—Isaaku Glikmanu,* ed. I. D. Glikman (Moscow: DSCH and Kompozitor, 1993), 93–95.

one-time payment upon draft into the Soviet army or navy; (8) support to a member's family in case of death of the member; (9) trips to resorts and sanitariums; (10) payments to support children in nurseries, kindergartens, and summer camps; and (11) loans for personal reasons (not the professional support covered above).[71] In some cases, grant amounts were specified and payments were supposed to be automatic, but equitable distribution proved to be a real problem.

Muzfond was the most important element of the infrastructure that provided composers' basic material support. Controlled by the Composers' Union leadership and modeled after the Writers' Union Litfond, Muzfond helped provide the basic material support that composers needed to live and practice their profession, from housing and financial support during creative work to such professional support services as score copying. In all of these tasks, Muzfond policy was set by the Composers' Union leadership and many of its practices were overseen or legislated by the professional leadership. Though membership in Muzfond provided composers access to resources not available to much of the Soviet population, in practice the distribution of those resources proved uneven. Through its highly centralized apparatus and professional control, Muzfond provided significant and appreciated professional and material support services to the composers and musicologists who comprised the Composers' Union's membership. Together, Muzfond and the creative apparatus thus administered composers' and musicologists' creative work.

A Stalinist Professional Organization

From the time the all-USSR Writers' Union was officially founded in 1934, creative unions were a new sort of Stalinist institution. Municipal composers' unions in Moscow and Leningrad and in cities from Kharkov to the Transcaucasian republics took the shape of proto-professional organizations, collecting, organizing, disciplining, and supporting the composers, musicologists, and performers who embodied the Soviet Union's collective musical expertise.[72] But they did not do so in an institutional vacuum. They fit into an expansive bureaucratic system that was characterized by conflict and integration governed by state regulation, interest politics, overlapping personnel, and informal networks. Examining the place of the Composers' Union within this terrain helps explain how a Stalinist professional organization differed from more common institutions.

71. RGALI, f. 2077, op. 1, d. 234, ll. 81–89 (temporary regulations on Muzfond disbursements, 7 Sep 1948); d. 339, ll. 69–77 (Protokol #41, 9 Sep 1949), pt. 3. The 1949 regulations provided very specific guidelines not seen in the temporary regulations.

72. For evidence that municipal composers' unions or their analogs had formed in Belorussia and Transcaucasia by 1933, see "K plenumu Soiuza sovetskikh kompozitorov," *Sovetskaia muzyka,* 1933, no. 3:155.

Neither the municipal composers' unions nor their more powerful successor were the only institutions devoted almost entirely to music. The Soviet Union maintained a huge network of performance institutions, ranging from the most grandiose opera, ballet, and operetta theaters to the smallest chamber music ensembles and touring soloists. In 1935 the state planning institution, Gosplan, released a report about the Soviet Union's symphony orchestras, bands, folk music ensembles, chamber music and variety music groups, and choirs. Gosplan counted 210 ensembles and some six thousand full-time musicians—not including those employed in music theaters and the film studios.[73]

Most of these performance ensembles were administered by the All-USSR Radio Committee (VRK), and most soloists were members of the State Association of Music, Variety Stage, and Circus Performers (GOMETs).[74] The system was originally overseen by the Arts Department of Narkompros, but in 1936 it was taken over by the much more powerful Committee on Artistic Affairs. Together with the Bolshevik Central Committee's cultural apparatus, the Committee on Artistic Affairs was supposed to provide guidance and control to all cultural institutions, but it followed earlier governmental precedent and focused the overwhelming majority of its attention on performance institutions, especially opera and ballet theaters.[75]

The Committee on Artistic Affairs was as close to an outside, nonprofessional control organization as composers and musicologists experienced, and the differences between it and the Composers' Union illustrate how the creative unions differed from government control institutions. First, the Committee on Artistic Affairs was part of an immense governmental bureaucracy. Creative unions were not. Juridically and formally, they were independent institutions that were supposed to participate in projects defined by government and party mandates, but that would do so without the structural accountability characteristic of government agencies. The significance of this distinction is most evident in discussions of the fiscally undisciplined control that the Composers' Union exerted over Muzfond, which is analyzed in chapter 8.

Most importantly, the Composers' Union was always run by professional musicians, not the professional politicians or bureaucrats who comprised the

73. "Sovetskaia muzyka v tsifrakh," *Sovetskaia muzyka,* 1935, no. 7/8:163–64. Belorussia, Azerbaidzhan, and Turkmenistan were inexplicably not included in the count.

74. Ibid.

75. This conclusion has been drawn from analysis of the structure of the Committee's archive (RGALI, f. 962, with its more than a dozen large *opisi*) and confirmed by detailed examination of its leadership body (op. 3), musical subsection (GUMU, or State Agency for Musical Institutions; op. 5), and secret department (op. 10s). The conclusion is also borne out by the Committee's reports to the Council of Ministers. For a particularly clear example, see the annual report from 1938: GARF, f. 5446, op. 23, d. 1811, ll. 67–69 (Nazarov to Bol'shakov, 26 Mar 1939); the entire report is ll. 58–77. For more details, see the following few examples of typical monthly reports: l. 87 (Jul 1939), ll. 112–13 (Feb 1939), ll. 216–17 (Dec 1939), and other monthly reports in d. 1811. The year 1939 was not atypical. While the Committee on Artistic Affairs was primarily concerned with arts policy, Rabis remained the main source of performers' material support. Theaters and performance ensembles mediated between performers and these other institutions in both cases.

Committee on Artistic Affairs. After Cheliapov's demise during the Great Terror, the overarching concern of Composers' Union leadership and rank-and-file members alike was musical production. Composers' Union leaders and members were always engaged in the actual composition of new music and writing of theoretical or critical works. On the other hand, the Committee on Artistic Affairs was not directly involved in creating music but in overseeing, monitoring, and coordinating the institutions that did the creative work, especially music theaters and performance ensembles. The clearest illustration of this distinction is the fact that the Committee on Artistic Affairs had to employ outside consultants from the creative unions whenever precise evaluation of artistic products was required. Rising professional influence eventually helped the Composers' Union supplant the Committee on Artistic Affairs.

The proximity of Soviet terminology for trade unions (*profsoiuzy*) and my claim that the Composers' Union functioned in Soviet society as a professional organization necessitates brief consideration of the relationship between the two. This necessity is further underscored by the institutional relationship between the trade union for art workers (Rabis) and the nonliterary creative unions in the early 1930s. Investigating the relationship between Rabis and the municipal composers' unions reveals the stark differences between the two types of institutions and the comparatively low level of prestige and material comfort that characterized composers' and musicologists' prewar activities.

The initial relationship between Rabis and the municipal composers' unions was determined by the two institutions' completely disparate access to material resources. The practical subjugation of the composers' unions to Rabis that this state of affairs encouraged was clear already in 1932. In July of that year the Moscow union approached Rabis's ruling body with hat in hand. The poor union's members were in an extremely sorry state because they lost any existing privileges immediately upon entering the new organization. Allocation institutions simply had not begun to provide resources for the new union, and the royalties system that should theoretically have provided for the most fundamental of composers' material needs worked too slowly and provided insufficient funds. Just as bad, the union wanted to hold meetings to celebrate the fifteenth anniversary of the Revolution, but it simply did not have and could not borrow enough money to do it. The new composers' union did not have the resources even to begin satisfying the basic professional, creative, or material needs of its members. Rabis did help by providing a temporary grant and applying concerted pressure on the Moscow city government to start funding the new union.[76]

Rabis's direct relationship with the municipal composers' unions continued for at least a year, but even during this time the overwhelming number of Ra-

76. GARF, f. 5508, op. 1, d. 1717, ll. 149–50 (TsK Rabis Protokol #33, 27 Jul 1932), pt. 5. For a report to Rabis on how the Moscow union used the money allocated in July, see d. 1848, ll. 20–21 (9 Oct 1932). For evidence that Rabis participated in the early organization of other creative unions, see d. 1853.

bis members were performers.[77] Consequently, Rabis primarily concerned itself with the Soviet Union's performance ensembles. Like other trade unions
across the Soviet Union, Rabis's raison d'être was material support, and it
worked with these other institutions and independently to provide that support.[78] Within these boundaries, composers had virtually no place. In fact, Rabis's music subcommittee did not even include composers in its 1933 plan.[79]

This lack of attention meant that the municipal composers' unions remained
in dire straits. Still, the Leningrad union discovered early on that not all attention was good attention. In 1934 one of the secretaries of the Leningrad union,
Vladimir Iokhel'son, wrote to Rabis to object to the unfavorable conclusions
of a visiting investigating commission that denounced collaborative meetings
between representatives from the Leningrad and Moscow unions as "drunken
parties." Iokhel'son angrily objected that such nonprofessional assessors completely failed to comprehend the conditions needed to facilitate scholarly and
artistic work.[80] His complaint garnered little attention at the time, but it prefigured later implicit justifications of professional control over financial institutions like Muzfond. It also asserted the importance of that hallmark of
professional organizations—that only professionals are competent to decide
professional questions.

Trade unions like Rabis were thus different from creative unions like the
Composers' Union. The trade unions existed almost exclusively to serve the material needs of their members. Creative unions eventually helped serve that function through control of their own funding institutions, but material support was
only one part of a much larger system of professional responsibility.[81] Besides

77. GARF, f. 5508, op. 1, d. 1718, l. 189 (TsK Rabis Protokol #39, 17 Nov 1932), pt. 8, in
which Rabis granted material assistance to the Leningrad Composers' Union; and d. 1971 (1933),
which provides statistical data suggesting that composers were still at least partly under Rabis auspices in 1933, but only in three cities, all with existing municipal composers' unions (Moscow,
Leningrad, and Kharkov). The statistical data also demonstrate that composers comprised an insignificant minority in the performance-dominated institution.

78. For a typical sample of these efforts, see the following Rabis protocols: GARF, f. 5508, op.
1, d. 1718 (May–Dec 1932). Meetings to promote a particularly ill-fated food-related issue, rab-
bit raising, took place throughout this period (l. 9 [17 May], ll. 58–60 [27 Jun], ll. 86–87 [7 Jul],
ll. 170–71 [13 Nov]). More typically, Rabis was involved in the process of getting awards and pensions for performers. Examples literally fill the file, but especially see l. 50ob. (title to operetta musician), l. 102 (pension to musician), and l. 128 (deny title to conservatory professor). Not a single
composer was considered.

79. GARF, f. 5508, op. 1, d. 2073, l. 41 (music, radio, circus, estrada group Protokol #1, 21
Oct 1933).

80. For Iokhel'son's angry point-by-point refutation of the investigators' findings, see ibid., d.
2230, ll. 1–8 (27 Aug 1934). For the argument that nonprofessionals cannot differentiate between
appropriate and inappropriate expenditures because they do not understand the conditions of creative work, see especially ll. 3–4. The "drunken parties" ranged from a banquet celebrating a creative meeting between Moscow- and Leningrad-based composers to a working meeting in which
alcohol was not present. Though Iokhel'son's ire was particularly raised by these alcohol-related
accusations, the charge of incomprehension was related more to publication issues and working
hours.

81. Besides Litfond and Muzfond, Khudfond (for the Artists' Union) was created in 1944, and

material support, the Composers' Union also provided a forum for the professional and creative activities of its members. Its ever-evolving system of creative subcommittees and working groups gave composers opportunities to discuss work in progress with their colleagues, to exchange creative opinions, and to develop their professional expertise.

Both trade unions and creative unions sought to represent their members in interactions with the government and party bureaucracies, but the bases of their representative functions were different. Whereas trade unions focused exclusively on their members' material existence, creative unions' representation was based on a fundamentally professional characteristic—the expertise that their members embodied. The sense in which creative unions represented their members was thus much broader, encompassing both material and professional realms. This broad coverage was reflected in the working conditions that each type of institution provided. Trade unions were always attached to a separate workplace, whether a factory or an opera theater. Even though most composers and musicologists also had separate salaried appointments as conservatory professors, research institute workers, or consultants, the Composers' Union provided the very forum for its members' most definitive creative activities: composition and music analysis.

The Composers' Union was also distinct from a final type of institution, the conservatory. As the institutional home of professional composers and musicologists, the Composers' Union depended on conservatories to produce new professionals. The Composers' Union and the conservatories shared personnel since the most authoritative Composers' Union members very often held teaching and administrative posts at the conservatories. Both institutions inherited prerevolutionary traditions of conservatory professionalism. Consequently, the creative visions that they instilled were often similar, but the institutions were not.

Conservatories were much more amenable to governmental control than the Composers' Union turned out to be. Composers and musicologists disciplined by the party in the postwar period often lost conservatory positions but almost never lost Composers' Union membership. As continuing members of the music profession, they could await the rehabilitation that they usually eventually received. By the end of the Stalin period, a sign of the Composers' Union's greatly expanded power was its decisive intervention in affairs relating to the conservatories.

The Composers' Union was thus a unique type of institution in the Stalinist music world. It was differentiated from performance institutions by the type of work its members did (head- versus handwork). It was differentiated from government control agencies like the Committee on Artistic affairs by priorities (creation versus control) and leadership (musician versus career bureaucrat). It

---

Arkhfond (for the Architects' Union) in 1949. GARF, f. 5446, op. 46, d. 2442, ll. 1–28 (SNK SSSR on Khudfond, 1944); op. 75, d. 8, ll. 1–3 (Tepferov to Voroshilov, 16 Nov 1949).

was differentiated from trade unions like Rabis by its scope, uniting as it did the trade union's material supplementary function with a massive creative apparatus that formed the venue for creative work. And it was differentiated from conservatories by primary mission (professional organization versus education), scope, and susceptibility to governmental control.

By the beginning of the war, the existence of the Committee on Artistic Affairs and the conversion of the municipal and republican composers' unions into one quickly expanding all-USSR Composers' Union led exclusively by professional composers and musicologists placed it on the verge of full-fledged professional status. It was governed by a specific type of expertise—the ability to create and interpret new Soviet music—distinct from a whole range of other types of musical and governmental organizations. It had gained control over its own rapidly expanding material support infrastructure, which enabled its members to remain steadily among the Soviet Union's materially privileged. And it was actively overseeing the admission of new members and maintaining a vast creative apparatus to enable and oversee their creative work. But crucial to the definition of a professional organization is monopolistic control over socially valuable work. The Communist Party always posited itself as the ultimate arbiter of social value during the Stalin period, and by the end of the 1930s the music realm had attracted scant attention, especially when compared to such high-profile artistic groups as writers, poets, and film makers. It would take the fiery cauldron of World War II for composers and musicologists to prove their worth. Consolidating its institutional structures along the way, the Composers' Union would emerge from the war a full-fledged professional organization.

CHAPTER 3

Composers on the March, 1941–45

On June 22, 1941, the military forces of Nazi Germany invaded the Soviet Union to begin what the Soviets would come to refer to as the Great Patriotic War. The invasion introduced a period in Soviet history in which the interests of the regime and the Soviet population coincided as perhaps never before or after as both struggled for their survival. The regime made a series of popular concessions by relaxing pressure on the church, promoting Russian nationalism, and appealing to popular patriotism. The population responded with a truly heroic war effort in which masses of eager recruits joined the party in displays of patriotic defiance in the face of Nazi orders to exterminate all Communist Party members.[1] It was a totally patriotic response to Hitler's "total war."[2]

From the beginning of the war, *Pravda* published articles addressing industrial workers, agricultural laborers, women, scholars and artists, and members of non-Russian nationalities as part of a campaign to promote patriotism in each sector of Soviet society.[3] By exhorting citizens to work especially hard at their regular jobs, these articles transformed everyday work into a patriotic activity. As more men were drawn into the army, however, civilians—especially women—were encouraged to take up new tasks to replace the labor that was being thrown into the fire at the front.[4] By August, merely working was not enough—institutions were encouraged to create special Defense Funds that

---

1. T. H. Rigby, *Communist Party Membership in the U.S.S.R., 1917–1967* (Princeton: Princeton University Press, 1968), 236–72. For one composer's decision to join the party, later bitterly regretted, see Grigorii Frid, *Dorogoi ranenoi pamiati* (Moscow: Prosveshchenie, 1994), 228–29.

2. On "Hitler's total war," see *Pravda* beginning in June 1941, especially "Narodnaia voina," *Pravda*, 11 Aug 1941, 1.

3. *Pravda*, Jun–Jul 1941, especially "Net bol'shogo vraga u zhenshchin, chem Gitler," *Pravda*, 18 Jul 1941, 2; "Rabotniki nauki i kul'tury protiv gitlerovskogo varvarstva," *Pravda*, 27 Jul 1941, 1; and "Velikaia druzhba narodov," *Pravda*, 29 Jul 1941, 1.

4. "Kazhdoe predpriiatie, kazhdyi dom—krepost' oborony," *Pravda*, 2 Jul 1941, 1; A. Riabov, "V raionnom tsentre," *Pravda*, 2 Jul 1941, 3; "Kolkhoznitsy—na traktor, na kombain!" *Pravda*, 13 Jul 1941, 1.

could be used to cover the costs of producing additional military materiel.[5] Institutions and individuals alike responded in patriotic outpourings.[6] The struggle against the Nazi invaders was to be carried on at every level of society, as much at the rear as at the front.

Service to the war effort provided the opportunity to fulfill the final requirement of professional organization, performing *socially valuable* work. Musicians actively participated in the patriotic effort right from the start. They entered the ranks of the Red Army or performed in frontline concert brigades and in opera theaters, orchestras, and choirs that were evacuated to the rear. They composed songs for the troops or symphonies for audiences in the rear, and they traveled to the front with performance brigades as hybrid performer-composers. In fact, musicians served the Soviet war effort as perhaps no other artistic group did. They proved the social value of their work and earned themselves entrance into the most privileged strata of postwar society.

During the war, the Composers' Union also consolidated its organizational status and secured its members the legal right to privileged access to scarce goods. It coordinated composers' efforts to write the music that is still a reminder of the society's struggle, and it popularized the musical products that they created.

The profession also faced new problems. The strains of evacuation and impoverishment worsened the already comparatively meager material conditions in which composers and musicologists lived. More lastingly, the Composers' Union's songwriters increasingly clamored for recognition and prestige, straining relations within the Union and helping to establish two loosely defined camps in the profession that comprised its postwar membership. This chapter traces these developments in three areas. It describes the chaotic evacuation at the beginning of the war, explaining how the Composers' Union took advantage of the evacuation to consolidate, centralize, extend its institutional reach, and become more integrated across the Soviet Union's large territory. It traces the profession's changing material conditions from early wartime impoverishment (worsened by evacuation) to comparative privilege by war's end. And it discusses prominent examples of composers' and musicologists' contributions to the war effort, including direct service, patriotic music history, and new music. Among these, war songs and Shostakovich's wartime symphonic trilogy receive special attention. During the war, the Soviet music profession proved its worth, consolidated its elite status, and created popular and highbrow musical products.

---

5. "Fond oborony—novoe proiavlenie sovetskogo patriotizma," *Pravda*, 1 Aug 1941, 1.

6. The SSK SSSR responded by donating one million rubles to tank construction, and a group of Stalin Prize laureates tried to donate money for a tank named "Laureat Stalinskoi premii." RGALI, f. 2077, op. 1, d. 71, l. 1 (11 Jan 1943); RGASPI, f. 17, op. 125, d. 119, l. 46 (4 May 1942).

Dispersal and Integration:
The War and the Evacuation

The first few months of the war were a military disaster for the Soviet Union. The Wehrmacht overran the incompetently led and ill-supplied Red Army at a remarkable pace, capturing Minsk in just six days and reaching Smolensk in less than a month. By early October the Wehrmacht drove toward Moscow, triggering a panicked evacuation, and in late November it closed to within fifteen miles of the capital. Military disaster provoked a massive evacuation, during which composers and musicologists formed lasting personal and professional ties, while their professional organization became more integrated geographically and more consolidated in its evolving institutional forms.

Evacuation was an enormous, chaotic, costly, and logistically difficult project that relocated key industries and their workforces away from the front. Arts institutions were among those evacuated, and expectations placed on them were colossal. Central Committee bureaucrats were unwilling to countenance extended inactivity, and they made it clear that artists were expected to create new art to celebrate Soviet heroism and that performance institutions were required to display exemplary artistic evidence of the specific cultural heritage that the heroism protected.[7] Soviet composers were able to fulfill these tasks particularly well.

The Committee on Artistic Affairs (VKI) took charge of evacuating the arts. Institutions, employees, and their families were broken up and scattered across the Soviet Union until November 1941, when as many as possible were relocated to Sverdlovsk, in the Urals.[8] Evacuation was extremely chaotic, with some especially low moments. For example, the Concert Tour Association (VGKO, the institution that oversaw all *estrada,* or variety music, artists) had not found a final location in early December, so it could not efficiently organize the *estrada* concert brigades that served Red Army troops. Worse, the Piatnitskii Folk Choir, which was thought to be touring the Caucasus, was lost all together. No one knew where it was, although it had last been spotted unexpectedly somewhere in Central Asia.[9] Despite the chaos and trauma, however, the evacuation allowed arts institutions to direct their creative powers to the war effort, which they did quite rapidly.

The Composers' Union began the evacuation process almost as soon as the

7. RGASPI, f. 17, op. 125, d. 75, ll. 78–79 (A. Makhtanov and Zueva to Andreev, 8 Dec 1941); V. L. Komarov, "Krasnaia armiia zashchishchaet mirovuiu tsivilizatsiiu," *Pravda,* 30 Aug 1941, 3.

8. RGASPI, f. 17, op. 125, d. 75, ll. 71–75 (Khrapchenko to Andreev, 24 Nov 1941). For details, see Kiril Tomoff, "Creative Union: The Professional Organization of Soviet Composers, 1939–1953" (Ph.D. diss., University of Chicago, 2001), 54–55.

9. RGASPI, f. 17, op. 125, d. 75, ll. 77–80.

war began. Despite serious hardships, it posed no major problems for the VKI or the Central Committee. Throughout the early months of the war, the Orgkom met at a feverish pace, often daily. The Orgkom members who acted in its name almost always included Reinhold Glier, Aram Khachaturian, Iurii Shaporin, Viktor Belyi, Vano Muradeli, and Dmitrii Kabalevskii. As attention shifted to the practical matters of evacuation and material survival in late 1941 and early 1942, these leaders leaned heavily on two assistants to the head of the Composers' Union, Levon Atovm'ian and V. A. Lempert. Atovm'ian was a composer and orchestrator, and Lempert had been a top staffer in charge of Muzfond construction projects since 1939.[10] Together, these two managed practicalities for the Orgkom and Muzfond leadership. After the evacuation, Khachaturian essentially assumed the helm of the Orgkom, since Glier rarely attended meetings again. Shaporin remained in Sverdlovsk with evacuated composers even after the Orgkom returned to Moscow, so Khachaturian's most regular consultants were Belyi, Kabalevskii, and Muradeli.[11]

The Orgkom immediately made provisions for evacuation and a war footing. It established five special Muzfond funds to support musical brigades, stimulate work on military themes, help evacuated composers, musicians, and musical collectives, support civil defense volunteers, and fund a pioneer camp for children evacuated in early July. A sixth, previously existing fund provided monetary assistance during periods of creative work unsupported by outside commissions.[12] The funds were administered by Atovm'ian, who in mid-July took administrative and coordinating authority over the Orgkom's entire institutional system, including Muzfond.[13]

By operating these funds the Composers' Union participated in and even funded projects suggested by the Committee on Artistic Affairs in addition to financing composers' work and providing for members' and their families' needs.[14] However, the small amounts allocated to these funds also demonstrate the leadership's optimism, shortsightedness, or simple lack of financial resources. Unfortunately, matters would get worse before they improved, as the pioneer camp proved inadequate and composers from Ukraine, Leningrad, and Moscow had to be evacuated. By the time the evacuation was complete, evacuated composers were scattered in Sverdlovsk, Tashkent, Molotov, Tbilisi, Erevan, Alma-Ata, Kazan', Frunze, Ashkhabad, Stalinabad, Baku, and Chkalov.

10. RGALI, f. 2077, op. 1, d. 22, ll. 3, 15 (Prikazy #7 and 32, 11 Feb, 8 Aug 1939).

11. See ibid., d. 37 (Protokoly, 1941), esp. ll. 62–62ob. (15 Nov 1941), pt. 3; and d. 51 (Protokoly, 1942), esp. ll. 16–18 (Protokol #4, 25 May 1942), pt. 4.

12. Ibid., d. 37, ll. 13–14 (Protokol #19, 3 Jul 1941); and for an increase in the first fund from 750,000 to one million rubles: d. 37, l. 50 (Orgkom Postanovlenie #37, 4 Sep 1941); d. 51, l. 71 (stenogram, 7 Sep 1942); d. 37, l. 12 (Protokol #18, 2 Jul 1941). Each civil defense volunteer who was either a member of Muzfond or employed in the Orgkom's administrative apparatus would receive 500 rubles; d. 37, l. 18 (Orgkom Postanovlenie #21, 7 Jul 1941).

13. Ibid., d. 37, l. 27 (Protokol #28, 16 Jul 1941).

14. In fact, Muzfond was later severely criticized for acting like a philanthropic organization precisely because it helped the VKI early in the war: ibid., d. 51, l. 71 (stenogram, 7 Sep 1942).

The largest concentrations settled in Sverdlovsk with the Orgkom and in Tashkent with the Leningrad Conservatory.[15]

Evacuation frequently entailed extreme deprivation. Individuals were separated from their families, and the institutions that were responsible for their material well-being found themselves out of contact and separated from their records. In December 1941, A. D. Skoblionok, an employee of Glavlit (the literary censor) and wife of the composer Sergei Riauzov, appealed to Moscow's military procurator with a complaint that reveals the chaos, misery, uncertainty, and anger that many felt in the early months of the war. Skoblionok explained that her husband had volunteered for military service in July 17, and from that point until mid-October, the Composers' Union had paid monthly maintenance for their two children, Irina (age eleven) and Vitya (three). Once Skoblionok was evacuated to Kuibyshev during Moscow's mid-October panic, however, the children had not received a kopek. The children were separated from her and from one another. Irina was relatively healthy and living with one of Skoblionok's sisters, a professor in Novosibirsk, but Vitya was in extremely tenuous conditions in Tomsk, where he was living with another sister, the widow of the well-known professor and Old Bolshevik E. M. Braudo. Vitya was near starving and had just been kicked out of kindergarten because they could not pay. His conditions were so miserable because his aunt had been laid off. She had been evacuated by the Russian Republic's Administration of Artistic Affairs, but lost her job presumably because there was nothing for her to do in Tomsk while performance institutions were scattered across Russia. She had found work in a cafeteria, but her salary and a pension for Braudo's son could not support their seven-year-old son, herself, her own aging aunt, and poor Vitya.

By not answering her pleas to send money to Novosibirsk and Tomsk, Skoblionok argued, the Composers' Union had abandoned its responsibility to the children of one of the few composers who had volunteered to fight rather than skittering off to the rear. She entreated the procurator to intervene and call the Union to task. Couched in her emotional appeal for help for her children was a tragically straightforward uncertainty and resignation about her husband's fate. "If S. N. Riauzov has been killed," Skoblionok concluded, "that is all the more reason the Composers' Union is obligated to provide for the children of the deceased, children who have been torn away from their mother as well." This appeal contains all of the elements of the hardships of the evacuation and the war that forced it: widespread material deprivation, separation from family members, institutional chaos, tension between the front and rear, and, lurking just below the surface, the constant fear of death.[16]

---

15. Ibid., d. 37, l. 60ob. (Protokol, [11] Nov 1941). For other details, including the size and distribution of the six funds see Tomoff, "Creative Union," chap. 2.

16. RGALI, f. 2085, op. 1, d. 1209, ll. 20–20ob. (A. D. Skoblionok to the Moscow military procurator, [N. F.] Teplinskaia, and R. M. Glier, 23 Dec 1941). Teplinskaia was the SSK representative in Moscow. The fact that this appeal ended up in Glier's personal files suggests that the message finally got through to Sverdlovsk.

This story has a perhaps uncharacteristically happy ending. Riauzov was not killed but taken prisoner early in the war. He spent most of the war in German prisoner-of-war camps, but he eventually escaped and joined the partisans. He survived the war to play a small but active role in the postwar life of the Composers' Union and write a memoir about music in Nazi concentration camps.[17]

The single group of composers that probably suffered most during the first half of the war consisted of those who were not evacuated from Leningrad before the onset of the famously horrific nine-hundred-day siege of the city.[18] Though no one who survived the siege did so without unthinkable deprivation, specific details of the Leningrad composers' experiences during the first winter of 1941–42 demonstrate how limited the Composers' Union's penetration of the privileged elite was before the war. Everyone in Leningrad was affected by lack of transportation, phone communication, and, more importantly, heat. Rations were cut to below starvation levels.

Even within these horrible conditions, however, there were gradations of access to goods, both through hierarchically assigned ration categories and through a system of closed distribution, which ran primarily through special cafeterias. The Leningrad chapter of the Composers' Union did not have such a cafeteria, and efforts to gain access to others were only partially successful. With difficulty, they arranged permission to eat some meals at a few theaters' cafeterias and at some local city government cafeterias, though they were never admitted to the Writers' Union's "well-stocked" cafeteria as they hoped they might be. They were eventually granted permission to open their own, but by that time they had no money to pay for the necessary capital renovations, and supplies to new institutions had long ago ceased anyway. As it was, many composers were not even in the highest ration category.

The composers' difficulties gaining access to elite cafeterias should be understood as a function of their insufficiently elite status before the war and not as an indictment of the institutions who excluded them. "Well-stocked" cafeterias were far from having enough resources to feed their own members even adequately. That composers managed to gain access to some theater and government cafeterias is already a sign that their status was improving. In fact, in November and December they received an additional eleven first-category ration cards, and by June 1942 the whole Leningrad chapter had managed to get on especially high "curative rations." Still, they were fed through an overtaxed cafeteria that only admitted its huge number of arts workers in two-week shifts. And these improvements came far too late for the twenty-one members who

17. S. N. Riauzov, "Muzyka v plenu," in *Muzyka na frontakh Velikoi otechestvennoi voiny,* ed. G. Pozhidaev (Moscow: Muzyka, 1970).

18. Harrison Salisbury, *The 900 Days: The Siege of Leningrad* (New York: Harper and Row, 1969); Cynthia Simmons and Nina Perlina, eds., *Writing the Siege of Leningrad: Women's Diaries, Memoirs, and Documentary Prose* (Pittsburgh: University of Pittsburgh Press, 2002).

starved to death, froze, or died of untreated disease during the winter of 1941–42.[19]

Outside Leningrad, material deprivation did not often reach conditions this extreme, but procuring the essentials for daily living and securing those that had been found became even more important—and difficult—than it had been before the onset of war. The Orgkom tried to keep in touch with members and arrange special deliveries of scarce goods such as vitamins.[20] The general mobility and upheaval of the evacuation also meant that securing one's personal effects back home, or even apartment, required special attention, if they were not already completely destroyed.[21] Beginning shortly after its return from Sverdlovsk in 1942, the Orgkom did what it could to preserve the abandoned apartments of Moscow-based composers, attempting first to resettle those who had moved in and then helping composers pay their monthly apartment dues. The Orgkom (and Muzfond) logic was that composers who lived in Tashkent or Stalinabad could not hope to pay for their apartments promptly, so Muzfond should help them cover those fees while they were evacuated, presumably because it would save the effort of helping them find new housing when they returned.[22] Despite these efforts, there was little that could be done to prevent squatters from moving in.[23] And the hardships were not just personal but professional as well. Valuable musical instruments were destroyed, buildings were bombed, and prewar professional advancement plans were short-circuited.[24]

The beginning of the war and the evacuation presented problems not just for individual musicians, composers, and musicologists but also for arts organizations as institutions. The Composers' Union responded, sometimes with unintended consequences, to the difficulties of the early war years by solidifying formerly porous and unelaborated boundaries of its membership, beginning to expand its contacts and services into the regions, and consolidating its institutional structure. These three developments solidified the bounds of professional membership and sowed the seeds of future intra-professional strife for years to come.

19. RGALI, f. 2077, op. 1, d. 51, ll. 41–45 (Protokol #9, 23 Aug 1942).

20. GARF, f. 5446, op. 44, d. 1117, ll. 106–7 (SNK correspondence with NKPishcheprom SSSR 15 Dec 1942). For complete failure, see RGALI, f. 2077, op. 1, d. 51, l. 42 (Protokol #9, 23 Jul 1942), on the end of Muzfond-supplied medicine in Leningrad during the winter of 1941–42.

21. RGALI, f. 2085, op. 1, d. 1209, l. 30 (power of attorney, Glier to V. N. Krylov and N. R. Glier, 9 Jun 1942). Krylov and N. R. Glier were his son-in-law and daughter. For the complete destruction of apartments, houses, and personal property of Leningrad composers, see f. 2077, op. 1, d. 51, l. 42 (Protokol #9, 23 Jul 1942).

22. RGALI, f. 2077, op. 1, d. 51, ll. 18–19 (Protokol #4, 25 May 1942); l. 64 (Protokol, 7 Sep 1942); l. 76ob. (stenogram, 7 Sep 1942).

23. GARF, f. 5446, op. 48, d. 2181, l. 43 (letter to Voroshilov, 17 Oct 1946).

24. Ibid., op. 46, d. 2425, ll. 162–68 (late 1944); RGALI, f. 2077, op. 1, d. 96, l. 52 (9 May 1944); and GARF, f. 5446, op. 46, d. 2419, l. 99 (Shebalin to SNK SSSR, 22 Feb 1944); op. 48, ll. 109–23, 120–23 (on replacement pianos, 1946).

It should be recalled that performers were excluded from the Composers' Union in 1944 after they led an unsuccessful bid to dissolve the Union into a proposed new Musicians' Union. At the same time, membership was extended to a growing number of musicologists and composers, especially songwriters. Exact data about changing membership during the war are impossible to find because the Composers' Union leadership itself did not know how many members it had, either before the war or during it. However, the Orgkom considered 184 membership applications during the war, admitted seventy-seven new members, rejected sixty-seven applicants, and postponed decisions on forty.[25] These data overlap because many of those about whom final decisions were postponed in one meeting were later either admitted or rejected for good. In many cases, however, decisions were postponed while the applicant completed conservatory training or a special series of finishing courses offered by the Composers' Union. Some of those decisions were probably postponed until after the end of the war. Even if these seventy-seven admitted by the Orgkom were the only additions to the Composers' Union, they constituted a roughly 10 percent increase in total membership.[26] That the actual increase was even larger is suggested by a financial report in which Muzfond leaders announced that they expected to receive dues from one thousand members.[27] Not all Muzfond members were admitted to the Composers' Union. Some conservatory students were admitted to Muzfond until they finished their studies, and occasionally other candidates were accepted into Muzfond and then referred to special professional training programs before being admitted to the Union. Still, it is doubtful that there would be two hundred Muzfond members not admitted to the Composers' Union.

So who were these new members? It is hard to tell for sure, but details of the Orgkom's growing unease about new members suggests that many of them were songwriters with questionable professional qualifications. In May 1942 and again in July, the Orgkom warned local chapters that new members' qualifications were expected to be very high, and the Orgkom would eventually have to approve all new members.[28] This anxiety about qualifications cloaked ap-

---

25. See the following protocols of Orgkom meetings at which membership decisions were enacted, 1941–45: RGALI, f. 2077, op. 1, d. 37, l. 61(1941); d. 51, ll. 7–9, 22–23, 31–33, 48–49, 54, 92, 95–97, 98ob. (1942); d. 71, ll. 1–2, 6–6ob., 21ob., 32ob.–33, 36–38ob. (1943); d. 96, ll. 22ob., 53, 62, 68–69, 73 (1944); and d. 120, l. 8 (1945).

26. RGALI, f. 962, op. 5, d. 531, ll. 28–29 (Orgkom work plan, 13 Feb 1941). Total membership at that time was estimated at roughly 800 members.

27. RGALI, f. 2077, op. 1, d. 51, l. 62 (Protokol, 7 Sep 1942). Later plans counted on fewer dues, but that was probably because of expectations that members would not pay rather than because there turned out to be fewer members than Muzfond thought in 1942. For criticism of their 1942 plan based on high percentages of members in arrears, see RGALI, f. 2077, op. 1, d. 51, ll. 66, 74, 76 (stenogram, 7 Sep 1942). For the later estimates, see d. 96, l. 43 (Protokol #6, 28 Mar 1944) and d. 120, l. 10ob. (Protokol #3, 20 Mar 1945).

28. Ibid., d. 51, ll. 15–16 (Protokol #4, 25 May 1942); l. 30 (Protokol #8, 18 Jul 1942). The May decision also noted that SSK members who lived in a city for any extended period of time (i.e., in evacuation) were to be transferred mechanically into that city's SSK chapter.

prehension about the professional credentials of songwriters, an issue that had worried the Orgkom even before the war.

This guarded apprehension burst into the open in a set of instructions that the Orgkom sent to the Uzbek Composers' Union in December 1942. It urged the Uzbek leadership to insist on high qualifications, *especially among tune-smiths.*[29] The Orgkom was even concerned about the qualifications of M. E. Tabachnikov, the composer who wrote "Let's Have a Smoke" ("Davai za-kurim"), a popular song famously performed by one of the Soviet Union's most beloved crooners, K. I. Shul'zhenko. The Orgkom initially held off on Tabach-nikov's membership application, noting that he was a fine songwriter and ad-mitting him to Muzfond, but asking the Military Commission to take a longer look at his songs and help organize a special training program for him.[30] The Orgkom considered it important to admit talented songwriters but harbored serious reservations about their professional qualifications. The resulting influx of songwriters would have serious implications for internal divisions within the profession after the war.

During the war, the Composers' Union clarified its centralized control over local chapters and the relationship between the Orgkom and Muzfond. Dis-persing evacuated composers throughout the rear also helped to integrate the Composers' Union informally. For example, the arrival of evacuated com-posers from Moscow and Leningrad in Tashkent was said to have helped the Uzbek Composers' Union by facilitating two-way creative exchange. Evacuees used Uzbek folklore materials in their compositions, and Uzbek composers benefited from direct collaborations with evacuees. Uzbek songwriters also be-gan to write war songs and marches only after the Muscovites and Leningrad-ers arrived.[31]

Evacuees also formed lasting bonds among one another. When they returned from evacuation, they sometimes divided themselves according to where they had been evacuated and continued associations formed in evacuation even af-ter the return. In his recollections of Miaskovskii, Vissarion Shebalin noted how other "Frunze-ites" entered the social circle that revolved around the fam-ilies of Miaskovskii and Pavel Lamm once they returned to Moscow from that Kirgiz capital. Similarly, many of the Soviet Union's most prominent com-posers later reflected on their time spent together at the Ivanovo creative re-sort in the war's latter years. In fact, vacationing together in 1944–45 seems to have cemented the insularity of the most authoritative, influential, and power-ful composers, including Prokofiev, Miaskovskii, Shostakovich, Khachaturian, and Kabalevskii.[32]

29. Ibid., l. 101ob. (Protokol #17/18, 16 Dec 1942). In this case, the word that I translate as "tunesmiths" is "*kompozitory-melodisty.*" The numbering of Orgkom meetings at the end of 1942 was inconsistent; I use the numbers printed on the protocols.

30. RGALI, f. 2077, op. 1, d. 96, l. 53 (Protokol #8, 18 May 1944).

31. Ibid., d. 51, ll. 50–51 (1942), a report by the representative of the Uzbek SSK.

32. Vissarion Shebalin, "Iz vospominanii o Nikolae Iakovleviche Miaskovskom," in Shlif-

Some results of that informal integration actually found institutional expression. For example, in the first couple weeks of the evacuation, Muzfond looked into establishing new chapters in Sverdlovsk and Ufa. Though the Orgkom thought it prudent to hold off on Sverdlovsk until matters settled, it immediately agreed to the Ufa branch.[33] In 1943 the Committee on Artistic Affairs also established a branch of the state's central music publisher, Muzgiz, in Sverdlovsk as a direct response to conditions created by evacuation.[34] This extension of institutional support to regions in which it had not previously existed was an important result of the evacuation because it helped integrate the regions with the center, extending the Muzfond expansion of 1940.

The Orgkom sought to capitalize on this integration, using it to continue prewar efforts to pay more attention to composers from outside Moscow. In 1940 and early 1941, the Orgkom had held a series of traveling plenary sessions in Kiev, Kazan', and Leningrad, and it planned to hold more plenary sessions in the Caucasus in late 1941.[35] These plans were disrupted by the Nazi invasion, but the Orgkom did make some effort to continue the process. In early July, it responded to a joint request from Composers' Union chapters in Kazakhstan, Kirgizia, Tadzhikistan, and Turkmenistan by dispatching a Muzfond representative to help establish a temporary institute to facilitate their organizational work.[36] After the war, the Orgkom again sought to implement earlier traveling plenary session plans.

Despite problems of chaos and material deprivation, the evacuation of the arts institutions was an impressive component of the monumental evacuation of much of the Soviet Union's industrial complex at the beginning of the war, impressive if for no other reason than that arts institutions were included at all.[37] Evacuation allowed arts institutions to continue to function even during the militarily disastrous first months of the war. By the time the second German offensive on Moscow began, the Bol'shoi had already begun to stage major operas in Kuibyshev, and by the time the Wehrmacht achieved its nearest approach to Moscow the conservatory had been holding classes in Saratov for three weeks. The German advance on Leningrad was much more rapid, thus trap-

---

shtein, *N. Ia. Miaskovskii,* 1:293; M. Mendel'son-Prokof'eva, "O Sergee Sergeeviche Prokof'eve," in *S. S. Prokof'ev: Materialy, dokumenty, vospominaniia,* 2nd ed., ed. S. I. Shlifshtein (Moscow: Gosmuzizdat, 1961); Shostakovich to Glikman, 23 Jul 1944, in Glikman, *Pis'ma k drugu,* 68.

33. RGALI, f. 2077, op. 1, d. 37, l. 33 (Joint Orgkom and Muzfond Protokol #29–30, 27–29 Jul 1941).

34. RGASPI, f. 17, op. 125, d. 216, ll. 73–74 (correspondence, VKI and OPA TsK VKP(b), 25 Jun to 4 Aug 1943).

35. RGALI, f. 962, op. 5, d. 531, ll. 26–27a (Orgkom workplan, 13 Feb 1941); numbers cited correspond to notations in the file; ll. 35, 41ob. (undated, probably Feb 1941).

36. RGALI, f. 2077, op. 1, d. 37, l. 22 (Protokol #23, 8 Jul 1941).

37. For an evaluation of the evacuation of industry, see J. Barber and M. Harrison, *The Soviet Home Front 1941–1945: A Social and Economic History of the USSR in World War II* (London: Longman, 1991), 127–32.

ping more artists in the city, but by late autumn Leningrad's arts institutions were also beginning to operate again, deep in the rear and out of harm's way.[38]

Paradoxically, the all-USSR Composers' Union consolidated in evacuation. It limited membership to those who engaged in the theoretical construction of Soviet music: composers and musicologists, some of whom even took advantage of the evacuation to spend extended time in regions in which they had already pursued ethnographic interests.[39] It also expanded its institutional coverage to new locations, consolidating ground accidentally gained during the evacuation. It clarified its relationship with its provincial chapters, and it established an institutionally based division of labor between its professional support functions and its resource allocation responsibilities. In all of these aspects of institutional consolidation, it affirmed that power was concentrated in the central Orgkom of the all-USSR Composers' Union and sowed the seeds of future regional-based tension within the profession.

At the Front and in the Rear: Wartime Service

These institutional developments were typically only secondary or tertiary considerations for composers and musicologists. Their primary concern was how to serve the war effort. And serve, they did, proving the value of their work and emerging as a fully formed profession.

According to their later recollections and their immediate actions, most composers greeted the beginning of the war with a combination of surprise and patriotism. Some entered the ranks of the Red Army as volunteers or draftees. Others joined local civil defense brigades that existed in the rear but served a purpose directly related to the fighting. The famous case of Shostakovich serving on his building's fire defense unit in Leningrad is just one example of this phenomenon, which was particularly common among composers who remained in Leningrad after the beginning of the siege.[40]

For most composers, however, the start of the war was a call to begin intense creative work directly inspired by the war effort. Many composers remembered that they initially thought their creative services were no longer relevant and only later realized how important a role music could play in the war effort. The initial reaction of Orest Evlakhov, a Leningrad composer and Shostakovich student, was typical:

38. For example, G. Popov, who was working on a film score, was stuck in Leningrad when he missed the evacuation of Lenfilm: "G. Popov," in G. A. Polianovskii, ed., *Sovetskie kompozitory—frontu: Samootchety-vospominaniia* (Moscow: Sovetskii kompozitor, 1989), 6–8.

39. RGALI, f. 2077, op. 1, d. 37, ll. 37–38 (list of evacuees, 29 Jul 1941).

40. Shostakovich first volunteered for the regular army: Fay, *Shostakovich*, 123. He eventually appeared on the cover of *Time* in his firefighter's uniform. For another example, see Polianovskii, *Sovetskie kompozitory—frontu*, 10. This volume is comprised of short autobiographical sketches written in the autumn of 1945 and winter of 1946.

> I remember that my first impression was a feeling of complete incapacity to compose. It seemed to me then that the danger for the Motherland was so serious and great that only direct involvement in the events might serve some sort of real use to the country. The work and creative production of a composer seemed to me completely unneeded. Only gradually did this difficult feeling recede, and I was able to return to my work that had been interrupted by the war. Besides that, the new situation imperatively demanded the most varied activity.
>
> In the hot, sunny days of July and August 1941, I served in the Leningrad Conservatory's agitation collective. The agitation collective had in its arsenal a string quartet which regularly accompanied vocalists in concerts. For this quartet, I arranged some classical arias, romances, and Soviet songs.[41]

Despite their initial sense that music was not an important wartime occupation, composers soon began to assert that their creative efforts could contribute something significant to the war effort. Those contributions took many forms. Composers served in the military and in music battalions, they traveled with the troops and recorded their amateur musical endeavors, they participated in a grandiose competition to create a new national anthem, and, of course, they wrote music, from popular songs to orchestral music.

Some Composers' Union members joined the army or navy and fought. By August 1941 twenty Moscow-based members had left for the front.[42] By July 1942 twenty-seven Leningrad-based composers (including conservatory students who were members of Muzfond) had entered the Red Army or Baltic Fleet.[43] Twenty Leningrad members had been killed at the front by mid-1943, at which time there were only thirty Composers' Union members left in the blockaded city, and that twenty does not count those who died of starvation or who froze to death during the horrendous winters of 1941 and 1942.[44] Of the 121 prewar members of the Ukrainian Composers' Union, 11 entered the Red Army, 37 remained in occupied territory, 69 were evacuated, and 5 died.[45] By

41. "O. Evlakhov," in Polianovskii, *Sovetskie kompozitory—frontu,* 10. Evlakhov was the student to whom Shostakovich turned to request the incomplete opera score of another student, Veniamin Fleishman, when he was killed at the front. The result was *Rothschild's Violin.* Elena Silina, "Veniamin Fleishman, Uchenik Shostakovicha," in *Shostakovich mezhdu mgnoveniem i vechnost'iu: Dokumenty, materialy, stat'i,* ed. L. G. Kovnatskaia (St. Petersburg: Kompozitor, 2000), 383.

42. RGALI, f. 2077, op. 1, d. 37, l. 37.

43. Ibid., d. 51, ll. 37–38 (Protokol #9, 23 Jul 1942). At that point, only two had been killed, three wounded, and five demobilized.

44. Ibid., d. 71, l. 25, pt. 1 (Protokol #7, 10 May 1943); A. V. Bogdanova, ed., *Pamiati pogib-shikh kompozitorov i muzykovedov 1941–1945: Sbornik stat'ei* (Moscow: Sovetskii kompozitor, 1985), 1:8–20, which consists of short biographical sketches of the twenty slain members. In the first, LSSK representative Bogdanov-Berezovskii divided the thirty living LSSK members into twenty composers and ten musicologists and performers.

45. RGALI, f. 2077, op. 1, d. 96, ll. 4–5 (Protokol #2a, 11 Jan 1944), report of F. E. Koznit-skii on activity of Ukrainian SSK. The numbers, though they do not add up, are as they appear in the original. For an earlier report that does not attempt such precision, see RGALI, f. 2077, op. 1, d. 51, ll. 103–3ob. (Protokol #18, 24 Dec 1942).

the end of the war, at least 44 Composers' Union members, more than 5 percent of the prewar membership, had died in the fighting.[46] The percentage may have been higher. There were 829 members of Muzfond in 1941, and by December 1943, 61 had been killed, 12 were missing in action, and 32 remained in occupied territory.[47] The 73 killed or missing in action amounted to almost 9 percent of the prewar membership, and the war would still continue for eighteen months.

The disparity between these sets of statistics can be explained partly by different reporting parameters, but it is mainly a result of the fact that members of Muzfond were not necessarily members of the Composers' Union. Since it was relatively standard procedure to admit promising but as yet unaccomplished composers to Muzfond while they sought to raise their professional qualifications to a level appropriate for full membership, the nonoverlapping group consisted primarily of young men—exactly that demographic group most likely to be killed in war. Inexact though they are, these statistics do provide a general sense of the scale of military service among Composers' Union members. Obviously, the scope of their sacrifice should not be underestimated. However, it was also much lower than the average for the entire Soviet Union, in which one in every seven died.[48] Considering that the overwhelming majority of Composers' Union members were male, we may have expected their mortality to be even higher than the national average.

That it was not can be explained in part by the fact that most composers, like professionalized elites in other belligerent societies, were significantly beyond the prime soldiering age, but that explanation is not entirely sufficient. Another contributing factor was the value placed on their professional activities, which were considered crucial to the war effort. This value entitled even budding professionals to exemptions from military service, though the exemptions were not unlimited. In 1944 the director of the Moscow Conservatory requested military service exemptions for about a hundred conservatory students, arguing that interrupting their studies would greatly harm their future potential. Military authorities argued against the exemptions, noting that the conservatory already had significantly more exemptions than other institutions of higher education.[49] Musicians' professional services were clearly highly valued by the re-

---

46. A memorial installation on the second floor of the Dom kompozitorov in Moscow names the forty-four who were killed, including twenty from Leningrad and sixteen from Moscow.

47. RGALI, f. 2077, op. 1, d. 99, l. 1ob. (stenogram, 12–24 Feb 1944).

48. For the "one in seven" number, see Barber and Harrison, *Soviet Home Front,* 41, where it is embedded in a discussion of the unreliability of estimates of Soviet civilian and military losses during the war. This number should be treated with some skepticism, but whatever the precise statistics, the Composers' Union suffered fewer losses than the population's average.

49. GARF, f. 5446, op. 46, d. 2419, ll. 124–25 (Correspondence, Shebalin, V. Tepferov, and A. N. Kosygin, 21–29 Feb 1944). Shebalin's request targeted performance students, but the conservatory's more-than-average exemptions clearly applied to budding composers and musicologists as well.

gime. But what exactly did those professional services amount to, and why were they so important?

The most celebrated service was participation in a music battalion that entertained the troops. In September *Pravda* complained that these brigades' repertoire was not yet popular enough, but it also reported impressive concert mobilization. In the second half of July and August, the Central Theater of the Red Army had staged a hundred concerts for the active army. Leningrad was even more productive; each of the many concert brigades that were formed at the start of the war to serve the Northern and Northwestern Fronts had put on an average of 160 concerts per month. The periphery was doing the same. In Rostov, 992 people in thirty-six brigades had given over five hundred concerts. And in the first ten days of the war, 250 concerts took place in Odessa, 140 in Ordzhonikidze, and 184 at mobilization points in Irkutsk.[50] The Composers' Union later reported that in the first year and a half of the war, two hundred thousand concerts and performances were given for the Red Army, and sixty thousand of those took place right at the front. In the month of February 1943 alone, artists performed for the Red Army fifteen thousand times.[51]

Though these concert brigades were comprised mainly of performers, some of them had a resident composer who both performed with them and wrote new material throughout the war.[52] Others served as organizations that composers visited when they came to the front to collect material for composition efforts that were conducted in the rear.[53] Sometimes these concert brigades assisted amateur musical groups that the Red Army soldiers formed themselves. Those groups then hosted professional composers during their trips to the front.[54] Beginning in mid-1942, the Composers' Union even began printing sample programs for amateur musical productions and packaging them with accompanying sheet music.[55]

In 1943 composers also participated in a grandiose competition sponsored

50. Viktorina Kriger, "Rabotniki iskusstv—Krasnoi Armii," *Pravda*, 4 Sep 1941, 3.

51. "Muzyka i muzykanty nashikh dnei," in *Sovetskaia muzyka: Sbornik stat'ei No. 1* (Moscow: Muzgiz, 1943), 4. The last figure may be somewhat misleading because it appears to count each individual artist's performance separately; so a string quartet accompanying a vocalist in a single concert seems to have been counted as five performances. For the other numbers, the counting procedure appears to have been more straightforward.

52. G. S. Frid was such a composer, an official member of the army who directed a folk instrument orchestra of the Central House of the Red Army, a concert brigade that performed directly before the troops at the front, in hospitals, in squares, and in train stations. See Frid, *Dorogoi ranenoi pamiati*, 207–12.

53. "V. Belyi," in Polianovskii, *Sovetskie kompozitory—frontu*, 27–28; "D. Vasil'ev-Buglai," in ibid., 30–31; and "N. Chemberdzhi," in ibid., 38.

54. See "D. Vasil'ev-Buglai," in ibid., 31; and especially "Iu. Miliutin," in ibid., 33. The Polianovskii volume contains short autobiographical statements written by eighteen composers of different creative proclivities, each of whom traveled to the front, often several times.

55. RGALI, f. 2077, op. 1, d. 51, l. 14 (Protokol #4, 25 May 1942). This decision empowered Muzfond to print programs and sheet music for four thematic sample concerts, each with a coordinating editor: Partisan (edited by Muradeli), Summer (Kabalevskii), Lyrical (Belyi), and Naval (Khachaturian).

by the party and government to create a new national anthem. This competition took precedence even over concert brigade service. When the army's chief political administration requested that leading Stalin Prize–winning composers visit the front in 1943, none answered the call. When the army complained, they were told that everyone was busy working on the hymn. I. O. Dunaevskii, the most famous composer of popular music in the Soviet Union as well as a member of the Orgkom, was sent to explain in person that no composers would be available to go to the front until the competition ended on 1 November.[56]

Though it may seem dodgy to claim that all prominent composers were working on the hymn, the later awards that were passed out to participants confirm the accuracy of the Orgkom's claim. Almost all previous Stalin Prize winners were included on the list of 165 composers who were officially thanked for their participation.[57] Other than the aging N. Ia. Miaskovskii, the only Stalin Prize–winning composers who were not listed were known (and rewarded) for their contributions to the musical culture of their specific national republics. They were likely involved in early efforts to create their republics' own anthems.

Participation was handsomely rewarded. The winning entry was submitted by A. V. Aleksandrov, the prominent mass song composer and founder of the Red Army Song and Dance Ensemble, who set a text by S. V. Mikhalkov and G. G. El'-Registan. Each of the winners received one hundred thousand rubles, the equivalent of a Stalin Prize, first class. For every unsuccessful variant submitted, composers received four thousand rubles, and for every variant that made the competition's first cut and was actually performed, they received twice that. Poets, too, received four thousand rubles per text, but only for those which a composer later set to music.[58] To put these prize incentives in perspective, the reimbursement for military songs that were approved for publication and performance in 1941 was set at five hundred rubles per song.[59] For merely participating most unsuccessfully in the national anthem competition, composers received eight times as much—per entry.

Besides these special services, composers and musicologists applied their professional skills to create specific types of musical products. In 1943 the editors of *Sovetskaia muzyka* summarized the importance of music to the war effort by describing a struggle between two cultures and then elaborating on composers' and musicians' contributions. Stalin Prize winners since 1941 were framed in the context of the war: "Our struggle with fascism is a struggle of two worlds: a world which is hostile to any kind of culture and a world which is fighting for all of the best achievements of human culture, and for its further flourishing."[60]

56. Ibid., d. 71, l. 36 (Protokol #10, 12 Aug 1943).

57. GARF, f. 5446, op. 46, d. 2419, ll. 1–3 (SNK SSSR Postanovlenie #2, 3 Jan 1944). In addition to the 165 composers, 41 poets also received official recognition.

58. Ibid., l. 3.

59. RGALI, f. 2077, op. 1, d. 37, l. 24 (Protokol #25, 8 Jul 1941).

60. "Muzyka i muzykanty nashikh dnei," 3. The Russian word choice conveys a sense of strug-

As evidence that the Nazis were "hostile to any kind of culture," the editors rattled off the cultural institutions that the German army destroyed during their advance into the Soviet Union:

> The disciplined murderers and robbers, upon crossing their Eastern border, with cynical efficiency set about the elimination of everything that somehow reminded them of civilization. They derided art works and monuments to their great creators, national feelings, and every expression of humanity and morality in people that they met on their robbers' path. With what words can we express our anger and outrage when we read about the savage and mocking plundering of Iasnaia Poliana, the Tchaikovsky House Museum in Klin, Rimsky-Korsakov's home in Tikhvin, Chekhov's cottage in Crimea, about the burned and destroyed theaters, conservatories, clubs, pioneer palaces, about the looted museums and libraries in Kiev, Kharkov, Odessa, Rostov-on-the-Don, Minsk![61]

A partial refutation of the Nazi argument that Russians could not achieve culture is already contained in this catalog of the cultural heritage that the invading armies destroyed. The juxtaposition was completed by a discussion of the wartime accomplishments of Soviet art:

> We can bravely say that our art withstood the ordeal, matured, came closer to the people, to the army, that it transformed itself into a sharp weapon which strikes the enemy and raises the spirit of our people at the front and in the rear. Our art derives strength from love for our motherland and hate for its enemies, and so these days it sounds with such a full voice that it strikes a fatal blow against the senseless fascist barbarians who expected it was within their power to destroy our culture and art.[62]

By merely continuing to exist, Soviet art and music confounded the Nazi effort to destroy Soviet culture. Music's contribution to the war effort was twofold: it "raised the spirit" of those fighting at the front and working in the rear, and it countered the Nazi claim that Soviet (or Russian, or Slavic, or non-Aryan) culture was subhuman and worthy only of complete eradication.

Musicologists engaged the second half of this project least publicly but perhaps most directly. The musicologists' main professional platform was the journal *Sovetskaia muzyka,* publication of which was discontinued during the war. Musicologists were left with only annual volumes of collected articles in which to make their contributions to the clash of culture and barbarism. The introduction to the first *Sovetskaia muzyka* volume cited above is one example, but the phenomenon pervades all of the wartime volumes.

---

gle even more than the English. *Vrazhdebno* has extreme coloration absent in the English "hostile," and *zavoevaniia* is not just an "achievement" but one that has been attained through struggle. In most writing about music, the Russian for "achievement" or "accomplishment" is *dostizhenie.*

61. Ibid., 4.
62. Ibid.

Another emblematic effort reveals a clear response to the rhetorical battle against the Nazis by addressing the clash of German and Russian artistic culture, especially music. In his essay "German and 'German' in Russian Music and Musical Culture," B. V. Asaf'ev, the dean of Soviet musicology, sought to strip German influence from Russia's musical heritage.[63] In his highly inventive article, Asaf'ev relied on the very cosmopolitanism of eighteenth- and nineteenth-century European culture to debunk the myth of the great German musical tradition, arguing that it was, in fact, mostly Italian, French, and yes, Slavic. He started by differentiating between two kinds of German music: German and "German." The first included pre-Viennese German music of the Enlightenment and the classical European Viennese school, including the romantic Schumann. The second, with "German" in quotes, included the "most varied trends of German nationalistic philistinism and its inherent forcibly organized and automatically schematic style of musical-artistic conjecture."[64] "German" music was modernism and its immediate antecedents.

The pre-Viennese German music of the Enlightenment, Asaf'ev argued, was born in part of a Slavic melodic tradition, in particular the Czech Hussite choral tradition of the Reformation. Likewise, the classic Viennese school was fundamentally international, blending the national song and instrumental cultures of Italy, the Tyrol, and Hungary in a Viennese melting pot. Furthermore, Mozart's genius was that he managed to form an international style that incorporated the "musics" of Italy, France, and neighboring Slavic countries. And Beethoven's contribution to the "European musical intellect" was the "idea of development," something born of the French Revolution. The successor to the tradition of Mozart and Beethoven was not the schematic German music of the late nineteenth and twentieth centuries, but Tchaikovsky. Tchaikovsky's affinity with Mozart was undeniable, Asaf'ev argued, but it was the international genius of Mozart's music that Tchaikovsky inherited, not his much less significant identity as a German composer. And Beethoven's legacy in Russian music (through Glinka to Tchaikovsky) was an idea of development that the great Russian composers combined with their own dramaturgical impulses.[65] The German in Russian music was thus what was European and international about both of them.

By peeling away and attributing to a broader European musical tradition everything that was good (in his eyes) about German music, Asaf'ev countered

63. B. V. Asaf'ev, "Nemetskoe i 'Nemetskoe' v russkoi muzyke i muzykal'noi kul'ture," in *Sovetskaia muzyka: Sbornik stat'ei No. 1*, 8–14. This article was part of Asaf'ev's longer cycle entitled "Cherez proshloe v budushchemu," which formed the cornerstone of the first two article compilations.

64. Ibid., 8–9. In the quote, the word that Asaf'ev used for "forcibly" is the same as the Russian for "rape," a double meaning which Asaf'ev must have intended.

65. Ibid., 9–12. Asaf'ev's argument about Tchaikovsky as a Mozartean composer prefigures a more recent theoretical repositioning of both Mozart and Tchaikovsky in Richard Taruskin, *Defining Russia Musically: Historical and Hermeneutical Essays* (Princeton: Princeton University Press, 1997), 239–307.

an unidentified German claim that anything that was good about Russian music and Tchaikovsky in particular was simply derivative of German musical culture. He left "German" music stripped of anything but the hated automatic and inhuman "schematism" of modernism. Though he may have repeated the very "shortsightedness" of German musicologists that he reviled in the article, Asaf'ev showed that his own professional resources could be engaged in the effort to contrast barbarian Nazis (or Germans) with cultured Soviets (or Russians).[66]

In later volumes, other themes were taken up, but their themes were never far from the war experience or the theoretical requirements of the war effort.[67] Composers and musicologists thus proved their value by volunteering to fight or entertain troops at the front or by engaging the rhetorical battle between Soviet and Nazi culture. But the composers' greatest contribution to the war effort was to compose war songs and symphonies, those genres that did most to "raise spirits" in the front and rear and to demonstrate Soviet high-cultural achievements at home and on the international stage.

War Songs

> How could I help my Motherland, at sixty years of age? I had never held a rifle in my hands and certainly was not a military specialist. And all the same I did hold in my hands a mighty weapon which could strike the enemy—it was the song! What could I give to the front—to the fighters, to the commanders, to the political workers? Songs!
>
> —A. V. Aleksandrov[68]

> It is our vital duty [to ensure] that generations who study the era of the Patriotic War will also know it by the songs which were worthy of this great epoch.
>
> —B. M. Iarustovskii[69]

Iarustovskii's wish would be fulfilled for at least three postwar generations, in no small part through Aleksandrov's song "Sacred War." From Victory Day celebrations to popular "Name That Tune" television game shows to current recordings by major international artists, songs written during the war remain

---

66. See Asaf'ev, "Nemetskoe," 9, for the allusion to the German claim and 13–14 for the attack on shortsighted German musicologists. For a discussion of those musicologists, see Pamela Potter, *Most German of the Arts: Musicology and Society from the Weimar Republic to the End of Hitler's Reich* (New Haven: Yale University Press, 1998), esp. 200–234.

67. For example, a changing conception of German barbarity was explored in A. A. Gozenpud, "Ideia zashchity Rodiny v russkom iskusstve," in *Sovetskaia muzyka: Vtoroi sbornik stat'ei* (Moscow: Muzgiz, 1944), 25.

68. "A. V. Aleksandrov," in Polianovskii, *Sovetskie kompozitory—frontu*, 24.

69. "Plenum Orgkomiteta SSK SSSR (Kratkoe izlozhenie dokladov, sodokladov i prenii)," *Informatsionnyi sbornik*, no. 7–8 (1945): 60.

an important part of Russian popular culture and of the way that the war is remembered.[70] They were perhaps Soviet composers' most powerful and enduring contribution to the war effort, successfully raising spirits at the front and in the rear and remaining as emblems of the struggle. But that success did not come without tremendous effort both by individual composers and their professional organization. From the very beginning of the war, much of the Composers' Union's creative and administrative efforts were designed to encourage the production of war songs. The resulting products provide a window into the changing demands of the audiences they addressed: soldiers and sailors at the front, and workers, families, and the party's ideological watchdogs in the rear.

Aleksandrov's reaction to the start of the war was not unusual. Many composers threw their energies into writing songs from the very beginning. Some later recalled that "we didn't have the opportunity even to think about symphonies and other large-scale works. [Leningrad] demanded from us efficient and quick work. Other composers and I wrote songs for Houses of the Red Army, for military ensembles, and for frontline amateur groups."[71] Another recalled that "the front demanded mass songs, and composers of all genres tried their strength at writing this literature." Kabalevskii agreed, and he counted himself as one of those who was never suited for writing mass songs but who nevertheless tried.[72] Others drew analogies to weapons production: "The front demanded new songs, and we wrote them without leaving our creative 'posts,' just like workers in military factories who were making bullets and shells."[73] At the end of the war, they looked back on this service with pride. "I too, a writer of songs," one wrote, "am not ashamed to look people in the eye. With a clear conscience, I can say: 'I did not live through the past years of the war in vain. Maybe I did very little, but I did everything that a musician of my abilities, my capabilities could have done.'"[74]

The Orgkom's initial response to the Nazi invasion was to hold daily meetings in which they listened to, discussed, and evaluated the songs that were being written so quickly by these energized, patriotic composers. The response was enormous. In just the first eleven days of the war, they evaluated 101 songs, accepting 57 for immediate distribution through performance, publication, or both. They also suggested that 20 songs be reworked and resubmitted, and rejected 24 as simply too poor for further attention. For those eleven days, the Orgkom did almost nothing else, discussing only two other issues—the evacuation of the children and the restructuring of finances discussed above.[75] By the

70. Examples for the domestic Russian market are legion; one product released for international consumption is baritone Dmitry Khvorostovsky's recording *Songs of the War Years*. Most of the songs were composed during World War II. Khvorostovsky, et al., *Pesni voennykh let*, Delos DE 3315 (Hollywood: Delos International, 2003).

71. "O. Evlakhov," in Polianovskii, *Sovetskie kompozitory—frontu*, 13.

72. "M. Matveev" and "D. Kabalevskii," in ibid., 20, 76.

73. "K. Listov," in ibid., 40.

74. "M. Blanter," in ibid., 37.

75. RGALI, f. 2077, op. 1, d. 37, ll. 1–15 (Protokoly #10–19, 23 Jun–3 Jul 1941). The chil-

end of July, the Orgkom had heard almost a hundred more songs, accepting about forty-five, rejecting about forty, and suggesting revisions for the remainder.[76] This flurry of activity around "defense songs" was repeated in regional chapters as well. For example, the Leningrad chapter routinely evaluated songs and marches every Monday and pushed seven song collections through to publication, either by Leningrad's Muzfond or by the Baltic Fleet's publisher, all by the end of 1941.[77]

Besides listening to songs and temporarily doing almost nothing else, the Orgkom established a system for evaluating and distributing them over the long term. Initially this system concentrated all authority and power within the Orgkom and, through a series of ad hoc decisions, subjugated the All-USSR Radio Committee (VRK) and the central music publisher (Muzgiz) to its decisions. The Orgkom coordinated the activity of these two powerful external institutions with that of their own Defense Commission, essentially oversaw their song-related activities, and occasionally transferred some publication duties to Muzfond when Muzgiz proved inadequate to the task.[78] This partial subjugation of Muzgiz and the Radio Committee to the Orgkom was very short-lived. It began to deteriorate as soon as the Orgkom's attention became occupied with questions of the evacuation and disintegrated near the end of 1941. In October the Central Committee stepped in to strengthen Muzgiz and the Radio Committee and to increase control over what was considered unreasonably slack criteria for the acceptance of new songs. Though it was implemented through an Orgkom resolution, it is clear that the impetus for the reform came from the Central Committee, which sent one of the cultural apparatus's top administrators, D. A. Polikarpov, to the Composers' Union to suggest the changes.

According to the new system, the committees that made decisions about accepting and rejecting songs in each of the three institutions (Orgkom, Radio Committee, Muzgiz) were to remain independent of one another, thus acting as a three-way system of checks. But the reform also strengthened the committees at Muzgiz and the Radio Committee by infusing them with Composers' Union members. After a piece had been approved by all three decision-making committees, it was to return to the Composers' Union for a broader hearing and

---

dren's evacuation and new funding structure appeared only at the last two of these meetings, on 2–3 July. These statistics are approximate, for some songs were heard more than once if they were originally sent back for corrections. For an example of reworked songs being accepted, see l. 8 (Protokol #15, 28 Jun 1941). Throughout this discussion "war song" and "defense song" are translations of the Russian *oboronnaia pesnia*.

76. Ibid., ll. 16–32 (Protokoly #20–30, 24 Jun–29 Jul 1941). The imprecision is the result of a meeting in which thirty-five songs by twenty-seven composers were evaluated and decisions were uncharacteristically made by composer rather than by song. The resulting numbers are necessarily inexact.

77. RGALI, f. 2077, op. 1, d. 51, ll. 39–40 (Protokol #9, 23 Jul 1942), report on the situation and activities of LSSK since the beginning of the war.

78. For more on the intricacies of this process, see Tomoff, "Creative Union," chap. 2.

evaluation at Tuesday evening concerts hosted by the Central House of Composers. Finally, the Orgkom was to continue disseminating and popularizing new songs through radio, film, recordings, publications, and the press.[79] Though this reform clearly undermined the initial ad hoc control that the Orgkom had established in June and July, it actually expanded professional composers' participation in the process by attaching them to the other institutions and confirming the Orgkom's leading role in evaluating and popularizing war songs.

The Orgkom also encouraged composers to write songs by providing real material incentives. As noted, they paid composers five hundred rubles for each acceptable song and agreed to pay the writers who wrote the lyrics as well. In September 1941 the Orgkom introduced a more visible incentive by holding the first wartime song competition. It empowered Khachaturian to call a meeting with all composers in order to explain the rules to as wide an audience as possible and suggested that the Moscow chapter give commissions to fifteen prominent song composers in order to guarantee participation at a high professional level. The Composers' Union also contacted the Writers' Union to request lyrics and offer an additional material incentive to writers. It proposed to pay 250 rubles for each *unsuccessful* text plus an additional 200 rubles to the lyricist of each published song. Besides that, six prizes would be awarded for a total of 22,000 rubles, 14,000 of which was earmarked for composers and 8,000 of which was reserved for writers.[80] That the Composers' Union extended this financial incentive to writers, especially considering the Writers' Union's vastly more extensive resources, demonstrates the seriousness of composers' commitment to the production of war songs and an early attempt to give writers a financial incentive to participate in musical projects.[81]

These competitions, a variation on a common prewar theme, were later emulated by local chapters around the Soviet Union. When Leningrad's chapter announced a competition for best song and march related to the twenty-fourth anniversary of the October Revolution, composers responded with more than a hundred songs and thirty marches. Four prizes were awarded. During that horrifying winter, they held another contest in connection with Red Army Day and received more than two hundred additional entries. In May 1942 another Leningrad competition gave incentives to prepare for the twenty-fifth anniver-

79. RGALI, f. 2077, op. 1, d. 37, l. 58 (Protokol #39, 4 Oct 1941).

80. Ibid., ll. 52–52ob. (Protokol #36, 13 Sep 1941). The fifteen composers were Blanter, Listov, the Pokrass brothers, Miliutin, Novikov, Kats, Kruchinin, Kompaneets, Buglai, Koval', Muradeli, Khrennikov, Belyi, and A. V. Aleksandrov. This decision also named the jury: Glier, Khachaturian, Kabalevskii, Shebalin, and M. A. Grinberg. Surin (VKI) was added at the next meeting. For that decision, see l. 53 (Protokol #37, 20 Sep 1941). The jury members were not song composers, but they were all members of the Orgkom; consequently, their placement on the jury says less about the preeminence of symphonic music over popular song music in the Union than it does about the influence of the Orgkom over both.

81. For one simple comparison of relative resource allocation between the two unions, see GARF, f. 5446, op. 46, dd. 2430–32 (Upravleniia delami SNK SSSR, 1944: Perepiska po voprosam Soiuzov sovetskikh pisatelei, khudozhnikov i kompozitorov, three volumes), passim.

sary of the Revolution.[82] In late 1942 the Sverdlovsk chapter held a contest for the best song connected with the same anniversary, and earlier that year they held contests for best *estrada* song and best mass song.[83] Through the Moscow chapter, the Orgkom repeated its own contest the next year.[84]

Many composers considered these contests important means of stimulating and supporting their work. The most dramatic example of stimulation comes from the Leningrad composer M. A. Matveev, who remembered one contest held during the siege:

> And so it's another day. The neighbor again promises to get to the window, to rip down the plywood and replace it with a piece of glass so that everybody could see the desired patch of the snow-covered embankment on the Neva by the Samsoniev bridge, which had been lit up by the native, gently pink Leningrad sun.
>
> On this memorable day, my hopeless despair was destined to disperse. Towards evening, the thin whisper of the radio announcer filtered through the pillow to my ears: "*Govorit Leningrad.*" And then he reported that the Leningrad competition for songs and marches had ended, and he listed the names of the winners: Timofeev, Leman, Bogdanov-Berezovskii.
>
> I remember how this news deeply excited me. Life! Somewhere quite near, my friends are living and not surrendering. They are continuing to work persistently. After this, was it possible to lie around thus, sunk in indifference? This fighting signal was enough to impart a new orientation to my thoughts.[85]

For others, it was not the results of the contest but the motivation to write for it that prompted them to creative activity, forcing them to write even during the most trying times. Others considered the prizes that they gave out as honors and probably means of sustenance. And still others thought of them as an opportunity to try their hand at composing in new genres.[86]

Outside of Moscow, the most significant type of support besides the contests was provided by local publishers. Some of these were controlled by Muzfond while others were branches of military publishers or Muzgiz. The aforementioned seven volumes of songs published by Leningrad's Muzfond and the Baltic Fleet's press were one of the only means of sustenance for Leningrad composers, who were cut off from the central Composers' Union and Muzfond.[87] In his re-

82. RGALI, f. 2077, op. 1, d. 51, ll. 41, 43, 45 (Protokol #9, 23 Jul 1941), in a report on the activities of LSSK during 1941 and the winter of 1941–42. The Revolution anniversary competitions were held jointly with the Leningrad branch of the VKI (UDI-Leningrad).

83. Ibid., l. 99 (Protokol #17, 26 Nov 1942). In this decision, the Orgkom overturned two prizes awarded by the Sverdlovsk SSK because they were given to composers who wrote the songs earlier and had not initially envisioned them as tributes to October. This decision underscores the fact that competitions were meant to encourage *new* works, not reward older ones. For earlier contests, see l. 58 (Protokol #11, 30 Aug 1942). The Sverdlovsk SSK also held competitions for symphonic, choral, and chamber music.

84. RGALI, f. 2077, op. 1, d. 40, l. 6 (competition announcement, [1942]).

85. "M. Matveev," in Polianovskii, *Sovetskie kompozitory—frontu,* 18.

86. "O. Evlakhov," "D. Vasil'ev-Buglai," and "D. Kabalevskii," in ibid., 12, 29, 79–82.

87. RGALI, f. 2077, op. 1, d. 51, ll. 40–41 (Protokol #9, 23 Jul 1942).

port to the Orgkom about wartime activities in Uzbekistan, the representative of the Uzbek Composers' Union repeatedly emphasized the role of the local publisher, noting proudly that 150 pieces had been accepted by the publisher and 60 had already been released. In fact, he complained that the publisher was really the only reliable source of income, and despite its laudable activities, it desperately needed more help.[88]

The results of this combination of self-motivation and institutional support to write war songs were impressive. War songs encompass a surprisingly broad sweep of genre, instrumentation, and style. Many were about the people who fought the war, like B. A. Mokrousov's rousing "Song of the Defenders of Moscow." Others directly addressed the war itself, like the one that, more than any other, became the emblem of the early war song, A. V. Aleksandrov's "Sacred War." "Sacred War" opens with a powerful chordal introduction strikingly reminiscent of the opening of the "Dies Irae" of Giuseppe Verdi's famous *Requiem* before launching into a musically interesting combination of a determined march feel with a three-four meter that expressed widespread feelings of defiance and hatred in compelling and militaristic musical language.[89]

Other songs helped to bridge the front and rear by expressing or portraying the thoughts and feelings of specific groups of fighters. Such songs included "March of the Artillery Men," "March of the Tank Drivers," and "Three Tank Drivers." Others, like "My Dear Capital" and "The City of Rostov," served to remind soldiers about the places they were fighting for and continue to be palpable expressions of local pride today.

Perhaps even more effective in bridging the gap between front and rear, however, were generically diverse, intimate songs, which ranged from dance music like M. G. Fradkin's "Accidental Waltz" and Tabachnikov's "Let's Have a Smoke" to songs styled after Russian folklore, like V. G. Zakharov's "Oh, the Clouds" (Oi Tumany). N. V. Bogoslovskii's "Dark Night," V. P. Solov'ev-Sedoi's "Nightingales," Iu. A. Levitin's "Field Post Office," the famous "Wait for Me" with its numerous songs of response ("I'll Wait for You"), and countless others were performed live and on the radio by singers accompanied by jazz or military band, folk orchestra, or a lone accordion. These sentimental songs about home, and about loved ones in the rear or at the front, became an imaginative bridge that helped all continue to fight.

88. Ibid., ll. 51–52 (Protokol #10, 18 Aug 1942). They were also pleased to announce that the publications were typically in both Uzbek and Russian rather than only one language, as had been the case before the war.

89. A. V. Aleksandrov, "Sviashennaia voina," perf. Krasnoznamennyi ansambl', *Sviashchennaia voina: K 50–letiiu Pobedy,* RDCD 00433 ([Moscow]: Russkii disk, 1995), track 1; Giuseppe Verdi, *Messa da Requiem,* perf. Chicago Symphony Orchestra, cond. Georg Solti, et al., BMG 09026–61403–2 (New York: BMG, 1993), disc 1, track 2.

Symphonic Music: Shostakovich's War Trilogy

The single most significant musical work produced during the war was Shostakovich's Seventh Symphony. Though he may have been thinking about the musical ideas that would fill the symphony before the war, Shostakovich began writing furiously in the early days after the Nazi attack.[90] He completed most of the symphony during the early months of the war, before he was evacuated from Leningrad. Dedicated to the city of Leningrad, it quickly became a powerful symbol of the heroic defiance of the Soviet population in the face of the Nazi invasion. Copies of the score were flown by military plane out of the Soviet Union so that the piece could be performed in Great Britain and the United States, performances which popularized the symphony the world over and symbolized the common struggle of the Allies. At home, the Seventh was premiered in Kuibyshev, where Shostakovich had completed it in evacuation, and then performed in Moscow and throughout the evacuated rear. In one of the most momentous performances in music history, a makeshift orchestra was pieced together for a defiant performance in blockaded Leningrad itself. These performances and the radio broadcasts of them had tremendous symbolic meaning that provoked such a powerful response that descriptions are rarely missing from any memoir of the war years. By the end of the war, the piece was entrenched in the Soviet cultural canon as a "chronicle" of the suffering of the Soviet population during the war.[91]

The appearance of the Seventh Symphony allowed a discursive shift in discussions of civilization and barbarism. Before the Seventh, arguments about the significance and excellence of Soviet civilization rested on the Russian cultural heritage. But the Seventh Symphony made the transition from Russian to Soviet; it was the first homegrown example of artistic accomplishment recognized unambiguously as such on both the domestic and international stage. As such, Shostakovich's Seventh Symphony demonstrated how Soviet symphonic music, not just popular songs, could serve the war effort.[92]

Demonstration of that importance was the primary accomplishment of the music profession during the war years, but it opened the door for intense scru-

90. In her authoritative biography, Laurel Fay notes that the Seventh Symphony we know was conceived at the beginning of the war, not before. Fay, *Shostakovich,* 313n7. That there are doubts is a result mainly of the *Testimony* controversy.

91. Fay, *Shostakovich,* 124–33. For a detailed contribution to the creation of the Seventh Symphony legend, see Sofiia Khentova, *Shostakovich: Zhizn' i tvorchestvo* (Leningrad: Sovetskii kompozitor, 1986), 2:7–122. For the earliest long review to appear in the professional rather than general press, see I. Martynov, "Rozhdennaia burei (O Sedmoi simfonii D. Shostakovicha)," in *Sovetskaia muzyka: Sbornik stat'ei No. 1,* 41–47.

92. The following was a typical claim for the importance of the Seventh Symphony clearly intended for an impressed foreign audience: "The Seventh Symphony of Shostakovich is significant beyond the bounds of a merely musical event. It has become a cultural entity of our people, a fact of political and social significance, and an impulse to struggle and victory." Professor K. Pavlov, *VOKS Bulletin,* 1942, nos. 7/8:49, quoted in Schwarz, *Music and Musical Life,* 180. The bulletin in which this statement appeared was published in English, clearly for foreign consumption.

tiny of Shostakovich's successive symphonies. The reception of his Eighth Symphony was particularly ambiguous. In discussions of the Eighth, Shostakovich was often praised for the tremendous technical accomplishment of sections of the symphony and for the emotional power of what was taken to be his depiction of despair.[93] The Eighth became an emblem of suffering and grief, but it was deemed problematic because it did not depict a heroic solution to the suffering, a triumphant victory.[94] In the course of the discussions, a nearly unanimous expectation was established: the Ninth would redeem the Eighth's pessimism by concluding the war with a triumphant symphony of victory, thus forming a wartime trilogy that encapsulated the war experience of heroic suffering, devastating tragedy, and exultant victory.[95]

These expectations were so strong that the early reviews of the Ninth even repeated them, as though the reviewers' expectations overcame their ears.[96] Soon, however, the Ninth's unheroic tone became the center of critical attention, and the piece was deemed a failure.[97] The power of expectations and the understanding of the Ninth as the final chapter in a heroic symphonic trilogy simply limited the possibilities of its reception. Its expected heroism *had* to redeem the suffering portrayed in the Eighth, so when it was sarcastic or comic,

93. The paradigmatic review was N. A. Timofeev's lengthy evaluation at the Orgkom's 1944 plenary session: RGALI, f. 2077, op. 1, d. 92, ll. 122–58 (stenogram, 28–31 Mar 1944). After asserting that Shostakovich's symphonies bore the responsibility of speaking to future generations in the voice of contemporary Soviet society (l. 133), Timofeev went on to give the Eighth a profoundly mixed review. He considered it a tremendous technical accomplishment but thought that it only succeeded in conveying unresolved grief. See also I. Martynov, "Novye kamernye sochineniia Shostakovicha," in *Sovetskaia muzyka: Sbornik stat'ei No. 5* (Moscow: Muzgiz, 1946), 21, the introduction to an article about the chamber music that followed the "tragic element, the Eighth Symphony."

94. Even in reviews that did not discuss Shostakovich's work, critics stressed the importance of balancing tragedy and optimism. For a model example, see Gozenpud, "Ideia zashchity Rodiny v russkom iskusstve," 31. Gozenpud claims that historically all Russian patriotic art had been primarily "courageous" and that "tragedy is always optimistic" in Russian musical culture.

95. Shostakovich himself contributed to this expectation: Fay, *Shostakovich*, 145–46. Just how powerful this impulse was can be illustrated by its resurrection even after the "comic" Ninth disappointed critics. L. Danilevich concluded his analysis of the Eighth by expressing hope that after the "intermezzo" that was the Ninth, Shostakovich would produce a Tenth Symphony that could fully justify all hopes that he could complete the joyous finale: L. Danilevich, "Vos'maia simfoniia D. Shostakovicha," *Sovetskaia muzyka*, 1946, no. 12:56–64.

96. See, for example, the editorial synopsis of D. Rabinovich's remarks at the December 1945 plenary session of the Orgkom, inserted before a more lengthy, published review of the Ninth: N. Timofeev, "Vpechatleniia muzykanta (O 9-i simfonii Shostakovicha)," *Sovetskaia muzyka*, 1946, no. 1:66n1 (anonymous editor's note). Rabinovich had presented a reading of the symphony that made it the capstone of a wartime trilogy, an opinion not shared by L. Mazel', the speaker assigned the primary report.

97. The process was complicated. In fact, Timofeev called for evaluation of the piece *not* based on its relationship with the Seventh and Eighth. He provided an extremely positive such evaluation and predicted that listeners would return to the Ninth very fondly: Timofeev, "Vpechatleniia muzykanta," 66–69. For the final failure, see the lead editorial in *Sovetskaia muzyka* following the first Central Committee resolutions of the *Zhdanovshchina*: "Problemy, sovetskogo muzykal'nogo tvorchestva," *Sovetskaia muzyka*, 1946, no.8–9:3–14. The discussion of the Ninth is on pp. 7–8.

not only was it doomed to at least critical failure, but the Eighth was left unredeemed, thus magnifying the offense.

But confounded expectations were only one of the reasons that sarcasm was unacceptable in the Ninth. The other reason was the actual musical content of the sarcastic gesture in the opening of the Ninth Symphony. That gesture, scored for piccolo, trombone, and snare drum close to the beginning of the first movement, could have been heard as a parody (intentional or not, it makes no difference) of a standard announcement of the entrance of evil in the lauded programmatic symphonic music during the war.[98] Several critically acclaimed and even Stalin Prize–winning pieces contained similar gestures, starting most famously with Shostakovich's own Seventh.[99] Though scored differently, Prokofiev's contribution to the early war effort, the symphonic suite *The Year 1941*, bears perhaps the most striking resemblance to the Ninth's sarcastic gesture. In the movement titled "In Battle," the English horn yelps a short staccato theme over constant rhythmic accompaniment in the strings and percussion.[100] The second movement of Prokofiev's critically acclaimed Fifth Symphony, his greatest symphonic contribution to the war effort, opens with a more complicated theme, but that theme develops similarly, bouncing around the high woodwinds over a constant pulse supplied by the strings, until horns and snare drum interrupt with a gesture similar to the trombone's announcement of the sarcasm in Shostakovich's Ninth.[101] Khachaturian, too, wrote a well-received war symphony that contained a similar gesture, which like Prokofiev's opened the second movement.[102] The reduction of the invader from grimacing evil eminence to object of derisive snickering could have been seen either as a parody of war symphonies and their heroism or an inappropriate denigration of both

---

98. The gesture is announced by the trombone, pickup to rehearsal six, but consists primarily of piccolo, snare drum, and timpani through rehearsal nine. Then other instruments are added, and the theme is developed. See Dmitri Schostakowitsch, *9. Symphonie, op. 70. Taschenpartitur* (Hamburg: Musikverlage Hans Sikorski, [1991]), 7–9 (mm. 45–68). Also published as Dmitrii Shostakovich, *Sobranie sochinenii*, vol. 5, *Simfoniia No. 9. Simfoniia No. 10. Partitura* (Moscow: Muzyka, 1979), 7–9.

99. See the grand repetitive march in the first movement: Dmitri Shostakovich, *Symphony No. 7, Op. 60* (Leipzig: Edition Peters, [1971]), 14–17 (rehearsal nineteen to rehearsal twenty-five). The flute and piccolo share the first repetition following the string opening, always over a constant snare drum. After rehearsal twenty-five, the theme begins to break up and pass between instruments, but it does not disappear until the end of the movement. Also published as Dmitrii Shostakovich, *Sobranie sochinenii*, vol. 4, *Simfoniia No. 7. Simfoniia No. 8. Partitura* (Moscow: Muzyka, 1981), 16–20 (mm. 145–214).

100. Sergei Prokof'ev, "*1940–i god*": *Simfonicheskaia siuita. Partitura* (Moscow: Muzgiz, 1973), 18–29, but esp. 18–23 (rehearsal seven to rehearsal nine).

101. Sergej Prokofjew, *Sinfonie Nr. 5, Op. 100* (Leipzig: Edition Peters, [1970?]), 51–64 (mm. 1–111), esp. 54–57 (rehearsals twenty-eight (mm. 23–30) and thirty (mm. 44–58)). Also published as Sergei Prokof'ev, *Sobranie sochinenii*, vol. 14b, *Piataia simfoniia, soch. 100* (Moscow: Muzgiz, 1963), 59–72.

102. Aram Khachaturian, *Vtoraia simfoniia. Partitura* (Moscow: Muzgiz, 1962), 71–74 (bar before rehearsal eight to rehearsal eleven), in which the upper woodwinds shout a theme in unison over a steady accompaniment in low strings, punctuated by muted trumpets in the role of Shostakovich's later trombone.

the evil of the enemy and the magnitude of the triumph. Either was clearly unacceptable.

The many forms of service discussed in this section exemplify a response to one of the characteristic features of Stalinist society—its frequent state of mobilization. With roots extending back to the Civil War, the Stalinist state of mobilization took many forms both before and after World War II. The war scare and cultural revolution in the late 1920s helped mobilize society for the twin campaigns of rapid industrialization and forced collectivization. And from 1936 to the end of the Stalin period, society was alternately mobilized to fight perceived spies and wreckers, enemies of the people, Nazis and shirkers, formalists and idealists, cosmopolitans, and renegade doctors. Some of these primarily party-driven campaigns were more effective than others, and the prewar campaigns were generally larger in scale than the typically more focused intellectual campaigns after the war, but there is no question that the most effective of all was the mobilization to fight the outside threat of the Nazi invasion. As the other mobilizations should remind us, however, the principle of mobilization was not limited to those directly involved in the struggle but extended throughout the population even outside the context of World War II's total war. It should come as little surprise, therefore, that the music profession's service to the military effort during the war took so many forms. Fighting, entertaining at the front, working on the national anthem, collecting "contemporary folklore," and writing war songs and symphonies were all considered laudatory service for the war effort and demonstrated the value of the music profession to Soviet society.

The Reward: Official Codification of Hierarchies of Privilege

By the end of the war, composers and musicologists who were soldiers, sailors, frontline entertainers, songwriters, and symphonic composers together comprised a music profession that had served admirably in the struggle of the Red Army against the Wehrmacht, of Soviet society against Nazi incursion, and of culture against barbarism. It had earned an elite place in a newly recodified hierarchical system of privilege.

In March 1944, Sovnarkom codified the stratification of privileged access to food and consumer goods designed to serve a new postwar Soviet elite. Politicians were already well ensconced in material privilege long before, but the new system recodified privilege for other elites: academicians, professors, industrial managers and chief engineers, titled artists and athletes, chief doctors and surgeons, leading journalists, the upper officer corps, and members of the creative unions.[103] The decree allowed them to shop without ration cards in special

103. RGALI, f. 2077, op. 1, d. 94, l. 10 (appendix #6 to SNK SSSR Postanovlenie #289, 18

stores with special prices that guaranteed a wide variety of high-quality food and consumer goods, and it gave them access to special restaurants at which they could eat and seek entertainment. Beginning in mid-April 1944, Moscow would acquire twenty special food stores, including eight general grocery stores that would sell food, wines, beverages, and tobacco products and twelve specialized food stores which would carry a wide assortment of specific goods: two fish stores, two meat stores, two dairy stores, two produce stores, a bakery, a tea shop, a tobacco store, and a wine shop. Beginning in mid-May, a new central department store would sell made-to-order clothes and shoes, accessories, linens, hats, haberdashery, and perfume goods. An additional four stores would specialize in hats, haberdashery, and perfume. Though the new special stores would be open to the general public, members of the scientific and artistic intelligentsia would receive a 25 percent discount on all purchases, and members of the upper officer corps would receive a discount of 35 percent, up to specified purchase limits.[104]

In mid-April fifty new restaurants would also open across Moscow. Thirty of them would be second-level establishments, located in train stations or scattered around the city and open from noon until midnight. The other twenty would be first-class night spots featuring live music and *estrada* performances until five o'clock in the morning. Eleven were open to the general public, but the other nine were restricted to especially exclusive groups. One of these nine was a restaurant for composers and musicians that would be located in the Central House of Composers. This restaurant or a successor became a nearly legendary meeting place for composers to gather and socialize over good, inexpensive food.[105]

Members of the groups served by the March decree might have expected an immediate improvement in their standard of living, but implementation turned out to be more complicated than anticipated. By mid-June the nonfood stores had not opened, and the privileges were substantially revised to lower discounts and increase the groups that the stores would serve when they opened in July. Purchase limits were cut in half, the discount for the scientific and creative intelligentsia was reduced from 25 to 10 percent, and the discount for the upper officer corps was reduced from 35 to 20 percent. Recipients of the government's highest military and civilian titles, Hero of the Soviet Union and Hero of Socialist Labor, were added to the list and given the largest discount: 30 percent. Two new groups were also added. Some white- and blue-collar workers who had earlier been granted limited-access coupon books (*limitnye knizhki*) were given the same 10 percent discount as the intelligentsia, and the rest of the officer corps was included with the same 20 percent discount as their superior of-

---

Mar 1944). For a complete list of qualifying positions and titles, see Tomoff, "Creative Union," 123–24.

104. RGALI, f. 2077, op. 1, d. 94, ll. 2–3 (SNK SSSR Postanovlenie #289, 18 Mar 1944).

105. Ibid., ll. 3–4; Alla Semenovna Sedova, personal communication, 16 Mar 1999. The actual restaurant Sedova referred to may have been a later replacement.

ficers. Hierarchy was maintained by limiting these new groups' purchases to half of the others.[106]

Though the June decree leveled the consumer goods privilege significantly, the motivation was almost certainly not egalitarian but a concession to supply problems. There simply were not enough haberdasher goods and perfumes being produced in 1944 to allow such a limited group to purchase so much at such significant discounts as the March decree envisioned and still have enough left to reward less-privileged groups. Consequently, the March decree should be understood as establishing the government leadership's ideal privileged group and the June decree as an acknowledgment of supply realities. More severe supply problems doubtlessly worsened the distribution in practice, but the fact remains that specific and specialized consumption outlets were being created in Moscow as the war neared its end to reward those who were considered to have contributed most to the Soviet victory. Composers and musicologists not only numbered among that group but were the only musicians who were included because of their profession rather than their individual accomplishments.[107]

This specific extension of privilege to composers and musicologists was underlined in March 1945, when Muzfond opened a multifaceted service center to supply members with everything from shoes, clothes, linens, and housing renovation supplies to blank score paper, published scores, and musical instrument repairmen. In the first year after the war, it did crisp business and split into two centers, one for professional supplies and one for everyday products.[108] Attaining this service center was a new development in the increasingly privileged distribution abilities of Muzfond.

Within the profession, access to goods was not uniform, even for such basic goods as food. In April 1943 the Orgkom released a hierarchical list of rations recipients divided into five categories: main meal A, main meal B, dry rations, suppers, and limited-access coupon books. Though it is not entirely clear from the Orgkom decree, it seems that the main meals were received directly from the Composers' Union and probably eaten at the cafeteria located at Composers' Union headquarters at midday. Sixty-seven composers and Orgkom administrators received A meals, and fifteen Orgkom employees got B meals. The division between A and B was not within the profession but between professionals and nonprofessional employees. Particularly valuable, skilled, or highly placed nonmusican employees, however, were fed at the same level as Composers' Union members. The A list also included the director of the House of

106. RGALI, f. 2077, op. 1, d. 94, l. 17 (SNK SSSR Postanovlenie #746, 21 Jun 1944).

107. On privileged access to goods before the war, see Sheila Fitzpatrick, *Everyday Stalinism: Ordinary Life in Extraordinary Times: Soviet Russia in the 1930s* (Oxford: Oxford University Press, 1999), 95–106; and E. Osokina, *Za fasadom "Stalinskogo izobiliia": Raspredelenie i rynok v snabzhenii naseleniia v gody industrializatsii, 1937–1941* (Moscow: ROSSPEN, 1998), esp. 120–27.

108. GARF, f. 5446, op. 48, d. 2177, ll. 43, 50–52 (correspondence between Upravlenie delami SM SSSR, SSK, MinFin, and VKI, 1946). The "service center" was actually a *kombinat*, which was formed on the basis of SNK SSSR Razresheniia #39-1, 28 Feb 1945. Turnover was 7 million rubles.

Composers and chair of the Composers' Union party cell (N. F. Teplinskaia, a librarian) along with the high ranking administrator V. A. Lempert.

Neither the A or B list included such prominent composers as Shostakovich, Prokofiev, Miaskovskii, Asaf'ev, Shebalin, or Shaporin. It would be extremely surprising if these most famous composers were not fed at the most privileged level, and they probably were. Only twenty-one members received dry rations, including, among those mentioned here, Glier, Khachaturian, and Kabalevskii, and twelve less famous but extremely prominent composers, among them A. V. Aleksandrov, soon to be named composer of the national anthem, Orgkom members V. A. Belyi, and M. V. Koval', and popular song writers Dmitrii Pokrass and V. P. Solov'ev-Sedoi. These twenty-one formed the most prominent group in the profession (plus Lempert) living in Moscow in 1943.[109] The dry rations were almost surely additional foodstuffs that could augment other rations.

Most composers and employees received suppers. There were ninety-two recipients in all, including almost all of those who received A meals and all but one of those who received dry rations. These dinners were also probably served on the spot—either at the House of Composers or the Composers' Union headquarters. Obviously, it was best to be on all lists, but only eleven actually were. However, those who received dry rations but not A meals surely took their midday meals at other institutions. In fact, the only dry rations recipient not on the dinners list was V. Ia. Shebalin, the director of the Moscow Conservatory. Surely he dined there.[110]

This hierarchy of rations suggests that the professional organization, including its support staff, was divided primarily along professional/nonprofessional lines while certain famous composers and particularly valued administrators sat atop the hierarchy. But one list is yet to be explained, the list for limited-access coupon books. Only fourteen composers received such books, six of whom were on all lists and only three of whom did not receive dry rations.[111] The most significant observation about these fourteen recipients, however, is not their relatively privileged access to goods within the profession but their relatively small number. In 1943 the Orgkom allocated only fourteen such books. Less than a year later, all Composers' Union members would receive them in connection with the opening of the special stores.[112] Though this expanded access to goods was a wider phenomenon, it demonstrates that the professional

109. For another measure of the "most prominent," see a list of seventeen composers for whom short "creative portraits" were prepared for international distribution through VOKS in 1942: RGALI, f. 2077, op. 1, d. 51, l. 36 (VOKS materials, 18 Jul 1942). Of the seventeen, thirteen are on this list of twenty-one recipients of dry rations and two more are listed as ration recipients in other cities—probably not eligible for dry rations issued by the Orgkom.

110. Ibid., d. 71, ll. 15–17 (Protokol #5, 5 Apr 1943).

111. Ibid., l. 16.

112. RGALI, f. 2077, op. 1, d. 94, l. 10.

organization moved more securely into official privilege by 1944.[113] The last requirement of profession formation had been met.

The war was an important moment in the development of the Soviet music profession. During a chaotic and traumatic evacuation, the Composers' Union expanded contacts and implicit commitments between the central body and local chapters, clarified the institutional relationship between its professional and resource distribution functions, and drew a solid boundary on membership by permanently excluding performers. At the same time, an influx of new members, mainly songwriters, changed the face of Composers' Union membership.

Most importantly, the Composers' Union's leadership helped to stimulate and support composers' and musicologists' response to the call to professional arms. The Composers' Union as a whole and its members individually produced just the sort of music that the war effort required. Their songs helped bridge the front and rear, raise spirits, and rally the troops. Their symphonic music helped demonstrate that even during wartime, Soviet society could produce a highbrow cultural product, thereby destroying Nazi *Untermensch* claims. Members of the Composers' Union successfully produced creative ammunition for both fronts in the battle of culture against barbarism.

For this service, the members of the Composers' Union gained lasting juridical access to a comparatively privileged strata of Soviet society. From a situation at the beginning of the war in which members of a local chapter could not even find a cafeteria that would feed them, members found themselves with the legal right to receive inexpensive, high-quality food and consumer products even outside the ration system. They became lasting beneficiaries of a codified system of privileged access to scarce resources. This service and its subsequent reward also demonstrate that by the end of the war the Composers' Union exhibited all of the defining characteristics of a modern professional organization, held officially sanctioned control over socially valuable labor that depended on expertise acquired through advanced education or professional training, and enjoyed a consequent elite status and material privilege.

The Composers' Union accomplished what it did with very little direct interference from oversight bodies like the party Central Committee apparatus. This is not to say that the Composers' Union received no direction from the party. Rather, composers and musicologists willingly responded to "the tasks laid in front of them by the party and the government," a phrase commonly used throughout the Stalin period whenever institutions discussed their raison d'être. When the party needed art that motivated people, exhibited a high cultural level, and unified the front and the rear, composers responded with highly successful songs and symphonies. They were amply rewarded.

---

113. For increases in VKI's allocation of *limitnye knizhki,* see ibid., ll. 15–16 (SNK SSSR Rasporiazhenie #9198p, 27 Apr 1944).

The war was a pivotal moment in the ongoing dance between the participants in interdependent fields of professional and political action. During the war the relationship between those fields was laid as bare as it would be at any other time. Without knowing the consequences, leaders of the Soviet state invested resources to evacuate the institutions and individuals who comprised the music profession. They counted on the profession as a repository of creative and intellectual expertise to create an artistic product that could be used in the struggle for civilization against barbarism. And they were pleased with the dividends that investment paid. As the war neared its end, professional musicians entered newly elite levels in a hierarchical system of material privilege, thus demonstrating the direct connection between professional service to the state and material rewards bestowed by it.

The nature of the wartime interaction established a precedent whereby composers and musicologists were left to their professional devices. They were materially supported while they pursued tasks that interested the party but which the party apparatus itself did not have the expertise to fulfill. It was an important precedent both for individuals, who valued their professional agency, and for the Composers' Union as the constitutive body of the music profession, which sought institutional control over the production of music.

These abstract wartime developments had real social ramifications at the individual level, and not just because Composers' Union members occupied such a high rung on the ladder of hierarchical access to scarce material goods. Union members, like their colleagues in most other spheres of life, joined the party in record numbers during the war years. For the entire period covered by this study, the mean year in which eventual party members joined the party was 1943.[114] As a result of this typically patriotic gesture, at the end of the war party membership, with its consequent loyalties and responsibilities, corresponded more closely than ever with Composers' Union membership, with its own loyalties and responsibilities. For the moment, individuals were willing to continue committing their professional energies to solving problems "laid before them by the party and government." When the party needed sophisticated professional descriptions and definitions of ideologically desirable art, musicologists and music theorists attempted to respond, revisiting questions of professional and party responsibilities and loyalties along the way.

114. For the statistical analysis from which this mean is derived, see chapter 7.

Part II

PROFESSION AND POWER, 1946–53

The all-USSR Union of Soviet Composers emerged from the traumatic upheaval of World War II as the constitutive body of a fully formed music profession. It controlled an independent funding institution that maintained its members in the Stalinist material elite, and it held a monopoly on the expertise required to create and interpret new Soviet music. Its members had also just demonstrated the importance of their intellectual and creative work by profoundly contributing to the Soviet war effort.

Immediately after the war, this professional organization was tested by a perpetually active, interventionist Communist Party. Intent on renewing ideological discipline after the lax war years, Stalin initiated a series of ideological campaigns that were led in the first years after the war by Andrei Zhdanov and his underlings in the Communist Party's cultural apparatus. Called the *Zhdanovshchina*, these campaigns culminated in an early 1948 public intervention into Soviet musical life. After Zhdanov's death in 1948, pressure on the Soviet cultural sphere did not relent. It took on a new character as earlier xenophobic and anti-Semitic strains came to the fore in the anticosmopolitanism campaigns that dominated Stalin's last three years. Again, the music profession did not escape attack.

Despite waves of political and ideological pressure, characterizing this time as the subjugation of musical life to Communist Party dictates fails to capture the complexity or even the essence of the relationship between the profession and the party in the postwar period. Notions central to traditional writing about the Soviet arts world and the modern profession, such as "subjugation" and "autonomy," are simply not conceptually useful tools for thinking about Soviet professions. The party did not have the expertise to articulate the manner in which it might subjugate the profession, and professionals did not conceptualize their autonomy from party dictates

95

even as a possibility. It is much more useful to think about Stalinist professions in terms of spheres of professional and political action. Professionals had the agency to define conduct, terms of debate, and musical value, to operate a professional apparatus, and to participate in state-sponsored projects.

Examining the Composers' Union's reaction to the early phases of the Zhdanovshchina, to the brouhaha of 1948, and to the anticosmopolitanism campaigns that followed demonstrates that even in the face of these waves of disruptive and traumatic campaigns, the Composers' Union experienced a long-term trend toward professional consolidation. By the end of the Stalin period, it had become the dominant institution in the Soviet music world. Understanding this process also helps us understand not just the similarities between the Soviet Union and its contemporaneous modern societies but also Stalinist society's uniqueness.

Ideology is often cited as a marker of Stalinist exceptionalism, but Stalinist ideology was fluid, mutable, and fundamentally dependent on institutional practices for sensible definition. Experts like the professionals in the Composers' Union were indispensable for defining, explaining, and enacting even the most ideological formulations.[1] However, economic and financial issues were just as often triggers for party intervention. Whether in the realm of ideology, economic planning, financial soundness, or cultural production, expertise was simply a requirement of postwar Stalinist governance. The same requirement that gave rise to professions as elite occupational groups in the Anglo-American and continental European societies did so in the Soviet Union. That necessity did not result in the ceding of an autonomous sphere (a nonsensical idea in Stalin's Soviet Union) but did open up the space for professional agency.

---

1. This claim is similar to that proposed by Ethan Pollock as an explanation for party intervention in the sciences: the party needed a scientific basis for its materialist ideology. See Ethan Pollock, "The Politics of Knowledge: Party Ideology and Soviet Science, 1945–1953" (Ph.D. diss., University of California, Berkeley, 2000).

CHAPTER 4

Zhdanovshchina and the Ogolevets Affair

On 9 May 1945, the Soviet population heard that the war was over. After the ecstasy of victory wore off, postwar reconstruction could begin on both the economic and ideological fronts. The groundwork for the postwar world had already been laid during the war, beginning at least as early as 1943. Until the war had truly ended, however, the Soviet Union's resources could not be fully redirected to postwar tasks. In 1945 that changed. Over the next several years, attention turned to rebuilding the country's industrial infrastructure, food supply system, and other basic elements of peacetime existence. The task of reconstruction was not accomplished easily, and the shocking material deprivation that much of the country faced did not really begin to subside until 1948. In fact, the famine of 1946 and 1947 made life more difficult in some places than it had been even during the last years of the war.[2]

Reconstruction did not apply merely to questions of material well-being. During the war, new recruits had joined the party in droves. Since party membership was often seen as an emblem of patriotism, new applicants were frequently accepted despite their lack of even rudimentary ideological education. After the war, party leaders realized that the party was far from the ideological bastion that they wanted it to be and initiated a campaign to reassert ideological control over the rank and file.[3]

This ideological reconstruction was not limited to the party. During the war, the party elite reckoned, the cultural intelligentsia had been allowed to range relatively far afield. Whatever contributions they may have made to the war effort were now spent, and it was time to reconstruct Soviet culture along ideological lines. Beginning in the fall of 1946, A. A. Zhdanov led a series of ideo-

---

2. Donald Filtzer, *Soviet Workers and Late Stalinism: Labour and the Restoration of the Stalinist System after World War II* (Cambridge: Cambridge University Press, 2002).

3. "Postanovlenie TsK VKP(b) ot 2 avgusta 1946 g., O podgotovke i perepodgotovke rukovodiashchikh partiinykh i sovetskikh rabotnikov," in *KPSS v rezoliutsiiakh i resheniiakh s"ezdov, konferentsii i plenumov TsK* (Moscow: Gos. Izd. Politicheskoi literatury, 1954), 3:476–84.

logical campaigns aimed at reestablishing a party line in the arts and in scholarship. Those campaigns have since born his name.[4]

The commencement of the Zhdanovshchina can be dated to the founding of a newspaper that would be the voice of the Central Committee's cultural apparatus until 1950, when the focus on ideology was supplanted by greater attention to personnel issues.[5] In the arts, the Zhdanovshchina began in earnest in August 1946, when the Central Committee issued three resolutions, on literature, theater, and film. The last of these was also the first to mention music, criticizing a score by the composer N. V. Bogoslovskii for being melancholy and "foreign" to Soviet audiences.[6] Like most Central Committee resolutions on the arts and scholarship, these three exhibited little technical understanding of the fields in question. Rather, they established the broad contours of a campaign, identified what were considered unacceptable examples of Soviet art, and instructed disciplined and unscathed artists alike to direct their efforts toward fixing the newly identified problems.[7] Starting with these resolutions, the defining characteristics of the early Zhdanovshchina were a call to valorize rather than pillory contemporary Soviet life, a rejection of Western art and a critique of Western artistic traditions, and, most importantly, increased attention to ideology and a consequent focus on criticism. Once these characteristics were identified by the Central Committee, arts organizations sought to fill in the contours with more theoretically meaningful content.

The Zhdanovshchina wound its way through scholarly fields as diverse as philosophy and cancer research before returning to the realm of the arts in February 1948, when the Central Committee published its final resolution of the Zhdanovshchina—an attack on the music field, the Composers' Union, the Committee on Artistic Affairs, and the Bol'shoi Theater. Even before this famous brouhaha of 1948, cultural discussions had been heavily theoretical and focused on the rigorous definition of ideologically sound literature, theater, film, and music.

During the war, the interests of Soviet composers and the party had coincided more perfectly than either before or after. With very little oversight, composers

---

4. For genesis of *Zhdanovshchina* in high politics, see Yoram Gorlizki and Oleg Khlevniuk, *Cold Peace: Stalin and the Soviet Ruling Circle, 1945–1953* (Oxford: Oxford University Press, 2004).

5. "Vyshe uroven' ideologicheskoi raboty!" *Kul'tura i zhizn'*, 1946, no. 1 (28 Jun): 1.

6. Postanovlenie TsK VKP(b) ot 14 avgusta 1946 g., "O zhurnalakh 'Zvezda' i 'Leningrad,'" in *KPSS v rezoliutsiiakh*, 3:485–88; originally published in *Pravda*, 21 Aug 1946; Postanovlenie TsK VKP(b) ot 26 avgusta 1946 g., "O repertuare dramaticheskikh teatrov i merakh po ego uluchsheniiu," in *KPSS v rezoliutsiiakh*, 3:489–94' originally in *Bol'shevik*, no. 16 (1946); Postanovlenie TsK VKP(b) ot 4 sentibria 1946 g., "O kinofil'me 'Bol'shaia zhizn,'" *Kultura i zhizn'* 1946, no. 8 (10 Sep): 1. Bogoslovskii was best known for his more than two hundred song compositions, but he wrote more than two dozen film scores and spent much of the 1940s working on musical comedies.

7. Definition by exemplar was also crucial to the formation of socialist realism in literature in the 1930s. See Katerina Clark, *The Soviet Novel: History as Ritual* (Chicago: University of Chicago Press, 1985).

and musicologists had set their own professional agenda and produced successful popular and serious music. In return, they were officially codified as a privileged rank of the Soviet elite. Though the party elite again seized control of the professional agenda during the Zhdanovshchina, enough wartime solidarity remained in the music profession to allow composers and musicologists to try to achieve the party's artistic and theoretical goals. However, the positive relationship forged with the party during the war was strained during the Zhdanovshchina, and for many it snapped in 1948.

One of the most striking developments of this process occurred in the midst of a lengthy, sophisticated musicological debate that took place in 1947, almost entirely outside publication. During this debate, leaders of the professional organization articulated a new definition of professionalism and a description of appropriate professional behavior. When the party increased its control over the Composers' Union's agenda, leaders of the Union tightened the reigns in an area they still controlled: professional conduct.

The professional agency that is so important to understanding the operation of the Soviet music profession and its relationship to political power depended on maintaining related but distinct professional and political spheres even during periods of ideological pressure, when the boundaries between the political and the professional, artistic, or creative were challenged. The Zhdanovshchina was just such a moment. Like the loyal party members that most of them were, Composers' Union leaders accepted the erosion of their wartime initiative and used their professional expertise and leadership to work on party tasks. In order to accomplish those tasks, they needed to establish clearly articulated boundaries between professional and political spheres. In 1947 the Orgkom defined appropriate professional behavior in a way that allowed developments within the profession to proceed without constant interference by the party elites. Unlike autonomy, which assumes the continuing operation of an independent professional realm, agency depended on *taking action*.

The definition of appropriate professional conduct that emerged in 1947 was surprising in two respects. First, it explicitly referred to the legacy of the prewar Terror in the early postwar period. Second, a clearly articulated boundary between political and professional discourses ensured that even in peak moments of ideological pressure when the party aggressively asserted its priority (never challenged) in the political realm, the professional organization quietly asserted the right to draw the boundaries that separated the two and to define the appropriate behavior of music professionals.

Professional Politics and Setting the Creative Agenda

The Zhdanovshchina's first big salvos effectively usurped the Composers' Union's power to set its own creative agenda, something that composers and musicologists had been accustomed to doing since the early days of the war.

How effectively the party elite seized control of the Composers' Union agenda can be seen in the planning discussions that led up to the Orgkom's plenary session at the end of 1946. Throughout that year the Orgkom repeatedly discussed plans for the All-USSR Congress of Soviet Composers, and those plans became the fodder for an internal struggle over the leadership of the Composers' Union and its membership. In early March, the de facto head of the Union, Aram Khachaturian, suggested that the Orgkom formulate a plan for the congress and present it for approval to the Central Committee apparatus and Committee on Artistic Affairs. The Orgkom appointed Khachaturian and two of the Orgkom's most experienced administrators, V. N. Surin and Viktor Belyi, to work out a detailed program.[8] It also decided to approach the same "directing institutions" with a request to expand the Orgkom to include six new members and to ask the Central Committee's arts sector (UPA, otdel iskusstv) to replace long-time organizational secretary Belyi with one of the Composers' Union's most successful wartime administrators, Levon Atovm'ian.[9] These personnel maneuvers indicate that the Orgkom was taking practical measures to shape the Composers' Union leadership after the congress. Freeing Belyi from his secretarial responsibilities while leaving him on the Orgkom gave him the time to focus on preparing for the congress. More significantly, adding six members to the Orgkom potentially disrupted the existing leadership structure and placed the new members in a position to continue in leadership posts after the congress. The six were approved by the Central Committee apparatus and the Committee on Artistic Affairs.[10]

This organizational change seems to have threatened Khachaturian. In a maneuver that clearly caught other Orgkom members by surprise, Khachaturian threatened to resign. In the commotion that followed, he reconsolidated his personal authority within Union leadership circles. Apparently without discussing the matter with his peers, Khachaturian sent the Central Committee a request in which he asked to be relieved of his responsibilities because of illness. The Central Committee did not claim the authority to grant this request; rather, they sent word to the Orgkom that they agreed with Khachaturian's decision. Surprised, the Orgkom decided not to resolve the issue until Khachaturian recovered and returned to Moscow.[11]

At the Orgkom's next meeting, Khachaturian confirmed that he had indeed asked to be relieved of his duties because of his illness and because "in his work, he had not met with the necessary support from members of the Orgkom." To

---

8. RGALI, f. 2077, op. 1, d. 139, l. 12 (Protokol #5, 11 Mar 1946), pt. 1. Surin was the unofficial liaison of the Composers' Union to the VKI, and Belyi was a composer and member of the Orgkom who had been a constant presence alongside Khachaturian during the war.

9. Ibid., ll. 13–13ob., pts. 3–4. The planned new members were composers S. S. Prokofiev, V. Ia. Shebalin, G. N. Popov, T. N. Khrennikov, L. A. Polovinkin, and L. K. Knipper. UPA was the name of the party's agit-prop administration; one of its divisions was the sector of the arts.

10. Ibid., l. 14 (Protokol #6, 5 Apr 1946), pt. 1.

11. Ibid., l. 14ob. (Protokol #6, 5 Apr 1946), pt. 4

replace him, the Orgkom's unofficial liaison to the Central Committee nominated either Dmitrii Shostakovich or Iurii Shaporin. Apparently alarmed, the Orgkom stated that Khachaturian's leadership to date had been very positive, and changing leadership so close to the congress was ill advised.[12] At the next meeting, Shostakovich read a collective letter from himself and two of the other most influential composers in the Soviet Union, Nikolai Miaskovskii and Vissarion Shebalin. The three giants argued that it was essential to press Khachaturian into remaining at least through the congress. Their resolution was approved, and the Central Committee was informed that Khachaturian would continue on in his powerful position.[13] What they did not need to say was that Khachaturian had managed to consolidate his personal authority within the leadership body, despite whatever threat its expansion may have posed.

He wasted no time before attempting to carry that authority through the congress. Just four days after agreeing to remain in power, Khachaturian proposed to hold a plenary meeting in June to approve the keynote address and hold elections in preparation for a December congress. This proposal was relatively bold, suggesting as it did that the matter of the congress, which had been up in the air for seven years, would suddenly be resolved in a month's time. Though seconded by the still powerful Belyi, Khachaturian's suggestion was rejected by the other Orgkom members who were present. Led by Dmitrii Kabalevskii, Lev Knipper, and L. A. Polovinkin, two of whom had just been appointed, these members argued that the elections should take place in the context of a "multifaceted examination and discussion of the creative work of Soviet composers." They opposed the June plenary session.[14]

Instead of convening such a session, the Orgkom effectively went on summer holiday, meeting just a few times between the end of May and the middle of September. During that time, the Central Committee issued its barrage of resolutions on the arts. When the subject of the 1946 plenary session next came up in September, the agenda had already been set, not by the professional leadership, but by the Central Committee. At issue was no longer the long-awaited All-USSR Congress, but the Central Committee resolutions on literature, theater, and film. This loss of power to set the professional agenda carried on well past the plenary session itself.

For the plenary session, the Orgkom decided to have Khachaturian deliver the keynote discussion of the three resolutions and to invite representatives from each national and autonomous republic to participate.[15] Khachaturian took time off to concentrate on his report, as did potential rivals and troublemakers such as Aleksei Ogolevets, who had recently attacked Composers'

12. Ibid., ll. 16–16ob. (Protokol #7, 29 Apr 1946), pt. 2.
13. Ibid., l. 17ob. (Protokol #8, 3 May 1946), pt. 2.
14. Ibid., l. 19 (Protokol #9, 7 May 1946), pt. 1.
15. Ibid., l. 57 (Protokol #17, 12 Sep 1946), pt. 1. Even the title of the protocol point acknowledges the shift in agenda setting: "O sozyve Plenuma Orgkomiteta SSK SSSR, v sviazi s postanovleniiami TsK VKP(b) o literature, teatre i kino."

Union leaders in the press.[16] Two weeks later, after the plenary meeting, the Orgkom met again to approve Khachaturian's report and prepare official resolutions about the session's results.[17]

The resolutions were approved later, but not without changes. Though they most likely seemed extremely minor at the time, those changes foreshadowed a much more spectacular definition of appropriate professional discourse that would take place a year later. Though the Composers' Union lost control over its agenda, it could still set the terms of professional behavior. In the draft resolutions, a number of prominent composers were singled out for specific criticism:

> Composers address such important, central themes [of contemporary, postwar Soviet life] only as a matter of exception. The rejection of these contemporary themes is notable in a few recent works even by the great Soviet composers; for example, in Shostakovich's Ninth Symphony, in Shaporin's cycle of elegies, and so forth.

Without explanation, the Orgkom changed the wording to a much more general, potentially less personally harmful statement:

> Even great composers who wrote remarkable pieces during the war, pieces that were imbued with heroic characteristics and the feelings of the Soviet people, after the war have not succeeded in composing new works that sufficiently reflect the most important themes of the postwar lives of the Soviet people.[18]

This rhetorical choice not to name names but rather to generalize critical remarks became an important element of the description of appropriate professional discourse that emerged in 1947. In 1946 it was merely a sign that Composers' Union leaders favored deflecting criticism from specific individuals, especially prominent ones.

At the same time, newly appointed members of the Orgkom began to assert themselves, though there is no evidence that they threatened the personal authority that Khachaturian consolidated in late May. After the plenary session, the Orgkom decided to implement two structural reforms. First, they wanted to reorganize the leadership body to follow the model of the Writers' Union. In order to work out the details, they appointed a commission of well-established powers in the Orgkom: Khachaturian, Belyi, Surin (the unofficial liaison to the Committee on Artistic Affairs), Gavriil Popov (a new member, but one closely allied in artistic temperament to Shostakovich), and Kabalevskii. Another perhaps even more important task, however, was entrusted to two new Orgkom

16. Shostakovich to Glikman, 24 Sep 1946, in Glikman, *Pis'ma k drugu*, 74–75; A. S. Ogolevets, "Perestroit' rabotu Soiuza sovetskikh kompozitorov," *Sovetskoe iskusstvo*, 20 Sep 1946.

17. RGALI, f. 2077, op. 1, d. 139, l. 59 (Protokol #18, 30 [Sep] 1946). The actual protocol is dated 30 October, but that must be a mistake. For the resolutions and description of the plenary session, see the published account in *Sovetskaia muzyka*, 1946, no. 10:3–96.

18. RGALI, f. 2077, op. 1, d. 139, l. 61 (Protokol #20, 16 Oct 1946).

members and an extremely respected songwriter who had long been on the Orgkom: Polovinkin, Tikhon Khrennikov, and Isaak Dunaevskii. These three were to reexamine the membership of the Composers' Union's creative commissions and think about possible structural changes.[19] This task entailed rebuilding the professional organization's creative apparatus. Khachaturian's personal authority was as high as ever, and his most recent composition (the Cello Concerto) was exalted in a normally critical press.[20] Still, he was not able to place his stamp on the Union's institutional forms.

The Central Committee continued to press on the professional sphere throughout 1947. The Orgkom's internal creative discussions and conflicts were frequently prompted by articles in the Central Committee's newspaper *Kul'tura i zhizn'*.[21] For example, a lengthy discussion of popular songs emerged as a direct response to an intervention by the Central Committee's cultural apparatus into the evaluation of works by songwriters in the Composers' Union. In January 1947 *Kul'tura i zhizn'* attacked professional songwriters in two articles, one that suggested that the quality of Soviet song writing had declined after the war, and one that celebrated the songs of a collective farm worker and amateur musician named Mariia Malkina.[22] In response to the first of these articles, the Orgkom met to discuss the Commission of Mass Genres and questions of Soviet songs, and eventually held a joint meeting of the Commission and Orgkom. For almost four weeks starting in mid-May, they heard more than forty songs that had been written in late 1946 and early 1947 by twenty-six composers. They issued generally optimistic evaluations but concluded by creating a series of subsections within the commission, so the result was another internal structural reform.[23] Though the Central Committee set the agenda, it was profes-

---

19. Ibid., ll. 60–60ob. (Protokol #19, 8 Oct 1946), pts. 1–3.

20. See G. Khubov, "Violonchel'nyi kontsert A. Khachaturiana," *Kul'tura i zhizn'*, 1946, no. 14 (7 Nov): 6. The article praised Khachaturian in positive language that mirrored the negatives of the Central Committee's *Zhdanovshchina* resolutions ("Listening to this new work by A. Khachaturian, we feel in it the breath of our present day") and characterized the piece as "sincerely melodic, filled with the spirit of folk singing, . . . and rich with beautiful harmonies."

21. RGALI, f. 2077, op. 1, d. 164, ll. 10–11 (Protokol #3, 5 Feb 1947), pt. 3; ll. 15–16 (Protokol #6, 24 Mar 1947), pt. 1.

22. I. Nest'ev, "O sovetskoi pesne," *Kul'tura i zhizn'*, 1947, no. 3 (31 Jan): 4. See also the lead article of the same issue which suggested that folk music and the music of the national minorities were particularly weak on the radio. G. Khubov, "Pesni kolkhoznitsy Marii Malkinoi," *Kul'tura i zhizn'*, 1947, no. 9 (30 Mar): 3. Nest'ev was the editor in chief of the Musical Broadcasts Administration of the All-Union Radio Committee. He was a musicologist who finished at the Moscow State Conservatory in 1937 and received an advanced degree from the same institution in 1940. He had been a party member since 1943. Khubov was a consultant on artistic broadcasts in the Central Committee apparatus. He was a musicologist who finished at the Tbilisi Conservatory in 1922 and took a second degree in piano and piano pedagogy at Moscow State Conservatory in 1930. He taught the first courses on the history of Soviet music while teaching at Moscow State Conservatory from 1934 to 1939. Like Nest'ev, he had been a party member since 1943. "Nest'ev, Izrail Abramovich," in *Muzykal'naia entsiklopediia*, vol. 3; "Khubov, Georgii Nikitich," in *Muzykal'naia entsiklopediia*, vol. 6.

23. RGALI, f. 2077, op. 1, d. 164, l. 11 (Protokol #3, 5 Feb 1947); l. 15ob. (Protokol #6, 24 Mar 1947); ll. 42–44 (performance programs).

sionals who typically determined the content and even institutional response. This pattern would continue until Stalin's death.

In the midst of their high-level, internal political jockeying, the Composers' Union leaders also sought to rid the professional organization of members who they considered insufficiently qualified. In March 1946 they contacted local and republican chapters to outline standards for membership before the approaching congress, stressing that members should only be those "professional composers and musicologists with the highest qualifications." Local leaders were to reexamine their membership and apply "the highest artistic and professional criteria." This effort primarily targeted those musicologists who were not highly trained theorists but who taught or popularized music and especially *melodisty,* or tunesmiths. Only those songwriters whose music "had achieved wide recognition either as mass songs or on the variety stage" were allowed to remain in the Composers' Union, and even those were subject to special approval of the Orgkom. If current members showed potential but had not yet realized it, they were to be transferred to candidate status and enrolled in a reorganized professional finishing institute under the auspices of the Composers' Union.[24]

This attack on popular music composers, many of whom had entered the ranks of the Composers' Union during the war, reveals tensions between loosely defined camps within the Union and demonstrates that the highly trained composers who held positions of authority within it sought to maintain it as an exclusive repository of expert knowledge. In fact, several of the most influential composers of highbrow music had long been trying to conduct a purge of the professional body, repeatedly asking the Central Committee apparatus for the go-ahead to do so.[25] Then in early March, the head of the arts sector of the Central Committee apparatus suggested that the Composers' Union reexamine its membership before holding the All-USSR Congress.[26] The Orgkom used the suggestion as a pretense to attack tunesmiths, but went too far.

From late April to mid-May 1946, about the same time that Khachaturian was making his power play in the Orgkom, the results of the local reexaminations began to come in. The Belorussian chapter cut its total membership almost in half, keeping nine full members, transferring six to candidate status, and kicking two out of the Composers' Union for "artistic unproductiveness and inactivity."[27] The Leningrad chapter was even more zealous. They retained fifty members, transferred twenty-five to candidate status, and ousted seven mu-

24. RGASPI, f. 17, op. 117, d. 609, ll. 225–25ob. (Glier and Belyi to local leadership bodies, 29 Mar 1946).

25. Ibid., l. 224 (G. Aleksandrov to Kuznetsov, 31 May 1946). Aleksandrov noted that Glier, Khachaturian, and Shostakovich had repeatedly contacted UPA with requests to "conduct a purge" of "accidentally admitted" members and had repeatedly been told that to do so would be improper.

26. Ibid., l. 223 (Nazarov to Kuznetsov, 28 May 1946). The suggestion apparently came from the head of the arts sector of UPA, Lebedev, in March.

27. Ibid., ll. 227–28 (A. V. Bogatyrev to Orgkom, 27 Apr 1946).

sicologists and twenty-five composers.[28] Confronted with these extreme results, the Orgkom retreated, but only slightly. It overturned the transfer of three of the Belorussian members to candidate status and suggested that a decision on a fourth should be made in Moscow since the member in question no longer lived in Belorussia. The Orgkom also upheld all twenty-five transfers of Leningrad members to candidate status, but it overturned the expulsion of ten others, ordering that they be transferred to candidate status and given the opportunity to polish their professional credentials. That left twenty-two former members out.[29]

This decision provoked a scandal that reached almost to the pinnacle of political power in the Soviet Union. When the head of personnel in the Central Committee apparatus learned of the decision, he quickly relayed his disapproval to Orgbiuro and Secretariat member A. A. Kuznetsov.[30] His objections were twofold. First, the Orgkom's decision was a thinly disguised purge based on internal professional disputes, or so it seemed from a telephone discussion that he had with the head of the Committee on Artistic Affairs, whose wife was also a Composers' Union member sitting on Moscow's membership review committee. Second, the "purge" was premature or unnecessary and should be decided only during the congress.

Zhdanov apparently agreed. G. F. Aleksandrov, the head of the party's cultural administration, also chimed in with his own considerably less detailed disapproval. On 8 June 1946, the Secretariat heard the issue and agreed with their officials in the apparatus. They found the Orgkom's actions improper and suggested that it adhere to its charter when expelling members.[31]

The Orgkom was forced to retreat further, and in mid-June, it passed a "clarification" of the earlier order and explained that the "verification" of members was not a "purge." Following the Secretariat's lead, it called chapters' attention to the existing bylaws of the Composers' Union and noted that members could be expelled only in exceptional, extreme circumstances. Finally, it overturned the decisions of the Leningrad and Belorussian chapters.[32]

There is nothing in the archival record to suggest that this assault on songwriters originated anywhere but in the leadership circles of the Composers'

28. Ibid., ll. 229–30 (LSSK protocol excerpt, 13 May 1946). The review committee was headed by the famous I. I. Dzerzhinskii, author of *Tikhii Don*, the most successful song opera of the late 1930s.

29. RGALI, f. 2077, op. 1, d. 139, ll. 52–52ob. (Protokol #13, 25 May 1946).

30. On 28 May, the Central Committee head of cadres, Nazarov, heard of the decision from the Orgkom's secretary, one Merzhanova; RGASPI, f. 17, op. 117, d. 609, ll. 226–26ob. (Merzhanova to Nazarov, 28 May 1946). His memo of objection was sent the same day; l. 223.

31. Ibid., l. 223; for Zhdanov's agreement, see marginal notation. Kuznetsov had forwarded Nazarov's letter to Zhdanov on 29 May; l. 224 (Aleksandrov to Kuznetsov, 31 May 1946); ll. 221–22 (voting record and draft resolution). The decision was sent to Aleksandrov, Khachaturian, Khrapchenko (head of VKI), and E. Andreev; RGASPI, f. 17, op. 116, d. 264, pt. 331g. (8 Jun 1946).

32. RGALI, f. 2077, op. 1, d. 139, l. 49 (Protokol #11, 12 Jun 1946).

Union, the Orgkom, or that it was motivated by anything but a concern for the credentials of Composers' Union members. The professional leadership had long been concerned about the qualifications of the *melodisty* admitted during the war, even forming consultation bodies to improve their expertise. Though it is possible that there was discomfort with the popularity and material success of popular song composers in general, those who were so successful to have potentially aroused the jealousy of Orgkom members were safe from the purge in any case. It is much more likely that they were simply concerned about professional qualifications.

The high-level intervention in response suggests that even as late as June 1946, party leaders were concerned primarily with personnel policy and upper leadership members, not with professional politics. In fact, when they approved the expansion of the Orgkom, and especially when they intervened to prevent the purge of the tunesmiths, the Central Committee ensured that the Composers' Union would be stylistically inclusive. It articulated as much in internal communications, reasoning that the Orgkom's attack on tunesmiths undermined "democratic principles" in the professional organization.[33] This inclusiveness did not extend to performers, however, for the apparatus never revisited that issue. It is also likely that the Secretariat, or at least members of the Central Committee apparatus, noticed the emerging contours of a split within the professional organization between members who placed the highest value on technical mastery and the expertise they thought should define the profession and those who were more eager to privilege political responsiveness. By supporting the tunesmiths, they kept the organization inclusive and curried favor with an already sympathetic group.[34] Within the year, the distinction between political and professional spheres within the Composers' Union was to become more sharply, clearly, and explicitly articulated.

The Ogolevets Affair

The immediate context in which the professional leadership articulated clear boundaries between party and professional discourse was an esoteric, complex, and highly theoretical musicological debate. Throughout much of 1947, the Musicology Commission of the Composers' Union was embroiled in a heated and protracted evaluation of the voluminous works of the musicologist A. S. Ogolevets. At the end of the discussion, Ogolevets's theoretical position was re-

---

33. RGASPI, f. 17, op. 117, d. 609, l. 223 (Nazarov to Kuznetsov).
34. In a personal communication to the author, 3 Jul 1999, G. S. Frid noted that songwriters often tended to put party loyalty first. Frid remembered the Composers' Union after the war as primarily divided into pro-party and anti-party groups. When asked if those divisions mapped at all onto professional proclivities, he agreed that indeed songwriters and pro-party types were strongly overlapping groups; however, there were plenty of songwriters who were more loyal to the profession, and, of course, some highbrow types who always privileged party loyalty.

jected, and the musicologist himself was nearly thrown out of the Union for unprofessional conduct. The description of Ogolevets's behavior and the consequences of continuing it amounted to an enunciation of the boundaries between the professional and the political and the professional's responsibility to maintain those boundaries.

The Ogolevets affair also demonstrated just how important the work of the creative commissions was to the professional operation of the Composers' Union, from simple evaluation of the work of its members to its policy statements about Soviet music broadly writ. That the Musicology Commission rather than the whole Composers' Union or even just the Orgkom was the primary focus of this conflict demonstrates that creative and political life in the Union depended on the system of commissions and sections of the creative apparatus. This conflict and others like it also demonstrate how professional authority operated within the creative apparatus. By concentrating professionals with the most authority in a specific category in one subcommittee and then filtering discussions about the category through that subcommittee, the Composers' Union sought to maximize the efficiency of its daily operations, its deliberations about issues that it thought were important, and its responses to issues that were considered crucial by the party elite.

Aleksei Stepanovich Ogolevets was born in 1894 in Poltava. One of the youngest of the prerevolutionary generation of professionals, he studied composition, piano, and music theory at the Moscow Conservatory from 1912 to 1916. He was a student of Boleslav Iavorskii, whose peculiar "modal rhythm" system of music analysis imparted several crucial components to Soviet music theory. Ogolevets's investigations into non-Western modes followed his own creative agenda, especially during the war. Before he turned to professional musicology, Ogolevets held a position in the Soviet police administration, and he also worked for *Pravda* from the early 1920s. He later used the experience and connections thus formed to intimidate his colleagues. In the 1930s he became a powerful and often controversial theoretical voice among professional musicologists. An ambitious administrator, he was active in the Composers' Union before the war and served as the wartime head of its Kuibyshev chapter.[35]

Before the end of the war, Ogolevets began seeking a quasi-independent institutional base from which to expand his authority over theoretical research. In October 1944 he proposed a Scholarly Research Department–Laboratory of Tonal Systems, which he planned to direct. The lab would investigate all questions of music in a theoretical way, but it would particularly focus on Eastern musical cultures, the translation and publication of tracts on Eastern and European music, and the differences between diverse tonal systems. It would also conduct studies in the area of Soviet music. Ogolevets appealed to an unutilized

35. "Ogolevets Aleksei Stepanovich," in *Muzykal'naia entsiklopediia,* 3:1083; Igor Belza, "Ogolevets, Alexey Stepanovich," in *The New Grove Dictionary of Music and Musicians,* ed. S. Sadie (New York: Macmillan, 1980), 13:519–20.

provision in the Composers' Union's charter to support scholarly research and form laboratories for that purpose. He also invoked the support of the figure-head chairman of the Composers' Union, Glier. The Orgkom accepted the proposal and ordered Ogolevets to develop a creative plan.[36]

Each year, the Orgkom revisited the lab's funding and creative plans, so it did maintain nominal control over the institution.[37] However, there is evidence that Ogolevets sought to establish himself as a theoretical force that would rival the institutional authority that the Composers' Union held over Soviet musicology. In July 1946 he submitted an ambitious plan to Kliment Voroshilov, a Politburo member, hoping that the latter would push it through the Council of Ministers. The plan called for the creation of an Institute for New Musical Problems. Ogolevets stressed the need to coordinate research on the "music of the future," including electronic music and recording technology. But his ambition was much greater. He proposed an institute that would contain three main departments: a Department of Musical Languages, Tone Rows, and Modes; a Creative Department of New Music; and a Department of Musical Technology. The institute would also subsume four additional subsidiary research institutions: the Laboratory of Tonal Systems that Ogolevets directed and three others that already existed under the auspices of the Committee on Artistic Affairs.[38] This institute would clearly pose a threat to the institutional authority of the Composers' Union, especially since it would subsume one of its subsidiary institutions and perhaps usurp some of its ability to coordinate the activities of Soviet composers and performers, which was one of the theoretical goals of Ogolevets's proposed Creative Department of New Music.

In retrospect, Ogolevets's grandiose scheme may seem like the delusional power grab of a marginalized crank, and so it may have been. But at this moment in postwar Soviet history, the grandiose schemes of ornery cranks were attracting the attention and sometimes support of high-ranking party officials just like Voroshilov. The most famous example of a successful crank who captured control of a scientific discipline is T. D. Lysenko. Lysenko was an agrobiologist whose theories about maximizing yields in wheat harvests were invalidated by internationally accepted genetics theories and experiments, but Lysenko adeptly defended his own work and attacked genetics on primarily Marxist ideological grounds. He was a constant irritant in the biology field in the 1930s and 1940s, when he developed a sizable following among his colleagues. He also cultivated close personal ties with members of Stalin's inner

---

36. RGALI, f. 2077, op. 1, d. 96, l. 67 (Ogolevets to Orgkom, 20 Oct 1944). Ogolevets probably prepared the groundwork for this request even earlier. In 1942 the Orgkom denied his request to establish a Scholarly Research Institute under the auspices of the Kuibyshev SSK; d. 51, l. 93 (Protokol #13, 12 Oct 1942), pt. r.3; d. 96, l. 71 (Protokol #14, 23 Oct 1944), pt. 6.2.

37. Ibid., d. 120, l. 22 (addition to Protokol #14, 5 Mar 1945); l. 23 (lab budget, 5 Mar 1945). The first of these asked for an increase in funding to support the lab, and the second was a budget drafted by Ogolevets and approved by Glier. Annual financial and creative plans were also approved for 1946; d. 139, ll. 9–9ob. (Protokol #3, 14 Feb 1946).

38. GARF, f. 5446, op. 48, d. 2181, ll. 61–67 (Ogolevets to Voroshilov, 16 Jul 1946).

circle, including Malenkov and perhaps Stalin himself. In a dramatic public discussion in 1948, Lysenko's theories received the endorsement of the Central Committee, and genetics was effectively relegated to the margins of Soviet biology, to great scientific cost.[39]

Unlike Lysenko's successful destruction of genetics, Ogolevets's scheme failed despite the fact that his theoretical views, though not dominant, were not as thoroughly discredited as Lysenko's. In fact, Ogolevets's proposal received much more than cursory attention. Initially, both the Ministry of Finance and the Committee on Artistic Affairs rejected the idea.[40] The Committee on Artistic Affairs reconsidered, however, and formed a special subcommittee to look into the matter. By then the plan was almost certainly reduced to one that would be less threatening to the Composers' Union, focusing as it did on research about the electronic music and recording technology that Ogolevets first mentioned.[41] Whether the new institute could have survived opposition from the Composers' Union we will never know. Before the committee could submit its findings, bureaucrats in the Council of Ministers realized that forming a new institute would violate a standing moratorium on starting new institutions, and the issue was dropped.[42]

Though unsuccessful, these machinations demonstrate that Ogolevets well understood what it took to accumulate power and authority in the Soviet system. He formed and cultivated unofficial, personal connections with high-ranking politicians, possibly including Voroshilov.[43] And he used those connections to try to establish something that was just as important as connections—an institutional base with its own source of funding and potential to dictate further developments in one's field. He was also well practiced in the politics of personal attack.

Ogolevets was a fiery character, later described by a contemporary as a "frightening man."[44] It is more from his behavior than from his ideas that he earned the reputation as a crank. On more than one occasion between 1941 and 1946 his presentations at large meetings of composers and musicologists had caused scandals because of his aggressive attacks against other professionals and the response those attacks elicited from Composers' Union leaders. For example, at the 1944 plenary session of the Orgkom, Ogolevets's written state-

---

39. Nikolai Krementsov, *Stalinist Science* (Princeton: Princeton University Press, 1997). The classic work on the Lysenko controversy is David Joravsky, *The Lysenko Affair* (Cambridge: Harvard University Press, 1970). For biology in the context of other science discussions, see Pollock, "Politics of Knowledge."

40. GARF, f. 5446, op. 48, d. 2181, l. 59 (Zverev to SM SSSR, 29 Jul 1946); l. 60 (Surin to Chadaev, 6 Aug 1946).

41. Ibid., l. 69 (Abolimov to Voroshilov, 28 Aug 1946).

42. Ibid., l. 70 (Abolimov, "Spravka," 10 Nov 1946).

43. Addressed to Voroshilov, Ogolevets's original appeal contained some of the language of a client's address to his patron; however, Voroshilov did not treat the appeal as he did those of less ambiguous clients.

44. G. S. Frid, personal communication, 7 May 1999.

ments for discussion were found so tendentious that Khachaturian refused to let him speak, suggesting instead that he tone down the remarks, remove the elements designed to create a row, and deliver his presentation the following day. Though Ogolevets took exception to that characterization, he did as he was asked, so the first set of remarks have not been preserved.[45] When he did present the next day, Ogolevets held little back, blasting his protagonist in very strong language and accusing him simultaneously of petty-bourgeois national chauvinism and "apopulism" because his compositions were characterized by "Western linearity" rather than being rooted in the traditional modal systems of one of the indigenous folk musics of the Soviet Union.[46]

Ogolevets's presentation was characteristic. He first described an artistic position that conflicted with his own and then characterized the adherent of that position in extremely strong terms, terms that amounted in the Stalinist lexicon to accusations of treason. This escalation of an attack from the realm of the professional to the criminal was what got Ogolevets in trouble with the professional leadership. In this case, Khachaturian allowed Ogolevets to finish, declared that his presentation had reached a "form" that was not appropriate for their discussion, and promised to return to Ogolevets's behavior at the end of the meeting.[47] When he did, he summarized the "sad episode" and scolded both participants. Ogolevets was chastised for not giving productive criticism but reducing his comments to bald insults that inhibited rather than promoted creative discussion. His antagonist was also scolded for failing to respond to the content of the professional attack and instead adding fuel to the personal fireworks by resorting to political formulations. The antagonist had already submitted a written apology for his behavior, and Khachaturian hoped that Ogolevets would do the same.[48]

Khachaturian concluded the affair by enunciating an early definition of appropriate professional discourse: "Our work in the SSK like the rest of our lives in the Soviet Union is based on the principles of friendship and the brotherhood of all peoples, and we are not permitted a single violation of those principles. We are not permitted a single artificial intensification of harmful instincts in whatever form they may be expressed."[49] In a later discussion of Ogolevets's behavior, this brief articulation would be greatly expanded.

45. RGALI, f. 2077, op. 1, d. 93 (Orgkom plenary stenogram, 1–7 Apr 1944), l. 248. The exchange between Ogolevets and Khachaturian was about Ogolevets's fourth presentation of the proceedings. His prepared remarks apparently started the row; a colleague (Iu. A. Levitin) answered, and as the tension mounted, civility declined.

46. Ibid., 290–96. I use the neologism "apopulist" for Ogolevets's "*anarodnost'*," which should not be confused with "*antinarodnyi*." In other words, he accused Levitin of taking an agnostic position regarding what he considered appropriately populist (not popular, necessarily) Soviet music, defined imprecisely as "*narodnyi*." Note that "*narodnyi*" does *not* mean "folk" in this case. Rather, Ogolevets meant "rooted in a modal system."

47. Ibid., l. 296.
48. Ibid., ll. 386–87.
49. Ibid., l. 388.

The 1944 plenum was not the only time that Ogolevets's behavior drew the attention and condemnation of his peers. In 1946, in fact, his presentation was considered so unacceptable that it was not fit to print in the professional journal's transcript of the discussion. His remarks were briefly excerpted, and members were still talking about it a year later.[50]

Despite his repeated outrageous behavior in public forums, Ogolevets was also a respected and prolific musicologist. He worked tirelessly throughout the war years and prepared several lengthy theoretical volumes for publication immediately after the war.[51] In 1946 the central music publisher issued the second of these texts.[52] The Musicology Commission decided to meet to discuss Ogolevets's collected thoughts on Soviet music theory, but the discussion did not actually begin until April 1947.[53] Once it did, musicological life revolved around Ogolevets for nearly six months while the Musicology Commission (headed by A. I. Shaverdian) met thirteen times to let more than thirty musicologists read reports lasting as long as several hours and running more than one hundred pages.[54] At the end of the discussion, the Orgkom even met several times to hammer out the details of the concluding resolution, which was then tucked away in a very brief announcement in the professional journal, the only published mention of the Ogolevets affair.[55]

It was in the context of this discussion that Khachaturian, other Orgkom members, and members of the Musicology Commission articulated a clear differentiation of professional and political spheres. This differentiation revolved around the issue of appropriate professional behavior, and it was a result of Ogolevets's behavior in the past and at a meeting on 6 October 1947 in which the final resolutions were approved. The repartee in that meeting both described and exhibited the two poles of antisocial and model behavior.

The issue of behavior first surfaced at the very beginning of the 6 October meeting, when Ogolevets gave his opening remarks. His belligerent comments reveal both the context of his unprofessional behavior and suggest an explana-

50. "Materialy Plenuma Orgkomiteta SSK SSSR," *Sovetskaia muzyka*, 1946, no. 10:68–69. The objectionable part of the presentation was probably his "sharp polemic" against the musicologist L. A. Mazel'. For a veiled reference to what must have been a less public scolding, see Khachaturian's remarks about inappropriate presentations in ibid., 88.

51. He received a sizable commission from the Composers' Union in 1942 for a project entitled "Tonal Music." RGALI, f. 2077, op. 1, d. 51, l. 23 (Protokol # 5, 10 Jun 1942), pt. r.3.

52. A. S. Ogolevets, *Vvedenie v sovremennoe muzykal'noe myshlenie* (Moscow: Muzgiz, 1946).

53. For Ogolevets's request to have the discussion postponed until the fall of 1946 because of his illness, see RGALI, f. 2077, op. 1, d. 139, l. 17ob. (Protokol #8, 3 May 1946), pt. 3.1.

54. For a complete record, see ibid., dd. 175–199. A particularly long report (115 pages) was presented by V. A. Tsukkerman on June 5; see d. 187, ll. 1–59ob. Like many participants, Tsukkerman began with a brief discussion of Ogolevets's contributions and then launched into a meticulously detailed criticism of his published work. Most reports were about fifty pages.

55. Ibid., d. 164, ll. 45–46 (Protokol #11, 20 Jun 1947), pt. 2; l. 54 (Protokol #15, 6 Oct 1947). Transcripts of the Orgkom discussions are RGALI, f. 2077, op. 1, dd. 198–99. The brief concluding announcement was *Sovetskaia muzyka*, 1947, no. 6:25–29, a much shorter summary of the resolution adopted by the Orgkom in October.

tion of the timing of what was to become a condemnation of him. Ogolevets was given the opportunity to defend his work against the overwhelmingly negative assessment proposed by the Musicology Commission. As he did so, he suggested that members of the commission were not qualified to criticize his philosophical position because they were not professional philosophers. Rather than accepting the commission's criticism, Ogolevets suggested that the issue be referred to the Institute of Philosophy. Ominously, he noted that "yesterday, I called Aleksandrov, with whom I am personally acquainted, about arranging such a consultation with me at the institute."[56]

Ogolevets's appeal to G. F. Aleksandrov was intended to intimidate his colleagues, but it also suggests an explanation for the timing of the stern resolution that followed. Ogolevets considered Aleksandrov to be a powerful protector, a patron who could extricate him and his work from criticism. What Ogolevets failed to consider was that Aleksandrov had just been criticized by Stalin himself and demoted from his position as head of the Central Committee's cultural oversight apparatus. This demotion landed him in the position of director of the Philosophy Institute, but he no longer wielded the power he had earlier. Knowing that Ogolevets's protector had recently been demoted, the Orgkom likely felt free to discipline him.

Khachaturian's reaction to Ogolevets's threatening response to the evaluation of his work is suggestive of the discussion about behavior that was soon to follow. Khachaturian first suggested merely softening the language of the Musicology Commission's draft resolution, changing all such phrases as "misuse and falsification" to "philosophical mistakes." Ogolevets replied aggressively: "No, I am not mistaken. Maybe the way I employ this or that thesis of Lenin is debatable, but I would like the very fact that I work on these theses to compel my comrades to work with me." Khachaturian and Lev Knipper, another member of the Orgkom, expressed the fundamental assumptions of the emerging definition of professional behavior in their reply:

KHACHATURIAN: From this day forward, a new era has begun—you will be a member of the collective.

KNIPPER: Many of us composers you have sternly rapped on the knuckles. From this, we have simply grown wiser.[57]

Willingness to place one's work in a professional context (rather than "compelling" others' attention) and avoiding abusive behavior were to become the two touchstones of the newly articulated definition of appropriate professional conduct. Later in the discussion, Khachaturian summarized the collective, or social, element of professional conduct when he emphasized that "Ogolevets the scholar, Ogolevets the public figure, and Ogolevets the man are one and the

56. RGALI, f. 2077, op. 1, d. 199, l. 27 (6 Oct 1947).
57. Ibid., l. 29.

same."[58] His scholarship could be criticized on its own terms, but it could not in the end be extricated from the social circumstances of its production and dissemination.

There was also an expressly personal element about the proceedings, one that Khachaturian expressed in surprisingly explicit terms. Throughout the discussion, Ogolevets challenged every negative characterization of his work, seeking in each case to change "false" and the like to "debatable" or something similar. In most cases the Orgkom decided on a middle ground, such as "mistaken."[59] After one such exchange, Khachaturian erupted: "If you were not such a pain, we would probably have just instructed the commission to remove all sharp expressions. It is because you have such a difficult character that we have to work through the whole thing. Why don't you just help us?"[60] Ogolevets's behavior was so consistently objectionable that Khachaturian reduced it to a question of character.

Though less explicitly, other participants in the debate also suggested that Ogolevets's character was such that he was incapable of participating in a professional organization. For example, Orgkom member Dmitrii Kabalevskii described what he considered the dangerous attitude that Ogolevets expressed in his objection about philosophy. Kabalevskii characterized that attitude as "staggering impudence." He argued that to say to the collective in which you work that no one is competent to judge your work—not even professional philosophers since they had so recently been scolded—is as much as saying, "I am an intelligent man, and you are all fools." It is profoundly insulting to colleagues, Kabalevskii continued, and "very dangerous to consider yourself smarter than everyone else."[61] Similarly, Knipper told Ogolevets that he did not think he was capable of true change, that even in the face of withering criticism he would not actually listen to what his colleagues were saying. He suggested that Ogolevets would just "sit there smiling and thinking that we are all a bunch of fools who do not have the right to criticize you."[62]

In the end, however, the complaints about Ogolevets boiled down to questions about his conduct. At the end of the discussion, Khachaturian opened the floor to thoughts about Ogolevets's presentation style, combativeness, and overall demeanor in professional settings. What followed was a litany of angry complaints that recalled the bleak days of 1937 by describing behavior commonly associated with the Great Terror and accusing Ogolevets of "ter-

58. Ibid., l. 53ob. I translate *obshchestvennyi deiatel'* as "public figure."

59. In Russian, the distinction between "false" and "mistaken" is sharper than in English because the word most commonly used in the discussion that I translate as "false" (*lozhno*) implies a degree of intentionality absent in my English translation.

60. RGALI, f. 2077, op. 1, d. 199, l. 35ob. The first clause of this quotation may be a paraphrase rather than direct quote. The Russian for "difficult character" (*kharakter tiazhelyi*) is considerably stronger than the English, especially in the typically staid context of this type of professional discussion, where it is actually quite jarring.

61. Ibid., ll. 53–53ob.

62. Ibid., l. 58ob.

rorizing" his colleagues. Vissarion Shebalin, director of the Moscow Conservatory, spoke on behalf of the conservatory professoriate, which considered Ogolevets's presentations "antisocial and perfectly out of place in the Soviet environment."[63]

Other members gave more specific descriptions of his unacceptable behavior. One Erokhin, a musicologist, produced a veritable laundry list of Ogolevets's scare tactics and first used the word "terrorize" to describe them. Erokhin charged that Ogolevets collected peoples' remarks and later used them to threaten them. It was well known that Shostakovich had thus been intimidated into refusing to take part in any discussion of Ogolevets's work. Before the 6 October meeting, Ogolevets had apparently seized each member of the committee, "terrorized [them] with phone calls and intimidation [by saying], 'it's agreed then, that I'll send telegrams to members of the Politburo.'" In fact, Ogolevets had called Erokhin and warned that he would send telegrams to the Politburo to inform them of a return of RAPP.[64] If those intimidation tactics proved insufficient, Ogolevets would shift course and say, "After all, I am a former police worker. I'll make mincemeat of one, I'll chase off another, and I'll do something or other with a third." In general, Erokhin recommended that Ogolevets "stop frightening people with the NKVD, with various telephone calls, with letters, and so forth." Erokhin claimed that even when everything was arranged for a purely comradely discussion, Ogolevets still insisted on "speaking various filth, scaring people, and other things." Finally, she summarized with an appeal:

> Once and for all you must walk away from these shameful methods by which you have been operating, from the system of intimidation, from the system of setting people against one another, from the system of scandals and rows, from the system of disgraceful facts. Either you take account of this . . . or we will gather all of the facts, starting with 1936 and up to last year, of your activities, and we will say to you: Aleksei Stepanovich, we warned you, we asked you, we talked to you, but apparently you and we are not on the same path, and apparently we must part ways.[65]

63. Ibid., 57–57ob.

64. RAPP was the Russian Association of Proletarian Writers, the literary organization that seized power during the Cultural Revolution of the First Five-Year Plan era but had been politically disgraced when it was eliminated in the 1932 resolution that called for the formation of creative unions. RAPP had a sister musical organization, RAPM, of which Erokhin was undoubtedly a member. In fact, "RAPM revival" was one of Ogolevets's frequent battle cries, in public and in secret, at least until 1951.

65. RGALI, f. 2077, op. 1, d. 199, ll. 59ob.–63. The Russian word that I have translated colloquially as "setting people against one another" (*natravlivanie*) can also mean "sicking" as in "inciting to attack." Erokhin may have intended this single word to cover Ogolevets's practice of poisoning professional debate by causing rows and threatening to incite police intervention. She also accused Ogolevets of other misconduct, including bribery, wondered if they should get the State Control Commission involved, and seconded Kabalevskii's denunciation of Ogolevets's attitude about philosophy and other professionals' competence to criticize him.

Though Erokhin's laundry list was the most extensive, other speakers added offenses to the catalog of outrageous behavior. Khrennikov told a story about how another composer had received an intimidating anonymous letter filled with racial slurs which, if it was not actually penned by Ogolevets personally, had clearly issued from his circle.[66] Khachaturian noted that "it is well known that you terrorize, threaten, blackmail. I know a few factors, and I believe that you have threatened people, [saying] that you would have them arrested, that you would annihilate them." And later, "I believe that if you want to indict someone, you say that 'in 1936, you said such and such, in 1937 thus and so,' and that you have clippings that document who said what at which meeting." Then he told the following story, to which Erokhin had likely already alluded:

I know about the following incident. I don't think that D. D. Shostakovich will blame me for this. He said that your conduct in relation to him called up in him, to a small measure, aversion to you as a person when you walked up to him, opened your little notebook, and said, "Now you will learn who are your friends and who are your enemies," and began to cite by number and date who said what when, who criticized his symphony and so forth.

After noting that everyone knew about Ogolevets's behavior "at the podium," Khachaturian continued to describe behavior that he thought would be new to some members: "you take the liberty to rummage through the dirty laundry of some of our comrades to search where there might be something to grab hold of in order to scare them and hold them in your own hands."[67] Khachaturian's tirade ended with a charge that resonates with the most evocative descriptions of life during the Great Terror:

You will never persuade me that [one of Ogolevets's colleagues at his laboratory] is a sincere follower of your scholarship. She is your ears around the [Composers'] Union. Everyone sees how she walks the corridors during intermissions and writes down what people say about you in order to deliver it to you. Is this really the behavior of a great scholar, the title to which you aspire? Excuse me for the fact that I'm reading you a moral lecture, but I must say this to you.[68]

All of these complaints about Ogolevets's conduct can be divided into two categories, public and informal. The public behavior consisted of personal or even professional attacks that contained charges of acts or opinions that were criminalized in Soviet society. Disturbing though they considered his public behavior, committee members seemed even more bothered by Ogolevets's informal conduct. This behavior entailed several interrelated practices of denunciation: collecting information, either by himself or through surrogates; keeping

66. Ibid., 63ob. The letter had apparently read something like the following: "If you don't stop saying such and such, I'll beat in your *zhidovskaia* mug."
67. Ibid., l. 70.
68. Ibid., ll. 71–71ob.

records of compromising utterances in official and unofficial settings; blackmailing and intimidating colleagues with that information; and actually denouncing them to the Politburo, party apparatus, or secret police.

Though Ogolevets was overly zealous, most of this behavior was something expected of a loyal party member. The mouthpiece of the Central Committee's cultural apparatus regularly called on cultural professionals to turn up the heat of criticism.[69] Khachaturian and the Composers' Union leaders often echoed these calls in their own public addresses.[70] But the professional leadership also reserved the right to define the boundaries of the criticism that was appropriate in the professional environment. The Ogolevets affair provided an opportunity to make those boundaries more explicit than they had been, and the Orgkom took advantage of that opportunity. As other observers of "Bolshevik criticism" have noted, self-criticism was a crucial component of the critical process.[71] The Composers' Union was no exception to this rule, as Khachaturian demonstrated at the very end of the discussion on 6 October.

Before turning the floor back to Ogolevets for a final word, Khachaturian gave him a veritable script for self-criticism. He said that he was allowing Ogolevets the last word in hopes that he would use it to admit his mistakes and promise not to continue them. He suggested that Ogolevets put aside fears about the publication of his latest book and try to convince the members that his contrition was sincere. And then he concluded by stressing the consequences of not doing so: "If you do not, I think that today's meeting was your last warning. Prohibiting you from composing, writing, creating, no one can do that, but keeping you in the organization—that we can do. And we can invite you to remain outside our ranks. You can write however much you want, but among the members of the Union you will no longer be."[72]

Undoubtedly shaken by the discussion, Ogolevets tried to follow Khachaturian's directions. He accepted the criticisms as "hard truths," and he promised to take a more active role in collective discussions and to submit his work to the Musicology Commission as quickly as he could. Though he begged not to be accused of bribery or paying spies, he promised not to appeal to "other organizations" to fight the Orgkom's decisions, despite the fact that he admitted having planned to do just that: "But I want to say that I deeply acknowledge my mistakes, and I will not submit appeals to anyone except the Presidium [of the SSK]. When I was walking here, I said to myself: I'll go in, the Presid-

69. In fact, this call was the fundamental task of the Central Committee apparatus's newspaper *Kul'tura i zhizn'*. See the lead article of the first issue: "Vyshe uroven' ideologicheskoi raboty!" *Kul'tura i zhizn'*, 1946, no. 1 (28 Jun): 1.

70. For example, see Khachaturian's closing remarks at the 1946 plenum: "Materialy plenuma," *Sovetskaia muzyka*, 1946, no. 10:89.

71. Alexei Kojevnikov, "Games of Stalinist Democracy: Ideological Discussions in Soviet Sciences 1947–52," in *Stalinism: New Directions*, ed. Sheila Fitzpatrick (New York: Routledge, 2000), 142–76.

72. RGALI, f. 2077, op. 1, d. 199, ll. 71ob.–72.

ium will probably approve that which has been prepared, and with a sense of being offended, I said to myself: 'Well, fine, I will appeal, I will write to the authorities.'"[73]

Ogolevets was not particularly adept at self criticism. He still refused to accept all details of the negative evaluation of his work, and he repeatedly paused to ask how he should proceed. Each time, Khachaturian suggested a continued self-critical tack, and Ogolevets agreed to his suggestion. The following is an example of such an exchange:

> OGOLEVETS: Now should I speak in the manner of a retrospective, or should I speak about my mistakes of a scholarly character?
>
> KHACHATURIAN: It would be in order [for you to say that] your future practice will be to ask for your comrades to help you correct them.
>
> OGOLEVETS: I'll say that straight away. . . .[74]

Despite these difficulties, the Orgkom decided that the self-effacement was sufficient to permit Ogolevets to remain a Composers' Union member. He was not expelled, despite repeated suggestions that he should be.[75] The result was that the Orgkom practiced what it preached, keeping criticism about scholarly work and professional conduct within the confines of the Composers' Union.

The Orgkom also modeled appropriately moderate criticism in its own modifications of the Musicology Commission's draft resolutions. And they did so quite consciously. One of the Musicology Commission's suggestions was to characterize Ogolevets's attitude toward past and contemporary musicology as "the most malicious reactionary propaganda." Shaporin suggested eliminating that phrase altogether because "there is a criminal law about such behavior." In other words, professional criticism should be expressed in professional terms, and scholarship deemed mistaken should not be criminalized. Despite others' reservations, Khachaturian agreed, and the damning language was excised.[76] Even in an issue that Orgkom members considered internationally significant, they decided to express their strong dismay verbally and to moderate the official, written resolution. Thus, Khachaturian informed Ogolevets that he had made a "frightening mistake," but the official resolution was a much milder description without invective.[77]

---

73. Ibid., l. 75ob.

74. Ibid., ll. 73–77.

75. Ibid., ll. 53, 63, 68ob.

76. Ibid., ll. 52, 54.

77. Ibid., ll. 49–50. The discussion was about Ogolevets's description of Azerbaidzhani modes, which he thought had been derived from Persian or Arabic sources. The implications of his findings were considered to be deleterious internationally, suggesting as they might that Azerbaidzhani musical thought was not independent but derived from Iran. In the Caucasus, such findings could also supposedly be used to bolster claims that the national cultures should fight off the influence of "superpower" Russian culture, though why that might be the case is not clear.

In the midst of his most severe criticism of Ogolevets, Khachaturian paused to explain how personal and professional enemies should be treated. Khachaturian noted that everyone has "enemies on principle," that is, antagonists whose creative and professional views differed from one's own. And he noted that Ogolevets had "unprincipled enemies," those who "don't like your nose or your glasses." Khachaturian promised that the Orgkom would help Ogolevets fight this latter group, but that Ogolevets had to tolerate the former: "We will give a rebuff to unprincipled critics who do not want to give you the opportunity to move ahead. But principled, serious, scholarly criticism, we will encourage. So, differentiate between your enemies and your antagonists. Enemies, we will all fight. Antagonists, we will hear out, even if we disagree with them."[78] By enunciating the distinction between professional antagonists and personal enemies, Khachaturian again separated the realm of potentially criminal accusations from the arena of professional discourse and asserted the right of the Orgkom to police the boundary of those realms and punish those who brought personal attacks into professional criticism.

While it was arguably within the Orgkom's purview to define the limits of acceptable professional criticism, they were on shakier ground when it came to their condemnation of Ogolevets's informal misconduct—denunciation. Denunciation was a tactic of which party leaders heartily approved. It may be objected that Zhdanov had condemned the practice at the Eighteenth Party Congress of 1939, just after the Great Terror. However, Zhdanov's condemnation stopped far short of even criticizing behavior like that attributed to Ogolevets. Zhdanov spoke out against "careerists" who used mass denunciations to climb the ranks within the party, convicting people through guilt by association. His concern was not the denunciation per se, but huge numbers of "conveyor belt" denunciations that led to mass purges.[79] In any event, almost ten years and a cataclysmic war had passed since the Eighteenth Party Congress, and the Central Committee cultural apparatus regularly took denunciations seriously.[80]

When Khachaturian and the Orgkom condemned the practice of denouncing fellow professionals, they sought to protect professionals from extra-professional censure or even, as the repeated invocation of the word "terror" suggests, arrest, deportation, or worse. They undoubtedly hoped to keep professional criticism relatively moderate and to reduce the danger involved in taking professional risks. However, they also constricted communication between the profession and the party leadership to those channels that they controlled,

---

78. Ibid., ll. 70–71. The last two sentences of this quotation may be paraphrased rather than directly quoted.

79. "Izmeneniia v Ustave VKP(b). Dokladchik t. Zhdanov," *XVIII S'ezd Vsesoiuznoi kommunisticheskoi partii (b), Stenograficheskii otchet* (Moscow: OGIZ, 1939), 520–21.

80. For one striking example, a repeat of which the SSK surely hoped to avoid, see the materials starting with an anonymous denunciation sent to Beria, which led to the 1946 TsK theater resolution: RGASPI, f. 17, op. 125, d. 465, ll. 121–64.

thus assuring that their own professional opinions would not be questioned by less expert but more powerful politicians. By doing so, they undermined one of the party leaders' most important sources of control and drew an explicit boundary between the professional and political fields.

The Ogolevets affair was not the only instance in which the Orgkom considered disciplining one of its members. In fact, it was not even the only such incidence in 1947. For example, a popular song composer who was accused of "unethical" behavior at a touring concert in the provinces had to submit a written explanation of that behavior. The Orgkom issued him a stern reprimand and warned that a repeat offense would result in "serious disciplinary action." The Orgkom underscored its license to police professionals' behavior when it attributed his impropriety to a "lack of understanding" about "norms of social conduct required of a Soviet composer." In another case, a local chapter expelled a member for "antisocial behavior: drunkenness, a prickly attitude about work, and un-Soviet relations with his family."[81]

There is a significant difference between these other disciplinary actions and the Ogolevets affair. Namely, in these other cases, the inappropriate behavior at issue was more akin to conduct unbecoming a professional. Disciplinary action was based on the principle that it reflected poorly on the profession as a whole when individuals who represented it were drunk or insulted audiences. As with exclusive organizations the world over, the Composers' Union enforced standards of behavior outside professional discourse. During the Ogolevets affair, on the other hand, the Orgkom described inappropriate behavior *within* the profession, behavior that it thought impinged on the integrity of professional discourse. And if that inappropriate behavior also happened to be in line with behavior expected of all vigilant party members, then those specific party obligations should be subjugated to professional ones.

This is not to say that there was a split between professional and party loyalty more generally. Each of the participants in the discussion about Ogolevets's improper, antisocial behavior was and remained loyal to the party. In particular, they continued to try to follow the agenda that the party had begun setting for the profession a year earlier. In fact, some even explicitly argued that Ogolevets's behavior—and the six-month discussion of it—detracted from the Composers' Union's ability to pursue those tasks.[82] In other words, party and professional loyalties were not considered incompatible. However, when the vigilant behavior expected of any party member conflicted with the moderate critical behavior expected of any professional, Composers' Union leaders were quite clear. Vigilance did not trump appropriately restrained professional conduct.

---

81. RGALI, f. 2077, op. 1, d. 164, l. 13ob. (Protokol #5, 12 Mar 1947), pts. 2–3; ll. 19–20 (Protokol #8, 11 Apr 1947), pts. 3.1–2. I have translated as *kolotnoe* as "prickly."

82. RGALI, f. 2077, op. 1, d. 199, l. 61ob. Erokhin noted that the Union should be spending its time preparing for the thirtieth anniversary of the Revolution celebrations, not mired in the Ogolevets affair.

Khachaturian and company were not to remain at the helm of the Composers' Union for long after the end of this discussion. In just a few months, they were collectively sacked and replaced with a new leadership body, headed by Tikhon Khrennikov. The available evidence does not in any way suggest that the Ogolevets affair and its attempt to draw a separation between political and professional spheres had anything to do with the 1948 brouhaha. Still, one may have expected the new leaders to dissolve once again the boundaries between the two spheres of authority and to cede priority back to the party. They did not.

While remaining completely loyal to the party and its leadership, the Composers' Union's new leaders continued to pursue policies that reveal the continued existence of this implicit separation between the political and professional realms. They insisted that they alone could identify and punish "cosmopolitans," thereby limiting punishment for professional mistakes to professional censure and preventing disciplined members from being expelled. This protection extended even to Ogolevets, whose age-old practice of denunciation began again in earnest after 1948 and included attacks on Khrennikov. But by the late 1940s and early 1950s, four years after he was first disciplined, Ogolevets's denunciations had lost their cachet. His appeals were dismissed as unprincipled and merely self-serving,[83] and Khrennikov's intervention was needed to save his career.

At the beginning of the Zhdanovshchina, the Composers' Union entered a period in which the party elite pressed on the boundaries between the professional and the political, implicitly threatening professional agency. The Composers' Union leadership lost control over professional leadership functions that they had enjoyed during the war. In a series of interventions, the Central Committee fought Composers' Union leaders' attempts to make the professional organization an even more exclusive repository of expert knowledge. They approved the expansion of the Orgkom to include several new members whose creative proclivities differed from the most powerful Composers' Union leaders. And they intervened to prevent the Composers' Union from excluding less-trained composers of popular music—tunesmiths—from its ranks. The party also usurped the power to set the Union's creative agenda, casting the profession into an intense theoretical discussion of ideologically sound music. In the midst of these encroachments, the Orgkom established a new definition of appropriate professional conduct that quietly asserted its right to draw and police the boundaries between the political and professional fields.

The processes and practices revealed in an analysis of the Ogolevets affair shed light on a fundamental aspect of the relationship between the Soviet creative intelligentsia and the party during the last decade of Stalin's life. The

---

83. See Ogolevets's denunciation of various figures (especially Kabalevskii) or entire circles of musicians: RGASPI, f. 17, op. 132, d. 243, ll. 1–19 (1949), 37–53 (1950), 54–78 (1951). For the memo dismissing any denunciation coming from Ogolevets, see l. 96 (Kruzhkov and Tarasov to Malenkov, 21 Feb 1951), which specifically rejects the attack on Kabalevskii but also notes that Ogolevets denounced anyone who attacked his own formalist work.

analysis helps steer through two familiar views of that relationship, one of which draws a sharp distinction between an antagonistic party and oppressed intelligentsia, and another that posits an intellectual and party elite with shared interests, or at least ideals. Elements that support each of these positions are present in the story of the Ogolevets affair. First it should be recalled that almost every actor who took part in the concluding discussion of the Ogolevets affair was a member of the party, which most members of the Composers' Union were not. Even these music professionals who were also party members conceptualized and articulated a distinction between appropriate professional conduct and the behavior of a vigilant party member. Despite recognizing that distinction, they did not think that party and professional loyalty were incompatible. Rather, they considered expendable—even punishable—those specific party obligations (like denunciation) that would impair the profession's ability as a whole to accomplish the larger tasks set by the party. They recognized and valued the importance of maintaining a discursive realm in which professional shortcomings were not construed as political mistakes. Thus, the Ogolevets affair illustrates how professionals began to cope with tensions between support for the Soviet system and dissatisfaction with the way it was functioning after the war. By 1947 they surely recognized those tensions, but they articulated them only as a defense of internal professional discussion, which was assumed to be a patriotic and loyal response to the new ideological tasks of the Zhdanovshchina.

This attitude is typical of the agency that I suggest best characterizes professionals' possibilities in the Stalinist Soviet Union. The music profession was not autonomous from politics or immune from direct party intervention. Its leaders never suggested that it should be immune, and they probably never conceptualized their administrative tasks as completely separate from politics. They acquiesced to the agenda established after the war by the party and its ideological campaigns, and they earnestly set about working on that agenda. But neither was the music profession completely subjugated by the party. From high-profile discussions to minor structural modifications, it was professionals who had the expertise to do the work required by the party campaigns. When the professional and political fields needed to be held separate in order to do that work, the Composers' Union leadership drew and maintained those boundaries.

CHAPTER 5

Brouhaha! Party Intervention
and Professional Consolidation, 1948

The external intervention that Khachaturian and his colleagues in the Composers' Union leadership sought to forestall with their code of appropriate professional behavior nevertheless arrived in the first two months of 1948. The brouhaha that ensued is one of the few events in the history of Soviet music to have attracted general attention. It has been described by music historians and journalists who witnessed the proceedings, and it is a watershed event in virtually every autobiographical, biographical, or systematic narrative of Soviet musical life, regardless of point of view.[1] All of these accounts together provide an adequate description of the events of 1948, but they fail to give a satisfactory explanation of why or how they happened. Such an explanation required investigating the archives when they opened after the collapse of the Soviet Union. What follows is the most complete explanation of these events based on archival sources, including some that have not previously come to light or been incorporated into English-language accounts.[2]

Party intervention in music was not an inevitable final stage of the Zhdanovshchina. Rather, explosive conditions of intra-professional and institutional competition intersected with a specific set of events to turn an unsuccessful staging of a new Soviet opera into a brouhaha that not only affected the music profession but also transformed the relationship between the Composers' Union and governmental and party oversight bodies. Paradoxically, the biggest disciplinary action that the party ever took against the music profession simultane-

---

1. For examples, see Alexander Werth, *Musical Uproar in Moscow* (London: Turnstile, 1949); Schwarz, *Music and Musical Life;* Harlow Robinson, *Sergei Prokofiev: A Biography* (New York: Viking, 1987); Fitzpatrick, *"Lady Macbeth* Affair"; Frid, *Dorogoi ranenoi pamiati;* Khrennikov, *Tak eto bylo;* Elizabeth Wilson, *Shostakovich: A Life Remembered* (Princeton: Princeton University Press, 1994).

2. Several key documents have been published in Russian, and their findings were incorporated in Fay, *Shostakovich,* 154–65. Other crucial elements of the genesis of the brouhaha, including the participation of prominent performers and conservatory professors, the indecision about *Velikaia druzhba* within the Committee on Artistic Affairs just before the storm broke, and especially the crucial financial aspects, have not to my knowledge been published in English.

ously strengthened the power of the Composers' Union and alienated many professionals.

The basic events of the 1948 party intervention are well known. In mid-January, Andrei Zhdanov convened a discussion of leading figures from the Soviet music world in the offices of the Central Committee.[3] Zhdanov announced that the Central Committee found completely unacceptable a new opera by Vano Muradeli entitled *Velikaia druzhba* (The Great Friendship), and it wanted to know what had gone wrong. The rest of the discussion was devoted to uncovering problems in Soviet music. Almost immediately after this meeting, the Politburo quietly passed a resolution that completely reorganized the Composers' Union leadership, removing Khachaturian, Muradeli, and Atovm'ian from the Orgkom and appointing a new Secretariat comprised of Tikhon Khrennikov, Marian Koval', and Vladimir Zakharov.[4] Two weeks later, the real blow fell when the Politburo issued a more far-ranging resolution that criticized *Velikaia druzhba* and attacked many of the Soviet Union's best-known composers: Shostakovich, Prokofiev, Khachaturian, Shebalin, Gavriil Popov, and Miaskovskii. These leading lights were accused of "formalism," the slippery definition of which boiled down to a "renunciation of the basic principles of classical music," propagation of "atonality, dissonance, and disharmony," and abandonment of melody, which in the eyes of the Central Committee resulted in "muddled, nerve-racking" sounds that "turned music into cacophony."[5] The change in Composers' Union leadership was reaffirmed and solidified at the First All-USSR Congress of Soviet Composers, and the attacks on the so-called "formalists," particularly Shostakovich, intensified to a feverish pitch, espe-

---

3. A transcript of the proceedings was issued with a circulation of fifty thousand less than two months later: *Soveshchanie deiatelei sovetskoi muzyki v TsK VKP(b)* (Moscow: Pravda, 1948), cited hereafter as "*Soveshchanie.*" See also drafts of corrected transcripts held in the Central Committee's archives: RGASPI, f. 17, op. 121, dd. 725–27 (one file per day, 10, 11, 13 Jan 1948). The published version differed mostly in trivial details from these drafts, which show that speakers were permitted to edit their statements, primarily for style and clarity, before publication. Leonid Maksimenkov has identified two changes in Zhdanov's speeches that indicate that Zhdanov used the editorial process to clarify his understanding of the music world as wracked by a battle between two camps—the bad, "formalist" one permeating even music administration. See Leonid Maksimenkov, "Partiia—nash rulevoi," *Muzykal'naia zhizn'*, no. 13–14 (1993): 6–8; no. 15–16 (1993): 8–10. My thanks to an anonymous reader for Cornell University Press for bringing this source to my attention. These changes challenge my characterization of the difference between the drafts and the published transcripts as "trivial." However, the addition of a phrase labeling administrative leaders as proponents of "formalism" in their music, which Maksimenkov identifies, occurred in the midst of a much larger discussion in which administrative, ideological, and political mistakes were all at stake. It is of debatable significance that Zhdanov chose a clear formulation of their conflation for the published version of his remarks. After all, Maksimenkov argues that Zhdanov's main concern was to reduce the complexity of the music sphere to his two-camp thesis.

4. RGASPI, f. 17, op. 3, d. 1069, ll. 3–4, pt. 4 (Politburo Protokol #62, 26 Jan 1948).

5. Ibid., ll. 42–49 (10 Feb 1948). The resolution was reprinted as "Ob opere 'Velikaia druzhba' V. Muradeli: Postanovlenie TsK VKP(b) ot 10 fevralia 1948g.," *Sovetskaia muzyka*, 1948, no. 1:4–5. The inclusion of Popov and removal of Dmitrii Kabalevskii from Zhdanov's earlier list has not been explained: Fay, *Shostakovich,* 158; Maksimenkov, "Partiia—nash rulevoi."

cially in a three-month series of articles in the profession's journal, *Sovetskaia muzyka.*[6] The musical implications of the brouhaha were temporarily extreme, though they faded with time. In the immediate aftermath, the most privileged genres were opera, folk music, choral music, and symphonic program music. The party intervention marginalized both complicated symphonic music and popular music that reminded party leaders of the West, especially jazz.

Many observers working without access to archival materials have assumed that this dramatic party intervention was the inevitable extension into music of the 1946 Central Committee resolutions on literature, theater, and film. The most flagrant example of this assumption appears in Ian MacDonald's polemical biography of Shostakovich. MacDonald suggests a periodization for Shostakovich's life that includes a single 1946–53 unit. He explains 1948 as follows:

> Prepared by the authorities in cahoots with Tikhon Khrennikov and the ex-Proletkult group, [the intervention] had probably been ready for some time (perhaps since 1946) and, when finally activated, needed to be given the illusion of spontaneity by attaching it to a current issue.... Convened in Moscow in January 1948, the First Congress of the Union of Soviet Composers was chaired by Andrei Zhdanov, who, fresh from purging science, was raring to lay down the law in classical music and dominated the conference with boorish gusto.[7]

Aside from its striking factual inaccuracy, MacDonald's account is notable for the clarity with which it expresses the more widely held assumption that intervention during the Zhdanovshchina was preordained. The emigré Russian musicologist Andrey Olkhovsky thus considers the brouhaha an inevitable stage in a single "crusade" that began in 1946. In her introduction to the collection of memoirs about the effect of the resolution on Shostakovich, Elizabeth Wilson explains the delay as a result of "music lagging a little behind in the Party's schedule of priorities." Even the impressive Boris Schwarz writes off the lag between the three 1946 resolutions and the 1948 intervention as "a considerable interval during which 'voluntary' compliance was tried."[8]

This assumption fails to account for a number of crucial aspects of the beginning of the brouhaha. If the 1948 intervention was *merely* an extension of earlier resolutions, why did almost eighteen months pass between the last of the 1946 resolutions and the music intervention? The lag requires some explanation. After all, if the party leadership had originally intended to intervene publicly, surely they would have done so in late 1946. Perhaps more importantly,

6. M. Koval', "Tvorcheskii put' D. Shostakovicha," *Sovetskaia muzyka,* 1948, no. 2:47–61; idem, "Tvorcheskii put' D. Shostakovicha (prodolzhenie)," *Sovetskaia muzyka,* 1948, no. 3:31–43; and idem, "Tvorcheskii put' D. Shostakovicha (okonchanie)," *Sovetskaia muzyka,* 1948, no. 4:8–19.

7. MacDonald, *New Shostakovich,* 190. The chapter is "Isolation: 1946–1953."

8. Andrey Olkhovsky, *Music under the Soviets: The Agony of an Art* (New York: Praeger, 1955), 9–10; Wilson, *Shostakovich,* 200; Schwarz, *Music and Musical Life,* 206.

why did the Central Committee choose an opera by a relatively minor Soviet composer as the occasion for its action? Faced with this second question, many commentators have thrown up their hands in bewilderment and written off the initial attack as yet another example of the party leadership's arbitrary capriciousness or the result of Stalin's anger at the libretto's glorification of Sergo Ordzhonikidze.[9] The search for answers to these questions must begin with an examination of the immediate context in which the intervention took place.

"I've Grown Weary of False Notes"

Since the publication of the Central Committee's theater repertoire resolution in 1946, the Central Committee apparatus had been applying sustained pressure to the government's arts watchdog institution, the Committee on Artistic Affairs. Much of that pressure naturally focused on the repertoire of the Soviet Union's drama theaters, but the preoccupation with theater programming extended to opera theaters as well. The resulting institutional wrangling between the Committee on Artistic Affairs and the Central Committee apparatus was one element of the context in which the 1948 brouhaha played out.

Another crucial element was significant infighting within the music profession. After their successful war efforts, composers and musicologists divided into two camps—populists and highbrow types—within the Composers' Union. These camps were so loosely defined that they should be understood not as competing factions but as vague associations determined by an often temporary convergence of professional opinion regarding a particular issue. They should also not be understood as corresponding easily to the even more artificial division between "formalists" and "realists" posited during the 1948 discussions. Adherents of each camp were both disciplined and promoted during the brouhaha. Considering their amorphous nature, defining the camps is an illusory exercise, but it is revealing nonetheless.

The populist camp temporarily and fleetingly united composers who were interested in a variety of issues that somehow touched on the musical life of the masses. It encompassed popular song composers, devotees of folk music performance and collection, and sometimes composers of the older generation who thought that folk materials were the essential building blocks of symphonic and vocal music that was accessible to the broadest possible audience. It included former members of the long-defunct Russian Association of Proletarian Musicians and some of their most visible opponents, the so-called traditionalists who followed classical traditions.

The highbrow camp equally fleetingly united composers who were concerned

9. The source of this latter, oft-repeated hypothesis seems to be Volkov, *Testimony*, 143. Ordzhonikidze was a former member of Stalin's inner circle who was probably saved from an official fall from grace by his suicide in 1937.

primarily with issues of professional mastery. Most composers who can be placed in this camp were best known for their compositions for symphony orchestra or chamber ensemble, and many of them valued technical exploration. However, applying the term "highbrow" to any group in the postwar Soviet Union is somewhat inaccurate. Almost without exception, the most prominent figures in this group also wrote in accessible genres, especially film music, and hoped that their music would be well received by general audiences. Despite the rhetoric of 1948, none of these composers sought to identify themselves with the experimental composers of the West.

These very broad positions overlapped substantially. A composer of serious symphonic music who valued most of all a connection with the classics of the Russian symphonic school could very easily fit into either camp, and such figures often did put their lot in with one group in one situation (symphony versus fox-trot) and with the other group in the next (technical manipulation versus traditional compositional rules). In the midst of the brouhaha, however, the positions in the populist camp found their clearest expression, clarified through the exaggeration that the general attack on "formalism" permitted. It is through a nonchronological examination of these statements that the various professional positions of the immediate postwar years can be described most accessibly.

At the January meeting, the first two permutations of the populist position were most clearly articulated by Zakharov, the longtime musical director of the Piatnitskii Choir and composer of songs patterned so closely on Russian folk songs that audiences rarely distinguished them from their traditional models. His vitriolic presentation before Zhdanov in the Central Committee chambers was perhaps more extreme and definitely more venomous than most, but it concisely laid out an argument that represented views held widely among Composers' Union members. The first permutation of this position was the most common, and it had been shared by party leadership since the early 1930s. Namely, Zakharov argued that the measure of a good, satisfied composer was the degree to which that composer's music was accessible to a general listening public: "I think that if any one of these composers just once tried to write a piece for the people, [a piece] which could be taken into a factory and there really, truly, and hotly met by the people, if it got through to the people, to the workers of that factory—that composer would experience a feeling of tremendous creative satisfaction."[10] This populism of reception had adherents who composed light dance music and popular songs and who wrote military marches and mass songs. It had been present in the Composers' Union in the 1930s, but strengthened during and after the war.[11]

Zakharov also expressed the second permutation of the populist position,

10. "Rech' V. G. Zakharova," *Soveshchanie*, 24–25.
11. RGALI, f. 2077, op. 1, d. 71, ll. 29–29ob. (Protokol #8, 28 Jun 1943).

though in such an extreme fashion that it prompted complaints at the time and indignant condemnation ever since. He argued that the *only* possible way to achieve this success was through the performance of folk music and composition of folklike songs. He asserted that all Soviet symphonic music had gotten stuck in a dead end because symphonic composers had abandoned folk music. Most controversially, he cast aspersions even at Shostakovich's otherwise untouchable *Leningrad* Symphony by suggesting that during the blockade Leningraders had asked not for recordings of the symphony but for folk songs.[12] Though no one else would spell it out with such totality, this preference for folk songs was something that many Composers' Union members shared.[13]

The third permutation of the populist position was most clearly articulated by Aleksandr Gol'denveizer, an eminent piano professor at the Moscow Conservatory. Gol'denveizer concluded his presentation at the meeting with Zhdanov by promising to submit a more complete report later. He did so, and the result was a thoroughgoing attack on virtually all elements of the Soviet musical establishment.[14] Gol'denveizer's basic stance was that of a conservative performance professor, who valued above all else the transmission of the Russian musical tradition to future generations. According to this position, all great composers began with a thorough understanding of the musical components of folk music and folk dance. For Russian composers, this meant understanding a lyricism identified by Pushkin and developed in the music of nineteenth-century greats Anatol Liadov, Anton Arenskii, and Sergei Taneev. It did not mean the production of music based solely on folk songs, like Zakharov's position, but the skillful application of "natural" harmonic rules derived from folk music and developed by composers in the West and in Russia from J. S. Bach to Sergei Rakhmaninov.[15]

Gol'denveizer summed up his position in one of the most famous remarks to emerge from the brouhaha: "But now I have grown weary of false notes. That music, which is written by our leaders and by the majority of other composers who follow them, violates the harmony that is dictated by natural musical sounds. The feeling of dissonance, that is, tension that somehow strives in the direction of its resolution, has been lost. Perfectly incompatible [notes] sound

---

12. "Rech' V. G. Zakharova," 23–24.

13. See, for example, E. V. Gippius's 1946 request for special funds to record folk music and preserve the huge folk music recordings collections then stored in dangerous conditions in Leningrad: RGASPI, f. 17, op. 125, d. 466, ll. 79–84 (Gippius to TsK VKP(b), [3 May 1946]). Gippius was the Soviet Union's most respected musical folklore expert. An even clearer example is RGALI, f. 2077, op. 1, d. 93, ll. 37–43, in which M. Shteinberg extemporaneously discusses the use of folklore and composition during the fifth day (1 Apr 1944) of an Orgkom plenary meeting.

14. "Rech' A. B. Gol'denveizera," *Soveshchanie*, 59; RGASPI, f. 17, op. 125, d. 636, ll. 11–36 (Gol'denveizer's report, 19 Jan 1948). Gol'denveizer's role—or at least that of "conservative, traditional musicians"—in the genesis of the brouhaha may have been rumored within Soviet music circles at the time: Dmitry Paperno, *Notes of a Moscow Pianist* (Portland: Amadeus, 1998), 63.

15. RGASPI, f. 17, op. 125, d. 636, ll. 11–13, 16; *Soveshchanie*, 54–56, 58.

simultaneously—outside any harmonic logic."[16] For Gol'denveizer and those who thought like him, Soviet culture would face grave danger if the next generation of musicians and audiences was raised on this "falseness" instead of the "natural" tradition.[17]

Adherents of the "highbrow" camp also made their case concisely during the January meeting with Zhdanov. First introduced by Shostakovich and then expounded at greater length by Lev Knipper, this position argued explicitly against Zakharov's exclusive view of appropriate Soviet music. Though bowing to the pressure of the brouhaha, Shostakovich and Knipper emphasized that music in any genre could potentially be appropriate to Soviet conditions. Some genres just required more skill than others.[18] Knipper articulated the catholicity of this position most clearly:

> Music, like literature, has many genres. There is opera, symphonic music, chamber music, the romance, the song, and so forth. And within each genre there are many different types. Each genre has its own specifics, and in the process of its composition, its own technical particularities. Do not lump all genres into one heap. And all genres are necessary, for you cannot lump all people into one heap. If you asked everyone sitting in the hall here right now what they love, it would turn out that one would need a song, another a quartet, and a third a symphony. Beyond that, one loves happy songs and others, sad ones. Further, one loves the freshness and transparency of "Snow White," and others, the complicated harmonic complexes of the late Rimskii in "Kashchei" or in "The Golden Cockerel." One cannot throw the late Skriabin out of Russian music. He is very complicated, but whenever a poster announces "Poem of Ecstasy" the hall is always full.[19]

Although Knipper's argument is based on reaching audiences of one type or another, his idea of an appropriate audience was much more expansive than Zhdanov's. By including Aleksandr Skriabin's late works in particular, he made the case for complicated music, but Gol'denveizer also included Skriabin in his list of good classical Russian composers. This agreement is an example of the overlap between the two very loose camps.

The increasingly antagonistic professional body was governed by a rather small group of composers who had an inordinate amount of control over the resources allocated to support all composers and musicologists. Creatively, these leading composers were a diverse group. The figurehead chair of the

---

16. RGASPI, f. 17, op. 125, d. 636, l. 13; *Soveshchanie*, 55.

17. Ibid., ll. 13–15, 17; *Soveshchanie*, 55–56, 58. In the published remarks, Gol'denveizer merely noted that it would be "sad" if this tradition was lost and argued that it in fact was being lost in the education of young Soviet composers. In his later report, however, he raised the stakes, repeatedly noting that the musical taste of both music producers and listeners was in danger of being "spoiled": RGASPI, f. 17, op. 125, d. 636, ll. 21–22, 34–35.

18. *Soveshchanie*, 53, 101–9, 160. Shostakovich noted that Muradeli lacked the skill to manage an opera.

19. *Soveshchanie*, 102–3.

Orgkom, Reinhold Glier, was a prominent and well-respected member of the older generation. His compositional style was directly derived from that of the late nineteenth-century giants whom the Soviets affectionately called "the Russian classics," but he was also active on the nationalities front, collaborating with younger composers from the Caucasus and especially Central Asia to create operas and ballets in the Russian tradition but based on national folklore. Khachaturian was an Armenian composer best known in the Soviet Union and abroad for his catchy, tuneful, and stylistic ballet music. The Orgkom secretary, Viktor Belyi, had been a member of the Russian Association of Proletarian Musicians, but he was best known after the war for his professionally impeccable song music and intellectually constructed suites. Other members of the leadership group included the famous Shostakovich and Miaskovskii, both of whom were known primarily for their symphonic music, though Shostakovich's musical language was considerably less traditional than the venerable Miaskovskii's.

If this leadership group can be said to have had a common vision for the music profession, it was a vision that depended less on stylistic similarity or generic exclusivity than on educational qualifications and appropriately circumspect professional conduct.[20] Nevertheless, when the party leadership intervened in musical affairs, these composers' control over scarce resources left all of them open to attacks from anyone who thought that they personally, or their preferred genre in general, was getting short shrift.

The Specific Mechanisms of Intervention

A context of increasing intra-professional discord still does not provide an explanation for why party leaders intervened the way they did, when they did. It merely describes the tinderbox waiting for the match. That match came in early January 1948, when Stalin and several other high-ranking politicians attended a special closed performance of the Bol'shoi Theater's production of a new Soviet opera, Muradeli's *Velikaia druzhba*.[21]

Velikaia druzhba was set in the Northern Caucasus during the Civil War. It was supposed to depict the revolutionary activities of Ordzhonikidze during the Bolsheviks' struggle for power. The hero and heroine of the opera are a Lezgin man and a Cossack woman. At the beginning of the opera, the hero sneaks into a Cossack village to meet the heroine. Discovered by a sentry, he is forced to kill the man, and he flees to be concealed in the heroine's hut. A group of Cos-

20. This statement requires the qualification that all of them disliked or mistrusted simple songs and dance music, much of which was very popular with general audiences, but not with the party elite.

21. See Khrennikov, *Tak eto bylo*, 195, the first page of an appendix containing excerpts from a transcript of a meeting between Zhdanov and participants in the private showing of *Velikaia druzhba*. The meeting was 6 January, the day after the showing.

sacks led by a White officer arrives to search the hut, loudly demonstrating their deep-seated loathing of Lezgins and other mountain-dwelling peoples who support Ordzhonikidze's attempt to establish Bolshevik power in the Caucasus. Accidentally exposed by the heroine's mother, the hero is attacked by the Cossacks. Just before the hero is killed, the White officer intervenes with a plan. He knows that the hero and heroine are in love, so he offers to arrange their marriage if the hero will agree to assassinate Ordzhonikidze. Out of desperation, the hero agrees, and he is sent off to the mountains.

He immediately encounters Ordzhonikidze enlisting the Lezgins in the revolutionary cause. Unaware of his son's plans, the hero's father arranges for him to act as Ordzhonikidze's guide, and on the road, the hero shoots at Ordzhonikidze but misses. Ordzhonikidze recognizes the hero's potential for decisive action and tries to persuade him that it is misdirected. That night, again in the Lezgin camp, Ordzhonikidze demonstrably, bravely, and trustingly turns his back on the hero as he goes to sleep. The hero is converted to the revolutionary struggle, and he returns to the Cossack village to find his lover. The hero and heroine meet and celebrate their conversion to the revolutionary cause, but the White officer intervenes again, this time threatening the heroine unless the hero carries out his promise to kill Ordzhonikidze. In the concluding scene, Ordzhonikidze rides triumphantly into the Cossack village, which has been mysteriously converted to the revolutionary struggle by the mountain dwellers, and the hero has his chance. When the White officer sees that the hero will not carry out his promise to kill Ordzhonikidze, he shoots at the commissar himself. The hero throws himself in the path of the bullet and is killed.[22]

There are not many descriptions of Muradeli's score other than the vague characterizations offered by the Central Committee resolution and the numerous public denunciations that followed it. However, the few professional evaluations written retrospectively after the collapse of the Soviet Union agree that the opera was inexpertly constructed. Musically, it appears to have been unsuccessful.[23]

Central Committee bureaucrats complained that the libretto presented Cossacks as a reactionary mass monolithically opposed to Soviet power and the mountain dwellers as a unified, monolithic revolutionary mass without any class differentiation. They found this characterization particularly problematic because of the nationalities politics involved. Namely, Russians were mono-

---

22. This synopsis is taken from a very critical review of the libretto by a Central Committee bureaucrat; RGASPI, f. 17, op. 125, d. 634, ll. 63–64 (Aleksandrov to Zhdanov, 1 Aug 1947). The entire report was prepared by OPA bureaucrat P. Lebedev and submitted to Aleksandrov, who never forwarded it to Zhdanov, as the address would suggest. See l. 62 (Shepilov to Zhdanov, 9 Jan 1948), which finally forwarded this old draft report to Zhdanov with the explanation.

23. See Khrennikov, *Tak eto bylo,* 123. Khrennikov notes that the opera was simply not well written. Though it was primitive, there was "nothing formalist about it." See also Frid, *Dorogoi ranenoi pamiati,* 261, in which Frid suggests that the opera is best forgotten. This evaluation corresponds exactly with Shostakovich's evaluation at the January meeting with Zhdanov; see *Soveshchanie,* 160–61.

lithic reactionaries and Lezgins were heroic revolutionaries. Ordzhonikidze was turned into a mountaineer and freedom fighter rather than a Bolshevik who united the poor laboring classes among Russians and mountain dwellers alike. Though this initial complaint presaged many of the later criticisms of *Velikaia druzhba*'s libretto, it did not extend in any large measure to the music. The report described the music as "successful, on the whole," though the musical language of the Russian characters was considered weak and often permeated by "Eastern intonations foreign to them."[24]

The Committee on Artistic Affairs leadership had been struggling to evaluate the opera since at least the end of October 1947. On 30 October, its Artistic Council met to appraise the new opera, and the head of the committee, M. B. Khrapchenko, decided that the opera needed further consideration before it could be evaluated.[25] The Bol'shoi's production was allowed to proceed: *Velikaia druzhba* would play to Moscow audiences for the first time during the celebration of the thirtieth anniversary of the Revolution on 7 November 1947.[26] A month after the Artistic Council convened, Committee on Artistic Affairs leaders demonstrated their insecurity by telling Voroshilov that they could not evaluate the new production on their own. Khrapchenko invited Voroshilov to watch the production and help decide whether it should be shown to general audiences. According to Khrapchenko, the opera was particularly important because it was intended to commemorate the thirtieth anniversary of the Revolution by "representing the struggle to install Soviet power in the Northern Caucasus" and "showing the growth and strengthening of the friendship of the peoples after the October Revolution."[27] With such a high degree of ideological importance attached to the new opera's production, the Committee on Artistic Affairs was vulnerable.

When the party leaders attended the performance, they were not pleased. But party leaders had been unhappy with operas, film music, and the like before, and they had not completely reorganized the leadership of the music profession.[28] This time, however, displeasure with the production of *Velikaia druzhba* started a series of events that led to the intervention in mid-January. The party leadership had been prepared to react more severely than in the past because of an inflammatory report submitted by the Central Committee apparatus just when Khrapchenko asked for help in evaluating Muradeli's opera.

In a brief post-Soviet reflection, the principal author of the report, Dmitrii

24. RGASPI, f. 17, op. 125, d. 634, l. 63 (Aleksandrov to Zhdanov, 1 Aug 1947).

25. RGALI, f. 656, op. 6, d. 73, l. 4 (VKI Artistic Committee Protokol #20, 30 Oct 1947). Khrapchenko came to this decision after hearing a report by Shostakovich, who consulted the VKI on musical matters.

26. V. I. Rubin, *Bol'shoi Teatr: Pervye postanovki oper na russkoi stsene, 1825–1993* (Moscow: Izd. Ellis Lak, 1994), 252.

27. GARF, f. 5446, op. 54, d. 42, l. 152 (Khrapchenko to Voroshilov, 15 Dec 1947).

28. Neither the 1936 attack on Shostakovich's opera and ballet nor the 1946 criticism of Bogoslovskii's film music resulted in the sort of institutional change that accompanied the 1948 intervention.

Shepilov, explained the circumstances in which he produced it. He noted that there was a general sense within the Central Committee, a sense that Stalin shared, that the Soviet victory during the war had not been adequately reflected in music, especially opera. Shepilov's image of opera was based on what he knew of Rakhmaninov, Tchaikovsky, and Verdi. By the late 1940s, he had decided that something needed to be done to promote the creation of an appropriately heroic Soviet opera. Shepilov's familiarity with Khrennikov's first opera, *V buriu,* and some of his theater music convinced him that Khrennikov's musical style was perfectly suited to the project. So, he decided to draw up a report that contained his recommendations about what to do in the music realm.[29]

That report would sketch many of the contours of the campaign to come, but Shepilov's chief preoccupations were significantly different from those emphasized later in the 10 February resolution.[30] Shepilov's report primarily targeted the genres of symphonic and chamber music and paid much less attention to individual composers. In fact, Shepilov praised some of the accomplishments of almost all of those eventually attacked in the Central Committee resolution (Shostakovich, Prokofiev, Miaskovskii, Khachaturian, and Popov) in addition to the songwriters who earned his most undiluted praise (Aleksandrov, Dunaevskii, Solov'ev-Sedoi, Novikov, and Blanter).[31]

Shepilov's report was primarily a policy recommendation accompanied by a detailed criticism of the music policy of the Committee on Artistic Affairs and the Composers' Union Orgkom. He criticized both groups for favoring "pure" symphonic music over forms that might appeal more easily to general audiences and amateur performers. He also implicated music critics whom he thought supported that music policy by heralding each complicated piece written by one of the country's leading composers as "a new triumph of Soviet music."[32]

In Shepilov's mind, the problem with this focus on symphonic and chamber music was twofold. First, its complexity was "opposed to the basic goals of communist education" because it was not accessible to the largest possible audiences. Second, its abandonment of "more democratic" genres, especially opera, violated the classical Russian tradition, a position that he backed up with a lengthy quotation from Tchaikovsky in which this prerevolutionary great wrote of his desire to reach "the entire people."[33]

29. Khrennikov, *Tak eto bylo,* 143–46. Shepilov's reminiscence is printed as a postscript to Khrennikov's memoirs.

30. Shepilov and P. Lebedev to Zhdanov, Kuznetsov, Suslov and Popov (Dec 1947), in Khrennikov, *Tak eto bylo,* 185–94. This is a reproduction of the report, published without archival citation. It is not paginated in the Khrennikov memoirs, so it will be cited as "Shepilov to Zhdanov" with the page number of the report.

31. Shepilov to Zhdanov, 1.

32. Ibid., 1–2. The critics implicated were Rabinovich, Shlifshtein, Mazel', Tsytovich, Polianovskii, and Ryzhkin. The particular beneficiaries of their praise were allegedly Prokofiev, Shostakovich, Miaskovskii, Kabalevskii, and Khachaturian.

33. Ibid., 2–3.

Shepilov also criticized the Moscow Conservatory for allowing or even encouraging its composition students to focus on music without text. He disparaged the country's leading opera theaters, the Bol'shoi and the Kirov, for their lack of attention to Soviet opera and their meager efforts when they did stage one. He castigated the Committee on Artistic Affairs for its commission policy, and he lambasted the Composers' Union Orgkom and the director of Muzfond for ignoring Union chapters in the national republics. Throughout the report, Shepilov continually and incessantly inveighed against the Committee on Artistic Affairs for overall incompetence, repeatedly noting its mistakes and inability to fulfill the Central Committee apparatus's direct instructions. In fact, one of the report's central conclusions was that "at the current time, the Committee on Artistic Affairs is completely devoid of competent specialists in the area of music."[34]

Shepilov may as well have leveled a similar accusation at himself. His report shares with virtually every Central Committee pronouncement on music an incapacity to speak in specific terms about the music that is disliked, other than to say that it is "inaccessible." More than the celebrated public pronouncements like the 1936 *Pravda* editorial that rejected Shostakovich's *Lady Macbeth* or the 10 February 1948 resolution, Shepilov's report is perfectly forthcoming about what constitutes that "inaccessibility"—the lack of a decipherable text, whether explicit lyrics or implicit program:

> In composers' circles, there is a well-known dissemination of the view that symphonic music in general should not be notable for its particular content. This "theory," which is hostile to Soviet art, denies works of prerevolutionary and Soviet music. Shostakovich's Seventh Symphony is an outstanding piece precisely because deeply and clearly, especially in the first movement, it reveals the idea of the Soviet people's battle for our homeland against the Fascist invasion. It is known that every talented, truly realistic symphonic work is notable for its deep richness of content.
>
> The infatuation with forms of symphonic music that are not understandable for the people has the inevitable result of a collapse of the work of leading Soviet composers in the areas of opera and other democratic genres that require the realistic depiction of the life of the people, their ideas, and their experiences.[35]

34. Ibid., 5–8, 10, the last of which is the most direct accusation of incompetence, but the shots appear on almost every page.

35. Ibid., 3–4. This inability to talk in detail about music was despite the fact that Shepilov claimed to have been assisted in its preparation by people who had an advanced musical education: Khrennikov, *Tak eto bylo*, 145. He names musicologist B. M. Iarustovskii, literary critic B. S. Riurikov, and musicologist Z. G. Vartanian. Iarustovskii and Riurikov had been part-time consultants in the TsK apparatus since 1946, and Vartanian was head of the Armenian branch of the Committee on Artistic Affairs until October 1947. All three would be promoted into the TsK apparatus in 1948, Vartanian as a consultant (E. S. Afanas'eva et al., eds., *Apparat TsK KPSS i Kul'tura 1953–1957: Dokumenty* [Moscow: ROSSPEN, 2001], 748–49, 769, 780). If they were involved in preparing the report, the fear of music without a text may have been a result of writing a report for an audience (the party leadership) that could not understand technical language.

Turning away from program music in symphonic genres led composers to abandon more "democratic" forms defined by their even more explicit texts. This is not just a call for more textually based symphonic music, but an effort to blame composers' focus on symphonic music for the lack of success in opera.

In his later recollections, Shepilov noted that he did not know what happened to his report once it was submitted, but it is now clear that it played an important role in the events that immediately followed. After all, Shepilov's concluding recommendation was to convene a meeting in the Central Committee with leaders in the music world from the Committee on Artistic Affairs and the Composers' Union.[36] This recommendation coincided with the call from the Committee on Artistic Affairs for help in evaluating *Velikaia druzhba,* and with a first meeting with musicians convened the day after the special performance. It was not the famous set of mid-January meetings with Zhdanov but a much smaller meeting with those responsible for the Bol'shoi's production, including Muradeli and his librettist, the director of the production, its conductor and eight performers with leading roles, and the director and artistic director of the Bol'shoi Theater. Also in attendance were Khrapchenko and two Central Committee bureaucrats, Shepilov and his assistant P. I. Lebedev.[37]

At this meeting, Zhdanov admitted in even starker terms than Shepilov that the Central Committee could not clearly articulate what about the music they did not like, but he insisted that their taste did represent that of a general audience.[38] Hardly a revelation, this statement merely demonstrates that powerful members of the party's highest leadership circles knew that although they could appreciate and sometimes evaluate music, they depended on professionals to fill out their vague impressions with specific musical content. That said, Zhdanov did attempt to convey what he did not like, sometimes coherently and other times nonsensically.[39] This dependence on expert evaluation was to play a critical role in the development of the Composers' Union in the aftermath of

36. Khrennikov, *Tak eto bylo,* 147; Shepilov to Zhdanov, 10.

37. "Zapis' soveshchaniia tov. Zhdanova s avtorami i ispolniteliami opery 'Velikaia druzhba' 6 ianvaria 1948 g.," in Khrennikov, *Tak eto bylo,* 195–201. Like "Shepilov to Zhdanov," this document is presented without archival or any other citation. Unlike the "Shepilov to Zhdanov" document, it is just a reproduction of the text, not the entire document (with marginalia, archival stamps, etc.). It also contains multiple ellipses. A more complete record apparently awaits greater archival access. I will cite it as "Zapis'" with the page number from Khrennikov's memoirs. Zhdanov referred to this meeting when he met with the larger group later. See *Soveshchanie,* 8.

38. "Zapis'," 195. Zhdanov notes that he does not consider himself a "specialist," but nor does he consider himself completely incapable of evaluating the success of music, especially when he can observe the reactions of other audience members.

39. Ibid., 196. Among his coherent remarks can be numbered his complaints about Muradeli's failure to use different musical languages to depict different types of characters. Perhaps his most nonsensical complaint was that the orchestration often left small groups of instruments or even individual instruments in isolation rather than having the orchestra perform "symphonically" all at once. Even basic familiarity with the opera orchestra repertoire reveals that this latter "complaint" could be leveled at any of the opera composers Zhdanov preferred. Zhdanov's implicit ideal of every member of an orchestra playing uninterrupted for the course of an entire opera is sadly laughable and would not suit his less ridiculous suggestions.

the brouhaha. It also explains the role of this first meeting of 6 January in the genesis of the larger brouhaha. Zhdanov needed to gather information to prepare for the larger discussion that would follow one week later.

Throughout the meeting, Zhdanov's angry remarks revealed his main motivation for calling it. He wanted to find out who to blame:

> How was this opera staged? We look upon the appearance of a Soviet opera not just as a serious artistic event but also as a political one. . . . What in the world happened with the production of "Velikaia druzhba"? The opera was prepared in secret from the Central Committee and government. Comrade Khrapchenko presented the Central Committee with a done deal. Suddenly on 7 November its viewing turns up. Nobody knew, no one had been informed about the staging of an opera. We in the Central Committee watch every new film before it reaches the screen, and here an opera has been hidden from the Central Committee. Really, isn't the Bol'shoi Theater collective interested in our help—in the help of the Central Committee and government? . . . Who here is more at fault—the Committee on Artistic Affairs or the Bol'shoi Theater? What is the story of the staging of this opera?[40]

Earlier warnings and complaints notwithstanding, Zhdanov was obviously angry about the Central Committee's lack of control over the production of a new opera, a situation that party leaders unsuccessfully sought to remedy for much of the rest of the Stalin period. From this outburst, it is clear that Zhdanov still thought that the problem with *Velikaia druzhba* was limited to one opera and two institutions—the Committee on Artistic Affairs and the Bol'shoi Theater. Both of those institutions fell under suspicion for attempting to hide the new production from the party leadership.

Those objections were quickly answered, and Zhdanov seems not to have returned to them. The librettist, the director of the Bol'shoi, the conductor, and one of the singers all testified to the sincerity with which they prepared for the premier. They assured Zhdanov that they had prepared in the normal way, and the librettist noted that versions of the libretto had passed through the Committee on Artistic Affairs and the Central Committee apparatus.[41]

Then the tenor of the discussion changed as Muradeli deftly accepted the criticism directed at him and suggested that Zhdanov should pass it on to all composers, composition professors, and music critics. In a long, cogent, and even well-organized statement that suggests some preparation, Muradeli argued that his acknowledged shortcomings were the result of a stifling professional organization and training program that favored originality over melodic composition. He claimed to have arrived in Moscow in love with folk songs and had that love squelched by his professional education.[42]

40. Ibid., 196. Ellipses in the "original."
41. Ibid., 196–98.
42. Ibid., 198–200. This is by far the least excerpted speech in the document, an editorial touch which may suggest a guarded attempt to pin the brouhaha on Muradeli. Obviously, the genesis of

As soon as Muradeli had finished, Shepilov supported his evaluation, repeating many of the exact arguments that he had first asserted in his report. He agreed that the Composers' Union was partly to blame for creating an atmosphere that favored abstract symphonic music, but he also laid some of that blame squarely on the shoulders of the Committee on Artistic Affairs leadership.[43]

The head of the Committee on Artistic Affairs spoke for the first time to defend himself by mentioning his own earlier criticisms of the opera, but Zhdanov would not let him slip off the hook. In a last effort to end up on the right side of the criticism, Khrapchenko supplied names to make more concrete the general picture painted by Shepilov and Muradeli: Shostakovich and Prokofiev for the prominence of their music and Miaskovskii for his influence on generations of composition students.[44] Armed with a newly confirmed, much broader conception of the *Velikaia druzhba* problem, Zhdanov adjourned the meeting.

A week later, Zhdanov convened the much more famous meeting in the Central Committee chambers to test the opinion that he had formed during this small meeting on a larger, more representative professional audience. After summarizing Muradeli's argument from 6 January, Zhdanov asked the assembled musicians if that assessment was fair and called for an open discussion about two issues: (1) the proper role of the classical heritage in Soviet music, and (2) the responsibility of the Orgkom of the Composers' Union for the bad state of affairs.[45] Zhdanov had already tipped his hand to the extent that the first question could not have been understood as anything but rhetorical. The second question was also loaded and leading, but it presented more elaborate possibilities for discussion. Specifically, Zhdanov wanted to know the following:

> It is also not clear what "forms of direction" exist in the Composers' Union and its Organizational Committee—whether or not there are democratic leadership forms based on creative discussion, criticism and self-criticism, or whether they smack more of an oligarchy according to which all matters are decided by a small group of composers and their true comrades-in-arms, music critics of the sycophantic type, as far from creative discussion, creative criticism, and self-criticism as the heavens are from the earth.[46]

---

the event was much too complicated to blame on one of the participants. Maksimenkov credits Muradeli with turning the tone of the meeting in a direction favorable to Zhdanov: "Partiia—nash rulevoi," pp. 7–8.

43. "Zapis'," 200.

44. Ibid., 200–201. In fairness, Khrapchenko did more than name names. He suggested that the real problem in Soviet music was that some composers had not yet broken with discredited views that prevailed during the 1920s. Miaskovskii was as much at fault for his associations then as for his conservatory professorship later.

45. *Soveshchanie*, 8, 10.

46. Ibid., 10.

Zhdanov sought information about the Composers' Union leadership, its control over resources, and its management of the Composers' Union creative apparatus. In the next two days, he received that information, though not by means of "open discussion." He also learned that the profession was sufficiently divided to provide significant support for a more thoroughgoing party intervention in the weeks to come.

In the days that followed, the Central Committee apparatus collected more evidence that supported the impression gained from the mid-January meetings. Besides the Gol'denveizer report, the Central Committee fielded a much longer, fifty-one-page report that crystallized many populist positions. One N. S. Sherman, a party member who was marginalized in the music world, launched an exhaustive denunciation of Miaskovskii, whose victimization in the Central Committee resolution has always been considered particularly mysterious.[47]

The report gave support to one of Shepilov's themes that had not been well substantiated in the mid-January meeting. Sherman's attack was based on a rejection of "intellectualism" in music. He divided music, musicians, and audiences into two "spheres," one for mass songs based on "simplicity of musical speech" and one for symphonic and chamber music based on "the high intellectual strata of musical art." Sherman rejected the latter sphere because it failed to touch a mass audience. Then in a protracted argument about long-term trends, Sherman blamed the predominance of "musical intellectualism" on Miaskovskii, who allegedly adopted it before the Revolution and successfully taught it to generations of composition students from his professorship at the Moscow Conservatory. Sherman argued at length that the influence of intellectualism inspired by Miaskovskii had corrupted the conservatories, the Composers' Union, and the press, and he suggested that its adherents had intimidated the Committee on Artistic Affairs into suppressing all criticism of leading composers, especially Miaskovskii.[48] "Musical intellectualism" and the symphonic music in which it was best expressed had completely dominated and damaged the music infrastructure.

Once Zhdanov had gathered these descriptions and denunciations, one final causal mechanism remained. It emerged when Stalin asked his minister of finance, A. G. Zverev, how much the opera cost to produce.[49] The response was essential to the genesis of the scandal. A week before Zverev's report, Zhdanov met with musicians in the Central Committee offices, and the first Politburo resolution on music was passed just one week after Zverev's memo arrived. In fact,

47. Paperno, Notes, 62–63.

48. RGASPI, f. 17, op. 125, d. 636, ll. 38–89 ("O sovetskom muzykal'nom tvorchestve," 13 Jan 1948).

49. Ibid., f. 82, op. 2, d. 951, l. 86 (Zverev to Stalin, [19 Jan 1948]). The date is taken from l. 85 (Zverev to Molotov), which is incorrectly dated 19 January 1947. Not just the context (i.e., *Velikaia druzhba* was not under production in 1947) but also the official stamps of receipt by the Central Committee apparatus confirm the 1948 date. This date, 19 January, should be considered the last possible date by which Zverev submitted the original report to Stalin; ll. 86–88 was a duplicate submitted to Molotov.

the memo was not archived until 11 February, the day after the Central Committee passed its final resolution.[50]

This incident reveals several things. First, as most observers suspected, Stalin indeed appears to have been personally involved in the decision to intervene in the music world in 1948.[51] Second, it suggests that financial and administrative concerns were as central a motivating force behind the intervention as issues of musical content and style, which were much more difficult for party leaders to gauge. In music as in most spheres of Soviet society, administrative and financial misconduct was often construed by party leaders as political error. Third and most importantly, it highlights an essential aspect of the brouhaha that has been largely missed by observers preoccupied with the effect of the resolution on prominent individual composers. Namely, it explains why so much of the actual force of the resolution fell on the Committee on Artistic Affairs and even spread to the Bol'shoi Theater.

Zverev described major theater funding procedures then in operation with a guarded grab for more power in his bailiwick. The Committee on Artistic Affairs decided all matters of funding and production plans for the country's most prominent theaters. The Ministry of Finance merely presented the Committee on Artistic Affairs with an annual lump sum, which the committee then distributed as it saw fit.[52] In practice, theaters actually maintained a good deal of control over their own repertoire; the Committee on Artistic Affairs seems merely to have overseen theater operations to protect against financial malfeasance and gross ideological errors, something that they were apparently trying to do when Khrapchenko invited Voroshilov to the staging of *Velikaia druzhba*.

Zverev also noted that the national average cost for a single production of

---

50. Ibid., l. 85, marginal notation.

51. Though such a conclusion can only be speculative, it is likely that Stalin's involvement explains the quirky circumstances responsible for the incomplete archival record of the events of 1948. The available record is an artifact both of Stalin-era filing procedures and post-Soviet era declassification practices. For almost every cultural decision in the postwar period, the Central Committee apparatus prepared materials and a recommendation, which they passed on to the Orgbiuro or Secretariat, often keeping copies in their own files. Then the Orgbiuro or Secretariat would make a decision, and if it required Politburo approval, they would send copies of the materials to the Politburo along with their decision. The Politburo would make the final decision, and the materials and copies all along the line would be sent to the archives. As of the writing of this study, researchers were allowed access to the materials of the Central Committee apparatus, the Orgbiuro, and the Secretariat, but not the Politburo. For this one major decision in the music realm, the Orgbiuro/Secretariat step of this process was skipped, and materials were sent straight from the Central Committee apparatus to the Politburo, apparently without the preservation of complete copies. Until Politburo materials are made fully available, the complete set of materials used to make the 10 February decision will not be available. A few well-connected Russian historians, however, have been permitted to comb the Politburo materials for document publications, a practice that has yielded many arts- and music-related documents but nothing on 1948, aside perhaps from the uncited documents published or excerpted in Khrennikov's memoirs and cited above. It is probably safe to assume that any other extant materials—if indeed they even exist in any quantity—do not contain particularly surprising revelations.

52. RGASPI, f. 82, op. 2, d. 951, l. 86.

an opera in 1947 was more than two and a half times greater than for a drama theater production and substantially more than 400,000 rubles, the planned expenditure per production in 1948. According to the Bol'shoi's plan for 1947, which Zverev was careful to point out had been approved by the head of the Committee on Artistic Affairs' Theater Administration, the theater's total expenditure on operas was supposed to be 4.5 million rubles, 600,000 rubles of which was allotted for *Velikaia druzhba*.[53] Molotov, at least, saw through Zverev's attempt to call the Bol'shoi's planned targets into question, implicitly wondering whether a new production at the Bol'shoi might be more costly than at a provincial theater, in which, for example, set construction cost less.[54] These production costs did not include performers' pay, which must have been included in their regular salaries.

But the financial problems with *Velikaia druzhba* did not stop with an expensive initial plan. Zverev noted that at the end of June 1947, the Committee on Artistic Affairs authorized the Bol'shoi to increase its *Velikaia druzhba* budget to 700,000 rubles; later, the Bol'shoi leadership increased it even further—to a final amount of 766,000 rubles.[55] Obviously, producing any opera was an expensive proposition, and producing *Velikaia druzhba* cost just less than twice the national norm. But the problem turned out to be more than just particularly high production expenses. Zverev catalogued a number of payments that simply violated the policy of even the Committee on Artistic Affairs. The composer's and librettists' pay exceeded the limits ordered by the VKI in 1945, sometimes by more than double. Worse, an audit of Muzfond uncovered the fact that Muradeli had contracted to write *Velikaia druzhba* with seventeen different opera theaters around the country. All told, these theaters had already paid him and the librettists far more than the equivalent of the Soviet Union's top artistic honor, a Stalin Prize, first class.[56]

Zverev concluded with a predictable plea for an increase in his own institution's power: "Extreme and unwarranted expenses of theaters on new productions testifies to the connivance and squandering of state funds on the part of the leadership of the Committee on Artistic Affairs and the Bol'shoi Theater. It also testifies that the workers of the USSR Ministry of Finance do not have sufficient control over the expenditure of resources that are spent by the government on art."[57] Zverev promised to conduct a financial investigation of both the Bol'shoi and the Committee on Artistic Affairs.

Considering subsequent events, one of the most striking things about this report is that it does not even mention the Composers' Union, except through an

53. Ibid.
54. Ibid., marginal notation.
55. Ibid., l. 87. The initial permission to increase the budget was sent on 20 June 1947 from the assistant head of the Chief Theater Administration of VKI (Gol'tsman) to the director of the Bol'shoi Theater (Bondarenko), but it had apparently been approved by Khrapchenko himself.
56. Ibid., l. 88.
57. Ibid.

indirect jab at Muzfond. It is scarcely surprising that Stalin and the other party leader who read it agreed to expand their suspicion beyond the production of *Velikaia druzhba* and into other major musical institutions. This crucial link underscores the fact that the main institutional targets of the brouhaha included the Committee on Artistic Affairs and the Bol'shoi Theater as much as the Composers' Union.

In the weeks that followed, Zhdanov prepared the resolution that would eventually be approved by the Central Committee on 10 February. That Zhdanov was the point man in the operation but that Stalin was also involved is not simply a matter of common sense. It can also be deduced from a set of materials that Zhdanov submitted to Stalin on 2 February.[58] Several weeks after his meeting with the musicians, Zhdanov presented Stalin and other top party officials with a copy of his introductory speech at the meeting, his presentation near the close of the meeting, a draft communiqué about it, and a draft of the 10 February resolution.[59] By the first week of February 1948, Stalin had received extensive reports from his ideology point man, Zhdanov, and his minister of finance, Zverev, about the failed opera and the state of affairs in music. It is probably safe to assume that he was personally involved in the final editing of the resolution, which differed even in some points of content from Zhdanov's draft.

If this assumption is correct, the differences between Zhdanov's draft and the final resolution reveal Stalin's personal priorities in the campaign.[60] As the query to Zverev demonstrates, Stalin was concerned about the financial ramifications of what all of the leaders agreed was an unacceptable state of affairs. A comparison of the two drafts of the resolution suggests that he was not interested in publicly spelling out a party program with specific instructions about how musical institutions should remedy the situation. Rather the resolution was a vehicle to set out broad principles that those institutions could apply later.

Though there were some minor editorial changes and reorganization in the long preamble, the most substantial changes were concentrated in the resolution.[61] Zhdanov's version contained eleven individual points that spelled out a

58. RGASPI, f. 17, op. 121, d. 724, l. 1 (Zhdanov to Stalin, 2 Feb 1948); f. 77, op. 3s, d. 142, ll. 2, 3 (Zhdanov's copy of same). Zhdanov sent copies to Molotov, Beria, Mikoian, Malenkov, Voznesenskii, Kuznetsov, Suslov, and G. M. Popov.

59. RGASPI, f. 17, op. 121, d. 724, ll. 2–13 (draft resolution); ibid., ll. 14–25 (Zhdanov's introductory speech); l. 26 (draft communique about the meeting, eventually published as *Soveshchanie*, 3, though in the published version the list of TsK participants is added); ll. 27–56 (Zhdanov's presentation at the meeting, 13 January).

60. Maksimenkov uses stylistic evidence and the fact that Zhdanov's bailiwick was criticized in the final draft to come to the same conclusion: "Partiia—nash rulevoi," 10.

61. The most interesting changes describe the position that formalist composers occupied in Soviet music. While both drafts note that they had gained control of the Composers' Union, Zhdanov first mentioned them in the following sentence: "The leading positions in Soviet musical art are occupied by composers who support a formalist, anti-popular tendency" (RGASPI, f. 17, op. 121, d. 724, l. 3). In the final version the phrase "leading positions" was removed, leaving the following: "The topic is composers who support a formalist, anti-popular tendency" (*Pravda*, 11 Feb 1948,

number of specific recommendations for further action. For example, Zhdanov suggested demanding the end of textless or nonprogrammatic instrumental music and ordering the Committee on Artistic Affairs and the Orgkom of the Composers' Union to make opera their top priority. Zhdanov also listed musical genres that would be acceptable fields for future work. Though the list was phrased in a way that suggests Zhdanov intended it to be *inclusive,* leaving it in the resolution would in practice have *excluded* those genres not in the Central Committee's list: symphonic, opera, song, choral, and dance music. That effect would have been amplified by another specific point: folk music would be the basis of composition in any of those genres. Furthermore, Zhdanov included several specific institutional recommendations, including ordering the Composers' Union to open up discussions to more of its rank-and-file members and cultivate a spirit of "Bolshevik criticism and self-criticism." He also suggested demanding that the Committee on Artistic Affairs completely reorganize musical education and publish mass editions of the Russian classics. And he wanted to instruct the Central Committee apparatus to use the press, radio, and lectures to popularize "the realistic tendency in music." In other words, Zhdanov's suggestions included a specific division of labor between institutions and a simultaneously detailed but vague set of musical recommendations.[62]

Most of these demands had been suggested in the preamble, but the final published version left them there. Rather than spelling out a series of specific measures, the final resolution ordered the Central Committee apparatus and the Committee on Artistic Affairs to take appropriate measures to "liquidate the shortcomings indicated in this Central Committee resolution and facilitate the development of Soviet music in a realistic direction." Likewise, composers were reminded that their task was to serve the tastes of the people, but they were not given specific instructions about which genres would fit that task.[63] In sum, the final resolution was significantly more open-ended than Zhdanov's draft. Consequently, it shifted more flexibility and responsibility for the future development of Soviet music onto institutions other than the Central Committee. Zhdanov's suggestions could serve as a blueprint for activity in the near future, but the Central Committee would not be publicly committed to any of them.

Echoes and Reactions: The Immediate Aftermath

Immediately after the release of the Central Committee resolution on 10 February 1948, the party leadership began collecting information about reactions

---

1; reprinted in *Sovetskaia muzyka,* 1948, no. 1:4). This may have been a simple editorial simplification, but it could be an attempt to reduce the impression of how influential those composers were. In both drafts, the next sentence contains the list of the "best representatives." Maksimenkov juxtaposes two additional variants of the resolution in "Partiia—nash rulevoi," 9–10.

62. RGASPI, f. 17, op. 121, d. 724, ll. 11–12.
63. *Sovetskaia muzyka,* 1948, no. 1:7–8.

in music institutions and audiences around the country. Though the leadership was continually collecting data about the mood of the population,[64] this is one of the few occasions in which those responses were retained along with materials related to the decision. The Central Committee apparatus monitored the situation unusually closely as news of the music resolution broke throughout the Soviet Union, which suggests that members of the apparatus may have been insecure about the reaction. The reports that they submitted show that there was fertile ground in the music world for party intervention, but they also suggest that insecurity was justified.

The most proximate reactions came from the all-USSR Composers' Union, the party cell of which was embroiled in a discussion of the meeting with Zhdanov when the resolution broke. That the party cell met at all to discuss creative issues was itself a new development, and one that many rank-and-file composers in the party cell welcomed.[65] Many composers took turns at the podium criticizing the Orgkom leadership for their exclusivity. When Khachaturian took the stage to acknowledge his creative mistakes, the assembly was annoyed that his self-criticism did not extend to his leadership activities. When another member of the Orgkom, Viktor Belyi, criticized Khachaturian's leadership, the rank and file turned on Belyi as well.[66] A frustrated and angry Khachaturian asked what had been wrong about his leadership other than its exclusivity (which he admitted). The question met with a stormy response in the hall as members referred him to the Central Committee resolution and accused him of intimidating his critics.[67] There was certainly support within the Composers' Union for the party's disciplinary action against the Orgkom.

Unsatisfying as they may have been to the composers in attendance, Belyi's accusations prefigured some of the complaints that were recorded elsewhere, and they gave party leaders a rationale for rejecting such complaints. Namely, Belyi noted that the well-known stylistic differences between the individual formalists (Shebalin and Shostakovich, Miaskovskii and Popov) were not de-

---

64. For a systematic study of one type of this monitoring activity, see Sarah Davies, *Popular Opinion in Stalin's Russia: Terror, Propaganda, and Dissent, 1934–1941* (Cambridge: Cambridge University Press, 1997). There are some serious differences between Davies's materials, mainly NKVD reports to the party, and those used here, mainly reports from local party figures not associated with the security forces, but the general practice is similar. The difference reverses the expectation of bias. In other words, whereas Davies's NKVD reports undoubtedly exaggerated the negative aspect of the mood of the population, the named sources in these party reports surely exaggerate the positive aspect.

65. RGASPI, f. 77, op. 3s, d. 142, ll. 9–10 (Shepilov to Zhdanov and Suslov, 13 Feb 1948). Shepilov reported on a three-day meeting, 10–12 February; the resolution was published in the morning papers on the eleventh.

66. RGASPI, f. 77, op. 3s, d. 142, ll. 10–11. The attack, led by Koval', included a VKI representative's proposal to name Belyi one of the main formalist facilitators. The issue was put aside only when the TsK representative (Iarustovskii) reminded everyone that the "chief formalists" were named in the TsK resolution.

67. Ibid., l. 11. Shepilov noted that the worst part of Khachaturian's speech was his defense of Atovm'ian, both as a composer and as a "sincere" hard worker in Muzfond.

cisive. What was decisive was that at every important juncture, such as Stalin Prize nominations and support of the Muzfond director Atovm'ian, they always supported one another and presented themselves as a single, organized group.[68] This organizational understanding of the "formalist group" was not understood by those further from the center of the discussion and became a source of one of the most challenging complaints about the resolution outside of Moscow.

The "echoes" reported by party officials elsewhere, like Minsk and Leningrad, fell into several categories. One common response was the meaningless positive reaction, short statements of support for the Central Committee resolution that did not contain any elaboration of the rationale for that support. Typical was the response of Leningrad-based composer and future Composers' Union Secretary Mikhail Chulaki: "The resolution strikes a decisive blow at formalism, which played such a pernicious role in the development of Soviet musical art. The resolution mobilizes all Soviet composers to the formation of pieces that are truly beautiful, truly popular, deeply rich in content, and worthy of our great epoch."[69]

However, most reactions did explain the respondent's support. The Leningrad report contained so many examples of one response that its author must have tailored it to drive that message home. Typical was the response of the head of personnel at a Leningrad railroad: "I am a man with higher education, and I consider myself a cultured person. But I was ashamed to admit to people that I do not understand Shostakovich's music. The resolution of the Central Committee of the Communist Party brought clarity and pointed out the antipopular nature of this music."[70] But not all nonmusical respondents exhibited such investment in the state of Soviet music. Some were much more dismissive: "I do not understand Shostakovich's music. It tires me out. It is an empty collection of sounds. After you hear Shostakovich's music with its rattling and noise—you get a headache."[71] The Central Committee resolution predicted this response, and the author of the report no doubt fashioned it to justify the assumption. Though possibly exaggerated here, it was undoubtedly common.

A number of other responses echoed and emphasized specific aspects of the Central Committee resolution. Some people were particularly taken by the call to follow folk music more closely, and others were especially gratified to hear

---

68. Ibid., l. 10. The attacks on Belyi supported this contention but included him in the group.

69. RGASPI, f. 17, op. 125, d. 636, ll. 162 (Popkov to Suslov, archived 24 Feb 1948). See also ll. 161 (two singers) and RGASPI, f. 17, op. 125, d. 636, l. 148 (M. Iovchuk and I. Makarov to Suslov, 16 Feb 1948). For similar empty praise from Muscovites, see RGASPI, f. 77, op. 3s, d. 142, ll. 11–12 (Shepilov to Zhdanov and Suslov, 13 Feb 1948). Popkov was secretary of the Leningrad oblast' and municipal party committees. Iovchuk and Makarov were high-ranking members of the Belorussian party organization.

70. RGASPI, f. 17, op. 125, d. 636, l. 164. See l. 161 for a similar response from a theater artist.

71. Ibid., l. 164. Such was the opinion of a naval artillery engineer. For four other extremely similar responses, see l. 149 and ll. 164–66.

the renewed emphasis on the Russian classics.[72] Almost all of the performers cited in these reports expressed a closely related if more professionally motivated sentiment. They were happy no longer to be forced to perform what they considered difficult and unsatisfying music.[73] This was probably a sincere response, reproduced in various forms by some performers faced with new music the world over, but it was not universal. The pianist Sviatoslav Richter publicly and defiantly refused to strike Prokofiev's music from his scheduled performances immediately after the publication of the resolution.[74]

No doubt the Central Committee apparatus expected these responses and others like them. They were neither a cause for concern nor could they have been particularly gratifying. On the other hand, composers' reactions were particularly interesting for what they revealed about the potential support—or lack thereof—within the profession for the party's intervention. The apparatus confronted mixed responses. Muscovite party members clearly supported it because of its potential organizational implications. Several Belorussian composers supported the contention that Composers' Union chapters outside the two cultural capitals of Moscow and Leningrad were not happy with central leadership. They noted that Belorussians were far less likely to suffer from formalism than their Muscovite counterparts, and they blamed what formalism did appear in Belorussia on visitors from Moscow.[75] They also concurred that popular genres had been slighted under the old regime, rebuking the Composers' Union for the 1946 attack on tunesmiths.[76] In Leningrad as well, song composers greeted the Central Committee resolution with relative enthusiasm. Resentment about the privileges that had been won by the composers named in the resolution also caused some to applaud it.[77]

72. Ibid., ll. 150, 161–62, 166.

73. The principal conductor of the Belorussian State Philharmonic reported that the orchestra musicians greeted the resolution particularly cheerfully because they did not enjoy performing the "empty, chaotic" pieces; RGASPI, f. 17, op. 125, d. 636, l. 148. A Belorussian opera singer also noted that it was "easier to study logarithms" than to sing music by some Soviet composers; l. 150. A Leningrad-based opera singer concurred, though less colorfully; l. 160.

74. Richter's behavior at public performances has been widely reported by memoirists and biographers. He was also defiant before these concerts: when asked to remove Prokofiev's "formalist" Third Piano Sonata from his program, Richter reportedly replied, "Then I will immediately go to Prokofiev's home and, as a sign of respect for him, I will perform his sonata." RGASPI, f. 77, op. 3s, d. 142, l. 13 (Shepilov to Zhdanov and Suslov, 13 Feb 1948). This conversation centered around a recital scheduled for 17 February. For one report on Richter's public behavior, see Robinson, *Sergei Prokofiev*, 473. Robinson describes a 28 February concert at which Richter and Nina Dorliak performed Prokofiev's settings of songs by Balmont.

75. RGASPI, f. 17, op. 125, d. 636, ll. 150–51. One composer blamed a critic from Moscow for a turn to "formalism," and another blamed a visiting official critic from the Committee on Artistic Affairs. Yet a third blamed his local chapter leadership. The sentiment was echoed by some Ukrainian composers as well. See RGASPI, f. 77, op. 3s, d. 142, l. 12 (Shepilov to Zhdanov and Suslov, 13 Feb 1948).

76. RGASPI, f. 17, op. 125, d. 636, l. 151. Other composers also noted that Belorussian composers should write more mass songs.

77. Ibid., ll. 161, 163, 168. A conductor at an operetta theater complained that some composers

On the other hand, a number of musicians exhibited their displeasure with the resolution. More than half of the Leningrad composers who were reported to applaud the resolution did so only with the assumption that composers would find the specific paths through the terrain laid out by the Central Committee. They noted that "everything depends on us" and that "sharp criticism . . . compels us to consider again and again our creative path."[78] Alone, these sorts of statements do not present a picture of discontentment, but their sentiments were amplified in more overt complaints as well. One Leningrad-based composer flatly disagreed with the Central Committee resolution's general thrust, preferring professional evaluation to Central Committee predictions about the future of popular taste: "This is how the government fights to regulate the tastes of the masses. After all, music that is incomprehensible to the masses today might become understandable to them in fifty or a hundred years. It is impossible to close the paths of innovation."[79] A Moscow Conservatory professor also asked in exasperation if they were to turn away from what was good about Shostakovich and Miaskovskii and consider as the ultimate musical development the music of Zakharov's Piatnitskii Choir.[80]

Other composers who may have agreed with the theoretical aspects of the resolution called attention to its inconsistencies and questioned the Central Committee's competence. One noted that there was absolutely nothing formalist about Muradeli's opera, and another wondered "how Khachaturian fell onto the list of formalists." This latter complainant rattled off a list of Khachaturian's pieces that were "examples of realistic music." He feared that conservatory students would be "hit like a thunderbolt" instead of being encouraged to think and reconstruct themselves.[81] Perhaps less cautious because they stood just outside the hottest flame of the resolution, a few other artistic intellectuals leveled the charge of incompetence at the Central Committee even more directly. An orchestra musician at the Malyi Opera Theater predicted that the storm would blow over and everyone would return to composing as before, especially because the opera that the Central Committee attacked was, as he knew from his own experience in the pit, not formalist and perhaps the best of the Soviet operas yet written. A conductor at the same theater noted that the resolution gave the impression that the Central Committee had just stepped into an opera theater for the first time in thirty years. And a writer summed up this angle of complaint most directly: "The Central Committee is not an art critic. . . . It would have been better if such a decision had emanated from composers

---

"looked at music through the monetary advance that they can most easily earn," and an unnamed questioner asked if the disciplined composers would have to return their Stalin Prizes.

78. Ibid., l. 162.

79. Ibid., l. 166. These were the thoughts of a composition teacher at the Leningrad Conservatory, I. B. Finkel'shtein.

80. RGASPI, f. 77, op. 3s, d. 142, l. 11.

81. RGASPI, f. 17, op. 125, d. 636, l. 167. The first of these composers was V. O. Vatlin, who noted that if Muradeli was a formalist, he figured he was too. After all, both wrote arias that could be easily sung. The second was V. N. Salmanov.

themselves. And so, I'm afraid, they will begin to raise to the head various traditionalists and ungifted people and to interpret the resolution as a signal to retreat backward."[82]

Taken together, these comments from supporters and detractors of the Central Committee resolution alike should be seen as symptomatic of an emerging consensus that music professionals were the only ones who could competently produce and evaluate Soviet music. But the professionals were not the only ones who challenged the Central Committee's competence in the musical arena, though they did so most directly and consciously. In a list of questions provoked by the resolution, the Leningrad party secretary included several that suggest that the resolution was received with skepticism even by general audiences. People wanted to know how a formalist opera had even made it to the Bol'shoi stage and how formalist composers had won Stalin Prizes. They wanted to know why attention had been turned to music so late, and they wondered why Shostakovich met with such international success. Perhaps most troublesome for the Central Committee apparatus, they wondered how they were to evaluate Shostakovich's tremendously popular Seventh Symphony and Khachaturian's highly praised "Song about Stalin." They even asked if there actually were any composers "of the realistic tendency," an indication that the questioners had heard only about the leading lights pilloried in the resolution.[83]

The last grand opportunity to provide musical content to the Central Committee resolution and to test the mood of the professional body was the First All-USSR Congress of Soviet Composers, which took place in the Hall of Columns on 19–26 April 1948.[84] The first task of the new Composers' Union leadership was to organize the congress in consultation with the party leadership. In early April, the Orgbiuro approved the new plan, including outlines of the keynote addresses that Asaf'ev and Khrennikov would read at the congress. In the meantime, bureaucrats in the Central Committee apparatus helped write those speeches, and the Composers' Union determined who would attend the congress as delegates.[85] As the congress approached, the new Secretariat met with heads of delegations from across the Soviet Union to decide who would serve on the congress's governing board, a symbolic body that included repre-

82. Ibid., l. 167. Ellipses in the original. The pit orchestra musician was D. A. Shevalin, the conductor was E. M. Kornblit, and the writer, N. A. Golubentsev.

83. Ibid., l. 168.

84. A transcript of the proceedings was published as *Vsesoiuznyi s"ezd sovetskikh kompozitorov: Stenograficheskii otchet* (Moscow: Izvestiia, 1948).

85. RGASPI, f. 17, op. 118, d. 22, ll. 81–82, pt. 455g. (materials to Secretariat Protokol #344, 3 Apr 1948). Khrennikov, *Tak eto bylo,* 130. Khrennikov reports that Iarustovskii led a team of musicologists who wrote the speech that he read at the First All-USSR Congress. For selection of the delegation, see RGALI, f. 2077, op. 1, d. 234, ll. 19–21 (General SSK Meeting Protokol #10, 15 Apr 1948). Most vigorous discussion focused on whether or not the former director of Muzfond, L. T. Atovm'ian, should be included in the list. It was finally decided not to include him. See also ibid., l. 32 (Protokol #12, 20 Apr 1948), a last-minute approval of extra delegates from Leningrad.

sentatives from the other creative unions, prominent arts institutions, the Committee on Artistic Affairs, and the Central Committee apparatus.[86]

The Central Committee again fielded reports from its observers at the meeting, including Shepilov and one of his assistants in the Central Committee apparatus, L. F. Il'ichev. Shepilov observed and reported on the first three days of the congress, in which all of the prepared reports were read to an assembly of nearly twelve hundred people: five hundred voting delegates from Composers' Union chapters and seven hundred guests from the creative intelligentsia, including writers, painters, opera performers, and other artists. Il'ichev reported on the discussion that took place after the third day and on the voting that concluded the congress.[87]

Shepilov also evaluated the speeches read by the heads of delegations from each national republic and assessed the mood of the participants as they negotiated the scheduled events. His assessment makes the report particularly revealing because it illustrates that composers were disgruntled with the Central Committee's clumsy intervention and that the party leadership was content to let the new professional leadership cope with this somewhat disgruntled professional body. After the 10 February resolution and its immediate aftermath, the Central Committee ceded control of the professional sphere back to the new professional leadership.

Shepilov briefly described the prepared speeches, all of which had been cleared by the party leadership. He allocated significantly more space to the reports read by leaders from each of the national republics, which had been approved by the republics' central committees, so the congress also provided the Central Committee a chance to get a glimpse at the results of their republican counterparts' oversight work. Shepilov complained that these reports resembled one another too closely, each giving a mere "snapshot" of the shortcomings and successes in the musical life of the respective republic. None reached beyond the republic's borders except to complain about the lack of attention paid the republic by the outgoing Orgkom.[88] That said, Shepilov singled out the delegations from Azerbaidzhan, Armenia, and Ukraine for their "concrete, qualified" analyses of the situation in their republics. He was annoyed that the Belorussians, Kazakhs, and Georgians intimated that the resolution did not apply to them because they had few or no formalists in their ranks, but he was particularly troubled by reports like that from Turkmenistan that misunderstood the thrust of the resolution and used it as an excuse to pillory any Russian composer who lived in the republic and all students who graduated from conservatories in Russia.[89] The brouhaha

---

86. Ibid., ll. 28–31 (Protokol #11, 19 Apr 1948). The complete list of the leadership (ll. 29–31) demonstrates that it was dominated by Muscovites despite efforts to include representatives from the other delegations.

87. RGASPI, f. 17, op. 125, d. 636, ll. 229–32 (Shepilov to Zhdanov, Kuznetsov, Suslov, and Popov, 21 Apr 1948); ll. 254–62 (Il'ichev to Zhdanov, Kuznetsov, Suslov, and Popov, 28 Apr 1948).

88. Ibid., l. 229.

89. Ibid., l. 230.

was seen by some participants as an opportunity to settle personal and professional scores. A similar but even more profound creative interpretation of central campaigns would wrack the Uzbek Composers' Union during the anticosmopolitanism campaign in the years to come.

Most of Shepilov's report was spent describing conditions that strongly suggest that many composers were unhappy with the proceedings. On the second day of the congress (the first in which representatives from the national republics read their reports), only 150–200 people of the 1,200 assembled actually attended the talks. The rest milled about in the foyer and corridors, carrying on their own conversations. After Shepilov met with the heads of all of the delegations and chastised them for the undisciplined behavior of their delegates, the composers behaved with much more discipline during the third day.

Still, throughout the proceedings, Shepilov noted that "the formalists" seemed to be ignoring the programmed activities. Of those mentioned in the resolution, only Muradeli and Shostakovich attended regularly. Khachaturian, Popov, and Prokofiev showed up for the first day and then left, and Shebalin did not turn up until the third day. Even when they were there, Khachaturian and Shebalin were most active in the corridors, not in the hall. They conversed with groups of their colleagues or individual delegates. On the third day, a large group of composers identified as former members of the Association of Contemporary Music (ASM) apparently gathered at Miaskovskii's apartment, though the professor was too ill to attend the scheduled events.

Some did not just ignore the proceedings; they actively provoked trouble. On the third day, a small book containing a "mistaken" article by Asaf'ev circulated along with whispers that *his* mistakes had not been subjected to sufficient criticism. The podium was barraged with anonymous notes that cryptically threatened members of the new Secretariat or defended the composers under attack. One note passed to Khrennikov criticized him for failing to acknowledge the positive contributions of Shostakovich and Prokofiev along with their mistakes. Another noted that "Khrennikov and Koval' will pass on, but Shostakovich and Prokofiev will remain in history."[90]

During the discussions that took place in the days that followed, "the 'corridor' activity of the 'friends' of the formalists did not fall quiet." In fact, the whispering support for the disciplined composers became even more explicit in the corridors. Gnesin and Shaporin were both overheard suggesting that the most aggressive speakers were mistaken when they attempted to orient Shostakovich and Miaskovskii to the works of other composers rather than to point out as exemplary the "progressive elements" in their own work. Many older composers who enjoyed respect for their accomplishments and were in good favor because of the return of the classics sought to soften the criticism directed at their "formalist" colleagues. Meanwhile, except for Shostakovich,

90. Ibid., ll. 230–31.

the disciplined composers continued to avoid the podium, causing many in the audience to call for more self-critical public reflection.[91]

This discontent finally expressed itself in limited form in the balloting that took place on the final day of the congress. Il'ichev provided party leaders with a brief account of how the ballots were prepared and a short explanation of the results. Despite the extreme control exerted over the proceedings, a striking amount of discontent still managed to seep through. On the morning of 25 April, representatives from each delegation gathered to discuss candidates for the newly organized governing board and auditing committee of the Composers' Union. The meeting was conducted by a few party members who led the delegations. They drew up a large list of candidates, and the assembled representatives objected to only four suggestions: the composers Ivan Dzerzhinskii, Anatolii Novikov, and Karl Rautio and the musicologist Tamara Livanova. Livanova was removed from the list because she concentrated on the prerevolutionary greats and not Soviet music. Novikov was replaced by another song composer, Boris Mokrousov, after allegations of unethical behavior sullied Novikov's candidacy. Despite significant support for another representative from the Karelo-Finnish Republic (Ruvim Pergament), Rautio remained on the list, as did Dzerzhinskii, without explanation.

In the final session of the congress, this list was presented to the assembled delegates, who sought to add Shostakovich, Khachaturian, Kabalevskii, Gol'denveizer, the stricken Novikov, and the unsuccessful Pergament. In the stormy discussion that followed, Shostakovich's candidacy was particularly vigorously championed by those in the room who "were satisfied" with his self-critical presentations in earlier days. Finally, a military band composer took the floor to ask how it would look "to the people" if, after all the discussion of the resolution, they reelected a "formalist composer." The question was called, Shostakovich was defeated, and Kabalevskii and Khachaturian withdrew their names.[92]

When the secret voting finally took place, Shostakovich still garnered thirteen write-in votes, and Pergament, who also failed to make the list, gathered forty-four. The absent Miaskovskii got six write-in votes, and Kabalevskii and Khachaturian each received two. Though these tallies pale in comparison to the 333 votes needed to be elected to the new governing board, they indicate that a significant group continued stubbornly to protest long after the whispers died down and the writing was on the wall.

The vote totals of the successful candidates also reveal stubborn manifestations of discontent. Of the fifty-one composers and musicologists elected to the governing board, most of those who had been named to the Secretariat by the Central Committee resolution of 26 January finished far back in the pack. The new boss, Khrennikov, did the best, but he finished behind sixteen other can-

---

91. Ibid., ll. 254–56.
92. Ibid., ll. 256–57.

didates, most of whom were uncontroversial selections from the national republics or well-respected senior composers like Gnesin, Dmitrii Arakishvili, and Sergei Vasilenko. The figurehead leader of the Composers' Union and keynote speaker, Asaf'ev, finished twenty-eighth, and no one else named by the Central Committee finished in the top forty. In fact, Shaporin, Dunaevskii, A. I. Shaverdian (the musicologist who helped lead the proceedings against Ogolevets the year before), and Leningrad's song king, Vasilii Solov'ev-Sedoi, all finished well ahead of the rest of the new Secretariat.[93]

Despite this significant display of dissatisfaction, the corridor talk, note passing, whispering, and undisciplined voting should not be construed as outright opposition, nor should they convey a picture of a professional organization up in arms against the party's intervention. In fact, most delegates supported the prospect of transforming the Composers' Union into a more "democratic" institution. Though many of the speakers took the opportunity to settle professional scores (some of them stretching back to the 1920s), a strong current of opinion interpreted that increased "democracy" as the more uniform distribution of resources. Representatives from outside of Moscow repeated a common refrain. Both in the formal presentations during the second and third day and in the more free-flowing discussions that followed, they demanded that more attention and more resources drift their way.[94] For these composers and musicologists, any change in leadership could present the opportunity to remedy past neglect. But the disruptive behavior does indicate that many composers and musicologists resented the clumsiness of the heavy-handed party intervention, a fact that was to become more apparent in the years ahead.

The famous brouhaha of 1948 had a profound influence on the development of the Soviet music profession and its constituent institution, the Composers' Union. Though it grew out of the volatile conditions of postwar Soviet culture shaped by Zhdanov's ideological campaigns, the brouhaha was not an inevitable extension of the Central Committee resolutions of 1946. Instead, momentum for the party intervention began with an unsuccessful, costly opera production and grew through a series of reports and meetings to encompass the Composers' Union, the Bol'shoi Theater, and especially the Committee on Artistic Affairs. Internal professional divisions caused many composers and musi-

93. Ibid., l. 257; ll. 259–62 (election results). Koval' finished forty-fifth with just sixty votes more than he needed to be elected; Zakharov finished forty-ninth, just fifty votes over the minimum. The Central Committee apparatus's music expert, B. M. Iarustovskii, finished forty-sixth, and the head of the Leningrad SSK, Chulaki, finished forty-second, the only one of these to receive more than four hundred votes. Of the others mentioned, Solov'ev-Sedoi finished highest (twenty-sixth). The top vote-getter was Dangatar Ovezov, a composer and conductor from Turkmenistan. Shostakovich, Khachaturian, Kabalevskii, Miaskovskii, and Pergament were far from the only write-ins. In fact, there were fifty, the vast majority of whom received just one or two votes. Only four others got five votes or more: M. B. Leviev (Tashkent), D. S. Vasil'ev-Buglai (Moscow), M. A. Grinberg (Moscow), and Ia. A. Eshpai (Marii ASSR).

94. *Vsesoiuznyi s'ezd sovetskikh kompozitorov*; RGASPI, f. 17, op. 125, d. 636, l. 255.

cologists to greet the party intervention with enthusiasm, but its clumsiness also caused many to become more disgruntled, vote against approved lists of candidates, grumble in corridors, and generally articulate vague dissatisfaction with the treatment of the most authoritative members of their profession at the hands of the party.

At no other time during the postwar Stalin period would it be so clearly demonstrated that professional composers and musicologists did not operate autonomously. Nevertheless, the genesis of the brouhaha demonstrates that the party leadership leaned on professionals for the preparation even of this most blatant intervention. At the height of pressure from the party, professional expertise was needed. In fact, during the brouhaha a Composers' Union member was appointed to the Central Committee apparatus for the first time. On 23 April 1948, Boris Iarustovskii was named head of the music sector of the Central Committee apparatus.[95] At the very moment the profession was most controlled by the party, the party apparatus professionalized itself.

That the party leadership harnessed professional expertise so clumsily and to such traumatic effect alienated many in the profession. But the intervention also opened up new opportunities. After all, it was not just the Composers' Union that was disciplined in 1948. The new professional leadership used the opportunity to expand the influence of the Composers' Union over areas of Soviet musical production previously outside their grasp. And by the end of the year, both leaders and rank and file in the Union began once again to guard their professional terrain from outside intervention. During the anticosmopolitanism campaign that began just a year after the beginning of the brouhaha, the Composers' Union actively deflected and even managed to avoid some directions from the party.

95. RGASPI, f. 17, op. 118, d. 37, ll. 31–32, pt. 577g. (materials to Secretariat Protokol #346, 23 Apr 1948). Iarustovskii had been a consultant in the apparatus since 1946, but this was his first full-time appointment.

CHAPTER 6

Anticosmopolitanism and the Music Profession, 1949–53

One of Stalinism's most consistent characteristics was a tendency to undertake periodic ideological campaigns to mobilize the Soviet population, campaigns like the Zhdanovshchina. Another crucial postwar campaign that has received less attention in scholarly work about Soviet culture is the struggle against cosmopolitanism.[1] The anticosmopolitanism campaign in the cultural professions was launched in earnest by an unsigned *Pravda* editorial in January 1949. Titled "On a Group of Antipatriotic Theater Critics," the editorial imbued the attack vocabulary of party discourse with a new concept, rootless cosmopolitanism. In the months to come, the press was permeated with editorials and news stories that filled out this new concept and explained how various groups were applying it to expunge their respective organizations of undesirable elements. After a period of intense discussion in early 1949, the anticosmopolitanism campaigns endured with occasional peaks of intensity until Stalin's death four years later.

Participants, victims, and historians alike have correctly understood the anticosmopolitanism campaigns as primarily anti-Semitic.[2] However, this understanding is incomplete. A close study of the music profession during the anticosmopolitanism campaigns demonstrates that anti-Semitism was an essential component of anticosmopolitanism, but in no sphere were the two coterminous. Instead, examining some of the organizational and practical battlegrounds

---

1. Anticosmopolitanism in music gets its most thorough treatment in Schwarz, *Music and Musical Life*, which focuses on the published reactions as an attack on musicologists.

2. Postwar official anti-Semitism has attracted significant scholarly attention since the opening of the Soviet archives: Gennadi Kostyrchenko, *Out of the Red Shadows: Anti-Semitism in Stalin's Russia* (Amherst, NY: Prometheus, 1995); Kostyrchenko, *Tainaia politika Stalina: vlast' i antisemitizm* (Moscow: Mezhdunarodnaia otnosheniia, 2001); Joshua Rubinstein and Vladimir P. Naumov, eds., *Stalin's Secret Pogrom: The Postwar Inquisition of the Jewish Anti-Fascist Committee*, trans. L. E. Wolfson (New Haven: Yale University Press, 2001); and Frank Grüner, "Juden und Sowjetstaat, 1941–1953. Vom öffentlichen Verschweigen der nationalsozialistischen Verbrechen an den Juden bis zur politischen Instrumentalisierung des Antisemitismus durch die sowjetische Staats- und Parteiführung" (Ph.D. diss., University of Heidelberg, 2002).

in which bureaucrats, party ideologues, and music professionals struggled with "cosmopolitanism" and "cosmopolitans" reveals that anticosmopolitanism had a diverse array of coexistent meanings, intended and unintended. Besides anti-Semitism, the most widely recognized feature of anticosmopolitanism has been fear of foreign influence,[3] but other essential meanings included a patriotic preoccupation with "contemporary reality," a pro-Russian bias in both cultural preferences (like the preference for popular music based on folk song rather than jazz) and personnel selection, and a surely unintended promotion of local national culture at the expense of Russian culture in many non-Russian republics.[4] The open-ended possibilities of ideological campaigns even at the peak of postwar Stalinism demonstrate the fragility and mutability of Stalinist ideology and the crucial importance of institutional practices to define, refine, and police centrally generated ideological constructs during these mobilization campaigns. Understanding these practices in the press, in music performance, in the Central Committee apparatus, and in music institutions themselves is crucial to understanding the meanings of the campaigns and their surprising failure in the Composers' Union.

All these understandings of anticosmopolitanism together shaped the landscape of cultural production in the last years of Stalin's life. They formed the context in which the Composers' Union once and for all solidified its authority, decisively squeezing the influence of the Committee on Artistic Affairs out of the production and control of Soviet music and expanding its direct connection with the Central Committee's cultural oversight apparatus. At the same time, musicians and politicians all across Central Asia used its ambiguous terminology to resist Russification, sometimes even promoting particular national "separate paths" of music development. In practice, the slogans of anticosmopolitanism translated into increased professional agency. The Composers' Union leadership in Moscow used its enhanced agency to combat unintended interpretations it disagreed with by applying the disciplinary authority of the profession in Central Asia. It also used that agency to minimize the effects even of an *intended* meaning of anticosmopolitanism which it disliked—anti-Semitism. By the time of Stalin's death, the professional organization of Soviet composers had come of age.

---

3. This strain is most prominent in studies of postwar Soviet science: Krementsov, *Stalinist Science*, which dates the turn against scholarly contacts with the West to July 1947 and the Kliueva-Roskin affair (131–43), for which see Krementsov, *The Cure: A Story of Cancer and Politics from the Annals of the Cold War* (Chicago: University of Chicago Press, 2002); David Joravsky, *The Lysenko Affair* (Cambridge: Harvard University Press, 1970); and Alexander Vucinich, *Empire of Knowledge: The Academy of Sciences of the USSR (1917–1970)* (Berkeley: University of California Press, 1984).

4. This last component receives only limited treatment in this chapter. I develop the theme fully in Kiril Tomoff, "Uzbek Music's Separate Path: Interpreting 'Anti-Cosmopolitanism' in Stalinist Central Asia, 1949–52," *Russian Review* 63, no. 2 (Apr 2004): 212–40.

Publicizing Anticosmopolitanism: The Cultural Press

When it burst into the discourse on cultural policy in January 1949, anti-cosmopolitanism engendered a new type of attack vocabulary. Before 1949, unhealthy cultural products were usually characterized as "formalist." Despite its prominence in official discourse beginning at least in the 1930s, "formalism" was a slippery concept, the definition of which depended on professionals who could and did manipulate the always loose understanding that they provided. Party bureaucrats were always vague when they wielded "formalism" in their public proclamations and in their more secret internal communications. After the beginning of the anticosmopolitanism campaigns, however, a wider gap opened between public and secret discussions. Perhaps because they were ashamed of the anti-Semitic element of anticosmopolitanism, the party's cultural administrators refrained from explicitly, publicly linking anticosmopolitanism to an attack on Jews in the cultural sphere. Instead, they used the terms "rootless" to characterize cosmopolitans and "antipatriotic" to characterize cosmopolitanism. This attempt to sidestep accusations of anti-Semitism opened the door for a misunderstanding of another crucial component of anticosmopolitanism: patriotism. Still, most of the cosmopolitans who were named in the press were Jewish, and astute readers could easily understand the anti-Semitic message. It is that guarded, but public, anti-Semitism that has been indelibly linked to the campaigns ever since.

Shortly after the *Pravda* editorial appeared, the party cultural administration's newspaper, *Kul'tura i zhizn'*, expanded the definition of cosmopolitanism and distinguished it from formalism.[5] Cosmopolitan criticism was far more dangerous than "mere formalism" because it was damaging, demoralizing, and debilitating. Whereas formalism was dangerous because of its inherent dependence on Western modes of artistic experimentation, cosmopolitanism actually praised unhealthy foreign influences and ignored Russian preeminence in any artistic sphere. Explicitly, the danger of cosmopolitanism was precisely that it was antipatriotic and glorified the West. *Pravda*'s less explicit anti-Semitic message was strengthened by *Kul'tura i zhizn'*, which ran an article that identified a Jewish theater critic who wrote under a Russian pseudonym.[6] Though the attack on Jews was recognizable, the importance of patriotic attention to Soviet (or Russian) cultural figures and accomplishments was still paramount.

In the next five issues of *Kul'tura i zhizn'*, the party's cultural administration systematically reported on the progress of the struggle waged by cultural institutions against cosmopolitans. At first, the attack remained focused on the initial group of theater critics and the attempts to undermine their influence in the

5. "Na chuzhdykh pozitsiiakh: o proiskakh antipatrioticheskoi gruppy teatral'nykh kritikov," *Kul'tura i zhizn'* (hereafter cited as *KZ*), 1949, no. 3 (30 Jan 1949): 2–3.

6. Kostyrchenko, *Red Shadows*, 153n1. Kostyrchenko meticulously identifies Jewish surnames; observant contemporary Soviet readers would surely also have understood the changes.

Writers' Union and at the country's leading drama theaters.[7] But soon it expanded to writers, composers, artists, and art critics.[8] By the end of March, *Kul'tura i zhizn'* had extended the attacks to literary critics in the Literature Institute, to the film industry, and to the fields of philosophy and architecture.[9] Each time, the range of fields under attack was expanded by an unsigned editorial, and details were furnished in follow-up articles or published letters by authoritative members of the field.

Very early on, the press campaign spread to the music realm. In late February 1949 an article attributed to Tikhon Khrennikov and Vladimir Zakharov, two top leaders of the Composers' Union, applied the lessons of the first two *Pravda* and *Kul'tura i zhizn'* articles to music by attacking music critics.[10] The choice of authors for this attack itself suggests crucial characteristics of the anticosmopolitanism campaigns. To speak of *choice* of authors is necessary, for it is doubtful that the two actually wrote the article. Khrennikov was known to consult with the more experienced Viktor Belyi on all of his public pronouncements, and there is evidence that this particular article was actually penned by two other musicologists, Iurii Keldysh and A. I. Shaverdian.[11] Both Khrennikov and Zakharov were members of the one-year-old Secretariat of the Composers' Union, and Khrennikov was its general secretary. Theirs were the official voices of the new, post-1948 music leadership.

The choice of Zakharov as Khrennikov's official coauthor is suggestive on

7. "Do kontsa razgromit' antipatrioticheskuiu gruppu teatral'nykh kritikov: Na partiinom sobranii SSP, v Akademicheskom Malom teatre, v Akademii obshchestvennykh nauk pri TsK VKP(b)," *KZ*, 1949, no. 4 (11 Feb): 3. See also A. Demen'tev, B. Chirskov, and M. Shuvalova, "Podgoloski estestvuiushchikh kosmopolitov," in the same issue.

8. "Na sobraniiakh pisatelei i rabotnikov iskusstv," *KZ*, 1949, no. 5 (20 Feb): 4; "K dal'neishomu rastsvetu sovetskoi dramaturgii i teatral'nogo iskusstva: Na obshchemoskovskom sobranii dramaturgov i kritikov," *KZ*, 1949, no. 6 (27 Feb): 4; "Sobranie moskovskikh khudozhnikov," *KZ*, 1949, no. 7 (10 Mar): 4. The last of these engendered a letter to the editor from an attacker and an apologetic response from one of the "cosmopolitans": V. Shleikho, "Formalisticheskie etiudy khudozhnika Bekhteeva," *KZ*, 1949, no. 7 (10 Mar): 4; and V. Bekhteev, "'Formalisticheskie etiudy khudozhnika Bekhteeva,'" *KZ*, 1949, no. 9 (31 Mar): 4.

9. On the Literure Institute, see V. Malov et al., "O kosmopolitakh i formalistakh iz Literaturnogo instituta," *KZ*, 1949, no. 5 (20 Feb): 4; and "O kosmopolitakh i formalistakh iz Literaturnogo instituta," *KZ*, 1949, no. 7 (10 Mar): 4. On film, see *KZ*, 1949, no. 7 (10 Mar), especially the lead editorial, "Sovetskoe kino—moguchee sredstvo kommunisticheskogo vospitaniia trudiashchikhsia" and "Za dal'neishii rastsvet sovetskogo kinoiskusstva" (ibid., 3). On philosophy, see "Razoblachit' propovednikov kosmopolitizma v filosofii" (ibid.), and B. Kedrov, "V redaktsiiu gazety 'Kul'tura i zhizn','" *KZ*, 1949, no. 8 (22 Mar): 4. On architecture, see "Burzhuaznye kosmopolity v arkhitekturnoi teorii i kritike," *KZ*, 1949, no. 8 (22 Mar): 4.

10. T. Khrennikov and V. Zakharov, "Burzhuaznye kosmopolity v muzykal'noi kritike," *KZ*, 1949, no. 5 (20 Feb): 3.

11. Khrennikov's consultations with Belyi were noted both by G. S. Frid (personal communication, 7 May 1999), who lived downstairs from Belyi, and by Khrennikov himself (personal communication, 30 Aug 1999), who noted that he would have been lost in the early years of his leadership without Belyi's level-headed guidance. On the charge that Keldysh and Shaverdian wrote this particular article, see RGASPI, f. 17, op. 132, d. 244, l. 37 (Vdovichenko to Malenkov, 17 Mar 1949).

another level. Zakharov was the artistic director and primary composer for the Piatnitskii Folk Choir, the very emblem of official Russian folk music performance.[12] Only the Red Army Song and Dance Ensemble could rival the Piatnitskii Choir's patriotism. Zakharov was an unmistakably outspoken proponent of folk music because it was popular and patriotic. Coupling Khrennikov and Zakharov indicated that the campaign was also binary. It was about promoting Russian patriotism while building institutions that were to maintain theoretical and practical discipline.

Khrennikov and Zakharov's article established the terrain of the public struggle against cosmopolitans in the music realm. It began with an attack on the Musicology Commission of the Composers' Union, a logical extension of the original criticism of theater critics and a sign that the new campaign was primarily theoretical.[13] The shift from antiformalism to anticosmopolitanism entailed, in part, a shift from criticizing practices of cultural production to criticizing the theoretical justification of those practices. As the institutional repository of music critics, music historians, and music theorists, the Musicology Commission was an obvious target of attack.

However, Khrennikov and Zakharov merely scolded the commission for inactivity. The real force of the criticism they directed at several individual music theorists and historians. This public attack opened up three fronts: the contemporary performance front, about which they had comparatively little to say; the historical front, about which they provided some more details; and the contemporary theoretical front, to which they devoted most of their attention. Their conclusions described a constellation of closely related but distinct areas of cosmopolitan deviation. Cosmopolitans devalued classical Russian music theory, which was steeped in Russian nationalism and emphasized the importance of folk materials in the composition of serious music. Authors of music textbooks misrepresented and underplayed the accomplishments of nineteenth-century Russian composers, characterizing their work as at least partially derivative of earlier advancements in the music of Western Europe rather than progressive and innovative in its realism. Cosmopolitans thus slighted the historical accomplishments of their Russian predecessors. In their writings about more recent musical developments, cosmopolitans praised abstract and formally complicated music, thus kowtowing to Western notions of progressive art rather than developing native Soviet ideals of realism. Finally, they espoused music theories that strove for "general human" relevance rather than rooting their evaluations in a specific national (Russian) heritage. This last element was part of the broader accusation of "rootlessness," a euphemism that was important for the unexplicit anti-Semitic understanding of the campaign and for

12. Susannah Lockwood Smith, "Soviet Arts Policy, Folk Music, and National Identity: The Piatnitskii State Russian Folk Choir, 1927–1945" (Ph.D. diss., University of Minnesota, 1997).

13. For an account of the SSK party organization meeting from which this article emerged, including Khrennikov's attack on seven supposed cosmopolitans, see "Na sobraniiakh pisatelei i rabotnikov iskusstv," *KZ*, 1949, no. 5 (20 Feb): 4. The "cosmopolitans" were L. A. Mazel', D. V. Zhitomirskii, S. I. Shlifshtein, I. F. Belza, Iu. Ia. Vainkop, A. S. Ogolevets, and I. I. Martynov.

its creative interpretation outside Moscow. Finally, most of the attacked musicologists were Jewish; though their nationality was never mentioned, the repetition of their names suggested an otherwise silent argument that Jews were suspect, inherently antipatriotic.[14]

Despite the near saturation of the cultural press with attention to anticosmopolitanism, however, there remained significant confusion about the meaning and application of the constellation of terms that surrounded cosmopolitanism and about the music that could serve to counter the perceived cosmopolitan threat. Over the course of the next few years, frustrated efforts to use music to combat cosmopolitanism, confusion about its possible remedies, and obfuscation about the "rootlessness" euphemism engendered a range of further struggles, especially anti-Semitic understandings of personnel policy and national understandings of "rootlessness" that generated an aggressive Russification by the end of Stalin's life. This chapter explores these areas of confusion and contestation.

Performing Anticosmopolitanism: Patriotic Music Programming and the Call of the West

The patriotic element of the anticosmopolitanism campaign was important from the start. Almost as soon as the campaign began, the party Secretariat considered new theater programming that would promote anti-American sentiment. As proposed by the Committee on Artistic Affairs (VKI), the programming would include new *estrada* repertory accompanied by a series of brochures and *Sovetskaia muzyka* articles devoted to the collapse of musical culture in the United States.[15] The Secretariat approved the proposals and instructed the VKI to implement the reform by administrative order rather than awaiting a formal Central Committee resolution.[16] The Writers' Union, the VKI, and the VKI's Music Theater Administration (GUMT) began constructing and staging this new repertory.[17] Anti-Americanism was seen as a ready antidote to potential antipatriotism. At least in the realm of popular musical taste, however, the patriotic call to reject Western popular music forms, if not the explicitly anti-American *estrada* programming, would fall on mainly deaf ears.

Anticosmopolitanism dictated a rejection of Western-style popular music and

14. According to the logic and practice of Soviet nationalities policy, Jewishness was a national identity. Though "Jewish nationality" grates on contemporary Western ears accustomed to thinking of Jewishness as a religious or cultural affiliation, the Soviet usage is sometimes unavoidable.

15. RGASPI, f. 17, op. 132, d. 234, ll. 27–28 (VKI memo from Lebedev to Malenkov, 30 Mar 1949); this memo was forwarded to the Secretariat on the next day (l. 26). "*Estrada*" covered a range of popular performance genres roughly equivalent to "variety show" genres more familiar to English-speaking audiences.

16. Ibid., l. 29 (Beliakov to Malenkov, 17 Jun 1949). Beliakov was an assistant sector head in OPA TsK VKP(b).

17. Ibid., ll. 50–62 (SSP and VKI to Malenkov, May 1949); ll. 67–68, 75–82 (VKI and GUMU to TsK apparatus, Oct 1949).

its characteristic focus on images of sex and violence that seem to appeal to young audiences the world over. When they investigated the young postwar generation's musical taste at the end of the 1940s, bureaucrats in the Central Committee apparatus were alarmed to discover that Soviet youth was no exception. Their internal report provides a nearly unique glimpse at the popular musical taste of Soviet audiences at the height of the anticosmopolitanism campaign.[18]

Nominally about the state of musical education in the Soviet Union, the report begins by praising the strides that Soviet culture had made since the February 1948 music resolution. More interesting—and alarming to bureaucrats—are the perceived remaining problems. The investigation revealed that Soviet youth did not have adequate knowledge of classical Russian music and had almost no understanding of the most elementary questions of musical aesthetics. Though middle-school children received adequate training in literary classics like Pushkin and Gogol, they learned almost nothing about such musical giants as Glinka and Tchaikovsky. Consequently, "the everyday life of a significant portion of the youth is dominated by Gypsy music [*tsyganshchina*], street songs, and even songs with pornographic content." To popular tunes by composers such as the former emigré romance composer Aleksandr Vertinskii or more upstanding Soviet composers, unknown authors composed alternate, inappropriately intimate lyrics, which then circulated from hand to hand and gathered a large following. For example, a song called "The Beggar Woman" described "the wanderings and misfortunes of a young homeless woman who can only watch the good life through others' windows." Other songs spoofed the great wartime romances either by describing light-headed wives who abandoned their husbands during the war or by assuming the voice of the abandoned husbands, who complained that the war had "spoiled all the women." Other songs glorified lives of violence and crime.[19]

While the texts of some of these songs were disturbing, their musical forms also bothered the report's authors, V. S. Kruzhkov and P. A. Tarasov. They carped about intimate tangos, fox-trots, and rhumbas, dances with titles like "Blue Eyes," "Champaign Spray," "It's Raining," and "Stella," all popular with youth audiences. In fact, the text of one of these "fox-trots of suffering" itself spoke of the importance of this form of dancing:

> I have no success in life
> And out of grief, I turned to drink

18. Ibid., ll. 102–10 (Kruzhkov and Tarasov to Suslov, 2 Nov 1949).

19. Ibid., ll. 102–4. A. N. Vertinskii was a popular singer and song composer before the Revolution who was known for his sentimental romanticism. He emigrated in 1919, lived in Paris, and performed throughout the world until he finally returned to the Soviet Union in 1943. (See G. Janecek, "Vertinsky, Aleksandr Nikolayevich," in *Biographical Dictionary of Russian/Soviet Composers*, ed. Allan Ho and Dmitry Feofanov [New York: Greenwood, 1989].) The report also singled out one Leshchenko and one Kozin, whose creative proclivities are not as easily discovered, but they were doubtless similar.

> Only because I don't know
> How to dance different fox-trots.[20]

What Kruzhkov and Tarasov found disturbing in these musical forms resonated with the patriotic preoccupations of anticosmopolitanism and painted an intriguing picture of how young Soviet audiences enjoyed musical entertainment: "Orchestras of four to eight individuals often perform at evening dances in clubs, movie houses, and so forth. [These orchestras] imitate the manner of playing of American jazz performers and get carried away with dry rhythms, harsh harmony, and music that is deprived of any melody. In the performance of dances, they often delve into 'special' Western 'styles' with the easy hand of some sort of 'connoisseur' of Western tastes."[21] Some of these dance bands had been forbidden to perform Western dances at the dance halls, but that sort of "administrative battle" did not work. After repeatedly requesting such music, young people gave up and held parties in their homes so that they could dance to the accompaniment of lone accordionists who could not be controlled.[22]

The party's cultural administrators thus were completely opposed to anything "Western," whether it was jazz or less-spicy dance music, precisely because it was Western. But more than that, they opposed the spread of this "Western" popular music because it was *imitative*. Just as in the public criticism of theater and music critics, youth audiences were criticized because they cultivated derivative musical tastes rather than pursuing what Kruzhkov and Tarasov would have considered more homegrown popular music, like the new anti-American *estrada* repertory. Finally and perhaps least surprisingly, party administrators were preoccupied with controlling the population's taste rather than catering to it. That obsession permeated discussion of how this underground popular music was disseminated by war invalids who traveled from city to city, by unauthorized recordings that were distributed under the packaging of more acceptable music, and from person to person in handwritten song books.[23] Since they could not suppress this music, they recommended drastically increasing the amount of basic music education to explain to young audiences why they should not be attracted to it.[24]

Revealing as it is about party administrators' fears of Western popular music, this report also illuminates a wildly unsuccessful element of the patriotic anticosmopolitanism campaign: a rejection of Western popular music that was

20. RGASPI, f. 17, op. 132, d. 234, l. 103.

21. Ibid., ll. 104–5.

22. Ibid., l. 105. For analysis of one segment of this Western-oriented youth milieu, see Mark Edele, "Strange Young Men in Stalin's Moscow: The Birth and Life of the Stiliagi, 1945–1953," *Jahrbücher für Geschichte Osteuropas* 50, no. 1 (2002): 37–61.

23. RGASPI, f. 17, op. 132, d. 234, ll. 103–5.

24. For their education plans, see ibid., ll. 105–8. For complaints about the "complete anarchy" that governed the supply of this "mass music" in clubs, dance halls, movie houses, and so forth, see ll. 108–10.

to remain important until the very end of the Soviet period. When coupled with the anti-American *estrada* programming, this uneasiness about Western popular music is an important reminder that whatever their theoretical preoccupations and personnel decisions, the predilections of the party bureaucrats in the Central Committee apparatus had real ramifications for the normative musical taste that they promulgated. The discomfort with Western popular music was also part of a long-standing ambivalence toward popular music in general in the Soviet Union.[25] Part of the ambivalence about popularity—the desire to sculpt popular musical taste rather than respond to it—is discernible in both the new stimulus to anti-American *estrada* and in the calls to improve music education.

The Composers' Union responded to the general assault on Western influence in popular music by sponsoring a two-day discussion titled "Soviet Mass Song and Images of Our Times" in mid-April 1949.[26] The discussion brought together three professional groups—poets, music critics, and popular song composers. However, it proved unfruitful because only two song composers (Isaak Dunaevskii and Vladimir Solov'ev-Sedoi) presented, and more importantly, the discussion quickly degenerated into a squabble between representatives from the Writers' Union and the Composers' Union.[27] Still, the discussion revealed the contours of a professional response to the patriotic pressures of anticosmopolitanism and its application to popular music.

The official keynote speaker from the Composers' Union, the critic Pavel Apostolov, explicitly situated the discussion within the context of the anticosmopolitanism campaign by noting that mass songs had been virtually immune to earlier attacks on formalism and academicism because of their inherently popular nature. This earlier immunity, however, made the mass song particularly susceptible to corruption by foreign influence (literally "Americanization" through use of jazz characteristics), condemned as cosmopolitanism. Noting, furthermore, that cosmopolitanism hinged on a differentiation between the personal and the collective, Apostolov suggested a joint focus on epic hymns for grandiose popular celebrations and on "more humble songs about life" that avoided individualistic, subjective, and simple lyrical content in favor of songs

25. S. Frederick Starr, *Red and Hot: The Fate of Jazz in the Soviet Union, 1917–1980* (New York: Oxford University Press, 1983); Kiril Tomoff, "The Illegitimacy of Popularity: Soviet Composers and the Royalties Administration, 1939–1953," *Russian History/Histoire Russe* 27, no. 3 (Fall 2000): 311–40.

26. RGALI, f. 2077, op. 1, dd. 381, 383 (stenogram on Soviet mass song, Day 1 [12 Apr] and Day 2 [14 Apr 1949]).

27. The most contentious speakers were the poet Kovalenkov, one of the official SSP discussants, and the musicologist A. I. Shaverdian, who exchanged increasingly vitriolic words on both days. See ibid., d. 381, ll. 31–36 (Kovalenkov), ll. 48–49 (Shaverdian); RGALI, f. 2077, op. 1, d. 383, ll. 21–23 (Kovalenkov), ll. 24–26 (Shaverdian). The nastiness was finally cut off by the chair, Terent'ev, before it spread further: see RGALI, f. 2077, op. 1, d. 383, l. 43. At issue was primarily the evaluation of the state of mass song (the poets thought things were fine) and who was to blame for the shortcomings, as each group blamed the other.

that would "resonate with the epoch through their lyrical-civic themes."[28] This thematic solution concentrated attention on collaboration with the poets in attendance and provided a baseline for the response of the few composers present.

In his response, Dunaevskii placed responsibility for interpreting anticosmopolitanism on musicologists within the Composers' Union and then used his own authority as the king of Soviet popular music to contradict the most concrete suggestion to emanate from the musicologists' earlier discussions. When he rose to speak near the end of the two-day discussion, Dunaevskii was the first composer to address the gathered experts. He did not apologize for himself or his colleagues, insisting instead that it was the composers' task to remain quiet and absorb the criticisms and suggestions directed to them. Dunaevskii argued that in order for composers to respond to the Central Committee's statements from 1946 through the anticosmopolitanism campaigns, they had to rely on musicologists to explain to them how those dictates applied to their field. After nodding to the theoretical brilliance of those assembled about him, Dunaevskii noted that the theoretical discussions were, in fact, of very little practical use to composers. Closer analysis of actual songs, he suggested, would be far more helpful. In the long first part of his presentation, Dunaevskii sought to excuse composers from interpretation of the political dictates of both Zhdanovshchina and anticosmopolitanism and then criticized the critics for not doing their interpretive job clearly enough.[29]

Then, in an abrupt but subtle rhetorical shift, Dunaevskii systematically refuted the most practical suggestion yet forwarded by those he accused of failing to suggest practicalities. He claimed that the use of jazz by Soviet composers should not be considered antipatriotic cosmopolitanism because the final products were not similar to American jazz. Dunaevskii claimed that American jazz artists simply would not recognize Soviet composers' work as jazz. He completed his defense through allusion to jazz elements in the works of three of the most authoritative figures in the field: himself, Khrennikov, and Solov'ev-Sedoi.[30] That this defense was a conscious gesture toward the greater authority of composers compared to the critics is suggested by the inclusion of Khrennikov, who was known primarily as a talented symphonic and musical theater composer and much less as a song composer. Dunaevskii's presentation thus sought to absolve composers from blame by resting responsibility to interpret solely with musicologists and then undermined the power of musicologists to influence popular music by using his superior authority to contradict their only concrete suggestions. The result was to leave the ground open for composers to utilize even jazzy language.

Solov'ev-Sedoi's seemingly compliant response, when examined carefully, also turns out to be similarly inclusive, striking a loud chord with the rhetoric

28. RGALI, f. 2077, op. 1, d. 381, ll. 1–30ob., here esp. ll. 4–4ob. and l. 6.
29. RGALI, f. 2077, op. 1, d. 383, ll. 52–58 (Dunaevskii), here ll. 52–56.
30. Ibid., ll. 56ob.–58. The references were to Khrennikov's "Proshchanie" and Solov'ev-Sedoi's "V lodke."

of anticosmopolitanism while quietly opening the theoretical field for stylistic diversity. He began by agreeing with Dunaevskii that composers depended on remiss musicologists to interpret the genre for them. Then he railed against unnamed formalists and cosmopolitans who welcomed enemy ideologies into Soviet ranks. He then launched into an extended discussion of mass songs, praising the epic songs of A. V. Aleksandrov, Dunaevskii, and Zakharov and the lyrical songs of Matvei Blanter and Boris Mokrousov. He criticized music publishers for seeking to popularize pieces never intended for wide distribution, and he practiced obligatory self-criticism. An optimistic tone pervades this criticism, however, for Solov'ev-Sedoi noted that only good songs would stand the test of time anyway.[31]

Finally, Solov'ev-Sedoi provided an extended discussion of the proper thematics and language for mass songs during the anticosmopolitanism campaigns. Soviet mass songs should be about the struggle to lead the "progressive democratic countries" in the name of peace and freedom against "reaction and lethargy." Songs should concentrate on the task of building a communist tomorrow and the feelings that task inspires. And that work should be done in a musical language that has a "national basis" and "light, life-affirming reflections of transfiguring, joyful labor written in major keys" in order "to show the spiritual and ideological growth of Soviet man, his valor and heroism." Sentimentality was right out.[32]

Solov'ev-Sedoi's presentation conformed with all of the major themes of the anticosmopolitanism campaign in the press, but without attacking Jewish composers. To a careful listener, however, a number of tricky rhetorical shifts and a final telling list of laudable performing ensembles served to narrow the applicability of these restrictions. The rhetorical shifts all related to song genre. Solov'ev-Sedoi spoke very explicitly about mass song, but earlier in his presentation he devoted attention to the subgenre of lyrical song. A good lyrical song, according to Solov'ev-Sedoi, was filled with "feelings of friendship, love, comradeship" expressed in "new, Soviet" language characterized by a "bright, joyful world view" and "ethical strength and optimism." The intimate characteristics attacked in earlier presentations, like love and friendship, in Solov'ev-Sedoi's view were redeemed by the Soviet context—if the musical language was sufficiently bright. The dangers of the lyrical song were not the result of subject matter but flowed from a certain lack of continued innovation.[33] This conclusion expanded the song genre to include not just the mobilization rhetoric of "peace and construction" but the more intimate topics "love and friendship."

The expansion of allowable musical language also entailed an even more subtle genre shift later in Solov'ev-Sedoi's talk. After a lengthy aside about the productivity of Leningrad-based composers (he was head of the city's Composers'

---

31. Ibid., ll. 65–70ob.
32. Ibid., l. 68ob.
33. Ibid., ll. 65ob.–66.

Union chapter), Solov'ev-Sedoi noted that Leningraders actively discussed not just the mass songs that were the subject of his talk but the closely related romance genre as well.[34] This almost parenthetical definition of genre, which introduced a new genre differentiated from mass song, sharply circumscribed the applicability of his earlier restrictions.

Solov'ev-Sedoi closed by listing the performance ensembles that represented the most promise for the future of Soviet song: "the Aleksandrov Soviet Army Ensemble, the choirs and collectives of the Radio Committee, the song and dance ensembles of the military districts, Utesov's orchestra, Knushevitskii's orchestra."[35] The military song and dance ensembles, along with the Piatnitskii Folk Choir, were the epitome of Soviet patriotic musical culture. By including L. O. Utesov, however, Solov'ev-Sedoi made a subtle gesture to the popularity and power of Soviet jazz. Utesov was one of the most prominent jazz musicians and bandleaders in the Soviet Union. Since 1946 his fortunes had plummeted drastically, but he had long since mastered the art of delivering anti-American lyrical content in jazzy musical packages.[36] Including his ensemble in this list was a subtle nod toward a stylistic inclusiveness that did not leave jazz beyond the pale.

Apostolov's mandates and Dunaevskii and Solov'ev-Sedoi's more authoritative responses demonstrate that the collective reaction of the Composers' Union to the dictates of anticosmopolitanism amounted to an incoherent definition of appropriate popular music. This lack of definition had the effect of validating a wider range of popular music by cloaking it in virtually nonsensical argumentation that nevertheless utilized the catch words of anticosmopolitanism. Though official productions during the peak years of anticosmopolitanism were more constrained than these theories may have allowed, anticosmopolitanism in popular music nevertheless failed to transform both popular taste and professional definitions of good songs.

A final component of anticosmopolitanism's effect on Soviet popular music is much more deeply shrouded in the details of the social composition of members of the Composers' Union. It is crucial to realize that many of the most successful composers of popular music before, during, and after the war were Jewish. Isaak Osipovich Dunaevskii, the brothers Dmitrii and Daniil Iakovlevich Pokrass, and Matvei Isaakovich Blanter were just a few of the prominent Jewish composers who wrote the Soviet Union's most popular songs. The existence of this long-standing ambivalence about popular music, the assumption that it was antipatriotic because derived from Western genres, and the accidental fact that many of its prominent practitioners were Jewish created the preconditions for a potentially disastrous convergence of the anticosmopolitanism campaign's many strains in what could have been a devastating purge of pop-

34. Ibid., l. 70.
35. Ibid., l. 70ob.
36. Starr, *Red and Hot,* esp. 144–56, 213–15, 224.

ular song composers in the Composers' Union. This convergence should not be forgotten in the following discussions of music personnel policies and the Union's response to anticosmopolitanism.

Anti-Semitism and Music Personnel

In the press, anticosmopolitanism was a call for theoretical patriotism. In popular music, it was a demand for homegrown musical forms that expressed anti-American content. In the more secretive sphere of the Central Committee apparatus, anticosmopolitanism engendered a series of decisions about the personnel composition and structural reconfiguration of arts institutions. Personnel policy thus became a battleground against cosmopolitanism as party bureaucrats, arts institution leaders, and citizens armed with denunciatory pens struggled to define, identify, and discipline individual cosmopolitans. Examining these struggles reveals that anti-Semitism was an important, though complex, component of the anticosmopolitan personnel policy practiced by the Central Committee apparatus. Motivated by a desire to increase the number and proportion of Russian music professionals, Central Committee bureaucrats were receptive to sometimes openly anti-Semitic attacks that made ascribed Jewish identity a liability throughout the last four years of Stalin's life. It also demonstrates, however, that the key authority to identify individual cosmopolitans resided almost exclusively with professional experts, namely, the leadership of the Composers' Union. Neither anti-Semitic denunciations nor attacks from government agencies could shake the growing authority of the Union.

Anticosmopolitanism in music developed in two phases. In the first wave of early 1949, the Central Committee turned its attention to the personnel composition of the Soviet Union's main arts institutions, including the Moscow State Conservatory and the Composers' Union. Both of these prestigious organizations were told to increase the percentage of Russians in their membership, faculty, or student body as the case may be.[37] The ramifications of these instructions were felt almost immediately as the Composers' Union struggled to respond to the party's call while simultaneously extending at least limited protection to its members and spreading its authority over broad swathes of the Soviet music world.

This first phase of the anticosmopolitanism campaigns lasted through the first few months of 1949, dying down in the press at the end of March and petering out in Central Committee discussions in May or June. During the first phase, the Central Committee concentrated on specific personnel matters and limited

37. I have inferred this instruction from later follow-ups: for the conservatory, see RGASPI, f. 17, op. 132, d. 420, l. 205 (Kruzhkov and Kiselev to Suslov, 23 Dec 1950); for the SSK, see d. 418, l. 206 (Kruzhkov and Tarasov to Suslov, 25 Oct 1950).

institutional change. But in late 1950 a second phase began when the Central Committee apparatus conducted a review to determine how successfully the personnel of arts institutions had been Russified. In this second wave, the apparatus's personnel policy became more explicitly anti-Semitic.

In order to comprehend the campaign during each phase, we must understand the nature of the Central Committee apparatus's Russifying goals and the struggles to define cosmopolitans that took place in the context of the attempts to realize those goals. But first, some attention must be paid to the consequences of being labeled a cosmopolitan.

In early March, the Central Committee began receiving pleas for leniency from the "cosmopolitans" who were attacked in the press during January and February and whose jobs were subsequently threatened. In his plea, Lev Mazel' sought to save his professorships at the Moscow State Conservatory and Gnesin Institute, which came under attack after the Composers' Union party organization voted to label him "antipatriotic" because of his earlier positive evaluations of Shostakovich's discredited music. Mazel' retreated from his support of Shostakovich, drew attention to the vast majority of his scholarly output not related to Shostakovich, embraced the Russian classics that the first anticosmopolitan editorials endorsed, and claimed that he had actively struggled for the institutional health of Soviet music theory by leading earlier attacks against discredited formalist musicologists. In his emotional closing, he professed his love of and loyalty to his Soviet homeland and noted how painful it was to be accused of lacking patriotism.[38]

The fate of Mazel's appeal illustrates how difficult it was to shake a label approved by the Composers' Union without informal assistance. The Central Committee bureaucrat Dmitrii Shepilov summarized the Composers' Union decision, Mazel's admission of past mistakes, and his efforts to reform. He did not even mention the content of the accusations or Mazel's lengthy self-defense. Instead, he noted that the Committee on Artistic Affairs had issued an order freeing Mazel' from his pedagogical work and suggested that Mazel's letter remain unanswered.[39]

Shepilov's complete lack of interest in the content of Mazel's defense suggests that the Central Committee apparatus was more swayed by the administrative decisions of institutions that it trusted than in arguments about the behavior of the individual accused. It may also have been the case that Mazel's Jewish identity was further grounds for dismissing his appeal. However, the anti-Semitism that may have implicitly come into play was not an explicit issue. Mazel' lost his professorships; however, his professional life was not completely destroyed

38. Ibid., d. 244, ll. 33–34 (Mazel' to Voroshilov, 6 Mar 1949). Voroshilov sent a copy of the letter to Shepilov and P. I. Lebedev for familiarization two days later (marginal notation, 8 Mar 1949).

39. Ibid., l. 35 (Shepilov to Voroshilov, 26 Mar 1949). D. T. Shepilov was assistant head of the Central Committee agitation and propaganda department (UPA TsK VKP(b)).

because he remained a member of the Composers' Union and retained the possibility of waiting out the storm.[40] This conclusion was typical. In case after case, cosmopolitans were disciplined, shamed, and often lost their jobs, but they always retained membership in the Composers' Union.

The terrifying but ultimately short-term consequences of being labeled "cosmopolitan" were partly a result of Central Committee bureaucrats' preoccupation not with individual cases but with the overall proportions of institutions' personnel. This preoccupation is evident in the initial instruction to the Composers' Union and Moscow Conservatory noted above, but it was also an unmistakable component of its later responses to denunciations and investigations of these two elite music institutions.

From the beginning, the anti-Semitism of the Central Committee's anticosmopolitanism found resonance elsewhere in the cultural realm. A barrage of denunciations flowed into the Central Committee apparatus over the next few years. They were prompted by a range of motivations, from professional jealousy to what appear to be paranoid discoveries of hidden Zionist musical codes.[41] The Central Committee apparatus usually dismissed these spontaneous anti-Semitic attacks with little or no investigation, suggesting that they continued to treat open anti-Semitism with some suspicion. Whatever the reaction to the denunciations, however, it should be noted that the anti-Semitism that accompanied the official if covert anticosmopolitanism espoused by the Central Committee apparatus found fertile ground among the population.

A review of the Moscow State Conservatory prompted by an unsolicited denunciation reveals the importance and character of anti-Semitism in personnel reforms but also demonstrates the limits of Central Committee attacks on Jewish musicians. In December 1950 a jealous mother with administrative experi-

40. He remained in the official Composers' Union directory long past the period of greatest danger. See *Spravochnik Soiuza sovetskikh kompozitorov SSSR na 1957 god* (Moscow: Sovetskii kompozitor, 1957), 23. As further evidence that he avoided professional ruin, see *Muzykal'naia entsiklopediia*, 3:392, which lists his Moscow Conservatory affiliation without interruption; in 1966, he was decorated with the honorary title "Honored Figure of the Arts" and assumed a position on the editorial board of *Sovetskaia muzyka*.

41. For an unusually complete and insistent case that runs the gamut, see RGASPI, f. 17, op. 132, d. 243, ll. 1–15 (materials relating to Ogolevets's denunciation of Kabalevskii and a group of musicologists, 1949); ll. 37–53 (Ogolevets's attack on Kabalevskii, 1950); and ll. 54–75 (Ogolevets's attack on Kabalevskii, 1951). These three sets of materials all impugn Kabalevskii's position as a musicologist—a primarily professional dispute. However, each attack increases the circle of people around Kabalevskii whom Ogolevets thinks are damaging, and they become increasingly anti-Semitic, finally ending with the accusation that Kabalevskii slipped the Zionist hymn into his music for children. The Central Committee apparatus dismissed all attacks as groundless. For a later, even more anti-Semitic example, see RGASPI, f. 17, op. 133, d. 395, ll. 34–36 (Ogolevets to V. S. Lebedev, 15 Feb 1953), in which Ogolevets attacks Kabalevskii, Khubov, and Khrennikov for criticizing him for his earlier attacks on the Jewish composer M. S. Vainberg. Vainberg had just been arrested for his association with Solomon Mikhoels, his father-in-law. The attack is characterized by casual anti-Semitism, professional opportunism, and a bit of paranoid delusion (in which he continues to insist that Kabalevskii encoded the Zionist hymn in his music for children). Vainberg was released almost immediately after Stalin's death.

ence sent a scathing letter to the Komsomol Secretariat in which she attacked the most prominent members of the conservatory's violin faculty (David Oistrakh and Abram Iampol'skii) for allegedly showing preference to Jewish students, from primary school through the allocation of the Soviet Union's rarest violins (Stradivariuses, Guarneris, and Amatis). Though she was pleased to note that measures had recently been taken to replace Jewish violinists with Russians in international competitions, she remained unsatisfied.[42]

This denunciation prompted an investigation of the entire Moscow State Conservatory, which was summarized by two Central Committee bureaucrats (Kruzhkov and A. V. Kiselev). They reported that after the Secretariat had intervened the previous year, the conservatory had begun admitting more Russians and fewer Jewish students. On most other counts, Kruzhkov and Kiselev dismissed the original complaints. Though they reported that the situation was still "unsatisfactory" overall, Oistrakh and Iampol'skii were cleared.[43] The party was serious about its efforts to increase the percentage of Russians at the conservatory *at the expense of* Jews, but it was not willing to do without accomplished Jewish musicians whose political reliability was not seriously questioned. Though they may have been forced to admit more Russian students and undoubtedly feared worse, the prominent Jewish violinists on the conservatory's faculty did not have to worry about their jobs.[44]

A remarkably similar preoccupation characterized a later investigation of personnel policy in the Composers' Union. Prompted by a denunciation of the Union by the Committee on Artistic Affairs, this investigation shows that the Central Committee apparatus's anti-Semitism proceeded explicitly from a Russification agenda and that it was expressed in the abstract terms of overall personnel distribution and did not specifically target individual Jewish professionals.

When they concluded their investigation, Kruzhkov and Tarasov, the two bureaucrats who usually handled artistic affairs, reported serious insufficiencies

42. RGASPI, f. 17, op. 132, d. 420, ll. 202–4 (Sharoeva to Mikhailov, 4 Dec 1950). For a probable victim's bitter account of anti-Semitic political intervention in a different division of the same 1950 competition, see Dubinsky, *Stormy Applause*, 14–23. For details regarding this incident, see Tomoff, "Creative Union," chap. 5.

43. RGASPI, f. 17, op. 132, d. 420, ll. 205–6 (Kruzhkov and Kiselev to Suslov, 23 Dec 1950). Suslov acknowledged and approved the report on 25 December, and the whole affair was archived with the note that Lebedev and Kaloshin (VKI) had been given instructions and Mikhailov (Komsomol) had been informed of the decision.

44. For an openly anti-Semitic review of the Moscow State Philharmonic (MGF), see RGASPI, f. 17, op. 132, d. 420, ll. 185–94 (review materials, Oct 1950–Jan 1951). The review was prompted by internal denunciations of Jewish mutual protection circles who were undermining financial discipline at the MGF; ll. 187–89ob. (twenty-four MGF members to Malenkov, 7 Oct 1950). It concluded with a Central Committee apparatus report that blasted MGF management, accusing them of entrepreneurial activity and political unreliability. Particular attention was devoted to the number of Jews in the administration, especially among leadership workers who planned concerts (of thirty-three, seventeen were Russian and fourteen were Jewish); ll. 190–94 (Kruzhkov and Tarasov to Malenkov, 2 Jan 1951).

in the personnel policies of the Composers' Union. These insufficiencies fell into four categories: (1) the second largest group of Composers' Union members by nationality consisted of "individuals not of root nationality of the USSR, namely: 435 Russians, 239 Jews, 89 Armenians, etc."; (2) only 20 percent of all Union members belonged to the party; (3) some chapters contained too many members without higher musical education; and (4) the Composers' Union administrative apparatus was inefficient and politically unreliable. Of these four categories, the last received the most attention later in the report, but inadequate "personnel work" was what most drew Kruzhkov and Tarasov's ire.[45]

The preponderance of Jews and lack of Russians in the Composers' Union was especially apparent in specific chapters. In Moscow, there were 174 Russians, 116 Jews, 16 Armenians, and fewer in other nationalities. In the Kazakh chapter there were 6 Kazakhs and 6 Jews; and in Moldavia 8 Jews, 5 Moldavians, and only 3 Russians. In Rostov there were 5 Russians and 5 Jews. Moreover, Composers' Union leaders had been pressed to admit more professionals to improve the overall personnel balance of the professional organization, but only 50 people had been admitted in the previous two years. Only 21 of them were Russians, 14 were Jews, 4 were Armenians, and 7 were spread among other nationalities. In the periphery, the state of personnel was particularly bad.[46]

Central Committee bureaucrats did not attack individual Jewish composers and musicologists as some of those who denounced Jews would have preferred. Instead, they encouraged the Composers' Union to admit more Russians and fewer Jews to change the relative percentages of the two groups within the organization. To accomplish this shift, they recommended that the Composers' Union admit more young professionals, including new conservatory students. The policy was a sort of affirmative action for Russians at the expense of Jews. The policy failed for two reasons: the composition departments of conservatories were under assault and failing to turn out new graduates; and the Composers' Union continued to pursue its own admissions procedure, which confounded the bureaucrats' demands for an increasingly Russian professional organization.

Important though it was, anticosmopolitan Russification was only one of the concerns that motivated Kruzhkov and Tarasov's investigation. They also lambasted the professional leadership for inefficiency and political unreliability. Though they attacked some individual Jewish administrators, it is clear that administrative efficiency, not nationality, was their primary concern. In a list of examples of mismanagement and corruption, only the complaints about Muzfond were directly tied to anti-Semitism, which manifested as an assertion that general corruption in Muzfond was *caused by* a supposed clique of "acciden-

45. RGASPI, f. 17, op. 132, d. 418, ll. 206–29.
46. Ibid., l. 206.

tal" Jewish administrators.[47] But most of the report detailed the inefficacy of the Composers' Union, including secretaries' work schedules, the comfy, unprofessional attitude that ruled in the Muzfond apparatus, and the fact that its working resort in Ruza had become a mere vacation spot where some composers lived year-round free of charge.[48]

The Central Committee apparatus was thus primarily concerned with the relative proportions of personnel in elite music institutions and with their administrative proficiency. However, many of the main battles of anticosmopolitan personnel policy revolved around the definition of individual cosmopolitans. In these battles the Composers' Union was able to fend off attacks from prominent journalists and the Committee on Artistic Affairs and establish its dominant authority over the music realm.

In a March 1949 appeal to Politburo member Grigorii Malenkov, the editor of the arts newspaper *Sovetskoe iskusstvo,* V. G. Vdovichenko, attacked a whole host of professional musicologists, seeking to expand the initial circle of publicly named cosmopolitans to include some of the most active leaders of the Composers' Union. Vdovichenko asserted that there was no artistic field in which criticism was so unhealthy as it was in music. "Factionalism, theoretical dissension, protection of cosmopolitans and formalists, lack of principle, and intrigue—that, in large part, is how the current condition of music theory and music criticism can be characterized." The situation was so bad, Vdovichenko noted, that mere pressure from the press was not sufficient; the intervention of administrative organs was essential.[49]

Vdovichenko's characterization of the problem reveals both the persistence of long-suppressed tensions from the 1920s and the insertion of more open anti-Semitism into the secretive language of anticosmopolitanism. He listed eight musicologists who were affiliated with RAPM and in a strangely anachronistic attack, accused them of being "Trotskyites." He noted those who had relatives who lived abroad, and he called attention to their Jewish nationality, either by labeling them "rootless cosmopolitans" or by revealing the Jewish names of those who used pen names.[50] Vdovichenko listed nine more Jewish musicologists without any indication of what shortcomings they had other than, implicitly, their nationality.[51] He then sought to demonstrate that the whole gaggle of cosmopolitans was exerting a nefarious influence on the Composers' Union through Khrennikov's Jewish wife, Klara Vaks. Apparently, only

47. Ibid., ll. 207–8.

48. Ibid., ll. 208–9.

49. RGASPI, f. 17, op. 132, d. 244, ll. 36–39 (Vdovichenko to Malenkov, 17 Mar 1949).

50. The eight were L. N. Lebedinskii, V. A. Belyi (identified as "David Aronovich Veis"), B. S. Shteinpress, S. I. Shlifshtein, Iu. V. Keldysh (identified as "Kaldyn'sh"), I. V. Nest'ev, D. V. Zhitomirskii, and A. I. Shaverdian. Of the eight, six or seven were Jewish (I have not been able to determine Keldysh's nationality) and one was Armenian (Shaverdian).

51. The nine were M. S. Pekelis, L. A. Mazel', G. N. Shneerson, G. M. Kogan, M. A. Grinberg, M. S. Bruk, N. S. Sherman, V. A. Tsukkerman, and G. B. Bernand. Several of these musicologists had been named in the initial *Kul'tura i zhizn'* article.

Khrennikov's private sympathies could explain why fellow Composers' Union members Belyi, Keldysh, and Shaverdian exerted such an influence over his public pronouncements.[52]

Vdovichenko's assault was not limited to the Composers' Union. He lashed out at the ranking music expert in the Central Committee apparatus, musicologist Boris Iarustovskii. Iarustovskii had apparently repeatedly defended Keldysh, Shaverdian, and Israil' Nest'ev from attack on the pages of *Sovetskoe iskusstvo*, and he even recommended Nest'ev for leading administrative posts. After acknowledging that Malenkov likely had already heard about the sorry state of affairs in music theory from Iarustovskii and his assistants, Vdovichenko closed by suggesting that the Composers' Union did not contain a single "real party man" who could liquidate all of the mistakes in music criticism and set musicology on the correct course. They needed serious support from the party.[53]

The initial response from the Central Committee apparatus was puzzlement. When Malenkov sent the letter to Suslov, he drew his subordinate's attention to Vdovichenko's claim that there were no "real party men" in the Composers' Union.[54] Suslov, who was likely more familiar with tensions in the music world, sent it on to Shepilov with the notation that "Vdovichenko tosses everyone into one and the same pile." He also questioned the inclusion of three names in the list: Keldysh, Nest'ev, and Shaverdian.[55] It is important to note that Suslov's skepticism applied to the only two in the group who were not Jewish, and to one who was but whose name did not make that immediately apparent.[56] Suslov was also apparently skeptical about Vdovichenko's claim that there were no "real party men" in the Union leadership. Khrennikov, Koval', and Zakharov had apparently proven themselves.

Vdovichenko's assault on musicologists completely backfired. Khrennikov asserted the Composers' Union's exclusive authority to define musical cosmopolitans, turning the tables on the newspaper man and extending his own attack to the VKI.[57] Khrennikov acknowledged the positive role of the press in the anticosmopolitan campaign, but he complained that *Sovetskoe iskusstvo* irresponsibly slandered honest, useful specialists, especially Keldysh, whose minor mistakes Khrennikov admitted and whose contributions he extolled. The

---

52. RGASPI, f. 17, op. 132, d. 244, ll. 37–38.

53. Ibid., ll. 38–39.

54. Ibid., ll. 36 (marginal notation), 39 (underline in same dark-blue pencil).

55. Ibid., ll. 36 (marginal notation, question about Keldysh), 37 (questions about Nest'ev and Shaverdian). Both notations are in the same light-gray lead pencil, as opposed to Malenkov's dark-blue one.

56. See my above reservation about Keldysh's nationality; I have here counted him as not Jewish.

57. RGASPI, f. 17, op. 132, d. 244, ll. 41–44 (two copies of Khrennikov to Malenkov, 25 Mar 1949). The reply appears only on the second copy, ll. 43–44. This memo was sent eight days after Vdovichenko's, about which Khrennikov may or may not have been aware. Explicitly, it was a response to what Khrennikov considered inaccurate and unfair attacks in *Sovetskoe iskusstvo*.

unfounded attacks on Keldysh were particularly damaging because the newspaper was silent about the real cosmopolitans: Zhitomirskii, Vainkop, Ogolevets, Belza, Mazel', Ginzburg, and the others who were condemned by the "musical public," by which he meant the Composers' Union. He registered a brief complaint about attacks in the newspaper *Trud* on N. Ia. Briusova, a senior Soviet musicologist and old party member, and on Zakharov and his Piatnitskii Choir.

In an aggressive counterattack, Khrennikov sought to hold individual VKI bureaucrats responsible for the incorrect attacks on professional musicologists, suggesting that the attacks were hindering attempts by the Composers' Union to reconstruct Soviet musicology. In a paragraph that attracted special attention in the Central Committee apparatus, Khrennikov claimed that Vdovichenko had long held unsound or even depraved positions on musical matters and suggested that *Sovetskoe iskusstvo* was due for a "decisive healing."

Khrennikov's counterattack is particularly interesting because of its implicit claims about authority and discipline in the music world during the anticosmopolitan campaigns, especially in the decisive realm of personnel policy. Khrennikov's assumption was that *only* the Composers' Union could decide who was a cosmopolitan and who was a once-misguided but now reformed, healthy, and loyal music professional. Treading on the Composers' Union's turf was a dangerous proposition that opened highly placed newspaper editors and bureaucrats in the government's arts administration to counterattack. That counterattack proved to be very effective. Suslov received Vdovichenko's and Khrennikov's letters on the same day. When he sent them to Shepilov for action, he noted his skepticism about Vdovichenko's claims and then, on Khrennikov's letter, suggested that they should immediately consult with Khrennikov about a new candidate, presumably for Vdovichenko's editorship.[58] Two days later, Vdovichenko suddenly asked to be released from his editor's duties so that he could return to school to complete a long-unfinished degree.[59]

The VKI did not capitulate so easily. Perhaps in support of Vdovichenko, the head of the VKI, P. I. Lebedev, wrote to Malenkov in early April in order to lay out the rationale of the attack against Keldysh. According to Lebedev, Keldysh was too slow to reform the curriculum of the music theory department of the Moscow Conservatory. The VKI had to criticize him and relieve him from his duties as head of the music theory department. Keldysh retained his professorship and leadership position in the Composers' Union, so he was not deprived

58. For Suslov's comment on Khrennikov's letter, see RGASPI, f. 17, op. 132, d. 244, ll. 43 (marginal notation), 45 (underlined juxtaposition of "Vdovichenko" and "depraved positions"). The notation is as follows: "To Shepilov. Suggest a candidate, the sooner the better. You should consult with t. Khrennikov. [signed] Suslov, 31 Mar 1949."

59. Ibid., l. 46 (Vdovichenko to Malenkov, 27 Mar 1949). Malenkov sent the letter directly to Shepilov on 31 March, the same day that Suslov sent him Vdovichenko's initial letter and Khrennikov's response.

of an active, influential professional life.[60] The VKI still had the institutional power to assert its control over some issues, but this incident demonstrates that personnel disputes allowed the Composers' Union to control the administration of its terrain increasingly effectively.

That control was again demonstrated in the response to another VKI attack in late 1950. The main thrust of this onslaught was against "people who have dubious political reputations" but who were working in the administrative apparatus of the Composers' Union or Muzfond.[61] Though this denunciation prompted the critical Central Committee investigation discussed above, it also proved again the exclusive authority of the Composers' Union to define professional cosmopolitans.

The VKI was most disturbed by the presence of M. A. Grinberg. They argued that he had twice been thrown out of the party, once in 1939 for connections to enemies of the people and again while he was working at the Radio Committee in 1948–49, for not following the party line in the selection of creative cadres. After Grinberg was dismissed from the Radio Committee, the VKI suggested that he be sent to the periphery, but the Composers' Union appointed him musical consultant to take advantage of his organizational abilities. The VKI report also attacked one of Khrennikov's administrative assistants (L. Veksler), the head accountant of the Composers' Union (G. Bleiz), various administrators in Muzfond's apparatus, the housing cooperative, and several people associated with the journal *Sovetskaia muzyka*.

For the most part, these attacks were limited to noncreative personnel, to the apparatus rather than the membership of the professional body. However, there were two exceptions. First, the VKI alleged that the Moscow Muzfond's Bureau of Propaganda regularly sent Lev Lebedinskii, Raisa Glezer, and Georgii Polianovskii (all Jews) to give lectures without exerting any control over what they might say. The three were probably suspect because they were Jewish, but the primary VKI complaint was that the Composers' Union did not exert sufficient oversight of the interpretive lectures that its members gave to the general listening public. In his reply, Khrennikov noted that the three had absolutely nothing to do with the work of the Muzfond Bureau of Propaganda (as the VKI charged); rather, their "lecturing" activities were limited to a few introductory remarks at mainly internal concerts featuring works by a colleague.[62] The Central Committee apparatus dropped the issue.[63]

The second area in which the VKI attack touched on the professional mem-

---

60. Ibid., ll. 47–48 (Lebedev to Malenkov, 9 Apr 1949). The memo was archived along with the Khrennikov-Vdovichenko exchange because the Secretariat had already ruled on Vdovichenko's removal; l. 49 (Parinov to Sukhanov, 11 Apr 1949).

61. RGASPI, f. 17, op. 132, d. 418, ll. 201–2 (Kaloshin and Anisimov to Suslov, early Oct 1950).

62. Ibid., l. 204 ("Spravka," Khrennikov [to Suslov], 14 Oct 1950).

63. See ibid., ll. 206–9 (Kruhzkov and Tarasov to Suslov, 25 Oct 1950). The party bureaucrats do not even mention the attack on the three musicologists, and Suslov signs off on all of their recommendations (l. 206, marginal notation, 26 Oct 1950).

bership of the Composers' Union was much more illustrative of the nature of anticosmopolitanism and the response of the Composers' Union, though the result was the same. The VKI noted that heads of four of the Union's creative sections and commissions were politically dubious. Aleksandr Veprik, Aleksandr Livshits, Grigorii Frid, and Viktor Vinogradov headed up the Symphonic Section, the Children's Music Section, and the Commissions on the USSR and RSFSR. The VKI noted that Veprik graduated from the Berlin Conservatory and once actively spoke out against Rimsky-Korsakov. Vinogradov was thrown out of the party for destroying his party card when in German captivity during the war, and Livshits had been a member of RAPM.

The first two of these accusations demonstrate that the VKI bureaucrats had learned the lessons of official, public anticosmopolitanism. Veprik's foreign education and personal antagonism with one of the classic Russian composers made him politically suspect in the patriotic Russian campaign. Vinogradov's purported disloyalty in captivity made his own Soviet patriotism questionable. The attacks on Livshits and Frid, on the other hand, demonstrate an understanding of the tacit anti-Semitic aspect of the campaign. Though Livshits had demonstrated creative sympathies that were no longer officially in favor, he was not a member of the even more problematic ASM, which had modernist sympathies and contact with the West. It is likely that the more important but unmentioned "dubious political characteristic" of which Livshits was guilty was his ascribed Jewish identity. This supposition is given greater credence by the inclusion of Frid, one of the few war veterans in the Composers' Union, without any mention of any possible political liability. Frid was Jewish, and that apparently made him unreliable enough to warrant mention by the VKI.[64]

It was not, however, enough of a charge to warrant a rebuttal from the Composers' Union. Khrennikov refuted the VKI's direct charges or provided information that somehow alleviated them. Khrennikov left indirect or implicit charges unanswered, but probably because Central Committee bureaucrats found him trustworthy, his refutation effectively limited further discussion to charges of political disloyalty and administrative incompetence.[65]

In most cases, Khrennikov simply provided short biographical sketches of the bureaucrats in the Composers' Union apparatus and noted when they had been appointed at the recommendation or order of the VKI, as was the case both with Veksler and Bleiz. For example, the VKI attacked one Gol'tsman, an organizational consultant to Muzfond who also happened to be Jewish. In his reply, Khrennikov noted that the VKI had in fact once fired Gol'tsman allegedly for turning in a fictitious autobiographical statement. However, the courts had overturned the VKI decision, so he was simply released for other work. The Composers' Union offered him that work and now defended him against VKI attack.

---

64. Ibid., l. 201.
65. Ibid., ll. 202–5 ("Spravka," Khrennikov to Suslov, 14 Oct 1949).

Khrennikov's defense of the heads of creative sections and commissions was cursory but followed the same strategy. Since the VKI had not actually accused Frid of anything, Khrennikov apparently did not think it was necessary to defend him. And in fact, Frid was not mentioned again. The purely anti-Semitic attack failed. Likewise, Khrennikov left the specific charges against Vinogradov and Veprik unanswered, noting only that Vinogradov was assistant head of the Commission on the USSR and that Veprik was secretary of both the symphonic and instrumental chamber music sections. For Livshits, whose loyalty was impugned because of his former affiliation with RAPM, Khrennikov provided a bit more information: he had been a party member since 1921 and had fought as a Red Guard and then a member of the Red Army during the Civil War in Ukraine, at which time he was seriously wounded and lost both legs. He was currently working as secretary of the Commission on the USSR.

Cursory though this defense was, bureaucrats in the Central Committee apparatus apparently thought that it was sufficient. None of the accusations against professionals in the Composers' Union were mentioned again.[66] This silence suggests that by late 1950 the Composers' Union had solidified its control over decisions about specific professionals.

The examples of the explicit or implicit campaigns against Jews at the Moscow Conservatory and in the Composers' Union administrative apparatus illustrate the terms of the anticosmopolitan campaign as it played out not in the press but in the more secretive realm of the Central Committee apparatus. First, the implicit anti-Semitism of the public campaign resonated with many bureaucrats and citizens, who denounced alleged cosmopolitans. They recognized that element and repeated it in their own attacks.

Second, the Central Committee bureaucrats were not motivated by explicit anti-Semitism directed against individual musicians. They did nothing to reduce the influence of performance superstars like Oistrakh or more humble professional leaders like Livshits or Frid. Rather, they directed their attention to the overall personnel composition of the institutions in question, forcing the Moscow Conservatory to admit more Russian students at the expense of Jewish applicants and encouraging the Composers' Union to do the same. This abstract anti-Semitism was explicitly motivated by Russification—an attempt to increase the percentage of Russian performers, composers, and musicologists in the Soviet Union's musical institutions. The fact that Jews represented the largest minority and that anti-Semitism resonated with people both inside and outside the apparatus all but guaranteed that they would be the primary losers in the campaign to promote Russians. Anticosmopolitanism should be seen not simply as a euphemism for anti-Semitism but as a set of practices that encouraged Russification at the expense of Jews.

Third, the consequences of being branded a cosmopolitan in the music profession were dire and frightening, but not, in the end, life threatening. Cos-

66. Ibid., ll. 206–9.

mopolitans were often fired from teaching positions and administrative posts, but they were not excluded from the Composers' Union. As continuing members of the Union, they were entitled to basic material support, which could sustain them until the campaigns ended and they could return to a more normal professional existence.

Finally, the authority to define who was and who was not a cosmopolitan on an individual basis resided primarily with the professional leadership of the Composers' Union, whose expert evaluations repeatedly overcame outside efforts to expand the campaign. This definitional power had its limits; it is inconceivable that the leadership could have said simply, "We have no cosmopolitans." Once the parameters of the campaign were set by the initial press attacks, the professional leadership could use its expert authority to choose the cosmopolitans and then provide the limited shelter of continuing membership in the professional body. This was no small power. This expert authority to define the specific applications of anticosmopolitanism was essential to the surprising failure of anticosmopolitan personnel policy in the Composers' Union.

Subverting Anticosmopolitanism: The Failure of Anti-Semitic Anticosmopolitanism

Despite the flurry of memos, reports, and instructions to Russify, the party's limited anti-Semitic personnel policy was an outright failure in the Composers' Union. This surprising failure hinged on two main factors: the underproduction of qualified composers and deliberate attempts to avoid the anti-Semitic elements of the campaign. The underproduction of qualified composers was the result of a struggle over conservatory enrollments, which the Composers' Union eventually won. More important was the Union's effort to thwart the anti-Semitic elements of anticosmopolitanism in its own ranks.

The first of these two factors demonstrates the remaining limits of the Composers' Union's institutional power in the late 1940s and early 1950s. Despite its increasing institutional clout, the Composers' Union was not able to block all changes with which it adamantly disagreed, especially if the proposals were slightly out of its official purview of professional composers and musicologists. This limitation was revealed and then overcome during a three-year struggle over the fate of the composition department at the Gnesin Institute and conservatories in Russia and Ukraine. The struggle was part of a VKI attempt to limit the influence of composers whom cultural bureaucrats considered either dangerous or incompetent while it restructured one of the Soviet Union's most prestigious music schools. It was also part of a larger and initially successful struggle to limit the production of new composers, a VKI goal that worked at immediate cross-purposes with the Central Committee's instructions to the Composers' Union to admit more young professionals. By engaging in the struggle and emerging victorious from it, the Composers' Union demonstrated its increasing influence over the production of new professionals and further marginalized the VKI.

This struggle took place over three successive academic years. In early 1949, the VKI and the Ministry of Higher Education (MVO) conducted a systematic review of the composition departments at all of the conservatories in the Russian and Ukrainian republics and limited the advanced training of composers to the Moscow, Leningrad, and Kiev conservatories. The department at the Gnesinka and those in eight other Russian and Ukrainian cities were forbidden to admit new composition students.[67] Despite the participation of Composers' Union members in the joint VKI-MVO investigation committee, the Union seems to have been caught off guard, but when the issue was revisited in 1950 Composers' Union leaders mobilized substantial political forces and authoritative arguments on behalf of the Gnesinka, the Urals Conservatory, and the Kharkov Conservatory. Composers' Union intervention helped the Urals and Kharkov conservatories readmit students in 1950, and the Gnesinka in 1951.[68]

Throughout this struggle, the well-connected head of the Gnesinka, Elena Gnesina, and the Composers' Union were pitted against the combined forces of the VKI and MVO in a pitched battle in the Central Committee apparatus. In 1949 Gnesina essentially fought alone, attempting to use the patriotic terms of the anticosmopolitanism campaign to save her institution's composition department. In appeals to the high-ranking party members Suslov and Kliment Voroshilov, Gnesina stressed the central role that her brother Mikhail played in training musical cadres throughout the Soviet Union and the living link to the Russian classics preserved by his status as the last surviving student of Rimsky-Korsakov. Gnesina complained about arbitrary accusations of anticosmopolitanism during the VKI-MVO review and stressed that her institute was the "only music pedagogy institution of higher education in the Soviet Union."[69]

Though the Gnesins' Jewish identity could not have helped their cause in 1949, VKI head P. I. Lebedev did not resort to anti-Semitism while defending the findings of the joint VKI-MVO commission. He stressed issues of institutional identity and professional authority, suggesting that the Gnesinka's composition faculty (with the exception of Mikhail Gnesin) was incapable of training first-rate composers and that composition departments should be filled not with graduates from pedagogical institutes but with professionals with conservatory educations.[70] In the Central Committee apparatus, this argument

---

67. This summary is gleaned from two reports: RGASPI, f. 17, op. 132, d. 238 (Lebedev to Tarasov, 3 Jun 1949), and d. 420, l. 148 (table compiled by A. Grigor'eva, 2 Aug 1950), which contains data on all nine discontinued departments.

68. I provide extensive details in Tomoff, "Creative Union," 301–14.

69. RGASPI, f. 17, op. 132, d. 238, ll. 56–62 (Gnesina to Suslov, with copies to Voroshilov, Kaftanov, P. I. Lebedev, and Khrennikov). Gnesina had a reputation for having contacts "at the top," most notably Voroshilov; Paperno, *Notes of a Moscow Pianist*, 133.

70. RGASPI, f. 17, op. 132, d. 238, ll. 63–65 (Lebedev to Tarasov, 3 Jun 1949).

proved decisive.[71] But shifting terrain to professional authority set the stage for overturning the 1949 decision over the next two years, when the Composers' Union mustered its professional authority on behalf of the conservatory departments, including the Gnesinka's.

When the Composers' Union entered the fray in 1950, it used its institutional authority and mobilized an array of other actors. The initial salvo was fired by Khrennikov, who argued to Suslov that the decision to liquidate conservatory composition departments was "deeply mistaken" because it would sharply reduce the preparation of composers and cut short the promotion of new, talented composers throughout Russia and Ukraine. He suggested that all local conservatory departments should be reopened.[72] Khrennikov also flexed the Composers' Union's muscle by soliciting support from one of the VKI's subsidiary institutions, the Russian Republic's Committee on Artistic Affairs, and from the provincial party secretaries in Sverdlovsk and Kharkov.[73] Gnesina repeated her earlier arguments, bolstered with a new one that stressed the dominant authority of the Composers' Union in the music realm: the Gnesinka's composition department provided an "immediate connection" to the Composers' Union. Without this link to the Composers' Union, creative preparation in the Gnesinka's other departments would suffer.[74]

The VKI and MVO twice defended the 1949 decision, repeating that the Gnesinka's pedagogical mission prevented it from training composers.[75] But by the end of August 1950, the combined forces marshaled by the Composers' Union, including a detailed critique of the VKI's composer training plans, forced the VKI to capitulate on the two most important conservatories that the Composers' Union defended, the Urals Conservatory and the Kharkov Conservatory. However, the VKI still held out on the Gnesinka, insisting that it needed to improve the faculty before new students could be admitted.[76]

When the Central Committee bureaucrats in charge of the case submitted

---

71. Ibid., l. 67 (Kruzhkov and Tarasov to Suslov, 5 Oct 1949).

72. RGASPI, f. 17, op. 132, d. 420, l. 156 (Khrennikov to Suslov, 24 Apr 1950).

73. Ibid., l. 154 (Silant'ev to Lebedev and Iarustovskii, 17 May 1949). Though this KDI RSFSR memo is dated 1949, that date is most likely a mistake. Even if it was not, its location in this file suggests that the Central Committee apparatus dredged it up again while reconsidering the case in the summer of 1950. Ibid., l. 146 (Kuroedov to Tarasov, 12 Jul 1950) and l. 147 (Shachneva to Tarasov, 27 Jul 1950). Kuroedov and Shachneva were Obkom party secretaries in Sverdlovsk and Kharkov, respectively.

74. Ibid., ll. 143–45 (Gnesina to Malenkov, 24 Aug 1950). Malenkov sent the letter to Kaftanov (MVO), Lebedev (VKI), Sinetskii (Biuro po kul'ture pri SM SSSR), and Kruzhkov (OPA), with instructions that the last prepare a report on the matter; l. 142 (28 Aug 1950).

75. Ibid., ll. 151–52 (Briushkov and Rushev to Kruzhkov, 26 May 1950). RGASPI, f. 17, op. 132, d. 429, ll. 149–50 (Samarin and Kaloshin to Kruzhkov, 22 Jul 1950).

76. RGASPI, f. 17, op. 132, d. 420, ll. 153–53ob. (Kukharskii to Iarustovskii, 24 Jul 1950). In marginalia on l. 153ob., Iarustovskii heavily emphasized Kukharskii's enumeration of the "appalling" numbers of students planned for admission in 1950. Ibid., l. 157 (Bespalov to Kruzhkov, 26 Aug 1950).

their final analysis to Suslov, they reported that the recently completed plenary session of the Composers' Union had protested against the VKI-MVO decision and a number of regional party secretaries had also complained. Since the VKI and MVO explanations had been completely unsatisfactory, they had been forced to reverse their decision. The VKI held the field until the next academic year (the argument about the Gnesinka's teacher-training mission was decisive), but in 1951 Gnesina trumped mission with authority, appointing Khachaturian to the faculty and persuading even the MVO and VKI that the Gnesinka department should reopen. Kruzhkov and Tarasov agreed, and the Gnesinka was cleared to admit five composition students a year, starting in 1951–52.[77]

The struggle over composition departments shows that the Composers' Union managed to win a key battle with the combined forces of the Committee on Artistic Affairs and Ministry of Education. Its only setbacks were due to an emphasis in the stated mission of the Gnesinka—the preparation of teachers rather than composers. Though forced to compromise on the number of conservatories that would reopen, it preserved the departments of the two for which it specifically campaigned. Besides demonstrating the increasing institutional power and decisive professional authority of the Composers' Union, the struggle over conservatory composition departments had ramifications for the success of the Central Committee's Russification campaign. It should be recalled that a crucial aspect of Kruzhkov and Tarasov's recommendations about the personnel policy of the Composers' Union was that a greater number of young Russian composers and musicologists should be admitted to the Union. That recommendation could not be followed if conservatories could not train new composers. Though this consequence was obvious—and argued by the Secretariat of the Composers' Union and by Gnesina—the Central Committee apparatus discovered it with some alarm only later.

In 1953 after it had been replaced by a new Ministry of Culture, the then former VKI was subjected to scathing criticism for so sharply reducing the production of young composers and musicologists. Central Committee bureaucrats A. M. Rumiantsev, Tarasov, and Iarustovskii noted that the creative environment in the Russian provinces was deplorable precisely because of the earlier decision to eliminate composition departments there. Graduates of the Moscow and Leningrad conservatories remained in the capitals rather than returning to the provinces, so provincial conservatories needed to produce their own composers. In the immediate future, however, the Central Committee *apparatchiki* suggested that the new Ministry of Culture should seek to assign fu-

---

77. Ibid., ll. 258–59 (Kruzhkov and Tarasov to Suslov, 31 Aug 1950); Ibid., ll. 160–61 (Kaftanov to Malenkov, 31 Aug 1950), which Malenkov set aside the next day; ll. 162–63 (Bespalov to Malenkov, 8 Sep 1950); l. 164 (Sinetskii to Malenkov, 2 Oct 1950); and ll. 165–66 (Kruzhkov and Tarasov to Malenkov, 16 Oct 1950). Sinetskii proposed the final solution: reconsider the issue in 1951 and suggest that Gnesina strengthen the faculty before then. For 1951, see RGASPI, f. 17, op. 133, d. 333, l. 120 (Kruzhkov and Tarasov to Malenkov, 12 Jul 1951), a response to an appeal that Gnesina sent to Malenkov.

Table 6.1. Nationality of Those Admitted to SSK SSSR, January 1949–August 1950

Chapter	Russian	Jewish	Armenian	Georgian	Other	Total
Moscow	16	6	3	2	3	30
Leningrad	0	2	0	0	0	2
Other RSFSR (6)	9	0	0	0	0	9
Other SSR or ASSR (7)	1	3	1	0	4	9
Total USSR	26	11	4	2	7	50

Source: RGALI, f. 2077, op. 2, d. 2, ll. 1ob.–2 (Svedeniia o kompozitorakh, podavshchikh zaiavlenie o prieme ikh v chleny SSK za period s ianvaria 1949 po 1.IX.50g. Priniatye v SSK).

Note: In the remainder of 1950, the following were admitted: six additional Russians, nine additional Jews, one additional other (see table 6.4).

ture conservatory graduates to provincial cities. Not only did the Russification of the Composers' Union not succeed, the creative atmosphere in Russia outside the capitals had actually gotten worse. What the bureaucrats never acknowledged was that the problem was largely a product of their own earlier support of the VKI and MVO's initiatives.[78]

The second cause of the Central Committee's failure to Russify the Composers' Union was the Union leadership's response to the pressure placed on its personnel selection policy. Beginning in late 1950, the Composers' Union prepared a series of reports for the Central Committee apparatus which presented statistics about changes in its overall personnel composition. Most of the reports have not been preserved in the party or Composers' Union archives, but the Composers' Union retained the statistical tables for their own records. Though they are not completely uniform, most tables or sets of tables contain information about the education, party affiliation, age, and nationality of newly admitted members of the Composers' Union. They allow a relatively complete reconstruction of the social changes within the Composers' Union from 1949 to the end of Stalin's life in March 1953.

A key component of that social change for understanding anticosmopolitanism was nationality. In the first two years of the anticosmopolitanism campaign, the Composers' Union admitted fifty new members, twenty-six Russians, eleven Jews, four Armenians, two Georgians, and one each of seven other nationalities (see table 6.1).[79] Despite Kruzhkov and Tarasov's protestations to

78. RGANI, f. 5, op. 17, d. 444, ll. 46–50, here ll. 46–46a, 50 (Rumiantsev, Tarasov, Iarustovskii to Pospelov, 14 May 1953). To be fair, it should be noted that the 1950 evidence suggests that within the Central Committee apparatus, Iarustovskii was probably an important supporter of the SSK position. As the probable author of this 1953 report, he was entitled to some license to criticize the earlier VKI decision.

79. RGALI, f. 2077, op. 2, d. 2, ll. 1–5 (data on membership applications received Jan 1949 to 1 Sep 1950, undated but probably Sep 1950). This is the same total that Kruzhkov and Tarasov cited in their report, though their specifics (twenty-one Russians, fourteen Jews, four Armenians, etc.) suggest that the Central Committee bureaucrats disputed the nationality of a few new members. The discrepancy also suggests that the Composers' Union materials should be understood as imprecise; however, they are certainly accurate enough to provide good evidence of the overall contours of change within the professional body.

the contrary, the Composers' Union pursued a policy of drastically increasing the rate at which they admitted new members. After the First All-Union Congress of Soviet Composers in early 1948, only four new members were admitted to the Union—two Russians and two Jews. In 1949, during the heat of the anticosmopolitan campaign, twenty-two new members joined, and in 1950 forty-four more. The peak of the growth was reached in 1951, when fifty-five new members were admitted. After that, the number of new professionals entering the Union fell to thirty. In four years, 121 composers and musicologists were added to the professional organization.[80] This admissions policy was at least partly in line with the Central Committee's demands.

An examination of one subset of these newly admitted professionals also demonstrates that the Composers' Union was partially following the instructions of the Central Committee. Between 1948 and 1953 the professional ranks swelled by forty-three, slightly more than half of whom were Russians, and only 16 percent of whom were Jewish. An additional 12 percent were Georgian, and the remaining 21 percent were scattered among various other nationalities.[81] Kruzhkov and Tarasov assumed that admitting young professionals meant Russifying the organization; this assumption was borne out by the national composition of young composers and musicologists who joined the organization in the last years of Stalin's life.

However, a closer examination of the specific nature and timing of this growth reveals that the Composers' Union actually foiled the spirit of the Russification drive. The national composition of the Composers' Union did not change over the whole period. In fact, Composers' Union leaders may even have managed personnel policy in a way that allowed them to continue admitting new Jewish members while eluding Central Committee detection of the fact that they were doing so. This is not to say that Jewish nationality was not a liability for new applicants at any time during the campaigns. It was. It is also not to say that there were no other ways of discriminating against Jewish professionals, new and old members alike. It is just to suggest that the Composers' Union's personnel selection successfully weathered the anti-Semitic elements of the anticosmopolitan storm.

The most intense discrimination against Jewish applicants occurred during the first twenty months of the anticosmopolitan campaign. Though Jews comprised 22 percent of those admitted to the Composers' Union during 1949 and the first two-thirds of 1950, Jewish applicants were rejected at a much higher rate than applicants of other nationalities. A third of those denied membership were Jewish (see table 6.2).

More Jewish applicants sought admission than any other group except Rus-

---

80. Ibid., l. 58 (data on SSK membership as of 1 Jan 1953, undated table prepared by Pomerantseva). The 1951 figure has been corrected from Pomerantseva's 54 by reference to ibid., ll. 11, 16–18 (other tables which all agree on the 55 figure).

81. Data taken from ibid., ll. 50–51 (data on members accepted between 25 Mar 1948 and 15 Mar 1953, undated report).

Table 6.2. Nationality of Those Denied Admission, January 1949–August 1950

Chapter	Russian	Jewish	Armenian	Georgian	Other	Total
Moscow	9	6	1	1	0	17
Leningrad	0	1	0	0	0	1
Other RSFSR/ ASSR (18)	14	7	0	0	2	23
Total	23	14	1	1	2	41

Source: RGALI, f. 2077, op. 2, d. 2, ll. 2ob.–4 (Svedeniia o kompozitorakh, podavshchikh zaiavlenie o prieme ikh v chleny SSK za period s ianvaria 1949 po 1.IX.50g. Otkazano v prieme).

sians, who comprised an even larger share of those denied admission. But the disproportionate number of unsuccessful Jewish applicants was not simply a function of volume. From January 1949 through August 1950 Jewish applicants had a significantly lower success rate than applicants of other nationalities. Only 44 percent of those who applied were admitted, as opposed to 53 percent of Russians, two of three Georgians, and four of five Armenians. This poor success rate was despite the fact that the Leningrad chapter admitted two of its three Jewish applicants (see table 6.3).

Jewish identity was clearly a liability for applicants to the Composers' Union during 1949 and 1950. However, when the admissions data are broken down further, an intriguing pattern emerges. In 1949, fourteen of the twenty-two successful applicants were Russian, and only four were Jewish (see table 6.4). Then in the first eight months of 1950 an additional twelve Russians and all of seven Jews entered the Union. Thus the first eight months of 1950 saw a dramatic increase in the success of Jewish applicants for Composers' Union membership. This pattern suggests that the Composers' Union membership committee felt the anti-Semitic pressure at least temporarily lessen at the end of 1949 when *Kul'tura i zhizn'* published an article that heaped praise on composers for their accomplishments since the February 1948 Central Committee resolution.[82]

On the other hand, it must still have been clear to those making membership decisions that the Central Committee was watching their personnel choices. After the Composers' Union report was submitted to the Central Committee sometime in September 1950, an additional six Russians and *nine* Jews were admitted. That brought the yearly totals for 1950 to eighteen Russians, sixteen Jews, and ten members of other nationalities.[83] The timing of the release of the reports and the admission of Jewish applicants suggests that the membership committee sought to admit Jews when the Central Committee's attention was not trained on their personnel policy, probably hoping that the anticosmopoli-

82. M. Chulaki, "Na puti muzykal'nogo tvorchestva," *KZ*, 1949, no. 36 (31 Dec): 2, which praised the Third Plenum of the SSK SSSR, marking an end to the pressure and scrutiny of the Composers' Union that had continued since 1948. See also "Plenum pravleniia SSK SSSR," *KZ*, 1949, no. 33 (30 Nov): 1.

83. These data were generated by comparing table 6.1 with table 6.4.

Table 6.3. Applicant Success Rate by Nationality, January 1949–August 1950 (percentage)

Chapter	Russian	Jewish	Armenian	Georgian	Other	All nationalities
Moscow	64	50	75	67	100	64
Leningrad	—	67	—	—	—	67
Other	42	30	100	—	67	44
All chapters	53	44	80	67	77	55

Source: Summary percentages from table 6.1 and table 6.2.

tan campaign would end before the next review. It did not, and 1951 saw a return to more balanced admissions: twenty-seven Russians and eleven Jews.

The 1951 figures also suggest another trend in the Composers' Union personnel decisions that reflected a larger tendency that was disturbing to Central Committee bureaucrats. In 1951 there was a significant surge in the number of composers and musicologists of titular nationality (e.g., Georgians in Georgia) admitted to chapters in the national and autonomous republics. While only eight had been admitted in the three years since the Central Committee resolution in February 1948, fourteen entered the ranks of the Composers' Union in 1951 alone, a trend that continued at least through 1952. The increase in non-Russian titular nationals can be at least partially explained by a shift away from Moscow. While the Moscow chapter accounted for virtually all of the growth of the Composers' Union as a whole in 1948 and 1949, by 1950 its share of admitted applicants had already shrunk to just over a third, and by 1952 less than 17 percent of those admitted to the Union entered the Moscow chapter (see table 6.5).

Though the Central Committee generally approved of the promotion of titular nationals, there was an aspect of this shift away from Moscow that disturbed them. Titular nationals seem to have been admitted to their local chapters at the expense of Russians. Though complete data about unsuccessful

Table 6.4. Nationality of Those Admitted to SSK SSSR, 1948–51

Year	Russians	Jews	Non-Russian titular	Other	Total
1948	2	2	—	0	4
1949	14	4	2	2	22
1950	18	16	6	4	44
1951	27	11	14	3	55
Total	61	33	22	9	125

Source: RGALI, f. 2077, op. 2, d. 2, ll. 13–18 (Spisok tvorcheskikh rabotnikov, priniatykh v chleny SSK).

Note: In 1952 and the first three months of March 1953, seven Russians, five Jews, and sixteen others were admitted. These figures have been surmised by comparison with RGALI, f. 2077, op. 2, d. 2, ll. 50–51 (Sostav chlenov SSK, priniatykh posle I-go Vsesoiuznogo s″ezda sovetskikh kompozitorov (s 25.III.48g. po 15.III.53g., undated report). "Titular" means those whose nationality is the same as the name of the republic in which they reside, e.g., Georgians in Georgia.

Table 6.5. Growth of Moscow Chapter and Growth of SSK SSSR, 1948–52 (335)

Year	Moscow chapter	Total SSK SSSR	Moscow as % of total
1948	4	4	100
1949	16	22	73
1950	15	44	34
1951	18	55	33
1952	5	30	17

Sources: Total SSK SSSR: RGALI, f. 2077, op. 2, d. 2, l. 58 (Undated table prepared by Pomerantseva, "Svedeniia o chislennosti i priroste chlenov SSK po sostoianiiu na 1.I.1953g.). Moscow chapter: RGALI, f. 2077, op. 2, d. 2, l. 57 (Na 27.I.53g., Spravka po Moskve, Rost organizatsii).

Note: The 1951 figure was corrected by reference to RGALI, f. 2077, op. 2, d. 2, ll. 11, 16–18 (other SSK tables, which all agree).

applicants were not preserved in the Composers' Union's central archive, the information contained in the Composers' Union's first report in 1950 does suggest that what was intended to be a Russification campaign completely backfired outside of Russian areas. At the peak of anti-Semitic, pro-Russian activity in 1949 and 1950, chapters outside Leningrad and Moscow admitted only 42 percent of Russians who applied for membership. This acceptance rate was lower than for any other group except Jews outside Moscow and Leningrad (table 6.3). Though the Central Committee no doubt approved of the promotion of titular nationals, they did not approve of the avoidance of the Russification drive that accompanied it.

This avoidance of anticosmopolitanism's Russocentrism was even more clearly displayed in a controversy over appropriate musical culture in the Central Asian republics that raged from 1950 until after Stalin's death. At issue was the interpretation of anticosmopolitanism's call to resurrect the musical classics and promote the culture of the Soviet Union's "root" nationalities. All across Central Asia, musical elites, often with the support of their political counterparts, used this call as an excuse to promote local musicians at the expense of the representatives of European musical traditions in their republics and to program a whole range of music based on a traditional Central Asian musical canon. Needless to say, neither of these trends sat well with bureaucrats in Moscow, who fought strenuously against both.

During this fight the Composers' Union again showed the decisive importance of its professional expertise. After discovering this maverick interpretation of anticosmopolitanism in Uzbekistan, the Central Committee apparatus depended on the disciplining power of the Composers' Union's professionalizing norms to define what components of Central Asian musical traditions could be considered national culture deserving of promotion and what components had to be considered "backward" in musical language or "feudal" in thematic material and worthy of eradication. The dispute raised a central contradiction of Stalinist nationalities policies and assumptions, which were stuck between efforts to promote "root" national cultures and modernizing efforts to combat supposed Central Asian backwardness. Since Composers' Union representatives in Moscow tended to share assumptions of Central Asian cultural backwardness with the Moscow-based political leadership, the Composers' Union could—and did—use heartfelt calls for professionalization to reassert an orientalist, Russifying cultural agenda throughout Central Asia.[84] Nevertheless, the statistics that demonstrate the increased promotion of titular nationals in the Composers' Union suggest that the interpretation of anticosmopolitanism that was first discovered in Uzbekistan found analogous expression all over the Soviet Union. In practice, anticosmopolitanism was used to privilege titular nationals over Russians.

So what were the final consequences of this series of personnel developments during the anticosmopolitan campaigns? Unfortunately, we do not have complete data about the nationality of Composers' Union members before 1949. But we do have complete information about the composition of the professional organization by nationality less than two weeks after Stalin's death. A complete breakdown of these data is given by nationality in table 6.6 and by nationality and local chapter in table 6.7.

In table 6.7, "Non-Russian titular" designates members of the titular nationality in areas outside of the Russian republic, Armenians in the Armenian SSK, for example. "Other" designates non-Russian, non-Jewish members whose nationality was different from the titular nationality, such as Armenians in Moscow or Ukrainians in Uzbekistan. We also have complete data about each individual admitted to the Composers' Union from 1948 to 1952.[85] Using these two data sets in combination allows a rough estimate of the personnel composition of the Composers' Union at the beginning of the anticosmopolitan campaign in January 1949 (see table 6.8). According to that rough estimate, the Composers' Union was comprised of 962 members, 37 percent of whom were Russian, 23 percent of whom were Jewish, 32 percent of whom were non-Russian titular nationals, and 8 percent of whom did not fit any of these categories. At the end of the anticosmopolitan campaigns four years later, those numbers were virtually unchanged: 38 percent Russian, 23 percent Jewish, 31 percent non-Russian titular nationals, and 8 percent other. The Russification campaign and its associated anti-Semitism both failed in the Composers' Union.

An analysis of late Stalinist cultural policy in the world of Soviet music reveals an array of intended interpretations of anticosmopolitanism—including anti-Semitism, fear of foreign influence, patriotic preoccupation with "contemporary reality," and a pro-Russian bias in the promotion of cultural forms and personnel—coexisting with rejection of anticosmopolitanism or creative, per-

---

84. Tomoff, "Uzbek Music's Separate Path."
85. RGALI, f. 2077, op. 2, d. 2, ll. 13–18 (list of accepted members). This list is summarized in table 6.4.

Table 6.6. Complete Composition of SSK SSSR by Nationality, 15 March 1953

Nationality	Members	Nationality	Members	Nationality	Members	Nationality	Members
Russian	420	Lithuanian	21	Kazakh	6	Ossetian	2
Jewish	256	Latvian	20	Polish	5	Gypsy	1
Armenian	90	Tatar	18	Bashkir	4	Italian	1
Ukrainian	72	Turkmen	11	Buriat	4	Korean	1
Georgian	60	Chuvash	9	Tadzhik	4	Lezgin	1
Estonian	27	Belorussian	8	Marii	3	Mordovan	1
Azerbaidzhani	22	German	8	Moldovan	3	Uigur	1
Uzbek	22	Kirghiz	8	Finn	2		

Source: RGALI, f. 2077, op. 2, d. 3, l. 52 (table prepared for report on membership, 15 March 1953).

Table 6.7. Composition of SSK SSSR by Nationality, 15 March 1953

Chapter	Russian		Jewish		Non-Russian Titular		Other		Total
Moscow	207	59%	111	32%	—	—	32	9%	350
Leningrad	62	54%	43	38%	—	—	9	8%	114
Gorkii	8	89%	0	0%	—	—	1	11%	9
Novosibirsk	9	90%	0	0%	—	—	1	10%	10
Rostov-na-Donu	6	55%	4	36%	—	—	1	9%	11
Sverdlovsk	12	75%	4	25%	—	—	0	0%	16
Other Russian cities	17	57%	11	37%	—	—	2	7%	30
Bashkir ASSR	0	0%	0	0%	4	44%	5	56%	9
Buriat-Mongol ASSR	0	0%	1	20%	4	80%	0	0%	5
Dagestan ASSR	0	0%	0	0%	0	0%	1	100%	1
Kabardin ASSR	0	0%	0	0%	0	0%	2	100%	2
Marii ASSR	2	40%	0	0%	3	60%	0	0%	5
Mordovian ASSR	1	50%	0	0%	1	50%	0	0%	2
Northern Ossetian ASSR	3	75%	0	0%	1	25%	0	0%	4
Tatar ASSR	3	21%	1	7%	9	64%	1	7%	14
Udmurt ASSR	2	100%	0	0%	0	0%	0	0%	2
Chuvash ASSR	2	22%	0	0%	7	78%	0	0%	9
RSFSR Total	335	56%	174	29%	29	5%	55	9%	593
Ukraine SSR	34	26%	38	29%	58	44%	3	2%	133
Belorussia SSR	7	30%	7	30%	7	30%	2	9%	23
Lithuania SSR	2	8%	1	4%	21	88%	0	0%	24
Latvia SSR	5	17%	5	17%	19	66%	0	0%	29
Estonia SSR	4	13%	0	0%	26	87%	0	0%	30
Karelo-Fin SSR	0	0%	3	60%	2	40%	0	0%	5
Georgia SSR	7	10%	0	0%	56	81%	6	9%	69
Azerbaidzhan SSR	4	11%	7	20%	22	63%	2	6%	35
Armenia SSR	0	0%	1	2%	55	98%	0	0%	56
Moldavia SSR	3	17%	8	44%	3	17%	4	22%	18
Uzbek SSR	10	26%	5	13%	17	45%	6	16%	38
Kazakh SSR	6	29%	4	19%	6	29%	5	24%	21
Kirgiz SSR	1	11%	0	0%	8	89%	0	0%	9
Tadzhik SSR	2	15%	1	8%	4	31%	6	46%	13
Turkmen SSR	1	7%	1	7%	11	73%	2	13%	15
SSK SSSR Total	420	38%	256	23%	344	31%	91	8%	1111

Source: RGALI, f. 2077, op. 2, d. 3, l. 52 (table prepared for report on membership, 15 March 1953).

haps unintended interpretations of it—including the adaptation of popular music forms understood to be Western and the promotion of titular national culture at the expense of Russian. To understand this complicated ideological terrain, we must understand the practices associated with it, and we must recognize that the onset of anticosmopolitanism corresponded to a shift in how solutions to problems in Soviet culture were perceived by political decision makers and bureaucrats in the party's cultural oversight apparatus. Whereas the problem of anticosmopolitanism was initially approached primarily in theoretical terms (for example, a preoccupation with criticism of cultural produc-

Table 6.8. Imprecise Measure of Membership, January 1949

Nationality	Estimated 1949	New members, 1949–52	March 1953
Russian	354 (37%)	66	420
Jewish	220 (23%)	36	256
Non-Russian titular	312[a] (32%)	32[a]	344
Other	76[a] (8%)	15[a]	91
Total	962 (100%)	149	1111

Source: Data extrapolated from table 6.4 and table 6.7.

Note: There were actually 989 total members in 1949; the difference can be accounted for by deaths and limited disciplinary expulsions from the Union.

[a]The division between Non-Russian titular and Other is estimated because 1952–53 data do not differentiate between the two.

tion rather than with cultural production itself), after Zhdanov's death in 1948 the Central Committee envisioned primarily personnel-based solutions rather than closer ideological control. Consequently, Central Committee bureaucrats expended a great deal of energy trying to Russify musical institutions in the abstract terms of overall personnel distribution, not in direct attacks against specific Jewish professionals. This shift to personnel-based solutions required—or at least coincided with—a shift of power from the ideologues to the professional leadership in the judging of cultural practitioners.

This general shift has profound implications for our understanding of late Stalinism. The multifaceted interpretive possibilities of ideological campaigns even at the peak of postwar Stalinism demonstrate the constantly shifting nature of Stalinist ideology and—here is the rub—the crucial importance of institutionally situated definitions, refinements, and disciplinary activities in the interpretation and dissemination of ideological constructs generated by the party elite.

From 1949 until 1953, the Composers' Union was able to circumvent aspects of ideological campaigns that its leaders considered particularly odious. The failure of anticosmopolitanism's anti-Semitic aspect in the music profession, exceptional though it may have been, suggests that authority derived from technical expertise provided cultural professionals with the agency they needed to shirk even the most strident ideological demands. This failure is particularly striking considering the ambivalence about popular music in the Central Committee apparatus, the discomfort that bureaucrats felt about the popularity of Western dance genres among Soviet youth, and the extreme prominence of Jewish composers among elite popular song composers. Stalinist ideology should thus be understood as flexible, mutable, and constitutive of the crucial power of interpretation, implementation, and limited avoidance that resided with the experts who comprised the Soviet cultural elite.

The anticosmopolitan campaigns also coincided with the culmination of the long rise of the Composers' Union from a marginal, inadequately provisioned group before the war to the most powerful institution in Soviet musical life upon Stalin's death. Though the party intervention of 1948 had been traumatic, that intervention had not fundamentally altered the importance of technical expertise in the postwar Stalinist system. Professionals retained agency during the anticosmopolitan campaigns that plagued Stalin's final years. They used that agency to complete the rise of the Composers' Union, marginalizing the Committee on Artistic Affairs and establishing themselves as the dominant force in Soviet musical life. This rise of institutional power and preservation of professional agency is further demonstrated by an examination of the results of party intervention and the professional response in areas outside the immediate glare of the ideological campaigns.

CHAPTER 7

The Results of Party Intervention

Zhdanovshchina, the brouhaha of 1948, and the anticosmopolitanism campaigns all pressed on the boundary between politics and professional life in areas of particular concern to the party elite. But these successive interventions also created general conditions that structured the development of the music profession in areas outside the immediate attention of the party. We have already seen how the Composers' Union and its leadership responded to the direct challenges of anticosmopolitanism, utilizing the expertise it embodied to enforce the Russification of musical culture in Central Asia while simultaneously blocking the most egregious anti-Semitic elements of the campaign in personnel circles and successfully fighting off the combined efforts of the Committee on Artistic Affairs and Ministry of Higher Education to limit the production of new composers at conservatories in Russia and Ukraine. We have seen how professional monopolization of expertise translated into professional agency in areas that received direct attention during party intervention throughout the postwar period. But how did party intervention affect the composition and activities of the professional organization outside these areas of special party attention? Answering this question requires attention to institutional changes, personnel transformations, and patterns of professional discussion in the Composers' Union after 1948.

An examination of these areas demonstrates that although the Composers' Union underwent substantial internal transformations in response to party intervention, it nevertheless maintained a sphere in which professional evaluation was decisive. Increasingly distant professionals exhibited their agency by shifting categories of expertise in the Composers' Union creative apparatus, by redistributing the concentration of creative authority within the Union, and by retreating behind opaque technical discussions in order to exchange artistic ideas and generate and deploy professional authority that was sometimes at odds with the dictates of the party agenda. The paradoxical result of this series of party interventions into musical life was a striking professional consolidation.

The Creative Apparatus

During the Stalin period, the Composers' Union categorized expertise and experts in two fundamental ways, according to the creative product (genre) and according to the creative producer (cadres). When it created categories, the Composers' Union institutionalized them in a creative apparatus that was intended to organize the professional activities of its members. The two fundamental principles were always present in one way or another, and the theoretical and practical tension between them was never completely resolved, but patterns of interaction between the two are clearly discernible. In 1939 the dominant paradigm was that of the creative product: it was a primarily genre-based system. During the war, the Composers' Union found this system inadequate and created a parallel system of consultation designed to address the professional development needs of individual composers and musicologists regardless of their preferred genres. Simultaneously individualized and overarching, the consultation system was the beginning of a more thorough shift to an organizational principle based on cadres. In the 1948 reorganization, the new Secretariat of the Composers' Union created a system that integrated both the genre and cadre principles into a complete dual creative apparatus of genre-based sections and cadre-based commissions. It took two years to delineate how the sections and commissions interacted, but by late 1949 it was clear that the Composers' Union's creative work would be done primarily by the genre-based sections while the cadre-based commissions would be critical institutional sites for helping the sections assimilate marginalized professionals from the periphery, musicologists, military musicians, and young composers.[1]

After the direct party intervention of 1948, this dual creative apparatus undertook several crucial new tasks. Some tasks demonstrated the extension of the profession's authority to areas it had earlier sought to influence with only partial success. For example, the Secretariat created a new Composers' Union editorial board, initially called the Commission for Publication and Print Institutions, to which the genre-based creative sections were supposed to recommend pieces for publication.[2] This reform had the effect of subsuming publication within the creative apparatus of the Composers' Union, though government publishing houses like Muzgiz still remained crucial publication outlets.

Other new tasks profoundly affected how the Composers' Union functioned internally. Most significantly, the all-USSR Composers' Union more successfully extended its reach outside the Russian cultural capitals of Moscow and Leningrad. The old Orgkom had always intended to coordinate the activities of all Composers' Union chapters, but it had never done so effectively, despite

1. For a detailed institutional analysis of this process as it emerged over time, see Tomoff, "Creative Union," chap. 6.
2. RGALI, f. 2077, op. 1, d. 238, ll. 14–14ob. (Protokol #6, 30 Mar 1948).

local chapters' frequent pleas for more attention and the additional resources they thought would accompany it.[3] Central attention was extended in large part through the new cadre-based Commission for the Direction of the Creativity of the Composers of the USSR and a similarly titled Commission for the RSFSR.[4] These new commissions were charged with what amounted to a new task for the Composers' Union.

In July 1948 the Secretariat established that the Commission for the USSR would render broad organizational and creative assistance to Composers' Union chapters in the national republics. The commission's leaders immediately familiarized themselves with works by the relevant composers and then prepared to host a ten-day music festival for composers from particularly neglected areas, such as the Transcaucasus, the Baltics, and Central Asia. They also resolved to call the most talented composers from many national republics to Moscow for consultation and to develop their own systematic travel plan whereby they could regularly visit each national republic and its Composers' Union chapter. Though the all-USSR Composers' Union had always maintained ties with its chapters everywhere, this was the first *systematic* plan designed to maintain and extend those ties in practice.[5]

Another early manifestation of this new, catholic interpretation of its responsibility to organize *all* professionals was the creation of personnel files for all creative cadres. In March 1948 the Secretariat ordered local unions to file comprehensive personnel information no later than early April.[6] Once this system of personnel files was in place, the central bodies began systematically sending representatives to the periphery. Experts in the commission system were sent to offer creative help, and other special representatives were sent to provide organizational assistance.[7] These trips were so frequent as to constitute a new phenomenon, distinguished, for example, from earlier trips to assist peripheral organizations prepare for special events, such as a plenary session.[8] The operation of the Commission for the USSR and the Commission for the RSFSR thus entailed a real change in how the Composers' Union functioned.

3. For examples, see the speeches of several composers from the national republics (especially Central Asia) during the 1946 SSK Plenum: "Vystupleniia k plenumu," *Sovetskaia muzyka,* 1946, no. 10:33–89. Similar sentiments were expressed in the earlier 1944 plenary meeting as well; RGALI, f. 2077, op. 1, d. 93 (Orgkom plenary session stenogram, 1–7 Apr 1944), esp. ll. 19–35, 41–48, 75–84, 213–16.

4. These are shortened hereafter as "Commission for the USSR" and "Commission for the RSFSR."

5. RGALI, f. 2077, op. 1, d. 238, ll. 54–55 (Protokol #23, 2–3 Jul 1948), pt. 1.

6. Ibid., d. 234, ll. 12–13 (Protokol #5, 19 Mar 1948). Personnel information included everything from name, address, autobiography, and party membership to a complete works list, to be updated quarterly.

7. Ibid., d. 340, ll. 12–13, 17, 26, 35, 48 (*Prikazy* sending commission representatives for creative help, 1949) and ll. 37, 42, 59, 61–64, 69, 101, 106 (*Prikazy* sending other representatives for organizational help, 1949).

8. Ibid., ll. 71–72, 74, 76–78, 81–83, 96ob., 99 (*Prikazy* ordering plenum preparation trips, 1949).

The revamped creative apparatus also significantly increased its activities in more mundane areas of professional life. For example, it became clear that the genre-based sections were supposed to maintain a collegial attitude between members and keep their interaction at an appropriately professional level so that squabbles would not make it to the Secretariat.[9]

The creative sections also became more systematically involved in securing funding for their active members. Though the creative apparatus had always occasionally supported requests to fund individual composers, this practice was not systematized until 1948. In Secretariat meetings throughout the year, more and more requests for funding were supported by creative sections or commissions.[10] At the end of the year, this ad hoc process was formalized to ensure that sections and commissions would determine whether a piece funded by the Composers' Union met the criteria of the original funding agreement and then pass their decisions on for approval.[11] Composers were to present their pieces to the leadership body (*biuro*) of the section or commission through which they had initially received funding. That *biuro*'s decision would then be approved by the secretary who was responsible for that section or commission and then be checked by the Finance Department before receiving final approval at a meeting of the Secretariat. In practice, section and commission decisions were almost never countermanded by the higher bodies.[12]

The creative apparatus of the Composers' Union thus experienced significant changes in its organizational structure and fundamental tasks after 1948. Such changes may suggest that party intervention successfully subjugated and subsequently dominated the Union. However, the new structure and tasks continued to be consistent with professionally determined priorities, and the newly solidified organizational system streamlined the production of new professionals as determined by existing leaders within the creative apparatus.

The Experts: Social Data about the Creative Leadership

Throughout their existence, the various systems of categorization of expertise in the Composers' Union incited professional and political conflict over whose authority would define good music. In order to understand that conflict, we must understand not just the professional and political differences between experts within the Composers' Union but the social divisions as well. This sec-

---

9. RGALI, f. 2077, op. 1, d. 238, l. 127 (Protokol #43, 6 Nov 1948), pt. 2.

10. Ibid., l. 118 (Protokol #40, 19 Oct 1948), pt. 3.; l. 130 (Protokol #44, 11 Nov 1948), pt. 2.

11. Ibid., ll. 146–47 (Protokol #48, 26 Nov 1948), pt. 2.

12. For one of few counterexamples, see RGALI, f. 2077, op. 1, d. 338, l. 72 (Protokol #13, 29 Mar 1949). The Secretariat overturned a Children's Music Section recommendation about a composer's working resort trip.

tion examines data on the nearly two hundred individuals who held positions of leadership on a commission or section during the first decade of the all-USSR Composers' Union.

There were three key areas in which composers and critics differed in *social* terms: party membership, age, and professional tenure. An examination of the leadership of sections and commissions within the Composers' Union in these three categories elucidates the influence of a combination of generational change and party membership on the social structure of the Union's creative apparatus. And if we focus further on a small group of the most influential professionals, we see that changes in this social structure coincided with a shift in the concentration of internal authority within the Union's bureaucratic apparatus.

Commission and section leaders in the creative apparatus formed a reservoir of internal professional authority, but not necessarily nonprofessional authority. This pool of leaders was less influenced by the intersection of the professional arena with other arenas in which authority was created and deployed. Such prominent figures as Khachaturian, Glier, and Khrennikov hardly figure in the discussion here because they rarely served on the sections and commissions or their directing leadership boards. Instead, the individuals about whom this discussion is relevant were those composers, theoreticians, and critics who were appointed to section and commission leadership panels by the Orgkom or Secretariat. Their appointments were managed entirely within the profession, and unlike the leaders of the Composers' Union as a whole, section and commission leaders were not approved by any outside group. Tracking them before, during, and after direct party intervention helps understand the profession's response.

The data that follow refer to people who were appointed to creative leadership positions at a given time and to an overall body of leaders. Careful readers will notice that the sum for all time periods is quite a bit larger than the total number of leaders. This apparent inconsistency results from the fact that many were appointed more than once and to more than one commission or section. Since this analysis is not concerned with the total number of individuals in the creative apparatus at any one time but with active changes in its social structure, each appointment cohort is treated as a distinct entity. A substantial number of repeat appearances are ignored. For the record, forty-six people were appointed in 1939, thirty-eight appointees were added during the war, thirty more in the immediate postwar period, fifty-two in 1948, and twenty-two in 1949.

The first social category that divided Composers' Union members was party membership. Of the 188 people who were appointed to commission and section leadership between 1939 and 1949, party membership data are available on 160.[13] Considering that my sources were likely to include composers and

13. The main biographical source for this section is the relatively comprehensive, six-volume

Table 7.1. Party Membership of Creative Apparatus Leadership, 1939–49

Appointment Period	Number of Appointees	Party Members at Appointment	Eventual Party Members
1939	46	2 (4%)	10 (22%)
1941–44	51	9 (18%)	12 (24%)
1945–47	73	14 (19%)	18 (25%)
1948	115	30 (26%)	38 (33%)
1949	94	20 (21%)	25 (27%)
Total	188	34 (18%)	49 (26%)

Sources: See note 13.

critics who were also party members, I have assumed that the remaining twenty-eight were not members. These data are summarized in table 7.1.

Thus, 26 percent of commission and section leaders were party members at some point in their lives. However, only 70 percent of eventual party members were party members when they were first appointed to a leadership position. As a rule, party members were considerably younger than their nonparty colleagues. In 1945 the average age of the party members regardless of when they joined the party was forty; the average age of their nonparty colleagues was forty-seven. Not surprisingly, considering this age difference, party members reached professional maturity at a considerably later date. Whereas nonparty leaders had been professionals for twenty-one years on average in 1945, party members had been practicing their profession for only thirteen years. This generational difference between party members and their nonparty colleagues is particularly significant in light of the interesting generational dynamics revealed below.

Party members made up just over one-quarter of the commission and section leadership. Though not surprising, these data become more interesting when they are charted over time. After reading traditional narratives about the party's domination of the arts, one might expect party membership of these crucial creative leadership bodies to increase steadily over time until 1948, when they would jump dramatically and then remain high. That is not what actually happened.

In 1939 forty-six composers and critics were named to the commissions and sections. Of those, only two were members of the party—just four percent. Of those appointed, ten (22 percent) would eventually join the party, making the 1939 cohort of appointees only slightly less party weighted than the average for the whole group. During the war, the Orgkom appointed fifty-one commission

---

Muzykal'naia entsiklopediia. The single most useful English-language biographical source, also drawn on here, is Allan Ho and Dmitry Feofanov, *Biographical Dictionary of Russian/Soviet Composers* (New York: Greenwood Press, 1989), which does not as a rule include party membership data.

and section leaders, and of those, nine were party members at the time of their appointment. That 18 percent of all appointees is a dramatic increase over 1939—more than a fourfold leap in party appointees. However, what seems like a monumental jump is really less spectacular when it becomes clear that only 24 percent of wartime appointees ever joined the party. That is only slightly more than the 1939 cohort and still slightly less than the average. The much larger apparent jump reflects the fact that Composers' Union members, like their counterparts elsewhere in Soviet society, joined the party at a much higher rate during the war than at any other time.[14] In fact, for the whole group of 188, the mean year to join the party was 1942.

In the years of increasing ideological tension between the end of the war and the 1948 brouhaha—a time when the party was actively and publicly trying to establish a "party line" in the arts and sciences, the percentage of appointees who were party members at the time of their appointment and who eventually became party members remained virtually unchanged. After the big wave of joining the party during the war, party members basically remained exactly as prominent in the section and commission leadership as they had been during it.

We would expect a big surge in party membership among creative leaders in 1948, and that is exactly what happened. In the thorough restructuring of the commission and section apparatus of 1948, the Secretariat appointed 115 people to leadership positions, fully a third more than at any other time. Thirty (26 percent) were party members in 1948, and a full third (thirty-eight individuals) eventually joined. It was no secret that the party sought to assert its power over the music profession, and so it did.

Much more surprising is how quickly those numbers decreased immediately after 1948, especially considering the commencement of the full-blown anti-cosmopolitanism campaign in 1949. That year, the Secretariat appointed ninety-four composers and musicologists to creative leadership positions, but only 21 percent (twenty individuals) were party members at the time of their appointment, and only 27 percent ever joined the party. The massive infusion of party members into the creative leadership of the Composers' Union dropped sharply. So rather than the slow-rise, big-jump, steady-level pattern that we might have expected, what actually happened was a big jump in the rates of musicians *joining* the party during the war in the midst of a relatively steady pattern of appointment of party members to creative leadership positions until 1948. In 1948 the expected big jump happened, but it immediately fell off in 1949.

The other major social factors to consider are the age and professional tenure of leaders in the creative apparatus. Analyzing these factors can determine whether or not a significant event in 1939–49 was the changing of the guard in generational terms. The mean age and professional tenure (figured from conservatory graduation or equivalent) of a member of the creative leadership in 1939 were forty and thirteen years, respectively. Four years later, in 1943, the

14. Rigby, *Communist Party Membership*, 236–72.

means were forty-five and eighteen, and in 1946 they were forty-six and nine-teen. In other words, these data suggest that the same generation was in power for the entire period from 1939 to 1946. This trend continued through the up-heaval of 1948, when the means were forty-seven and twenty—one year later, one year older. In 1949, appointees got even older—the means were forty-nine years of age and twenty-three years of professional activity. The generation that was in power in 1939 remained in power in 1949, with only slight oscillations in the general mix. In fact, for the entire period the mean year of birth ranged only from 1898 to 1901, and the year of graduation (or equivalent) only from 1925 to 1928. Not much change in generation. Or so it would seem.

Closer examination of the data, however, reveals an entirely different—and significant—story. When the appointees are divided into those trained before and after the Revolution, a whole new, quite complicated story emerges. Ac-cording to that account, the most significant social development in the creative apparatus during the 1940s was not exactly a generational *shift* (that is, a re-placement of one generation with another) but a generational *split* (a widened gap between two concurrent generations), which suggests a subgenerational shift within prerevolutionary professionals.

In order to demonstrate this complicated development, two factors must be examined. The first factor is the percentage of prerevolutionary professionals among appointees in a given period. The second factor is the mean year of pro-fessional maturity among the two different groups. Analysis of the percentages of members of different generations shows a steady four-to-one ratio of new to old professionals at the beginning and end of the decade, with a sharp decrease in the number of old professionals after the war and a big resurgence of the older generation in 1948 and especially 1949. Analysis of conservatory gradu-ation dates demonstrates that within this overall pattern, the old generation was getting even older, and the younger generation was getting younger.

From 1939 through almost the end of the war in 1944, prerevolutionary pro-fessionals comprised roughly 20 percent of the commission and section leader-ship. As the profession restocked its commissions and sections to face the challenges of the postwar world, the relative number of prerevolutionary pro-fessionals appointed to those commissions and sections dropped by nearly half—to just 13 percent. In the tumultuous 1948, the older professionals made something of a rally, rising to 16 percent of the appointees, but in 1949 they truly reasserted themselves, jumping by almost a third to 21 percent of all ap-pointees. There were relatively more prerevolutionary professionals appointed to leadership positions in 1949 than there had been a decade earlier!

At the same time, those older professionals got much older while the younger professionals got younger. In 1939 the mean year of professional maturity among the older generation was 1910, and among the younger generation it was 1929. During the war years, the mean for the older generation climbed to 1911, where it stayed until 1948. At the same time, the mean for the younger generation remained unchanged and then moved up a year to 1930 for the immediate postwar period. Then, in 1948, something strange happened. The mean year of professional maturity among the older generation *dropped* fully three years to 1908 while that for the younger generation rose to 1931. In 1949 the older generation's mean stayed at 1908 while the younger generation's dropped just a year to 1930. In other words, in 1948 a small, younger group within the older generation seems to have been replaced by a larger, older group. As we shall see, this was an important development. At the same, members of the younger generation either hung on or were replaced by contemporaries of roughly the same age.

So party membership among appointees stayed relatively stable until it leaped in 1948 and then dropped off again in 1949, and there was a complicated generational shift happening throughout the postwar period. Was there a correlation? A significant one. In the immediate postwar period, there were *no* party members among those in the older generation who were appointed to creative leadership positions. That was not a surprise, for there had only been one appointed, ever, and he was appointed in 1939 before he joined the party. On the other hand, 24 percent of younger appointees were party members, and 29 percent eventually joined. In 1948, when the older generation began its comeback, none of the appointees were party members, though one was to join later. And when older composers reasserted themselves in 1949, they still had only one party member in their ranks. Significantly, the older generation never contributed party members to the creative leadership.[15] On the other hand, in 1948, 35 percent of younger appointees were party members, and fully 42 percent eventually joined. Though those numbers dropped back a bit (to 30 percent and 38 percent) in 1949, they still remained much higher than both the average for the whole group and for any other period except 1948 itself. Taken together, these two developments demonstrate that the 1948–49 period saw older members of the older generation replace younger ones while party members among the younger generation replaced their contemporaries. The striking significance of this development is revealed in the next section's analysis of professional politics.

Within this larger group of creative leaders, a much smaller group of composers and musicologists garnered the most professional authority within the Composers' Union. Because they used their leadership positions to disseminate their visions of good music, all 188 members of the section and commission leadership had significant professional authority. To be appointed to a leadership position in the creative apparatus was a sign that one's colleagues respected one's creative vision and ability to execute it and to evaluate others' competence. In other words, the creative apparatus leadership was the profession's reservoir of internal authority.

---

15. Lack of party representation among prerevolutionary professionals was a constant feature of Stalin-era musical life. Amy Nelson has pointed out that in the 1920s and 1930s, when prerevolutionary professionals were the only available top administrative experts, the Moscow Conservatory was often the *only* institution of higher education in the Soviet Union not directed by a party member; Nelson, *Music for the Revolution*, 243.

Within that reservoir, however, a group of seventeen composers and critics were the most prominent and respected in the profession.[16] At the top of the list, a tiny group stood out in a nearly dominant position. The composer and musicologist Boris Asaf'ev was the most prominent single individual, respected by all camps within the Composers' Union. Next most prominent was a troika of composers whose authority was clearly higher than the rest—Shostakovich, Prokofiev, and Miaskovskii. The music or activities of each of these four received repeated attention in many more major articles throughout the Stalin period than anyone else.

In terms of the social data presented in this section, these seventeen most authoritative professionals were not representative of the rest of the creative apparatus's leadership, to which most of them belonged (fifteen held a leadership position in at least one section or commission). A higher percentage of them (29 percent) were professionals before the Revolution, and more of them (47 percent) were, or eventually became party members. Members of the older generation had been professionals for longer than the average for their contemporaries over the whole period, but they were slightly less experienced than the

---

16. The seventeen were the following: Boris Asaf'ev, Nikolai Miaskovskii, Sergei Prokof'ev, Dmitrii Shostakovich, Aleksandr Vasilievich Aleksandrov, Reinhold Glier, Dmitrii Kabalevskii, Aram Khachaturian, Marian Koval', Iurii Shaporin, Vissarion Shebalin, Isaak Dunaevskii, Ivan Dzerzhinskii, Grigorii Shneerson, Vasilii Solov'ev-Sedoi, Viktor Vinogradov, and Vladimir Zakharov. In order to isolate this group, I conducted a statistical analysis of major articles in *Sovetskaia muzyka* to determine authority by measuring the attention that a professional's musical opinion commanded, that is, the praise required if a piece was considered good and the need to refute that opinion if a piece was considered bad. I also used my impressionistic evaluation of other sources (too numerous or far-flung to count precisely) to make minor adjustments to the list, to which Kabalevskii and Shaporin were added. These additional sources include prominence in articles about groups of composers, leadership appointments in professionally significant but not self-contained institutions (like conservatories), and editorship of the journal.

The following is a summary of how I used *Sovetskaia muzyka* appearances as a measure of internal authority. I developed an overall score for each Union member who appeared as the subject of a major article or as the author of three significant articles in a given year and who appeared again in at least one other year. For composers, the score was simply the number of major articles about the individuals or their work, including a number of Stalin Prize–related articles. Unless an article strictly compared two individuals, articles that discussed the music of several different composers have not been included. For critics, theorists, and historians, the score was the number of significant articles to appear in *Sovetskaia muzyka,* though heavily weighted in favor of policy-setting articles (multiplied by three for major policies; multiplied by two for minor ones). Only those who penned three articles (at least one of them major) in a single year and appeared in other years are listed. The count does not include editorials, though for that reason all editorial board members were added to my list and subjectively boosted when I went from this artificial score to a less mechanistic evaluation. Crossover types were categorized by their primary occupation (e.g., Asaf'ev as a musicologist, Khrennikov as a composer, Koval' as a musicologist, Shostakovich as a composer), though some extra weight was added for crossover appearances (especially for Asaf'ev and Khrennikov). Strictly position-related articles were not included (e.g., articles written by Khachaturian and Khrennikov *because of* their leadership positions). Years of coverage were the following: most of 1939, all of 1940 by index but not by close examination (therefore less accurate for composers than for musicologists), most of 1941, the war bulletins (except for issue 3, which was completely historical), and 1946–49 in full.

post-1948 cohort. Their mean year of conservatory graduation was 1909. Similarly the members of the younger generation were more experienced than their contemporaries—their mean year of professional maturity was 1927. On the other hand, more members of the younger generation eventually became party members than even their contemporaries in the party-dominated appointee cohort of 1948. Fifty-eight percent eventually joined the party, though only 27 percent were party members when they were first appointed to a leadership position within the creative apparatus.

These data do not reveal anything particularly surprising about the most authoritative professionals—they were older, more experienced, and more likely to be members of the party than their less prominent colleagues. Still, party membership even within this most prominent group was not overwhelming. Less than half were party members. In fact, though Shostakovich joined the party in 1960, none of the most dominant four were party members during the Stalin period, and three of them (again Shostakovich is the exception) were professionals before the Revolution. These observations demonstrate that a composer could reach the pinnacle of respect within the profession without joining the party. But what about assuming a leadership position within the creative apparatus?

Up to this point, I have not discussed the upper leadership bodies of the all-USSR Composers' Union, the Orgkom (1939–48) and the Secretariat (1948 on), because as institutions they did not embody any category of professional expertise and because membership on them did not necessarily constitute creative or intellectual authority. This is not to say that members of the Orgkom and Secretariat could not and did not exercise a great deal of power from their positions, just that those positions were not necessarily indicators of *professional authority among their colleagues*. However, analyzing the membership of these two institutions with an eye to the seventeen most internally authoritative professionals reveals a significant shift in the distribution of the internal professional authority within the Composers' Union's bureaucratic structure.

The most prominent professionals were packed into the Orgkom but not into the later Secretariat. When it was established in 1939, the Orgkom's twenty-four members included ten of the seventeen experts who had the most authority within the profession, and most of the others represented non-Russian republics and enjoyed tremendous authority there. The mainly figurehead chairman of the Orgkom (Glier), the de facto head (Khachaturian), and the assistant chairman (Dunaevskii) all numbered among the seventeen, and three of the four most prominent composers were members of the Orgkom (only Prokofiev was not).[17] When the Secretariat was approved by the Politburo in 1948, it contained just six members, three (two in 1949) of whom were among the seventeen most prominent professionals. However, only Asaf'ev was in the top four,

---

17. RGALI, f. 2077, op. 1, d. 21, l. 1 (Postanovlenie SNK SSSR #611, "Ob organizatsii Soiuza sovetskikh kompozitorov," 4 May 1939).

and he was too elderly and ill to be more than a figurehead until his death in January 1949.[18] Later, an additional member was added, and he (Vasilii Kukharskii) was not among the most respected professionals.[19] Even those who were well respected (Vladimir Zakharov and Marian Koval') were not nearly of the same internal stature as many of those who had been replaced during the transformation of the Composers' Union in 1948. Though the percentage of the most authoritative seventeen in the main leadership body changed little, the drop in the size of the Secretariat from the Orgkom and the departure of the big four entailed a dramatic decrease in the concentration of internal professional authority in the upper leadership body of the Composers' Union after 1948.[20]

On the other hand, an increasing number of these most prominent composers appeared as leaders in the creative apparatus over time. In 1939 only five of them were appointed to the creative apparatus, and among the big four, only Miaskovskii held such a position. During the war a majority of these professionals were appointed to the creative apparatus for the first time. Three were appointed in 1943, and six more in 1944, mostly in connection with the creation and expansion of the consultation system. Since the goal of that system was to put experienced, well-respected professionals in contact with young, developing ones, even members of the Orgkom were pulled into the creative apparatus for the first time. By 1944 fourteen of the seventeen, and all four of the most prominent, had been in the apparatus, though one (the international music specialist Grigorii Shneerson) had dropped out, never to return. Since two were never appointed, it is clear that the high-water mark was reached at the end of the war, when ten of the seventeen were in the Orgkom and thirteen were in the creative apparatus.

I have already demonstrated that 1948 saw a decrease in the concentration of those with the most authority in the Union's upper leadership body. But what of the creative apparatus? During the complete restructuring of 1948, ten of them, including two of the big four, were reappointed to leadership positions in the apparatus. Because three of the big four were singled out for special attack in 1948, and since songwriter and military conductor A. V. Aleksandrov died in 1946 (thus removing a likely beneficiary of the 1948 transformation from the mix), this high number is somewhat surprising. In 1949, when the authority of the Secretariat became even more watered down after the death of Asaf'ev, six of the seventeen were reappointed to the creative apparatus and another two did not come up for review. In other words, by the end of 1949 only

18. RGASPI, f. 17, op. 3, d. 1070, l. 34, pt. 124 (Politburo Protokol #63, 12 May 1948).

19. RGALI, f. 2077, op. 1, d. 339, l. 122 (Protokol #53, 18 Oct 1949).

20. Tikhon Khrennikov attributes the success of the Composers' Union to what he called a concentration of the most authoritative composers in the Soviet Union in these upper-leadership bodies—a direct contradiction of my argument here. However, as evidence, he cited composers who were in leadership positions in the 1960s and 1970s, when the balance of creative authority may indeed have returned to the upper leadership (personal communication, 30 Aug 1999).

fifteen of the seventeen were still alive, and eight of them were still in creative leadership positions. When coupled with the fact that two of the remaining three most prominent figures were reappointed and none remained in the Secretariat, this relatively high number demonstrates that there was a shift in the location of professional authority within the Composers' Union from the upper leadership to the creative apparatus.

This shift can be summarized quite simply. In 1939 the most prominent composers were primarily concentrated in the Orgkom. During the war, they retained their Orgkom presence while expanding their participation in the creative apparatus. After 1948, the most prominent composers were no longer members of the professional organization's top leadership body, the Secretariat, but they were still significant members of the creative apparatus's sections and commissions. The slight decrease in the percentage of the seventeen most prominent composers in the creative apparatus coincided with a sharp increase in the number of prerevolutionary professionals. Considering the general respect paid older professionals within the Soviet music profession, this sharp increase in their numbers more than compensated for the slight drop in the membership of the most prominent composers in the creative apparatus. The concentration of internal professional authority thus shifted from the central body to the creative apparatus after going through a critical wartime phase in which the most authoritative professionals occupied both areas. Understanding the significance of this shift requires a brief rehearsal of the contours of professional politics before and after the peak of postwar party intervention.

Professional Politics and Expertise

The subcommittees of the creative apparatus in the Composers' Union were sites for professional and political conflict. Conflict within and between the creative sections and commissions often touched on the most fundamental divisions within the profession. The winners could potentially dominate their expert opponents and impose their musical visions on the profession as a whole. Though the authority of certain individuals, such as the seventeen discussed in the previous section, transcended them, these professional conflicts therefore established the contours of hierarchies of internal authority between groups of experts.

Composers' Union members typically fell into two groups, which I call "highbrow" and "populist." Partial holdovers from long-standing professional conflicts that reached their most vociferous polemical level in the late 1920s, these groups were sometimes more, sometimes less visible and confrontational.[21] From a nascent institutional presence in 1939, they went through a

---

21. For musical politics in the 1920s, including a tripartite categorization of divisions within the music world, see Nelson, *Music for the Revolution.*

period of peaceful and productive coexistence during the war, though the social conditions of the war itself fundamentally altered the contours of the group and prepared the way for open conflict after the war. In the immediate postwar period, two roughly defined camps emerged to struggle for preeminence in the profession. At stake were both the power to define good music in Soviet society and access to the scarce resources distributed by the Soviet state. The party intervention of 1948 brought this conflict to a head, and in the aftermath of the intervention, the conflict restructured the creative apparatus of the Composers' Union in ways we have already seen. But how was professional conflict institutionalized in the Composers' Union, and what does that conflict tell us about expertise, experts, and the distribution of authority within the professional organization after party intervention?

Though the division between highbrow and populist composers never assumed an official institutional structure, it virtually defined the contours of professional conflict all the way through the brouhaha in 1948. Highbrow composers tended to compose music in the traditional forms of symphonic and chamber music, while populist composers tended to compose songs, dance music, and military marches. Consequently, the categorization of expertise by genre led to the unofficial institutionalization of competing professional viewpoints.

Through the war and the early years of the Zhdanovshchina, an uneasy balance between these camps was maintained through a series of often counteracting institutional reforms.[22] The party intervention of 1948 was, on the whole, a victory for the populists, but not completely so. Populists gained control of the Secretariat, the new governing body of the Composers' Union. But highbrow sections continued to exist, and highbrow composers continued to hold leadership positions within the creative apparatus. More importantly, the "party line" definition of good music contained a component that was not just significant but critically important to some highbrow composers and critics. The praise that the Central Committee paid the Russian classics and the call to continue to develop the classical tradition meant that some composers of serious symphonic music, choral music, and even chamber music were explicitly encouraged to continue to write the music that they sincerely thought was best.

In fact, the appointment of these highbrow composers to leadership positions within the creative apparatus explains the odd generational dynamics detailed earlier in this chapter. Encouraging composers who perpetuated Russian classical traditions meant appointing composers who were trained by the prerevolutionary greats Nikolai Rimsky-Korsakov, Sergei Taneev, and Anatol Liadov. They were the oldest composers in the Composers' Union in 1948 and 1949, but their time had come again. They replaced their somewhat more adventurous, slightly younger colleagues among the prerevolutionary professionals.

Examining professional politics helps to explain both the changing author-

---

22. For details of these institutional machinations, see Tomoff, "Creative Union," chap. 6.

ity between competing groups in the midst of changing institutional forms and the odd shifts in the social structure of the leadership of the creative apparatus. As we have seen, during the postwar years the Composers' Union shifted its organizational paradigm, sustained a complicated generational split that placed young professionals who were party members alongside the oldest prerevolutionary professionals in the leadership of its creative apparatus, and shifted the concentration of the most prominent, authoritative professionals from its top leadership body to the creative apparatus. Taken together, these developments suggest that the Composers' Union underwent a significant transformation in the way it administered the expert knowledge that was its main reason for existing.

Such a significant transformation prompted by party intervention may seem to undermine my contention that the Composers' Union was a professional organization that utilized its monopolization of musical expertise to dominate musical production and preserve a sphere of professional agency. Not so. After all, this profession certainly did not act autonomously of political power or party intervention. Instead, in the face of that intervention, professionals used their agency to adopt strategies that simultaneously allowed them to participate in party-directed projects or, increasingly, to avoid those projects, and to preserve a realm of professional action. One of those strategies was to preserve the reorganized and expanded creative apparatus as a professional sphere.

By the end of the 1940s, the upper leadership body sat atop a system that sought to incorporate all types of composers from all over the Soviet Union and to direct their creative activity. The Secretariat had become an administrative body, a professional control center that coordinated the professional work carried out by the creative apparatus. At the same time, its own internal professional authority was surpassed by the creative apparatus that it administered. The Secretariat thus oversaw a bureaucratic structure that allowed competing viewpoints to survive even in the context of the partial victory of one camp over the other. In so doing, it put in place an institutional structure that preserved professional agency and helped its professionals produce music that was meaningful to audiences at home and abroad during the ideologically tense atmosphere of the late 1940s, throughout the virulent anticosmopolitanism campaign, and far beyond the Stalin period.

Profession Ascendant, Distant Professionals

Even in the months immediately following the party intervention, the new leadership tried to improve the status of the professional organization. The Secretariat sent delegations to Composers' Union chapters all across the Soviet Union and vigorously sought control over ever greater realms of musical production, mostly at the expense of the now rapidly declining Committee on Artistic Affairs. By the end of 1948, the Composers' Union was the most powerful institution in the music realm, but individual composers were more alienated than ever.

During the 1948 realignment of the Composers' Union and Muzfond, the Committee on Artistic Affairs, the Bol'shoi Theater, and the Central Committee apparatus, the Composers' Union expanded and solidified its institutional control over areas of music policy that had previously been out of reach. One of the most dramatic exhibitions of this new institutional power took place in late July 1948 when representatives from the Moscow Philharmonic and the Committee on Artistic Affairs presented the Composers' Union Secretariat information about the concert series that were due to begin in the autumn of that year. That the Philharmonic and VKI had to report to the Composers' Union at all was a new development that indicated the professional body's power was increasing. The Secretariat's decision cemented that power, both rhetorically and in practice. It cast itself as the authoritative interpreter of the Central Committee resolution's ramifications in the realm of music performance. The Secretariat claimed that the Philharmonic had never adequately popularized compositions by Soviet composers, and its concert plans for the 1948–49 season did nothing to remedy that past oversight.[23] The Composers' Union leadership thus made the rhetorical case for its supremacy of judgment.

More significantly, the Secretariat also flexed its new institutional muscle in practical terms. It formed a commission comprised of three Composers' Union leaders and one member of the Moscow Philharmonic to draft a new concert series that included the most valuable works of Soviet composers over the preceding thirty years. A representative from the Secretariat (Aleksei Ikonnikov), the heads of two Composers' Union creative subcommittees (the composers Aleksandr Veprik of the Symphonic Music Section and Sergei Balasanian of the Commission for the USSR), and just one representative from the Moscow Philharmonic (K. K. Sezhenskii) were to determine the Philharmonic's programming for the next season.[24] The Secretariat also placed the Philharmonic's club concert activities in the hands of the Mass Musical Genres Section of the Composers' Union and its head, Boris Terent'ev.[25] The decision was not just temporary; the Philharmonic and Committee on Artistic Affairs were both instructed to create a special bureau within the Philharmonic to develop three-year plans to increase the exposure of new Soviet music.[26]

In mid-August the move was solidified when the Secretariat approved the list prepared by the special commission and even set out a series of subscription

23. RGALI, f. 2077, op. 1, d. 234, ll. 64–65 (Protokol #27, 28 Jul 1948).

24. A. A. Ikonnikov was a musicologist and long-standing Composers' Union member; A. M. Veprik was an instrumentation specialist who completed his composition training at the Moscow Conservatory as a student of Miaskovskii in 1923; and S. A. Balasanian was a heavily decorated Tadzhik composer.

25. B. M. Terent'ev completed his composition training at the Moscow Conservatory in 1937 as a student of R. M. Glier and G. I. Litinskii. During the war, he voluntarily joined the navy and developed a reputation as a patriotic song composer.

26. RGALI, f. 2077, op. 1, d. 234, l. 65.

concerts. The list of pieces for performance included twenty-one new symphonic works, twenty-five rarely performed works from the past, and seven new chamber music pieces by composers ranging from Shostakovich, Khachaturian, and Miaskovskii to Khrennikov, Koval', and Boris Mokrousov.[27] Both those who benefited from the intervention and those who were most penalized by it could hypothetically profit from the professional organization's increased control.

This increased power was subject to one important caveat. In a subscription series conducted by Evgenii Mravinskii, the commission suggested replacing Shostakovich's Fifth Symphony with a symphonic suite by the same composer, but only with Mravinskii's permission, which had not yet been secured.[28] This caveat demonstrates the extent to which prominent performers could always control their repertoire. The Composers' Union did not completely monopolize programming even after its power expanded; instead, it displaced and subjugated the Committee on Artistic Affairs.

Concert programming was the most significant area in which the Composers' Union expanded its previous power, but it was not the only one. On 11 February 1948, the new leaders of the Composers' Union (Khrennikov) and the Committee on Artistic Affairs (Lebedev) wrote to Zhdanov to ask for substantially more resources for the music profession's only journal, *Sovetskaia muzyka*. Besides changing the journal's editor, they asked to increase its output from six to twelve issues per year and to increase its circulation from five thousand to twenty-five thousand copies per issue.[29] Composers' Union leaders had been complaining about the limited print space devoted to musical questions since the 1930s. In 1948 the new leaders finally received what they wanted. In March, the number of issues per year was doubled.[30] In September, the Composers' Union alone secured approval to increase circulation to thirteen thousand copies beginning in 1949.[31]

On a more informal, ad hoc level, the Central Committee apparatus began to depend on the expert opinion of the Composers' Union when faced with one-time decisions in the music realm. This informal reliance sometimes touched even the selection of personnel for institutions that did not fall under the Union's jurisdiction. For example, in February 1951 the Politburo approved the appointment of K. K. Sakva to the position of head of musical broadcasts at

27. Ibid., ll. 68, 71–72 (Protokol #28, 13 Aug 1948 and the appended list). B. A. Mokrousov completed his composition training at the Moscow Conservatory as a student of Miaskovskii. He was best known as a composer of songs and musical theater scores.

28. Ibid., ll. 73–74 (appendix to Protokol #28).

29. RGASPI, f. 17, op. 118, d. 21, ll. 6–7 (Khrennikov and P. Lebedev to Zhdanov, 11 Feb 1948).

30. Ibid., l. 1, pt. 342g. (materials to Secretariat Protokol #344, 3 Apr 1948). The decision also raised the prestige of the journal by placing its editorial board in the *nomanklatura* of the Politburo and increased the wage scale for the journal's workers. The size of each issue did not decrease; in other words, this decision meant a real increase in print space.

31. Ibid., d. 168, l. 6, pt. 3 (materials to Secretariat Protokol #379, 22 Sep 1948).

the All-USSR Radio Committee. Crucial to the decision was an opinion solicited from the Composers' Union.[32]

More typically, the Central Committee relied on the Union's expert opinion when it made one-time decisions about special cases. An example from the very end of the Stalin period illustrates this reliance and the ascendancy of the Composers' Union over the Committee on Artistic Affairs particularly clearly. In late 1952 the Italian composer Raffaello Monti dedicated a hymn to Stalin and sent it as a gift through the Soviet embassy in Rome.[33] The hymn caused a veritable furor in the Central Committee apparatus as the bureaucrats scrambled to decide what to make of the unexpected gift. Opinions were solicited from the Radio Committee, the musically trained members of the apparatus, and the Composers' Union.[34] In their concluding report on the matter, the Central Committee bureaucrats only reported the Composers' Union's evaluation, noting that "according to the conclusion of the Composers' Union, R. Monti's 'Hymn to Peace' is a celebratory composition. The music is noble, melodic, and filled with national colorations. The hymn was written sincerely, at a good professional level." Considering this evaluation, they recommended sending the score to the Committee on Artistic Affairs to organize recordings and performances on the stage and radio.[35] The expert opinion of the Composers' Union set the policy, and the Committee on Artistic Affairs was instructed to implement it.

The increased power of their professional organization was not so striking to most Soviet composers while they lived through the brouhaha of 1948. For some of them, the brouhaha meant a dramatic improvement in their personal positions, but for others it was a frightening period of uncertainty and abandonment. Shostakovich and Miaskovskii lost their conservatory positions. Shebalin remained on as director of the Moscow Conservatory for several months, but he too was demoted in August 1948.[36] Firings and demotions were not the only personal ramifications of being branded a formalist.

The subscription series discussed above illustrate another example of the negative consequences that the disciplined composers faced. Miaskovskii, Khachaturian, and Prokofiev all saw prominent pieces cut in favor of more traditional

32. RGASPI, f. 17, op. 119, d. 241, ll. 86–89, pt. 563s (materials to Secretariat Protokol #547, 8 Feb 1952). Musicologist K. K. Sakva completed the Moscow Conservatory and advanced education at an Academy of Sciences institute; a Red Army veteran, before this appointment, he also had extensive administrative experience as the one-time head of the VKI's musical ensembles administration and editor at the central government music publisher.

33. RGASPI, f. 17, op. 133, d. 368, l. 133 (Monti to Mozzhenko, undated). The occasion was the Congress of the Peoples, to begin on 12 December 1952 in Vienna.

34. Ibid., l. 130 (Kruzhkov and Iarustovskii to Mikhailov, 15 Jan 1953); l. 131 (Vlasov to Shevliagin, 13 Dec 1952); and l. 132 (Vartanian's analysis, 20 Dec 1952).

35. Ibid., l. 134 (Grigor'ian and Kruzhkov to Mikhailov, 23 Dec 1952).

36. Ibid., op. 118, d. 190, ll. 177–81, pt. 77 (materials to Secretariat Protokol #385, 11 Oct 1948), a follow-up action that removed him from the Ministry of Higher Education's attestation commission because he was no longer director of the conservatory.

or younger composers, and Shostakovich and Miaskovskii had their famous earlier pieces replaced by newer works.[37] In fact, restrictions on these composers' works were even harsher. In mid-February the theater censor issued its only order explicitly banning the performance of specific musical pieces, all of which had been composed by composers listed in the Central Committee resolution. That ban remained in effect for more than a year.[38]

As the actual party intervention faded, composers and musicologists settled back into their routines, and the disciplined composers were eventually rehabilitated, sometimes quickly. Those routines suggest that many of them, and not just the "formalist groups" of February through April, resented the clumsiness of the brouhaha and actively sought to avoid a repeat occurrence. Until the end of the Stalin period, major composers stopped working on operas, thereby continually frustrating the party leadership.

Less frustrating to party bureaucrats because not so noticeable to nonexperts was another development. Over the next five years, composers and musicologists dutifully flocked to general meetings in which they discussed vague Central Committee pronouncements on the arts. However, at those meetings they seem to have stopped trying to flesh out those vague decrees with meaningful musical content. Though it was exhibited most clearly in the Union's surprisingly successful attempt to avoid the anti-Semitic elements of the anticosmopolitanism campaigns, the continuing professional reluctance to participate in the ongoing discussions suggested by party resolutions was also discernible in theoretical discussions that occupied the attention of the Composers' Union during the last four years of the Stalin period. These discussions either commented on seminal theoretical articles about Soviet culture (such as an article by Stalin on linguistics) or proceeded from internal discussions (like how to write appealing popular music that was also ideologically sound).[39] In contrast to the ideological discussions of the immediate postwar years, composers and musicologists steadfastly avoided defining the characteristics of acceptable Soviet music, cloaking the broadest, most inclusive definitions possible in circular theoretical constructs of ideological catchphrases.

One example of such discussions we have already discussed: during the anticosmopolitanism campaigns the popular music composers Dunaevskii and Solove'ev-Sedoi used subtle shifts in generic reference and contextual arguments to preserve the breadth of theoretically acceptable popular music even in the context of a direct attack on popular music. This was not an isolated incident. In a discussion meant to define *narodnost'* (roughly translatable as "folkish-

37. RGALI, f. 2077, op. 1, d. 234, ll. 73–74.

38. For one copy of the ban, see ibid., d. 335, ll. 14–15 (Glavrepertkom Prikaz #17, 14 Feb 1948). The ban was declared illegal and lifted, and Glavrepertkom was reprimanded, when Stalin found out about it in late 1949; l. 13 (SM SSSR Rasporiazhenie #3179r, 16 Mar 1949). This singular event is discussed at length in chapter 10.

39. RGALI, f. 2077, op. 1, d. 736, ll. 1–164 (SSK stenogram on linguistics, 18 Mar–16 Apr 1952); d. 737, ll. 1–95 (same, 10 Apr 1952); d. 633 (stenogram on mass song, 3 Mar 1951).

ness"), it was proposed that this positive trait essentially boiled down to Bolshevik party loyalty. Bolshevik party loyalty, in turn, was defined as the propensity to compose works characterized by their *narodnost'*.[40]

In another discussion meant to elucidate the relationship between artistic mastery (*masterstvo*) and ideological soundness (*ideinost'*), the vast majority of the meeting was spent on organizational matters and entreaties to the creative apparatus leadership to redouble its efforts to promote (undefined) Bolshevik criticism. Artistic mastery came up only occasionally. Khrennikov himself opened the meeting by proposing that the question of ideological content and the perfection of form (the preoccupation of the "formalist") were one and the same issue. In the same opening remarks, he called on the leadership of the genre-based creative sections to focus attention on "principled creative problems" while avoiding any remaining elements of "formalism" in their critical discussions.[41] A later speaker stated the circular problem even more directly, though also without offering an intelligible solution: the representative of the Symphonic Music Section, V. M. Iurovskii, said that so much attention in his section was paid to "external" questions of musical form, language, and style that the "spirit of a work, its thought, its idea," was ignored.[42] Though Iurovskii's formulation suggests a shift in the object of analysis from musical form to some undefined ideological "content," neither Iurovskii nor Khrennikov nor any other speaker defined the specificity of that content or even how to identify it. One speaker even complained that without direction from composers, musicologists at the Soviet Union's music schools did not know how to instruct students about realism. For example, was realism *determined* by form or was form completely irrelevant and, if one was a "realist," a good piece would merely happen?[43] Participants were left with Khrennikov's opening formulation: content was determined by the perfection of form.

In 1952 the Composers' Union revisited the question of artistic mastery on the occasion of discussions of Stalin's article on linguistics, his last major ideological pronouncement. Moscow-based musicologist V. V. Vanslov drew a distinction between "formalist" understandings of mastery and a new conception. To the "formalist," mastery consisted of technique and the possession of the sum total of the resources of musical expression—that is, mastery of musical language. The postformalist understanding consisted of the ability "to reflect the truth of life and to express deep ideological content in simple artistic form." Crucial to this ability was command of musical language (the subject of the larger discussion), which could help a composer create a musical form "rich in content," in which "lifelike images were embodied."[44] These circular defini-

40. Ibid., d. 777, ll. 1–92 (stenogram on *narodnost'*, 25 Apr 1952), esp. ll. 40–70 (Sh. S. Aslanishvili).

41. Ibid., d. 372, ll. 1–6 (Moscow chapter stenogram on *ideinost'* and *masterstvo*, 18–20 Oct 1949).

42. Ibid., ll. 52–58 (Iurovskii).

43. Ibid., ll. 68–74 (S. S. Skrebkov).

44. RGALI, f. 2077, op. 1, d. 737, l. 7 (stenogram on linguistics, 10 Apr 1952).

tions of artistic mastery, musical form, and ideological content deftly employed the ideological language of Stalinist cultural politics without providing clarity. In discussion after discussion, professional mastery, *narodnost'*, and good musical language were defined as that which was "ideologically sound," but no musical characteristics of ideological soundness emerged.[45]

Both collectively and as individuals, composers engaged in an analogous practice when they wrote new music, composing some pieces that were direct responses to the party's call for programmatic vocal music and others that retreated entirely into introspective chamber music for sophisticated, primarily professional audiences. For example, Shostakovich's paean to Soviet reforestation schemes, the cantata *Song of the Forests,* was composed in the midst of work on his Fourth String Quartet and before he began work on his major piano cycle, the Twenty-four Preludes and Fugues. *Song of the Forests* completed Shostakovich's post-1948 personal rehabilitation, earning him a Stalin Prize, First Class, in 1950.[46] The chamber pieces—and the many others like them composed by Shostakovich's colleagues—kept creative discussion alive within the confines of the professional organization.[47] But the public face of Soviet music after the intervention emphasized programmatic vocal music, especially heroic cantatas and oratorios like those that dominated the 1949 plenum, when the entire profession was congratulated for its progress since the 1948 party intervention.[48]

At the same time, many public and professional discussions revolved around the familiar practices of criticism and self-criticism, but there was an observable change in attributing liability. In the years after 1948, blame for shortcomings was shifted from individual composers and musicologists to the professional organization as a whole (or sometimes to its leadership), thus reducing the danger that disciplined individuals might have suffered.[49] Both of these developments suggest that individual composers and musicologists were increasingly less eager to participate in the regime's theoretical projects. The growing stature of the Composers' Union allowed the institution to absorb criticism without risk of elimination. As it grew more powerful, the professional organization became less penetrable and even more protective of its sphere of expertise.

45. For one explicit acknowledgment that there was a great distance between their theoretical discussions and actual composition practice, see ibid., d. 736, l. 138 (Nest'ev, 1952).

46. Fay, *Shostakovich,* 174–80.

47. For other examples of this intensification of work on chamber music and oratorio, see Prokofiev's reedition of his Piano Sonata no. 5 (1952–53) and a cello sonata (1949), surrounding an oratorio "Na strazhe mira" and a vocal-symphonic suite "Zimnii koster" (both 1950); Miaskovskii's Piano Sonatas nos. 7–9 and Thirteenth String Quartet (1949), though this can be considered a continuation rather than intensification of Miaskovskii's consistent attention to chamber music forms; and Shebalin's Trio (1949), in the midst of two pieces for unaccompanied choir (1949, 1952).

48. M. Chulaki, "Na puti muzykal'nogo tvorchestva," *Kul'tura i zhizn',* 1949, no. 36 (31 Dec): 2. See also "Plenum pravleniia SSK SSSR," *Kul'tura i zhizn',* 1949, no. 33 (30 Nov): 1, a positive evaluation of the Plenum while it was in progress.

49. RGALI, f. 2077, op. 1, d. 565, ll. 1–82 (stenogram of a discussion of a *Pravda* article criticizing an opera by Zhukovskii, 24 Apr 1951), esp. ll. 1–13 (Chulaki's presentation).

A much less formal development illustrates this point even more clearly by revealing shifts or reaffirmations of the authority and prestige within the profession of composers who were directly involved in the events of 1948. In 1952 two Central Committee bureaucrats reported to Malenkov about the preparation of students at the Moscow Conservatory. The vast majority of students regularly chose to register for composition classes taught by composers who had been disciplined in 1948, most notably Shebalin and Khachaturian. On the other hand, Kabalevskii, who had escaped mention in the 1948 resolution, had a difficult time persuading any students to study with him. One of the principal institutional beneficiaries of the party intervention, Khrennikov, had not even been invited to teach at the conservatory.[50] Students also actively pursued alternative means of studying music that had been condemned by the 1948 resolution. They gathered in private apartments, listened to foreign radio broadcasts, and praised the experimental music they heard there.[51] This analysis of budding composers' educational choices demonstrates that condemned music retained a professional fascination, and being subjected to party discipline in 1948 came to be something of an informal marker of prestige. According to the Central Committee bureaucrats, the Composers' Union was doing nothing to fight this tendency, and other professionals teaching at the conservatory even encouraged it.[52] Though they may not have known it, this alternative study of music that was officially out of favor had long been carried out under the direction of conservatory professors. Miaskovskii's enormous personal collection of scores was well known in professional circles to contain music by such composers as Schoenberg and Stravinsky, anathema to Stalinist officials.[53]

All of these developments demonstrate that even under the direction of the new leadership, the Composers' Union maintained a realm in which professional determinations held priority. One final example suggests that Khrennikov personally, like Khachaturian in 1947 before him, intentionally sought to preserve that realm. While remaining completely loyal to the party and its leadership, the new leaders in the Composers' Union continued to pursue policies implying a separation between the political and professional realms. We have already seen how during the anticosmopolitanism campaigns that began in January 1949, the new leadership continued to operate according to the principle that only they could identify and even punish "cosmopolitans" within their ranks.[54] And when disciplined "cosmopolitans" were threatened with expulsion from the Composers' Union, Khrennikov used his influence to keep

50. RGASPI, f. 17, op. 133, d. 368, ll. 74–77, here l. 75 (Kruzhkov and Tarasov to Malenkov, 31 Jul 1952).
51. Ibid., l. 74.
52. Ibid., ll. 75–76.
53. Khachaturian, "Iz vospominanii," 301–2.
54. RGASPI, f. 17, op. 132, d. 244, ll. 36–49 (correspondence between V. Vdovichenko, Malenkov, Khrennikov, the VKI, and OPA, Mar–Apr 1949).

them in, again limiting punishment for professional mistakes to professional censure.[55]

Just as important, while evaluating professional work in mid-1949, the Union's new leaders and probably Khrennikov himself actually articulated the separation of realms. In April 1949 the Composers' Union Secretariat reviewed plans to publish a pamphlet written by Daniel' Zhitomirskii, a Jewish musicologist who had just been singled out for attack in the anticosmopolitanism campaign. The content of the pamphlet was deemed to be acceptable, but the Secretariat denied its publication anyway, citing Zhitomirskii's recent political trouble.[56] Two months later, the question was revisited and the decision reversed. This time, the Secretariat emphasized that there was nothing wrong with the brochure in question and it should therefore be published.[57] What changed? The evidence suggests that Khrennikov was responsible for the shift. He was on vacation when the first decision was taken and had returned just days before the second. It is likely that at his initiative the question was revisited, and the decision itself is in keeping with his earlier documented attempts to maintain control and discipline within a professional realm at least partially distinct from the political. The result was that creative merit and not political criticism was selected as the criteria for publication of musicological works.

After the dramatic party intervention in 1948, the Composers' Union consolidated its power as the dominant institution in the Stalinist music world. By making serious forays into previously inaccessible administrative terrain, like the programming practices of performance ensembles, and supplanting the Committee on Artistic Affairs on matters grand and small, the Composers' Union ascended to the peak of Stalinist music administration. At the same time, the professionals who comprised its membership adeptly sought to avoid repeated interventions by ceasing work on high-profile musical genres (like opera), interspersing composition of grand political pieces for wide consumption with work on complicated chamber music for professional consumption, by engaging in obtuse and circular argumentation that failed to provide meaningful guidance for following ideological dictates or identifying the oft-mentioned "content" of musical works, and even by quietly suggesting that professional work should be judged by professional criteria rather than political reliability. As the profession consolidated its dominance in the Stalinist music sphere, professionals were ever more distant. As a result, Composers' Union leaders in the Secretariat and in the creative apparatus, along with rank-and-file composers and musicologists, used their agency to preserve a professional realm distinct from—though never antagonistic toward—the political.

---

55. Ibid., d. 243, ll. 21–36 (correspondence regarding expulsion of Ogolevets and Shlifshtein, 1949). Neither was expelled thanks to Khrennikov's last minute memo to Malenkov.

56. RGALI, f. 2077, op. 1, d. 338, l. 76 (Protokol #15, 1 Apr 1949), pt. 3.

57. Ibid., l. 103 (Protokol #22, 30 May 1949), pt. 2.

Despite waves of political pressure, the postwar Composers' Union saw its power consolidated and its professional priorities preserved. Traditional studies of the Stalinist cultural world have looked at these party interventions and understandably seen the complete subjugation of cultural life to political prerogatives. Certainly some subjugation occurred. However, when the structural relationship between composers, musicologists, and political leaders is examined over the long first decade of the all-USSR Composers' Union's existence, it becomes clear that the expertise that defined the professional organization never ceased to be decisively important. Despite the dramatic moments of intervention that punctuate this period, the postwar period saw the consolidation of a professional organization that determined who could become a music professional, how the professional organization would be organized, how that organization would structure creative work, and how Soviet music—in the end— would be produced and interpreted.

The distribution of creative authority among professionals within the creative apparatus and leadership body helped to preserve professional agency, even as the Composers' Union expanded its institutional power and accommodated party intervention. As complicated generational and party membership dynamics unfolded, internal professional authority shifted from the administrative, top-leadership group to the creative apparatus. Professionals asserted their agency to define the theoretical contours of acceptable Soviet music through inaccessibly technical discussions, circular argumentation, and sometimes outright assertion that professional priorities should determine professional success. Though this definitional power was always circumscribed and cannot be understood as evidence of professional autonomy, it provides a significant illustration of the agency that accrued to experts by very virtue of their expertise.

The same can be said of the overarching limits of creative production within which these discussions took place. The party certainly placed ultimate limits beyond which discussion during the Stalin period simply was not possible. At no time during the Stalin-era existence of the Composers' Union did Soviet composers and musicologists attempt to justify the composition of serialism, for example. And at certain times (like 1948–50), public performance and promotion of even much less adventurous music was severely restricted. But even during those times, significantly broader professional discussions and professional composition took place within the confines of the Union, insulated as it was from political intervention by a technical abstraction that required professional expertise for interpretation. The result was somewhat analogous (though I emphatically do not suggest that it is an equivalent experience) to the market marginalization of mid-century "serious art" music from the listening public in the West and the retreat of modernist composers into the American academy. Professional consolidation took place in the midst of party intervention.

A number of scholars have recently insisted that the Soviet Union is best understood in the context of other modern states. Parts I and II of this study demonstrate that by mid-century the Soviet Union shared with other modern states the development of a profoundly modern elite occupational group, the profession. As in Western Europe and North America, the Soviet profession had a monopoly on the expertise required to perform socially useful work—composing and interpreting new music. In this realm the Soviet Union was characteristically modern.

But most observers of the Soviet Union also consider that its command economy and political system, directed by a single party with ambitions to control its population as completely as possible, make the Soviet Union profoundly different from its contemporary societies governed by capitalist parliamentary systems. As we have seen, one important ramification of that difference was that the Soviet profession did not operate autonomously. The Communist Party leadership always could and sometimes did intervene to disrupt the Composers' Union and assert its priorities. Nevertheless, the Union's collective control of socially significant expertise afforded its members the agency to preserve a realm for professional discussion and creative production. This agency enabled the profession as a whole to mobilize its expertise in support of both their own professional projects and the ideological and political projects mandated by the party leadership. Agency, not autonomy, thus provides the best characterization of the underlying principles governing the possibilities of the Soviet professional elite.

This finding suggests something unique about the Soviet Union among modern societies. Occupational groups that formed professions in North America and Western Europe did not necessarily experience analogous professionalization in the Soviet Union. Instead, it was a creative union, a body comprised of representatives of the creative intelligentsia, that fulfilled this structural function in the Soviet Union. That music—and not, say, dentistry—emerged as a site of professionalization suggests that the crucial link between mind work and social value in the Soviet Union was forged not primarily in legal or health fields but in cultural production. Soviet cultural professions thus helped define and interpret the way in which the Soviet state and its citizens viewed the world.[58]

58. Sheila Fitzpatrick first noted this phenomenon as the counterintuitive relationship between the Bolsheviks and the intelligentsia in "Cultural Orthodoxies under Stalin," in *The Cultural Front: Power and Culture in Revolutionary Russia,* ed. Fitzpatrick (Ithaca: Cornell University Press, 1992), 238–56.

Part III

PROFESSIONALS AND THE STALINIST CULTURAL ELITE

In the postwar period the Soviet Composers' Union asserted its agency by increasing and consolidating its control over the production of Soviet music and maintaining a separation between political and professional realms, even in the face of repeated party intervention. We now turn to a study of professionals and the authority they accrued from a number of different audiences to bolster their collective and individual agency. This agency had powerful cultural and social causes and results. In cultural terms, the preferences of the professional leadership (composers and musicologists all) established the criteria by which musical production was judged and often funded by Muzfond. Professional preferences also determined the assignment of value in the more prestigious and higher-profile area of exemplary musical production, typified by the awarding of Stalin Prizes. This cultural domination (though not absolute control) of musical evaluation simultaneously created and reinforced a markedly hierarchical social system within the profession and in Stalinist society generally, according to which an individual's place in the hierarchy of prestige and material privilege was determined by the accrual of authority among a variety of authority-granting audiences.

The study of this hierarchical social system helps answer more general questions about the formation of the cultural elite. How did social, economic, and prestige hierarchies form and what role did expertise play in producing intellectual or creative authority among nonprofessional audiences? How did cultural elites create points of articulation between the professional, political, and social spheres? How important were informal networks for members of the Soviet elite? Answering these questions requires us to consider other cultural elites that interacted with composers and musicologists.

Doing so allows us to trace the relationship between professionals and various authority-granting audiences. Creative authority translated into the power to set the terms of musical judgment and social hierarchy. Multiple interfaces between the professional and political realms simultaneously reinforced professional agency and prevented it from becoming autonomy, as autonomy is understood in the West. An analysis of the powerful definitional effects of professional agency helps to resolve the paradox inherent in many earlier descriptions of the Soviet arts system, which lauded artists' accomplishments while decrying their complete subjugation to the party-state.

To understand how autonomy and complete subjugation were precluded, we must examine how boundaries between the political and the professional were dissolved along a number of crucial interfaces. One of these interfaces was created by the ubiquitous informal networks that permeated the official bureaucracy, including within the profession. Another was embodied by the Stalin Prize Committee, which translated the opinion of the Soviet Union's cultural and intellectual elite into officially sanctioned markers of excellence, prestige, and material privilege and called into question the legitimacy of popularity with more general audiences.

The study of hierarchies in the music world also elucidates the nature of the professional organization that the Composers' Union embodied and the power and authority of its leaders. Authority, prestige, and privilege were extremely concentrated at the top of the Soviet music world. A small governing clique of authoritative and well-connected musicians played a dominant role in determining musical value and prestige, in distributing resources and privilege, and in managing informal networks. This highly centralized authority is typical of Stalinist institutions but peculiar among professions, an example of the Soviet Union's particular experience of modernity.

Finally, the processes of cultural and material elite formation reveal limits to some of the features commonly understood to define the specificity of Soviet governance. We shall see that the inefficient and ineffective bureaucracy could only function through the operation of personalized networks, both within the profession and across the line dividing profession from politics. We shall see how a few composers benefited from market-based economic forces in the midst of the centrally planned economy. And we shall see that a governing elite, bent on almost complete domination of Soviet society, nevertheless depended on crucial informal and institutional interfaces with such cultural elites as the professionals of the Composers' Union. Rather than the battered and completely subjugated artistic group familiar from most traditional studies of the Soviet arts, the music profession actually constituted an indispensable component of the Stalinist elite.

CHAPTER 8

Muzfond, Royalties, and Popularity

During the Stalin period, a two-part institutional system provided most composers and musicologists with their fundamental material support apart from what they earned in jobs at research institutes and conservatories or as consultants for performance ensembles and government institutions. The two components of the system were the financial institution controlled by the Composers' Union leadership, Muzfond, and the royalties and copyright administration. Each was a continual source of concern for party leaders and professionals alike. The Composers' Union leadership's virtually unmonitored, unregulated control over the substantial resources managed by Muzfond prevented it from functioning as a disinterested funding institution. Instead, it often distributed resources unevenly based on the personal preferences—and connections—of its leaders. Still, Muzfond provided the most fundamental material support available to music professionals and operated efficiently enough to maintain the entire professional body in the Soviet elite. Despite repeated findings of malfeasance and fiscal indiscipline, the Muzfond system was never substantially reformed. Leaving it alone ensured that the Composers' Union leadership would exercise its practical discretion in determining hierarchies of basic support.

The Copyright Administration provided basic material support to composers who had pieces performed, and it also became the focus of prolonged attacks. Struggles over comparative royalties rates during the Stalin period reveal a shift in the underlying conceptions about labor, intellectual property, and remuneration, and the tremendous disparities in the resources that the Copyright Administration distributed troubled policy advisors almost continuously. The extraordinarily high royalties that a very few composers earned were tainted by a sense of illegitimacy.

One of the consistent features of Soviet ideology was its emphasis on modernization and cultural development. An important internal measure of that development was the material basis that was established and maintained to support the creation of a particular product that the leadership valued. One of the categories to which this internal measure was applied was artistic production, a fact amply illustrated by a self-congratulatory survey of the history and state of the arts in the Soviet Union between 1939 and 1951, which was penned in 1951 by V. S. Kruzhkov, the head of the newly reorganized and renamed Central Committee Department of Literature and the Arts (OKhLI).[1] Kruzhkov contended that "there is no other country in the world which could compare to the Soviet Union in terms of the quantity of theaters, art exhibits, and films that serve audiences every year."[2]

Kruzhkov supported this proud proclamation with a discussion of the base of material support that the state provided to artists and their audiences. He cited governmental budget figures to show that since 1939, the state had spent 8.6 billion rubles on the arts, almost 5.1 billion in the years 1946–50 alone. The government also allocated the Ministry of Film an additional 12 billion rubles in the same eleven-year period, nearly 7.7 billion in 1946–50. In the postwar years, Kruzhkov bragged, the state rebuilt fifty-seven museums and galleries and thirty-seven theater buildings, for a total of thirty-two thousand seats. Since the end of the war, many cities had built concert halls, conservatory buildings, and arts schools. The result of this attention was that "at the current time, the USSR possesses the broadest system of theaters in the world," a system that encompassed more than 1,000 major theater and performance institutions, including 526 theaters, 123 philharmonics and variety show organizations, 183 musical collectives, 52 circuses for 124 circus collectives, and 85 art museums and galleries.[3]

Whether or not Kruzhkov's global comparative claims are accurate, they exemplify the intimate connection between the Communist Party leadership's understanding of its cultural mission and the material base allocated to support it. This understanding implicitly legitimated the creation of a comparatively privileged group of musicians, including the music professionals of the Composers' Union, concertizing soloists, and the performers of the USSR's many orchestras, choirs, and musical, opera, and ballet theaters. That Kruzhkov framed his discussion in terms of "serving audiences" also indicates that a crucial aspect of this relationship was determined by the party's interpretation of an authority-granting audience outside itself—the listening public. Indeed, party leaders and bureaucrats like Kruzhkov sought to mold the tastes of that audience, often speaking in the name of the "Soviet public," but they also repeatedly revealed that it was important to them to recognize authority gained within that audience. The shaping of public taste, the recognition of authority, and the construction of a material base were intimately related in a complex system of royalties, honorary titles, and official prizes. Within that already comparatively

---

1. RGASPI, f. 17, op. 133, d. 306, ll. 43–70 (8 Sep 1951). For the Politburo order that reorganized agit-prop, created OKhLI, and appointed Kruzhkov to head the new department, see ibid., op. 3, d. 1086, l. 84, pt. 462 (Politburo Protokol #79, 30 Dec 1950).
2. Ibid., l. 69.
3. Ibid., l. 67.

elite system, distinctions of legitimate and illegitimate prestige were vigorously contested.

Muzfond: Personalistic Provision of Basic Material Support

Muzfond was established in 1939 to fund the basic professional support that the Composers' Union provided its members and to assist them in times of material need. Through its oversight of Muzfond, the Composers' Union leadership controlled a vast material infrastructure that included a score-publishing service, supply depot, creative resorts, vacation spots, clubs, restaurants, and performance venues, in addition to more liquid assets like grant and loan funds and large reserves of money allocated for professional funding. Theoretically, these resources were to be distributed to all Muzfond members according to their needs and agreements with the Muzfond leadership, always overseen by the Orgkom or Secretariat.

From the very beginning, however, it was clear that even such an elite institution as the Composers' Union did not have the resources it needed to meet all of its obligations.[4] Muzfond too was part of the Soviet economy of shortage. As a result, when they decided who would receive funding and for what, Muzfond and Composers' Union leaders were forced to make choices. Whether allocating space in the coveted system of creative resorts, awarding grants or loans to provide support during the creative process, or handing out temporary and ad hoc emergency material support, they often did so according to undefined and often personalistic criteria. Other than its charters and a few general instructions, Muzfond never published objective funding requirements. As a result, every audit of Muzfond from the war until Stalin's death found evidence of malfeasance, favoritism, and other forms of financial impropriety. Nevertheless, final control over the material resources allocated to the professional organization was never removed from the professional leadership. Throughout the Stalin period, professional leaders distributed resources as they saw fit, and always efficiently enough to maintain the privileged status of Composers' Union members.

One of the most appreciated components of the Muzfond professional support infrastructure was its system of creative resorts (*doma tvorchestva*). The creative resorts were designed to provide Composers' Union members with shelter from their hectic, almost exclusively urban lives and other professional responsibilities so that they could concentrate on composing or writing. According to Composers' Union policy, the resorts were available to composers for up to four months per year. For as many as two months a year, Muzfond

---

4. RGALI, f. 2077, op. 1, d. 31, ll. 8–10, 13–15, 17–20 (Muzfond stenogram, 26 May 1940), speeches by Muzfond leaders P. N. Zimin and V. I. Muradeli.

would pay all expenses associated with the stay, including food. For the other two months, composers had to pay forty-two rubles a day, unless they were working on a "fundamental" composition, in which case they would also receive a 50 percent discount for the second two months. The minimum stay was two weeks, and the maximum, four months. Composers' families and collaborators (like librettists and lyricists) could also accompany them to the creative resort, but they were required to pay. In the summer months, pioneer camps with a capacity of fifty children were set up at Ruza and Ivanovo. All told, between these two main resorts, the Secretariat planned on three hundred stays for a total of nine thousand occupant-days in 1949.[5] In at least some creative resorts there was a further distinction between the expense-free two months and the paid occupancy: during the former, a composer also had exclusive use of a piano.[6] Upon their return, composers had one month to give a full account to the Composers' Union leadership of what they accomplished during their stay. If their report was not satisfactory, the cost of the trip was converted into a six-month loan.[7]

Despite the attraction of this perquisite, the creative resorts were not always used to the fullest. In 1947 the Orgkom complained that only 193 of the planned 250 one-month stays in Ivanovo actually came to fruition.[8] At the end of 1949 the Composers' Union actually decided to eliminate a vacation resort in Riga because it was only used at 67 percent capacity.[9] When they investigated, the Secretariat discovered that Composers' Union creative resorts were poorly distributed geographically. A number of creative resorts in the national republics had been reassigned by governmental decree. For example, the Composers' Union resort in Armenia was given to the Ministry of Internal Affairs. As a result, composers in a whole host of national republics and in the Far East did not have access to any creative resorts while some of the Union's resorts (like the one in Riga) were operating at far below capacity. The solution: rent spaces at more geographically proximate resorts run by the Writers' Union, the Artists' Union, and the Architects' Union and purchase musical instruments for those resorts if necessary.[10] But as we shall see, the problems did not stop there.

Muzfond also administered a frequently changing system of direct funding

---

5. Ibid., d. 338, ll. 57–59 (Protokol #11, 22 Mar 1949). These rates represented an increase. In 1945 the cost of a visit to the central creative resort in Ivanovo was set at twenty rubles per day, a sum that included food, and the same amount was set a year later. See ibid., d. 120, ll. 10 (Protokol #3, 20 Mar 1945), pt. 2; and d. 139, l. 20 (Protokol #10, 11 May 1946), pt. 1.

6. G. S. Frid, personal communication, 3 Jul 1999. In all other details, Frid's recollections square exactly with the policy sketched out here. He noted that the most pleasant arrangement was to group two years' entitlement together so that one could spend September through April at the DTK every other year.

7. RGALI, f. 2077, op. 1, d. 339, l. 71 (Protokol #41, 9 Sep 1949), pt. 3.

8. Ibid., d. 166, l. 10 (Prikaz #10, 20 May 1947).

9. Ibid., d. 339, l. 166 (Protokol #61, 13 Dec 1949), pt. 2.

10. Ibid., l. 174 (SSK Auditing commission Protokol #11, 7 Dec 1949), pt. 4.b.; l. 171 (SSK Protokol, 11 Dec 1949), pt. 5.

for creative work. Officially, this direct funding was governed by regulations passed by the Orgkom or Secretariat, the first of which were issued in 1943 to bring order to the previously chaotic wartime funding procedures. The 1943 regulations did not set specific payment levels, but they did provide general guidelines. For accomplished professionals, the level of a grant was determined by the amount of an analogous commission, and for fledgling professionals, it was set according to a special pay scale, which unfortunately was not included with the regulations. Once Muzfond members received this money, they were required to report to the Creative Commission three times. They had to present a thematic plan for the work upon receipt of the first payment; they were to submit excerpts part way through the creative process; and the entire piece had to be presented for evaluation upon completion. At least one member of the Creative Commission examined the score and submitted a review to begin the evaluation. If the review was favorable, the Commission convened to evaluate a performance of the piece, which determined whether or not the composer had complied with the terms of the agreement.[11] If this panel of experts considered the piece too unpolished, the composer could be sent back to work on it further. If not, the piece was accepted, and the composer was eligible to apply for further support for a new piece.

As we have seen, the creative apparatus in which the evaluative stages of this process took place changed over time. Though the general structure of creative assistance laid out in 1943 remained basically the same, these specific regulations underwent a series of modifications. In 1944 the Orgkom centralized the final decision to accept or reject a piece as fulfillment of obligations incurred by professionals from the periphery. Though they would listen to recommendations of local committees, the final say fell to consultation committees in the central apparatus.[12] Later in 1944 the Orgkom acknowledged the increased outside funding opportunities that the impending end of the war would bring and decided to cut back substantially on the number of payments Muzfond could make to support creative work, limiting them to particularly needy, young, or fledgling professionals. Introducing a blurry element, the 1944 decision also permitted payments to composers and musicologists who worked according to a thematic plan approved by the Orgkom.[13] These principles were reaffirmed in 1946, when the Orgkom allocated 1.2 million rubles to support all composers in their first two years out of the conservatory and, as individual exceptions, both young and elderly composers who could not win governmental commissions for one reason or another.[14]

---

11. RGALI, f. 2077, op. 1, d. 71, ll. 23–23ob. (regulations on creative assistance, 28 Apr 1943). For date and approval, see l. 21 (Protokol #6, 28 Apr 1943), pt. 2.

12. Ibid., d. 99, l. 4 (Orgkom stenogram, 2 Feb 1944).

13. Ibid., d. 96, ll. 65–66, 70–71 (Protokol #14, 23 Oct 1944 and draft proposal approved thereby). In the final decision, Muzfond leaders were heavily praised for the role their funding played in musical production during the war.

14. Ibid., d. 139, ll. 5–6 (Protokol #2, 5 Feb 1946), pt. 3.

After the big shakedown of the music world in 1948, Muzfond was reorganized, and the new Secretariat passed an expanded set of regulations that governed all payments to Muzfond members. These new regulations were intended to be a temporary stopgap until the system could be carefully reconsidered one more time. Muzfond began anew the practice of paying grants to support composers while they were working. However, the 1948 regulations clarified the distinction between money given as a grant and that issued as a loan. Funding levels were set at up to two thousand rubles per month, or three thousand rubles per month in exceptional cases and only with the approval of the Secretariat. As before, all payments were associated with work on a specific piece. If the composer had not received a commission from elsewhere to work on that piece, Muzfond money (up to eight thousand rubles) was considered a grant. If the piece had been commissioned, Muzfond money (up to ten thousand rubles) was considered a loan to be repaid when the composer received the commission payment. In either case, composers were required to present a progress report every two months. The 1948 regulations also provided free trips to creative resorts, research travel support, and payments for consultation sessions, translations, copy services, and even some performances.[15]

In 1949 these regulations were twice amended for the last time in the Stalin period. The new regulations reaffirmed policies regarding loans, paid research travel, trips to the creative resorts, and payments for consultations, translations, and performances. However, they cut creative grants once and for all, transforming them into those other sorts of support.[16] The most substantial regular support that composers could receive while they worked on a piece that had not been commissioned by a performance institution was an expenses-paid trip to a creative resort. This state of affairs lasted only a few months. In September 1949 the Secretariat passed a final version of the regulations which reaffirmed the cancellation of all grants but suggested that composers could receive loans. Only in exceptional cases did the approval of such loans require assurances of payment from a performance institution.[17]

Muzfond also administered a substantial fund from which it issued loans and grants to cover personal emergency expenses or provide help in major life-changing events. Many of these grants were supposed to be automatic. For example, in 1944 the Orgkom approved standard one-time "material help" payments to all members who were called into the army (up to one thousand rubles) or gave birth to a baby (three thousand rubles) or to a member's family

15. Ibid., d. 234, ll. 81–89, here ll. 82–84 (temporary regulations, 7 Sep 1948). For date and approval, see ll. 79–80 (Protokol #30, 7 Sep 1948).

16. Ibid., d. 338, ll. 2–4 (Protokol #1, 4, 7 Jan 1949), pt. 4.

17. Ibid., d. 339, ll. 69–70 (Protokol #41, 9 Sep 1949), pt. 3. These instructions basically affirm the 1948 state of affairs but provide more specific details. For example, loan amounts were determined by genre: working on an opera, ballet, musical comedy, symphony, cantata, concerto, or oratorio, or a large musicological work, entitled a composer or musicologist to ten thousand rubles over one year, whereas song cycles, etudes, romances, and marches gained a composer three thousand rubles over four months. Other genres fell in between these extremes.

if the member died (two thousand rubles).[18] Even for an elite institution like the Composers' Union, however, resources were too scarce to fulfill all entitlements. Even after the postwar boost in composers' material status, only 30 percent of them had their own pianos, though all of them were theoretically entitled to one.[19] Consequently, the vast majority of these extraordinary material assistance payments were decided on an individual, case-by-case basis in response to specific circumstances, whether professional (need of a piano) or personal (need of a loan to cover moving expenses). Though they decided all such special cases, the Composers' Union leaders never established clear criteria on the basis of which they could justify those decisions. In fact, the only rule that appears to have governed them was that there were no set rules.[20] Not surprisingly, utilizing personal connections was probably the most reliable path to these special funds.[21] That there were no standard criteria is perhaps best demonstrated by the fact that the leadership almost never even provided an explanation when they granted or denied a request.[22]

As a predictable result of this personalistic, individualized decision making, virtually every investigation of Muzfond's activities from the war to the early 1950s found evidence of corruption or profoundly deficient financial discipline. These findings came from investigations conducted by the Composers' Union and by external organizations. The first thoroughgoing criticism of Muzfond's financial practices was the result of an internal audit in September 1942.[23] The audit was called when the Orgkom leadership noticed that Muzfond was missing a significant amount of paperwork that should have documented its activities. The very scope of the audit spoke to pervasive bookkeeping problems; the

---

18. Ibid., d. 96, l. 54 (Protokol #8, 18 May 1944), pt. raznoe.4.

19. GARF, f. 5446, op. 49, d. 2829, l. 157 (Glier to Voroshilov, 20 Nov 1947).

20. For example, compare RGALI, f. 2077, op. 1, d. 96, l. 52 (Protokol #7, 9 May 1944), which grants A. S. Ogolevets money to repair his piano, damaged during the Nazi occupation, with RGALI, f. 2085, op. 1, d. 1209, l. 57 (V. V. Bunin to R. M. Glier, 11 May 1946), which complains that his repeated requests for one-time assistance from Muzfond had been denied. Bunin's apartment had been burglarized and cleaned out; the burglars had even taken clothes, shoes, linens, and so forth, and Bunin could not afford to replace the stolen goods for his wife and three children at market rates.

21. For two clear examples of patronage interventions that ensured the success of a request, see RGALI, f. 2077, op. 1, d. 139, ll. 70–71 (Protokol #25, 4 Dec 1946), in which Shostakovich asked for and received a pension for the widow of a colleague and ibid., d. 99, l. 26 (Orgkom stenogram on Muzfond, 24 Feb 1944), pt. raznoe, in which Shostakovich asked for and received a pension for the family of one of his best friends (Ivan Sollertinskii), who had just died. In many of these cases, material assistance was provided to close associates of Composers' Union leaders: ibid., d. 71, l. 39ob. (Protokol #12, 20 Oct 1943), which gives N. Ia. Miaskovskii a pension; and d. 139, ll. 64–65 (Protokol #21, 1 Nov 1946 and G. N. Popov to Orgkom, 1 Nov 1946), in which Popov receives a sixty-thousand-ruble, four-month loan to buy furniture since all of his was destroyed during the occupation.

22. Either the Orgkom or the Secretariat made such decisions at almost every one of their meetings. Most take the form "approve the request of member X." Examples are too numerous to warrant even a cursory list.

23. RGALI, f. 2077, op. 1, d. 51, ll. 65–90ob. (Orgkom stenogram, 7 Sep 1942).

auditor was only able to examine documents from one-third of the eighteen-month period of his charge. In that six-month period, he discovered a profound lack of financial discipline: Muzfond had doled out money too liberally and based on the decision of only one person, regardless of plan or documentation.[24]

The man responsible for the daily operations of the financial institution was Muzfond's chief administrator, Levon Atovm'ian. A composer, cellist, and pianist by training, Atovm'ian joined the party in 1920 and served in the Red Army from 1919 to 1929. In 1929 he became involved in musical administration for the first time as the head of the composers' department of the All-Russian Theater Society, a position he held until the municipal composers' unions took over in 1932. Besides his administrative duties, Atovm'ian was an active composer and, especially, arranger and orchestrator.[25] His personal loyalties lay with such prominent, serious composers as Shostakovich, who was known to count on him in administrative affairs.[26]

Even Atovm'ian's defense against charges of poor bookkeeping and liberal expenditures demonstrates the extent to which decision making was a personalistic affair. He noted that waiting for approval or paperwork was a waste of time. After all, if a composer came with a plea for help, Atovm'ian knew the situation (because he knew the composer), knew it was true, and did not need an independent cross-check.[27] Under such conditions, personal acquaintance with Atovm'ian was obviously crucial to receiving any special aid, and friendly relations probably helped as well.

Accusations of financial indiscipline, insufficient bookkeeping, and poor documentation were leveled again three years later, when Muzfond was instructed to adhere more closely to regulations governing the use of creative resorts and travel grants. In another complaint that would be repeated for years, the Orgkom called Muzfond to task for giving successive loans to individuals before they had repaid earlier loans. Only the Orgkom could allow an exception to that rule.[28]

During the brouhaha of 1948, Muzfond was subjected to an extensive investigation by an outside institution, the Ministry of Finance. Aleksei Kosygin, the ministry's representative, found not just personalistic, ad hoc decision making, but also such extremely disproportionate distribution of resources that he thought it amounted to corruption. Thus, more than 40 percent of all of Muzfond's loans during 1947 went to members of the Orgkom and Muzfond leadership. More than half of that went to just four individuals, often in single loans that far exceeded the legislated maximum.[29] Muzfond was also subsidizing some leaders' automobiles, practically giving away pianos, and simply wasting

24. Ibid., ll. 66–68ob.

25. *Muzykal'naia entsiklopediia,* 1:243.

26. Fay, *Shostakovich,* 364. Atovm'ian also arranged some of Shostakovich's orchestral suites from ballet and film scores; see 180, 241.

27. RGALI, f. 2077, op. 1, d. 51, ll. 74–75.

28. Ibid., d. 120, ll. 14–15 (Protokol #6, 23 Apr 1945).

29. Ibid., d. 233, ll. 39–41 (A. Kosygin to Biuro SM SSSR, 14 Jun 1948). Of the 722,000 rubles

money on administrative issues rather than direct support to Muzfond members.[30] Kosygin's findings echoed complaints that had been overheard within the Composers' Union earlier that year.[31]

Not surprisingly, Muzfond leadership changed in 1948.[32] But even after the new leaders had purportedly gotten the ship in order, internal investigations continued to uncover evidence of financial indiscipline and personalistic decision making. Loan repayment continued to be a problem, and in November 1948 the Secretariat of the Composers' Union approved a Muzfond plan to bring law suits against those who had not repaid loans.[33] In late 1948 and early 1949, the Secretariat began enforcing its new, stricter loan policy, demanding return of funds for uncompleted works; but this stricter enforcement was accompanied by yet another internal investigation, which discovered that the problem had not been remedied. Composers' indebtedness to Muzfond was growing. Though beginning to come under control, the loan situation was still considered an extreme problem even in the middle of 1949.[34]

Outside institutions also continued to hear complaints about the personalistic nature of Muzfond decisions. In 1950 the Central Committee apparatus conducted an investigation of artistic celebrations of Lenin and Stalin. In their report they noted that decisions to publish specific songs about the two leaders were not made on the basis of approval within "the composing public," but because of the personal relationships between "accidental people" in the publishing apparatus and specific composers.[35] Also in 1950, the Central Com-

---

loaned to Orgkom and Muzfond leaders, 440,000 allegedly went to just four. Though the maximum loan was set at 10,000 rubles, some of these reached as high as 75,000 rubles.

30. Ibid., ll. 40–41. The automobiles belonged to Glier, Khachaturian, and Shostakovich. The almost 1.3 million rubles that Muzfond spent on administrative expenses in 1947 amounted to 25 percent of its entire budget, but in some locations that percentage was as high as 57 percent.

31. RGASPI, f. 17, op. 121, d. 728, ll. 25–30 (Informational report on SSK party cell, 12 Feb 1948). Complaints included the accusation that Atovm'ian ran Muzfond as a sort of second Composers' Union only for "most respected composers," and that too much money had been "wasted" on Prokofiev and others.

32. Atovm'ian took the fall for Muzfond in July (RGALI, f. 2077, op. 1, d. 234, l. 65 [Protokol #27, 28 Jul 1948], pt. 3), but he had been replaced long before that. RGALI, f. 2077, op. 1, d. 234, l. 4 (Protokol #2, 2 Mar 1948); and d. 235, l. 18 (Orgkom Prikaz #25/l, 3 Mar 1948). N. N. Kriukov replaced Atovm'ian as the head. See also ibid., l. 69 (Prikaz #78, 16 Sep 1948), which ordered specific measures for the continuing reorganization of Muzfond.

33. RGALI, f. 2077, op. 1, d. 234, ll. 34–35 (Protokol #14, 8 May 1948), pt. 1. Muzfond leaders were congratulated for being united and incited to remain so as they enacted a decisive break with the past; l. 142 (Protokol #46, 19 Nov 1948), pt. 2. See also ll. 146–47 (Protokol #48, 26 Nov 1949), pt. 2, which established tighter restrictions for loan repayment.

34. RGALI, f. 2077, op. 1, d. 234, l. 152ob. (Protokol #50, 17 Dec 1948), pt. 3a. Several rank-and-file composers were ordered to repay advances; d. 338, l. 9 (SSK Auditing commission Protokol, 27 Dec 1948). The report also called attention to the unacceptable financial state of Muzfond's publishing operations; ll. 80–82 (Protokol #16, 15 Apr 1949).

35. RGASPI, f. 17, op. 132, d. 418, l. 24 (Kruzhkov and Tarasov to Suslov, 4 Apr 1950). The entire report is ll. 22–25. The phrases they used are *"kompozitorskaia obshchestvennost'"* and *"sluchainye liudi,"* a phrase usually applied to administrators who were not chosen for their ideological soundness or political credentials.

mittee apparatus complained that the creative resort in Ruza was not used appropriately; rather, the family and favorites of Muzfond workers used it all the time.[36]

Such consistent complaints of corruption and financial indiscipline suggest an administrative culture common to the Composers' Union leadership before and after 1948. Unofficial, personalistic networks pervaded the entire arts administration system, intertwining with official institutions to gain legitimate status and to facilitate the operation of a resource allocation system suffering from chronic and endemic shortages. Aside from merely participating in this pervasive system of unofficial, personalistic networks, however, Muzfond's personalistic tendencies and especially its lack of financial discipline suggest two other explanations.

The first explanation was provided by Muzfond leaders in one of their earliest defensive meetings and then repeated in the 1942 audit. The musical experts who directed Muzfond's activities were simply not as knowledgeable about what it took to run a large funding institution as they were about music.[37] When they tried to justify an early failure to fulfill a plan, the leaders noted that "this shortfall can be explained, apparently, by insufficiently substantiated planning which was committed in Muzfond's first year of work."[38] This "insufficiently substantiated planning" could come as no surprise either to those involved or to one who reads through the confused muddle of an early planning discussion. Even a member with eight years experience with Gosplan could not bring order to a discussion that sought to establish estimates on which to base the plan for Muzfond.[39] Though perhaps common to all central planning work, the inaccuracy of estimates must have been fundamentally exacerbated by the lack of experience and expertise of those doing the planning.

Though this explanation probably became less applicable as Muzfond officials gained planning experience, another, more personalistic explanation undoubtedly applied even well beyond the Stalin period. In many cases, those composers who sat on Composers' Union committees and commissions, and who could have enforced financial discipline by rejecting unfit work, simply felt more loyalty to their colleagues and friends than they did to abstract concepts of financial discipline or allegiance to a government from which many of them felt increasingly alienated. Thus, no matter how lousy a particular composition was, members of the evaluation committee could decide that they liked its com-

36. Ibid., ll. 201–9 (OPA report on SSK, 1950).
37. For the auditor's comment, see RGALI, f. 2077, op. 1, d. 51, l. 69ob. The auditor, named Balaban, notes that the financial problems he uncovered would meet with harsh treatment by Goskontrol′, but standards of financial discipline could not be so high in an *obshchestvennaia organizatsiia* staffed with "comrades" rather than financial experts. In other words, it was a question of competence, not malfeasance.
38. Ibid., d. 33, ll. 1–14, here 14 (explanatory report, 1940).
39. Ibid., d. 31 (Stenogramma soveshchaniia v Muzfonde SSSR, 26 May 1940), esp. ll. 25–38, a confused discussion of the nature and process of planning, in which the auditor Balaban announced his Gosplan experience and unsuccessfully tried to bring clarity to the discussion.

poser, and they knew he or she needed the money. So they described the work in glowing terms and accepted it.[40]

Whatever the explanation, Muzfond simply did not operate as a disinterested funding bureaucracy, mechanistically fulfilling creative plans set by the Composers' Union and responding to personal emergencies with appropriate material assistance. But it did provide composers and musicologists fundamental and extremely valuable material support while they were engaged in artistic production and as they attempted to negotiate the material difficulties they faced in their daily lives.

From Labor to Intellectual Property: The Copyright Administration

If funding from Muzfond was supposed to support all composers and musicologists who were actively engaged in creative activity, another source of material support—royalties—was intended to provide financial remuneration to those whose work was performed in public. From the late 1930s until the end of the Stalin period, the institution that managed both copyright and royalties for works of music, theater, and literature was the All-USSR Administration for the Preservation of Authors' Rights (VUOAP, the Copyright Administration).[41] Centrally administered by a governing council of composers, playwrights, and writers, the Copyright Administration's tasks were to administer copyright protection for the publication and public performance of literary, dramatic, and musical works, to collect royalties from publishers and performance institutions, and to pay authors and composers those royalties.[42]

By its own count at the beginning of its operations in 1938, this centralized bureaucracy was supposed to administer a system that included eight thousand writers, playwrights, and composers spread across eight republic-level agencies and over twelve hundred local branches.[43] Not surprisingly, the Copyright Ad-

40. G. S. Frid, personal communication, 7 May 1999. Frid attributed insincere positive evaluations both to the sort of instrumental funding thinking that I suggest here (i.e., "he needs the money") and to the discomfort associated with telling friends that their pieces were not good.

41. The literal translation of the phrase *"avtorskoe pravo"* is "authors' rights," but it means "copyright." This explains the difference between my literal translation of VUOAP's name (*Vsesoiuznoe upravlenie dlia okhraneniia avtorskikh prav*) and my shorthand (Copyright Administration).

42. Except where otherwise noted, the institutional information provided in this paragraph was provided by the introduction to RGALI, f. 2452, op. 2 (page 1), which was written by junior *sotrudnik* Rozenberg. For a much more detailed discussion of VUOAP, its activities in musical life, and the arguments summarized here, see Tomoff, "Illegitimacy of Popularity," 311–40.

43. RGALI, f. 2452, op. 1, d. 19, l. 31 (A. Tolstoi to Kondakov [OPA], Dec 1938). Tolstoi asked permission for Glavlit to publish a quarterly bulletin of decrees, instructions, and so forth to help administrators keep abreast of developments in copyright and royalties legislation. By 1949, VUOAP claimed to represent as many as ten thousand composers and playwrights; ibid., op. 2, d. 30, l. 2 (Leonov, Pogodin, and Verta to Voroshilov, 1949).

ministration kept busy in each of its areas of activity. For example, in 1938 it stepped in to threaten manufacturers of gramophone records with legal action if they did not check attributions on their records more carefully. Songs on records released in several national republics had apparently been incorrectly attributed, thus violating the actual authors' and composers' "moral and material rights." The record manufacturers were instructed to seek VUOAP clearance before going to press in the future.[44] Besides providing an idea of the mundane troubleshooting that the Copyright Administration could provide, this example demonstrates that at stake for royalties administrators were both the "material rights" and the intellectual or creative property ("moral rights") of authors.

The Copyright Administration also sorted through the tangled issues of royalties for theater music and managed conflicts and exceptions that touched on the payment of royalties. Despite its extensive reach, the Copyright Administration did not decide all matters that related to the practical workings of the royalties system. On particularly touchy issues, VUOAP administrators preferred to defer to other institutions. As it performed these tasks, the Copyright Administration was continually the center of controversy caused by perceived problems with the basic legislation on copyright and royalties. That legislation was passed in 1928 but was already considered archaic after the war.[45] Like almost all copyright legislation, the 1928 law was based on literary works and extrapolated to other artistic products from the literary example. This law was a continual source of frustration for composers, librettists, writers, royalties administrators, and even party bureaucrats. Arguments about its problems reveal an intriguing shift in the underlying conceptions governing the payment of royalties.

Royalties were always paid on the basis of use. If a theater performed an operetta by a Soviet composer, it had to pay royalties. This basic conception remained unchanged throughout the Stalin period, but within this general,

44. RGALI, f. 2452, op. 1, d. 19, l. 29 (A. Tolstoi [pred. soveta VUOAP] and Khesin [Direktor VUOAP] to Grammplasttrest, 21 Nov [1938]). This matter came to Khesin's attention through the efforts of two more junior members of the VUOAP apparatus, Iu. Khait and one Zhilinskaia, who argued that at stake was accuracy in "undoubtedly the best means of propagandizing and popularizing drama and musical works." See ll. 30–30ob. (Khait and Zhilinskaia to Khesin, 15 Nov 1938). For a short history of record royalties, see RGALI, f. 2452, op. 1, d. 93, ll. 155–55ob. (Kolesov [Direktor VUOAP] to VUOAP Sovet, 12 Oct 1951). For another complaint spearheaded by VUOAP, see RGALI, f. 2452, op. 2, d. 30, l. 3 (Zverev [MinFin] to SM SSSR, 19 Apr 1949) and ll. 8–8ob. (Abolimov and Artamonova to Voroshilov, 29 Apr 1949). The dispute continued well into the 1950s as it became part of the general discussion on royalties reform. For further VUOAP participation, see RGALI, f. 2452, op. 2, d. 34, ll. 5–6 (Lebedev, Leonov, Khrennikov, and Gavrilov to Voroshilov, 11 Apr 1950), which contained a draft SM SSSR resolution to resolve the matter.

45. For the full text of the basic law, see "Postanovlenie TsIK i SNK SSSR, 16 May 1928," *Svod zakonov SSSR*, 1928, no. 27, st. 245–46; reprinted in *Avtorskoe pravo na literaturnye proizvedeniia: Sbornik ofitsial'nykh materialov*, ed. L. M. Azov and S. A. Shatsillo (Moscow: Gosizdat Iuridicheskoi literatury, 1953), 7–15. For one accusation that the 1928 law was "archaic" twenty years later, see RGALI, f. 2452, op. 2, d. 27, l. 6 (Khesin to SSP SSSR and SSK SSSR, 21 Jun 1948).

pay-by-use system, there were graduated royalties rates for different kinds of artistic production. Insistent complaints about the graduated rate structure established in the basic copyright legislation were not only prompted by increasingly intense political pressure to produce new Soviet art but also reflected changing conceptions of the relative importance of labor and intellectual property in determining legitimate remuneration for artistic production.

In the beginning, copyright laws and the rules regulating graduated royalties payments were based on a conception that privileged labor as the fundamental basis for any remuneration. The amount of work required to produce a piece of music or a work of literature determined compensation. Though it was supported throughout the Stalin period by the trade unions and, to a lesser extent, the Ministry of Finance, this notion initially came under attack before World War II as too easy to manipulate for self-interested personal gain or in ways that undermined the party's instructions about artistic production. As a result, the head of the Copyright Administration proposed changes in policies that implicitly suggested that royalties should be used as a tool to stimulate artistic production along lines suggested by the Soviet Union's political leadership. The big change in the underlying conception that governed royalties rates, however, was a shift championed by both the Composers' Union and the Writers' Union. These two creative unions sought to stress the value and protection of intellectual property more than labor. Most writers and composers—creative union leadership and rank and file alike—agreed with this fundamental conception. They thought that royalties should be compensation for the production of an intellectual product that remained the original author's intellectual property even after it had been translated into another language and even if it continued to earn royalties, year after year, without any additional labor inputs from the playwright, writer, or composer.[46]

The royalties system thus proved to be fertile ground for disputes about the relationship between material compensation and artistic production, but throughout the Stalin period, the Copyright Administration understood its task to encompass *both* the protection of intellectual property and the provision of material support. As part of its overall contribution to the provision of material support, the Copyright Administration collected contributions from performance institutions' box office receipts and delivered them to Muzfond. In other words, performance institutions paid one cut to VUOAP to cover individuals' royalties and another to contribute to Muzfond.

The Copyright Administration's contribution to Muzfond's financial system was significant. Table 8.1 provides total budgetary figures for 1940, broken down into categories according to musical genre, box office receipts, royalties, and deductions for Muzfond. These budget predictions were undoubtedly in-

46. For the Writers' Union position on copyright and royalties claims regarding translated works, see RGASPI, f. 17, op. 133, d. 346, ll. 28–48 (SSP report [Fadeev], 30 Aug 1952). For the Composers' Union position on the legitimacy of collecting royalties as long as works are performed, see ibid., ll. 213–36 (Khrennikov to Suslov, [Oct 1954]), here 213–16.

Table 8.1. Royalties and Muzfond Deductions (in Rubles), 1940

Genre	Box office receipts			Royalties paid to composers[a]	Deductions for Muzfond[b]
	Total	VUOAP composer	Non-VUOAP composer		
Opera	16,000,000	9,700,000	6,400,000	294,200	322,000
Operetta	18,900,000	15,200,000	3,700,000	759,600	378,000
Philharmonics and estrada	34,000,000	34,000,000	0	1,000,000	680,000
Clubs, Houses of Culture	11,100,000	11,100,000	0	332,500	222,000
Outside theaters	2,600,000	2,000,000	600,000	98,500	53,000
Funds from previous years	7,200,000	5,400,000	1,800,000	277,100	145,000
Total	89,900,000	77,400,000	12,500,000	3,100,000	1,800,000

Source: RGALI, f. 2452, op. 1, d. 45, l. 12 (Tablitsa uslovnykh koefitsientov dlia ischisleniia po dannym avtorskogo gonorara, sborov i otchislenii v Litfond i Muzfond na 1940g., approved by Khesin, 28 Feb 1940). See table 8.2 for details of the Muzfond section of this table.

Note: A "VUOAP composer" was a living composer whose works were protected by the VUOAP.

[a] Royalties paid to composers totaled 5 percent of the box office receipts in all categories except Opera and Clubs and Houses of Culture. For VUOAP composers of opera, the original table notes a royalties rate of 3.5 percent, but the actual royalties are figured at 3 percent. For Clubs and Houses of Culture, Muzfond received 25 percent (of which, 3 percent was paid as royalties to composers), Litfond received 50 percent, and the status of the remaining 25 percent is unclear.

[b] Muzfond received 2 percent of box office receipts

accurate. They assume that 60 percent of box office revenue for operas would come from Soviet operas, a number which must have been far too high. Similarly, predicting that all philharmonic receipts would come from composers covered by VUOAP was simply absurd. However, these data are still quite useful because they provide a sense of the scale of royalties payments before the war. The nearly five million rubles in direct or indirect royalties payments was a significant source of material support. As table 8.2 demonstrates, royalties contributed as much to Muzfond at the end of the period covered by this study as they did at the beginning, but in the late 1940s VUOAP deducted a percentage of Muzfond's total royalties to support its own operations. Though VUOAP was always supported by contributions from the total royalties paid, that number is absent from the 1940 data. These data are most useful for the general idea that they give of the scale of royalties paid to composers during the late Stalin period.

The Copyright Administration oversaw one important element of the system that provided basic material support to music professionals, especially composers. Unlike other types of funding institutions, most of the funds that it administered were earmarked for individual composers rather than for music professionals as a corporate group. Since those funds were tied to theater box office earnings and specific pieces, they proved a lightning rod for discussions

Table 8.2. Copyright Administration Collections (Millions of Rubles), 1948–52

Year	1948 (actual)	1949 (actual)	1950 (plan)	1951 (plan)	1952 (plan)
Royalties paid	34.3	35	36	40	43.2
Funds to Muzfond	7.9	5.8	6	6.5	6.8
Funds to Litfond	7.3	7.2	5.5	8.5	9.8
Publication royalties	10.9	10	7.5	13	12.3
Subtotal: Regular collection	60.4	58	55	68	72.1
Other funds	15.1	13	12	10	9.5
Total collection	75.5	71	67	78	81.7

Sources: RGALI, f. 2452, op. 1, d. 93, ll. 78–80 (tables showing fulfillment of 1949 plan, compared to 1948); ibid., ll. 65–66 (Plan sbora avtorskogo gonorara i otchislenii v Litfond i Muzfond SSSR i postuplenii ot summy po realizatsii dogovorov na 1950g., 28 Feb 1950); ibid., ll. 112–15 (Plan sbora avtorskogo gonorara i otchislenii v Litfond i Muzfond SSSR i postuplenii ot summy po realizatsii dogovorov na 1951g., 31 Mar 1951); ibid., ll. 157–58 (Plan sbora avtorskogo gonorara i otchislenii v Litfond i Muzfond SSSR i postuplenii ot summy po realizatsii dogovorov na 1952g., 27 Oct 1951).
Note: When columns do not total, errors are due to rounding.

of appropriate compensation in the arts world. Those discussions shifted the justification for graduated royalties rates from labor to intellectual property. Though controversy raged on well after the end of the Stalin period, the Copyright Administration continued to provide an important share of music professionals' basic material support. For a very few composers, that material support eventually became much more than basic, and their astronomical earnings repeatedly called into question the legitimacy of the entire system.

Historians and historical economists have noted that the Soviet economic system was unlike its capitalist counterpart in a number of ways. One of the most notable differences between the two economic systems, it has been argued, was the disparate role of money in generating privileged access to goods and services. According to this view, salary or income from such sources as those described in this chapter were utterly unreliable measures of an individual's actual material status or means in Soviet society.[47] Rather, status was determined by a system of privileges that provided variable access to scarce goods and services and the hierarchies of prestige that accompanied that access.

This view of the Soviet system of privileges is not inaccurate, and chapter 9 explores just the sorts of honors and awards that conferred the highest elite status in the Soviet cultural world. Yet this view is incomplete.[48] There were alternate paths to material privilege in the Stalinist music world, only one of which was the official hierarchical system of honors, awards, and prizes that legitimated one sort of material privilege. Another path open to composers was

47. Janos Kornai, *Economics of Shortage* (Amsterdam: North Holland, 1980); and Osokina, *Za fasadom "Stalinskogo izobiliia."*
48. In fact, Julie Hessler has demonstrated the importance of both cash incomes and markets to the Soviet economy more generally: Julie Hessler, *A Social History of Soviet Trade: Trade Policy, Retail Practices, and Consumption, 1917–1953* (Princeton: Princeton University Press, 2004).

writing music that appealed to general, popular audiences and collecting the sometimes extremely high royalties that such music earned. Though few composers enjoyed this path to material comfort, those who did frequently became the objects of intense scrutiny and resentment. The material privilege of popular song composers who earned astronomical royalties was often considered illegitimate by professional colleagues and policy makers alike.

As is the case elsewhere in the world, the implicit logic of the Soviet royalties system was that popularity should be rewarded. When the royalties system was reviewed and restructured in the 1950s, among the major participants in the debate only Tikhon Khrennikov articulated that logic. He argued that popularity with the general listening public ought to entitle composers to continue earning royalties for the same popular piece year after year.[49] Crucial to Khrennikov's position was also a realistic defense of a system that he thought was being attacked for its exceptional rather than typical results. In short, the Soviet royalties system distributed earnings unevenly, as all royalties systems must, heavily rewarding some composers while leaving others to seek material support through other channels. For example, Khrennikov noted that 88 percent of all Moscow-based composers at the end of the Stalin period earned less than forty-five thousand rubles in royalties annually, and just over half earned none at all.[50] According to a separate, earlier report generated by the Copyright Administration, 93 percent of all royalties earners (not just composers) reportedly earned less than a thousand rubles per month while just over half a percent earned more than ten thousand. Three, including an extremely popular songwriter, earned over twenty-five thousand rubles a month.[51] Some of these earnings could be astronomical, as a 1954 Ministry of Culture report complained. Again, the popular song writer led the way by earning 2.4 million rubles "for performances of his operettas and popular songs" between 1951 and 1953.[52] These data show that composers of popular songs and operettas could amass tremendous fortunes.

Another group of musicians who earned terrific royalties was the performance elite, who grossed huge sums of money by collecting royalties from radio performances. Between 1950 and 1952 two prominent conductors each averaged well over 100,000 rubles per year; a musical director of an opera theater topped out at nearly 177,000 rubles in 1951. In 1950 a top violinist grossed over 125,000 rubles, and in 1952 the same violinist made over 75,000 more. Opera singers and conductors also frequently pulled in 20,000 to 40,000 rubles

49. RGASPI, f. 17, op. 133, d. 346, ll. 213–23, here l. 215 (Khrennikov to Suslov, [Oct 1954]).
50. Ibid., ll. 213–23.
51. RGALI, f. 2452, op. 2, d. 30, l. 12 (report on 1948 prepared by Vvedenskii, 6 Oct 1949).
52. RGASPI, f. 17, op. 133, d. 346, l. 257 (explanatory note to draft SM SSSR resolution, prepared by Kemenev [MinKul'tury], 2 Nov 1954). In this case, I translated "*estradnye proizvedeniia*" as "popular song." The report includes multiple composers of popular songs and a host of playwrights.

per opera performed on the radio.[53] As in every other case when high royalties were described, the proposal that accompanied these data suggested drastically cutting royalties, this time for radio performances.

This nearly constant concern about huge earnings from royalties reveals a deep-seated suspicion of the material privilege that royalties could produce. Unlike the official but extraordinary rewards like honorary titles and Stalin Prizes, high royalties reflected success with the broadest, most general of audiences. Political leaders and fiscal watchdogs alike seemed to mistrust such a general audience's reliability to confer prestige and material privilege, and they turned that suspicion on the theaters, composers, librettists, and playwrights who wrote "for the box office."[54] Besides being produced by suspect audiences, material privilege from royalties earnings was also considered illegitimate because it did not reward an artistic product that was judged exemplary by professional standards. Worse, it sometimes resulted in the emergence of an elite culture of conspicuous, even competitive consumption, as in the case of Isaak Dunaevskii's attempts—eventually unsuccessful—to outdo his one-time friend and film collaborator Grigorii Aleksandrov in displays of luxury items, foreign goods, and flashy summer houses.[55] This spectacle of a fantastically lavish lifestyle surrounding some artistic figures was also apparent in the early post-Stalin period, as government administrators fell from power in scandals associated with their high-living hobnobbing with wealthy writers and other artists.[56]

Composers and musicologists were funded by a basic material support system comprised of two elements, Muzfond and royalties. While the Copyright Administration collected royalties and delivered them to individual composers, Muzfond was responsible for material distribution to music professionals as a corporate group. Both institutions were highly centralized. In disbursing Muzfond resources, the Composers' Union leadership in Moscow sought to maintain control over its scattered chapters, even at the expense of developing ties between its various subsidiary institutions in the periphery.

As they performed their distribution tasks, both Muzfond and the Copyright Administration became the focus of controversy. Investigations that uncovered personalistic decision making and a profound lack of fiscal discipline in Muzfond revealed a deep-seated uneasiness with the arbitrary and uneven distribution of resources by the system's basic material support institution. Despite

53. Ibid., ll. 238–39 (explanatory note to draft SM SSSR resolution, from G. Aleksandrov [Min Kul'tury SSSR] to TsK KPSS, 2 Nov 1954).

54. For two of the clearest articulations of this mistrust, see RGASPI, f. 17, op. 125, d. 11, ll. 30–34 (Aleksandrov and Polikarpov to A. A. Andreev, Zhdanov, and Malenkov, 1 Nov 1940) and op. 132, d. 234, ll. 87–88 (Tarasov to Kruzhkov, 30 Aug 1949).

55. D. Minchenok, *Isaak Dunaevskii: Bol'shoi kontsert* (Moscow: Olimp, 1998), 461. The competition between the two men is the framing device for the entire chapter "Veter sud'by," which ends with Dunaevskii's final victory through his immortal music. The melodrama is characteristic.

56. "Ellochka i drugie liudoedki," *Nastoiashchee tainoe*, [May 1999], 5–7.

observers' and investigators' uneasiness, however, the professional leadership remained in complete, almost unmonitored control of the significant resources and material infrastructure of the Muzfond system.

Struggles over the royalties system revealed uneasiness with a distribution system that awarded composers of popular songs and operettas with huge royalties. In the continuous discussions about what to do with the graduated rate structure of the royalties systems, various participants exhibited changing conceptions about the place of legitimate material compensation in the music world. Some increasingly thought of royalties as a tool that could be used to promote the ideological goals set by the party. Others fought over the relative legitimacy of labor and intellectual property as a justification for compensation.

The Copyright Administration and Muzfond thus formed the backbone of the material support infrastructure that sustained music professionals throughout the Stalin period. They performed the essential task of distributing resources to the profession, often according to personalistic decisions and preferences. Despite the uneven distribution, the basic support of Muzfond and royalties was extensive enough to maintain Composers' Union members as a privileged elite within Soviet society. Within that elite, however, there were extensive hierarchical distinctions that played out in a system of extraordinary honors, titles, and prizes, all of which contributed to the material privilege of their recipients.

CHAPTER 9

Elite Hierarchies

Elite hierarchies in the music world were constructed and justified through a system of extraordinary honors, prizes, and awards that formed a capstone of prestige and material privilege. Though diverse audiences granted the authority required to qualify for these extraordinary awards, the criteria by which they were granted were essentially determined by the professional elite, especially members of the Stalin Prize Committee. This committee formed a crucial interface between the Stalinist political leadership and the creative intelligentsia. The musical elite's agency to interpret musical value was used to translate creative authority into social hierarchies and material privilege.

Extreme royalties and extraordinary honors afforded those who obtained them unusual material comfort, and both simultaneously acknowledged and reproduced creative authority. The audiences that granted that authority were quite distinct, however, and there was a pronounced difference in the perceived legitimacy of the respective privileges. Though the composers of songs and operettas who benefited most from the royalties system enjoyed remarkable popularity among general audiences, that popularity did not translate into unquestioned legitimacy. Elite opera singers, classical music performers, and highbrow composers enjoyed authority among an informed cultural elite. The highbrow preferences of this elite, including the Composers' Union leadership, ensured that purveyors of symphonic music, chamber music, operas, and ballet would occupy the pinnacle of status and privilege in the Stalinist music world.

Composers versus Performers

Before World War II, the Stalinist Soviet Union developed a system for displaying and rewarding outstanding contributions to its culture and society. Through honorary titles, orders, medals, and prizes, the music world figured prominently in this system of displayed excellence and prestige. After the war, the scale of recognition and reward, though not the form, expanded drastically; and the place of culture in these honor roles remained especially high, since the exclusive prewar titles and prizes remained the restricted terrain of the cultural and technical intelligentsia.[1] Several different types of official recognition were offered to musicians throughout the Soviet period. Titles, prizes, orders, and medals all had their place in a system of honors that drastically improved recipients' material conditions, reproduced or reinforced hierarchies of authority, and translated them into hierarchies of prestige within and outside the profession. These honors legitimized hierarchies of material privilege that favored traditionalist, high-art prejudices and the performers who were most suited to producing it, especially opera singers.

Perhaps the most significant type of extraordinary reward was the honorary title. Besides their prestigious cache, titles often conferred drastically improved housing access, medical care, and retirement pensions.[2] After 1936, musicians could receive four titles: People's Artist of the Soviet Union (Narodnyi artist SSSR), People's Artist of the Republic (Narodnyi artist respubliki; for example, Narodnyi artist RSFSR), Honored Figure of the Arts (Zasluzhennyi deiatel' iskusstv), and Honored Artist (Zasluzhennyi artist). The most prestigious and seldom awarded title was People's Artist of the Soviet Union, the only one issued by the all-USSR government.[3] Within the various republics, the highest title was People's Artist of the Republic. Honored Figure of the Arts and Honored Artist were less prestigious and more commonly awarded.

The second most significant type of reward was the Stalin Prize. Announced at the end of 1939 in honor of Stalin's sixtieth birthday, the Stalin Prize was a large cash payment, but it also carried the prestigious title "Stalin Prize Laureate."[4] Though its three classes carried monetary awards ranging from twenty-five thousand to a hundred thousand rubles, all three imparted the title on the winner. To put these amounts in perspective, in the first full year of its operation, Muzfond allocated an average of just over two thousand rubles per member in direct creative and material support, and this sort of allowance proved to be the envy of performers.[5] Stalin Prizes were awarded in creative categories,

1. At the Uzbek *dekada* of 1937, for example, participants were awarded 13 Orders of the Labor Red Banner and 25 Sign of Honor Orders; whereas, at the Uzbek *dekada* of 1951, 6 awardees received the Order of Lenin, 26 the Order of the Labor Red Banner, 59 the Sign of Honor Order, and 117 the Medal for Labor Excellence; *Izvestiia*, 1 Jun 1937, 1; *Vedomosti Verkhovnogo Soveta SSSR*, 1951, no. 49 (13 Dec): 2.

2. Juri Jelagin, *Taming of the Arts*, trans. N. Wreden (New York: E. P. Dutton, 1951); Galina Vishnevskaia, *Galina: Istoriia zhizni* (Moscow: Gorizont, 1993); RGASPI, f. 17, op. 133, d. 367, ll. 162–68 (Bespalov to SM SSSR, 18 Sep 1952, and response). Pensions for musicians with titles were decided on a case-by-case basis by the Council of Ministers. Levels depended on the honorary title and tenure of service.

3. *Izvestiia*, 8 Sep 1936, 1. The first potential recipients were thirteen theater personalities, eleven of whom were People's Artists of their respective republics, and two of whom were Honored Artists: RGASPI, f. 82, op. 2, d. 954, ll. 8–10 (Kerzhentsev to Molotov, 5 Sep 1936).

4. *Izvestiia*, 21 Dec 1939, 1.

5. RGALI, f. 2077, op. 1, d. 28, ll. 5–7, 8–8ob., 11–12, 14–16ob., 19ob–21, 22–22ob. (Muzfond Protokol #2–3, 5–8, 5–10 Feb, 26 Feb, 7 Mar, 13 Mar, and 25 Mar 1940).

three of which touched composers: (1) large staged musical and vocal compositions (opera, ballet, oratorio, cantata), (2) large instrumental compositions, and (3) compositions of small forms. Beginning in 1944, performers fell into a fourth subcategory within the music group, concert performance activity, and into separate opera and ballet groups.[6]

The least significant and most frequently issued types of awards were orders and medals. The Order of Lenin, the Order of the Labor Red Banner (Orden Trudovogo krasnogo znameni), and the Sign of Honor Order (Orden "Znak pocheta") were regularly issued to reward participants in large musical and theatrical events such as ten-day festivals (*dekada*) of national minority art, concert tours, and major institutional anniversaries.[7] Finally, individuals were awarded orders in celebration of major accomplishments or milestones like birthdays or anniversaries of premiere performances.[8] Besides the orders that were issued to the theaters' most prominent members, soloists, and directors, several different less prestigious medals were available to virtually all other participants, especially after the war.[9]

These awards provide a useful marker of the music world's prestige hierarchies when recipients of orders are compared with honorary titleholders. One sample demonstrates that composers from national republics often carried the most prestigious titles among visiting delegations, but performers received the vast majority of orders (104 of 146). The two most prestigious titles, People's Artist of the USSR and People's Artist of the Republic, were common to all mu-

---

6. *Sobranie postanovlenii i rasporiazhenii Pravitel'stva SSSR*, 1946, no. 3 (15 Mar), st. 39, "O prisuzhdenii Stalinskikh premii za vydaiushchiesia raboty v oblasti iskusstva i literatury za 1943 i 1944 gody." The concert performance category was created by SNK SSSR on 13 March 1943. For the first of these new awards, see RGASPI, f. 17, op. 125, d. 233, ll. 28–29, 35–36 (Khrapchenko to Stalin and Molotov, 1 Apr 1944).

7. For the Kazakh *dekada*: *Izvestiia*, 27 May 1936, 1; Uzbek *dekada*: *Izvestiia*, 1 Jun 1937, 1; Azerbaidzhani *dekada*: *Izvestiia*, 18 Apr 1938, 1; Kirghiz *dekada*: *Izvestiia*, Jun 1939, 1; Armenian *dekada*: *Izvestiia*, 5 Nov 1939, 1–2; Belorussian *dekada*: *Izvestiia*, 21 Jun 1940, 1; Buriat-Mongol *dekada*: *Izvestiia*, 1 Nov 1940, 1; Tadzhik *dekada*: *Izvestiia*, 24 Apr 1941; Georgian *dekada*: *Vedomosti Verkhovnogo Soveta SSSR*, 1950, no. 37 (22 Nov): 1; Ukrainian *dekada*: *Vedomosti Verkhovnogo Soveta SSSR*, 1951, no. 24 (19 Jul): 1–4; and a second Uzbek *dekada*: *Vedomosti Verkhovnogo Soveta SSSR*, 1951, no. 49 (13 Dec): 2; the Kiev Theater of Opera and Ballet: *Izvestiia*, 24 Mar 1936, 1; the Bol'shoi: *Izvestiia*, 3 Jun 1937, 1; and *Vedomosti Verkhovnogo Soveta SSSR*, 1951, no. 15 (5 Jun); the Leningrad Malyi Theater: *Izvestiia*, 24 Sep 1937, 1; the Leningrad Conservatory: *Izvestiia*, 8 Apr 1938, 1 and 18 Jun 1938, 1; the Red Army Ensemble of Song and Dance: *Izvestiia*, 17 Jan 1939, 1, and *Vedomosti Verkhovnogo Soveta SSSR*, 1949, no. 8 (16 Feb): 1; the Moscow State Jewish Theater: *Izvestiia*, 1 Apr 1939, 1; the Moscow Conservatory: *Izvestiia*, 8 May 1940, 1–2; and *Vedomosti Verkhovnogo Soveta SSSR*, 1947, no. 1 (5 Jan); 1; and a variety of visiting Leningrad groups, including theaters and the Leningrad Philharmonic: *Izvestiia*, 2 Jun 1940, 1–3.

8. For the award to I. O. Dunaevskii for film music: *Izvestiia*, 1 Jan 1937, 1; the folk singer Dzhambul Dzhabaev on his seventy-fifth birthday: *Izvestiia*, 20 May 1938, 1; the tenor I. S. Kozlovskii for outstanding service in opera: *Izvestiia*, 19 Jul 1939, 1; A. F. Kobzova, V. S. Arsen'ev, and V. G. Borisov for folk dance: *Izvestiia*, 3 Aug 1939, 4; and the pianist A. F. Gedike on his seventieth birthday: *Vedomosti Verkhovnogo Soveta SSSR*, 1952, no. 13 (15 May): 1.

9. *Vedomosti Verkhovnogo Soveta SSSR*, 1951, no. 15 (5 Jun): 1–2; *Vedomosti Verkhovnogo Soveta SSSR*, 1950, no. 9 (15 Mar): 2; no. 37 (22 Nov): 1.

sicians. The other two were almost mutually exclusive. Performers dominated the Honored Artist category (60 of 68), while composers, artistic directors, conductors, and teachers held most Honored Figure of the Arts titles (32 of 37).[10]

Another measure is provided by the sixty-five recipients of the title People's Artist of the USSR between 1936 and 1947. Almost half (thirty) of them were musicians, and the rest were major theater figures. Nearly half (thirty-one) were from Moscow, while fifteen came from Ukraine, six from Leningrad, six from the Caucasus, five from Central Asia, and one each from Belorussia and the Buriat-Mongol Autonomous Republic.[11] People's Artists of the Soviet Union were evenly divided between theater and music and between Moscow and the rest of the Soviet Union.

The distribution of these highest of honorary titles demonstrates that among the musicians, performers, especially opera singers, comprised a much larger group (twenty-four) than did composers (seven).[12] The dominance of opera is particularly striking, as all but *two* were affiliated with opera in one way or another.[13] Nineteen were singers (twelve sopranos, six basses, and a tenor), and the other four were either conductors or directors who specialized in opera theater.[14] Opera obviously opened the most prestigious—and privileged—doors.

Though it is an extremely small sample, the distribution of these titles over time suggests a shifting emphasis during the war. After proving their worth during it, composers received more titles after the war. Of the thirty-two musicians who were named People's Artist of the Soviet Union, twenty received their titles before the war, and twelve received them during or after it. Thus more than 60 percent of all titles to musicians were rewarded before the war. However,

---

10. Lists of order recipients in *Izvestiia*, 1936–41, and *Vedomosti Verkhovnogo Soveta SSSR*, 1946–52, yielded 269 titleholders in the music field, of whom 146 also had professional labels. The remaining 123 were members of the Bol'shoi Theater, so they were mostly opera and dance performers and probably represent a large number of duplicates since the Bol'shoi received two sets of awards in this period (without professional labels either time). For a detailed breakdown of the *Vedomosti Verkhovnogo Soveta SSSR* data, see Tomoff, "Creative Union," 475–78.

11. RGASPI, f. 17, op. 125, d. 499, ll. 156–58 (prepared by P. Lebedev, 1947), the apparent beginning of a Committee on Artistic Affairs campaign to issue more titles. For appeals, see ll. 143–78 (various project decrees and supporting materials addressed to Stalin, 1947).

12. One of these recipients, A. B. Gol'denveizer, strode the line between the two categories. He was a pianist and professor at the Moscow Conservatory who had entered the Composers' Union before the professional organization excluded performers. Though primarily a performer and teacher, he also composed for the piano, so he could count in either category. In the discussion about the difference between performers and composers, he has been excluded from both. The resulting thirty-one musical People's Artists include two crossover opera theater directors, counted as performers. The seven composers were B. V. Asaf'ev, R. M. Glier, V. G. Zakharov, N. Ia. Miaskovskii, L. N. Revutskii, U. A. Gadzhibekov, and A. Maldybaev.

13. K. N. Igumnov, a pianist, and Gol'denveizer.

14. The most obvious example was S. A. Samosud, who was named People's Artist of the Soviet Union in 1937, the year after his Malyi Opera Theater in Leningrad took Shostakovich's *Lady Macbeth of Mtsensk* and Dzerzhinskii's *Tikhii Don* on tour to Moscow, earning Stalin's praise for *Tikhii Don* and precipitating the Lady Macbeth affair. The other conductors and theater directors were A. M. Pazovskii, N. V. Smolich, and G. Ts. Tsydynzhapov.

four of the seven composers (plus Gol'denveizer) received their titles either in 1944 or 1946. Before the war, the only three composers who had been named People's Artist of the Soviet Union were known for their efforts to build national minority operatic culture.[15] The composers awarded during or after the war were typically members of the older generation of composers who sought to extend the traditions of Russian classical music.[16] If extrapolation from such a small sample is possible, it suggests that during and after the war the emphasis was shifting in favor of composers as a group and traditionalist, highbrow types in particular.

The fact that there was a much larger pool of performers to draw from may make this sort of numerical comparison unconvincing, but two more factors support these conclusions. First, the emphasis on opera severely limits the overall pool of performers. Even such world-famous musicians as pianist Emil Gilels and violinist David Oistrakh did not garner this most coveted title. Second and more significant, these conclusions are bolstered by a brief examination of title-holding Stalin Prize recipients, which paints a similar picture of the relationship between composers and performers.

Between 1941 and 1949, sixty-one Stalin Prizes were awarded to fifty-one composers; twenty-four prizes to twenty-seven non-operatic performers; and thirty-one to groups or individual opera performers.[17] The opera prizes were awarded to multiple musicians for one production, so eighty-seven received the thirty-one opera prizes.[18] Since recipients' titles were listed, we can compare composers and performers of roughly equivalent standing according to the hierarchies established by the Stalin Prize. This comparison is represented in table 9.1.

Stalin Prize–winning performers held titles at a much higher rate than composers. Opera singers were a particularly highly rewarded group, as 21 percent held the Soviet Union's top title and only 19 percent had never received a title.

15. R. M. Glier, though Moscow based, was widely recognized as one of the founders of Soviet nationalities opera in the Caucasus and especially in Central Asia. U. G. Gadzhibekov (Azerbaidzhan) and A. Maldybaev (Kirgizia) were similarly prominent in their respective republics.

16. This was especially true of B. V. Asaf'ev and A. B. Gol'denveizer, though to a significant extent it characterizes N. Ia. Miaskovskii and L. N. Revutskii as well. V. G. Zakharov was the lone exception; his Russian folk choir was a tremendously popular sensation during and after the war. His own compositions were nearly impossible for most of his audience to differentiate from traditional anonymous folk songs.

17. In 1941 the first batch of prizes was retrospective to 1936; *Izvestiia*, 16 Mar 1941, 1. For 1943 to 1949, see *Sobranie postanovlenii i rasporiazhenii Pravitel'stva SSSR*, 1946, no. 3 (15 Mar), st. 39; no. 9 (12 Aug), st. 162; 1947, no. 4 (25 Jun), st. 71; 1948, no. 3 (21 Jun), st. 35; 1949, no. 6 (24 Jun), st. 52. Coverage in the *Sobranie* skips from 1949 to 1957.

18. This figure has not been corrected for a small number of duplicates. When multiple people were awarded a single prize, the protocol for splitting the award was as follows. If two artists received a single prize, they were to split it in half; if three received a prize, the leader of the collective received half of the prize and the other two each received one-quarter; if four or five received a single prize, the leader collected one-third and the others split the remainder evenly, etc. RGASPI, f. 17, op. 117, d. 689, l. 46 (regulations, 1947).

Table 9.1. Titles of Stalin Prize Recipients, 1941–49

Occupation	Prizes awarded to People's Artists of the USSR	Prizes awarded to People's Artists of the Republic	Prizes awarded to Honored Figures of the Arts	Prizes awarded to Honored Artists	Prizes awarded to artists without titles	Total Stalin Prizes
Performers (total)	19	28	20	32	26	125
Opera performers	13	13	4	20	12	62
Instrumentalists and conductors	3	5	12[a]	4	3	27
Artistic directors and theater conductors	3	10	4	8	11	36
Composers	2	2	22	1	24	51

Source: Sobranie postanovlenii i rasporiazhenii Pravitel'stva SSSR, 1946, no. 3 (15 Mar), st. 39; no. 9 (12 Aug), st. 162; ibid., 1947, no. 4 (25 Jun), st. 71; ibid., 1948, no. 3 (21 Jun), st. 35; ibid., 1949, no. 6 (24 Jun), st. 52.

[a] Of these twelve, eight were members of two string quartets who probably received their prizes for service in education.

Compared to other performers or composers, they clearly formed the top of the officially rewarded musical elite. Composers, on the other hand, tended to have been less highly decorated than expected, considering the rising prestige and power of their professional organization. This is not to say composers were a neglected lot—they too received a great deal of recognition.

These data also help clarify hierarchies by creative preference within the ranks of the Composers' Union. Though most of the fifty-one Stalin Prize–winning composers from 1941 to 1949 wrote music in multiple categories, Stalin Prizes were typically awarded in categories for which they were best known.[19] Of the twenty-seven composers who received Stalin Prizes for instrumental music, fourteen did not have titles. Only one, R. M. Glier, was a People's Artist of the Soviet Union, but twelve were Honored Figures of the Arts. This group was by far the single largest in the profession and can be seen as a benchmark.

Composers of operas, ballets, and oratorios received titles at a greater rate than this benchmark. Of the ten composers who received Stalin Prizes in this category, only three were untitled, and two were People's Artists of the Soviet Union or Republic.[20] On the other end of the spectrum, composers of songs had strikingly few titles. Of the seven song composers who received Stalin Prizes, one was a People's Artist of the Soviet Union, one was an Honored Figure of the Arts, and the remaining five had no title.

19. Shostakovich is a striking exception to this characterization—the three Stalin Prizes he received before 1953 were for a piano quintet (1940), a trio (1943–44), and a cantata (1950), though he was best known for his large-scale symphonic works, film music, and (officially unsuccessful) operas. In my schema, he fits into the instrumental music category.

20. These numbers include two crossover composers—Prokofiev and Karaev, each of whom received a prize for an opera or ballet and for a large instrumental piece.

These Stalin Prize data suggest a hierarchy of rewards among composers. Music that accompanied a libretto or text stood atop the hierarchy. This most decorated form of music was led by opera and, to a lesser extent, ballet, but it also included large-scale choral works like oratorios and cantatas. "Serious" symphonic and instrumental music in traditional forms like the symphony, string quartet, and trio formed the middle of the hierarchy, and songs filled out the bottom.

The shakeup in the Composers' Union following the party intervention in 1948 revealed an intriguing paradox. The most frequently praised and highly decorated musicians were precisely the ones most open to attack, and the Central Committee decree prompted attacks from the composers of popular songs, who were the least frequently titled composers, on the symphonic music of their more prominent colleagues, especially when it had attracted international acclaim. In fact, it should be recalled that the most outspoken, Vladimir Zakharov, was the only song composer to have attained the People's Artist of the Soviet Union title. These previously less-decorated composers may have expected to climb the hierarchy of official titles and rewards, but no new composers were named People's Artist of the Soviet Union until 1954. When the title was reinstated, three of the 1948 "formalists," Shostakovich, Shebalin, and Khachaturian, received the honor.[21] Rather than overturning the established hierarchy of titles and prizes, the brouhaha merely caused a hiatus in the promotion of any composers to the society's highest cultural title.

Traditionalist, high-art prejudices thus became enshrined in hierarchies of material privilege through prizes and titles that were most frequently awarded to performers, especially opera singers. Though less frequently rewarded in these high-prestige areas, composers were rewarded roughly according to the same prejudices. Their internal hierarchies ranged from composers of the simultaneously highbrow and popular genres of opera, ballet, oratorio, and cantata through the more "serious" composers of symphonic and chamber music down to popular song composers. High-art traditionalism, which ensured that elite performers would be the music world's most highly decorated, prevented song composers from receiving the highest awards. Furthermore, even when party and government oversight institutions were at their most meddlesome, "serious" composers remained the most highly rewarded. These claims require an important caveat: all of the distinctions discussed here operated only within the elite of the profession. Everyone here occupied a high spot on the society's overall system of privilege, and no one suggested that they should not.[22]

---

21. *Vedomosti Verkhovnogo Soveta SSSR,* 1954, no. 16 (22 Aug), st. 349 (2 Aug).
22. The criticism leveled at privileged composers even during the 1948 brouhaha was short lived. Many disciplined composers were again awarded Stalin Prizes or honorary titles within a couple years.

Honorary Titles and the Making of Musical Elites

The system of honorary titles and Stalin Prizes reveals a pervasive preference for performers and highbrow symphonic and especially operatic music, even though honorary titles and Stalin Prizes were granted after very different decision-making processes. An investigation of those processes reveals how different audiences could help construct music professionals' authority and the hierarchies of status and privilege that followed. For honorary title recipients, the crucial audience was the government body that oversaw their field. For all musicians including composers and musicologists, this body was the Committee on Artistic Affairs. The original statutes that created the various orders and medals that paralleled honorary titles reveal how the awarding process for all of these types of rewards was supposed to work.[23] Passed between 1924 and 1935, these statutes created the Order of Lenin (1930), Order of the Red Banner (1924), Order of the Red Star (1930), Order of the Labor Red Banner (USSR, 1928; RSFSR, 1929), and Sign of Honor Order (1935), and they were all revised at least once before being codified in 1936, the same year that the last honorary title "People's Artist of the Soviet Union" was created.[24] Of these orders, two (Red Banner and Red Star) were exclusively military decorations, but civilian composers and performers were eligible to receive all others. The Order of the Labor Red Banner RSFSR specifically targeted writers, artists, and scholars, among others.[25] The process by which they were awarded established that nominations were supposed to come from the nominee's institutional base according to standards established there.[26]

A couple specific examples from different time periods illustrate how this process worked in practice. In 1942 the Presidium of the Supreme Soviet of the Russian Republic (that is, the parliament) sent Andrei Andreev a list of thirty-one honorary title nominees in science, art, and health, each accompanied by supporting materials provided by "the corresponding ministry."[27] For musicians, the "ministry" was the Committee on Artistic Affairs, which passed on Moscow Conservatory nominations for the world-famous violin professor David Oistrakh and the renowned composition professor Vissarion Shebalin.[28]

23. These statutes created orders and medals, not honorary titles; however, the two groups of rewards were almost always awarded together, especially when an entire institution and the artists who peopled it were honored. The only significant difference between the processes is eligibility: institutions could receive orders and medals but not honorary titles.

24. RGASPI, f. 17, op. 125, d. 78, ll. 126–39ob. (9 Oct 1942).

25. Ibid., l. 135 (VTsIK and SNK RSFSR decree, 14 Jan 1929), pt. 1.

26. Ibid., ll. 127, 129, 131, 133–35. Standards were so vague as to require significant clarification in each area.

27. Ibid., ll. 61–88ob., here 61 (A. Badaev to A. A. Andreev, 30 Sep 1942).

28. Ibid., ll. 62–64 (list of artists). These materials do not explicitly name the Moscow Conservatory as the original source of the nominations, but the likelihood is overwhelming considering the combination of Shebalin with Oistrakh and V. V. Sofronitskii (a pianist and professor at Leningrad Conservatory) in a list of Honored Figure of the Arts nominees. Performers (including the eight opera and musical theater figures here) were typically nominated for the title Honored Artist.

Each nominee's dossier included a short biographical sketch phrased to support the nomination. Though Shebalin's sketch is lost, Oistrakh's reveals the sorts of "outstanding service" that the Committee on Artistic Affairs thought deserved recognition in the form of an honorary title.

Three elements typify the reputations of honorary title holders: talent ("brilliant performer of the classical violin repertory") and tangible competitive accomplishments ("laureate of all-USSR and international violin competitions"); service (he frequently played the Russian classics and premiered new Soviet works); and external authority ("the artistic name of Oistrakh is one of the most popular in our country and has wide fame abroad"). This last element almost always played an important role in helping musicians receive a prestigious title. Oistrakh also displayed extremely important wartime service: "In addition to concert work and radio broadcasts, Oistrakh systematically performs for the ranks of the Red Army and in hospitals."[29] This typical example shows that the three elements of a successful nomination were certifiable professional skill, demonstrable service to state or society, and popular recognition.

It also demonstrates that the process often worked according to the legislation, but dozens of other cases suggest that a somewhat more complicated nomination procedure was more common. It operated as follows. Step one: a local institution, union, or arts control organization sends a letter to the local division (UDI or KDI) of the Committee on Artistic Affairs or, sometimes, straight to the VKI. Sometimes, those local letters go directly to the Central Committee apparatus or even to top-ranking politicians like Politburo members Andrei Zhdanov or Kliment Voroshilov. Step two: the UDI or KDI presents the VKI or Central Committee apparatus with nominations that it deems acceptable. Step three: the VKI passes on its recommendation to the Central Committee apparatus (or sometimes Zhdanov).[30] Step four: the Central Committee apparatus passes its list to the Secretariat with attached comments and recommendations. Step five: the Secretariat passes provisional decisions to the Politburo.[31] Step six: a report is sent to Stalin, complete with drafted resolutions.[32] Step seven: the resolutions are enacted by the Supreme Soviet.[33]

The case of conductor Evgenii Mravinskii typifies this more complicated process. In March 1947 the Leningrad Philharmonic director A. Ponomarev

29. Ibid., l. 69.
30. RGASPI, f. 17, op. 125, d. 499, ll. 39–40 (about Dziga Vertov), l. 91 (about Golovanov [from radio committee head]), complete with the biographical sketch, autobiographical statement, and a personnel report from the Department of Personnel, sent to Zhdanov.
31. See notations at the bottom of virtually every case in RGASPI, f. 17, op. 125, dd. 499, 589.
32. Ibid., d. 78, l. 151 (Zhdanov, Kuznetsov, and G. Popov to Stalin, 18 Dec 1947); ll. 153–55 (Khrapchenko to Stalin); ll. 156–58 (report on existing titles, signed by Lebedev); ll. 159–63 (set of materials signed by Zhdanov, Kuznetsov and Shepilov), which accompanied ll. 164–68 (draft resolution, 20 Dec 1947).
33. For selected examples that basically conform to this description, see RGASPI, f. 17, op. 117, d. 654 (1946); d. 853 (1947); RGASPI, f. 17, op. 125, d. 305 (1945); d. 402 (1946–47); d. 589 (1948); RGASPI, f. 17, op. 133, d. 370 (1952); RGASPI, f. 17, op. 125, d. 306 (performers, 1945–46). The last case also provides examples of the process for collectives from the periphery starting with a note from the local party chairman.

and principal conductor Mravinskii nominated several musicians for honorary titles.[34] The head of the Committee on Artistic Affairs, M. B. Khrapchenko, supported their nominees and sent them on. But Ponomarev tried to add Mravinskii's name by appealing to Central Committee Secretary A. A. Kuznetsov, explaining that "in our opinion, E. A. Mravinskii deserves the title People's Artist if one pays attention to his considerable weight in Soviet music and the multinational acknowledgment of his talent, which permeates this outstanding artist's every performance." As a member of the Philharmonic's nominating board, Mravinskii could not nominate himself, so he was excluded from the original request.[35]

This explanation reaffirms the criteria suggested in the Oistrakh example: talent and widespread recognition were crucial to justify an honorary title nomination. It also demonstrates that the award process could be more complicated than the legislated path. In this case, the director of the Philharmonic first communicated with the head of the Committee on Artistic Affairs, who approved the nominations, added logistical support, and passed them on to the Central Committee.[36] Then the director appealed to a member of the Secretariat to amend the nominations. Kuznetsov requested a new set of materials, which received their own consideration first by the relevant Central Committee department and then by the Secretariat.[37] In the end, the Secretariat failed to approve the nomination, and Mravinskii would have to wait another seven years to be named People's Artist of the USSR.[38]

A final example demonstrates how this sort of last-minute denial could take place. Also in 1947, a group of prominent composers sought to nominate one of their colleagues, Sergei Vasilenko, for the title People's Artist of the Soviet Union in celebration of his seventy-fifth birthday.[39] Though it originated with a group of colleagues, the official nomination was submitted by the Committee on Artistic Affairs, who could claim jurisdiction over Vasilenko because of his post at the Moscow Conservatory. After Voroshilov, Zhdanov, and their staff opined, the Secretariat approved the honorary title, pending (as all such decisions did) Politburo confirmation. However, on the voting protocol that

34. RGASPI, f. 17, op. 125, d. 499, ll. 9–10 (Ponomarev and Mravinskii to Khrapchenko, 26 Mar 1947). Khrapchenko was a bureaucrat, literary scholar, and eventual member (well after the Stalin period) of the Academy of Sciences; Afanas'eva et al., *Apparat TsK KPSS i Kul'tura*, 775.

35. RGASPI, f. 17, op. 125, d. 499, l. 8 (Ponomarev to Kuznetsov, 31 Mar 1947).

36. For logistical support, see ibid., ll. 15–24 (personnel file: M. A. Mravinskii), including ll. 23–24 (biographical sketch, G. Orvid, 8 Apr 1947). The packet was resubmitted 15 Jul 1947 (ll. 17–18).

37. Ibid., l. 8; ll. 12–13 (G. Aleksandrov to Kuznetsov, Jul 1947). Aleksandrov supported the nomination, noting that Mravinskii's service included premiering Shostakovich's Seventh Symphony, conducting popular lectures and concerts during the war, and transforming the Leningrad Philharmonic into a first-class musical collective; ibid., l. 14 ([P. I.] Lebedev to Kuznetsov, 22 Sep 1947); l. 11 (draft Secretariat approval, prepared by Lebedev).

38. "Mravinskii, E. A.," *Muzykal'naia entsiklopediia*, 3:716–17.

39. RGASPI, f. 17, op. 117, d. 737, l. 28 (Aleksandrov to Zhdanov, 29 Mar 1947). Aleksandrov summarizes the request, which originated with Glier, Miaskovskii, Shaporin, Khachaturian, and Shostakovich but came from the VKI.

was sent to the Politburo, Molotov wrote, "I doubt this. The title People's Artist of the *RSFSR* would be sufficient." Though the original decision was stamped with his approval, Zhdanov added a final handwritten note agreeing with Molotov's reservation.[40] Vasilenko was never named People's Artist of the USSR.

Vasilenko's case exhibits the various authority-granting audiences that were important to a composer's title-winning hopes. In order for composers even to enter the process, they had to earn the respect of their peers within the profession and gain some popularity with the broader listening public. They could not actively promote their own cause and depended on colleagues to make their case. In order to succeed, that case had to be at least partly based on popularity or, phrased differently, on authority within the music-listening public. Once the initial case was made, the nomination had to garner the support of a governmental institution. This step both acknowledged and made official the less tangible authority on which the initial case was made. But this acknowledgment was still not sufficient to ensure that a title would be won. The application had to run the gauntlet of an ideological review in the Central Committee apparatus and then pass the scrutiny of both the Secretariat and the Politburo. It was at these later stages that the authority-granting power of the title came into play, as high-ranking politicians considered whether or not the nominee was entitled to the status, prestige, and authority that receiving a certain title would convey. On the one hand, the hierarchies created by honorary titles were profoundly structured by politicians in the Central Committee Secretariat and Politburo. On the other, their decisions also confirmed or acknowledged hierarchies of authority that were constructed by professional and popular audiences. The entire process thus simultaneously created and reproduced hierarchies of authority and legitimized the material privilege that accompanied them.

For at least some of the players who came into the game late in this process, it was important that potential title recipients run the entire gauntlet. In June 1952 the Central Committee Department of Literature and the Arts (OKhLI) proposed a change in the procedure for deciding honorary titles in the arts at the republic level to bring it in line with the apparently more effective awards procedures for honorary titles in medicine and education. OKhLI bureaucrats also aligned the new procedures with those described above pertaining to the most prestigious title of all, the People's Artist of the Soviet Union. OKhLI's justification for the change is telling: it insisted that without the new procedures it was deprived of crucial information that should be provided by local, regional, and central governmental organs. Authority at the local and regional level was an essential precondition for entering the final stages of consideration in the Central Committee.[41]

---

40. Ibid., l. 29 (Voroshilov to Zhdanov, 28 Mar 1947); l. 28; l. 27 (*strogo sekretno vypiska* from the Secretariat protocol to the Politburo), marginal notations. Molotov's emphasis.

41. RGASPI, f. 17, op. 133, d. 367, ll. 116–17 (Kruzhkov, Tarasov, and [P. V.] Lebedev to Malenkov, 19 Jun 1952).

Vasilenko's case also demonstrates how interrelated the system's different strategies of material compensation and privilege were in the minds of the participants—or recipients. In his autobiographical statement included in the VKI's nomination materials, Vasilenko listed his many awards and honors:

> In 1927, I received the title Honored Figure of the Arts. In 1939 . . . People's Artist of the Uzbek SSR. On 23 March 1940 . . . People's Artist of the RSFSR (certificate #8). On 7 September 1940 . . . scholarly level Doctor of Arts, without defense of a dissertation. In 1930, Sovnarkom gave me an apartment for life. On 1 August 1943, I was decorated with the Order of the Labor Red Banner (order book #111947). On 11 August 1947, I was decorated with a second Order of the Labor Red Banner. On 23 March 1931, I was awarded a personal pension for life, in the sum of 225 rubles. On 1 February 1937, [the pension] was raised to 239 rubles.[42]

This list is striking precisely because of the way it intermingles seemingly mundane material support, like an apartment and a pension, with his extraordinary awards: honorary titles and orders. At least this recipient understood the latter as part and parcel of the regime's self-proclaimed efforts to provide the material basis for the flowering of cultural production, and not unreasonably so. The most famous of all Soviet composers, Dmitrii Shostakovich, was allocated such an unusually large apartment that housing administrators had trouble finding a suitable space.[43]

Stalin Prizes and the Making of Musical Elites

Whereas honorary titles were a career achievement award, the system of honors and extraordinary awards also contained an extremely significant element that targeted single accomplishments, the Stalin Prize. Unlike honorary titles, the decision to award Stalin Prizes was initially taken by a government body convened precisely for that purpose, the Committee on Stalin Prizes (KSP). Officially, this committee considered, nominated, evaluated, and selected candidates for Stalin Prizes in the arts and, later, science and technology. However, the committee was also an essential interface between those who wielded political power and those who held intellectual and artistic authority in Soviet society. It was a vehicle for producing, legitimating, and—very occasionally—censoring professional authority and for translating professional achievement into material privilege and prestige. It was even used by Stalin as an instrument

---

42. Ibid., op. 117, d. 737, ll. 33–34, here 33 (Vasilenko's autobiographical statement).

43. TsMAM, f. 2433, op. 5, d. 8, l. 36 (25 May 1946). In July the issue was resolved when a construction firm was given orders to combine two three-room apartments to fill the order; l. 38 (11 Jul 1946). Shostakovich was only the most striking example of a number of composers who received some of the largest apartments allocated in postwar Moscow. Laurel Fay describes the apartment in Fay, *Shostakovich*, 149.

to shape opinion, sometimes including his own image, within the creative intelligentsia.

The Stalin Prize Committee was one of the primary points of contact between political power and creative authority, and both politicians and artists were aware of the blurred boundaries that the contact created. As the first postwar reorganization of the Stalin Prize Committee demonstrates, the Central Committee conceived of the Stalin Prize Committee as the enshrinement of creative authority in governmental power. In January 1947 the Secretariat considered changing the composition of the Stalin Prize Committee for the first time since 1944 and to confirm its membership for the first time since 1943.[44] The proposed change originated with the committee's head, Writers' Union chief A. A. Fadeev, but his request was reviewed, modified, and endorsed by the Central Committee's cultural oversight department (UPA).[45] Besides the four members who had died since 1943, Fadeev sought to remove an additional seven for lack of participation, either because they no longer represented their previous institutions or because they did "not have serious creative authority among those who work in the arts."[46] Though UPA bureaucrats preserved the identical rationale for membership, they shifted the weight of the cuts to stress the importance—even over active participation—of institutional representation and "creative authority."[47]

In music, the brunt of the "low authority" criterion fell on the composer Isaak Dunaevskii, who apparently interpreted this attack as the beginning of the deterioration of his official position.[48] That the "lack of authority" com-

44. RGALI, f. 2085, op. 1, d. 1210, l. 21 (SNK SSSR Post. #1066, 29 Sep 1943).

45. RGASPI, f. 17, op. 116, d. 292, pt. 403g. (Secretariat Protokol #292, 9–14 Jan 1947); op. 117, d. 689, ll. 24–25 (undated unsigned memo to Stalin included in materials to pt. 403g [13 Jan 1947]); op. 125, d. 400, ll. 34–35 (same). Considering the materials with which each memo was accompanied, it seems likely that the memo in the UPA materials (op. 125) was part of Fadeev's original request, and the memo in the Secretariat materials (op. 117) was the UPA endorsement and restatement (with slight modifications). The op. 125 memo will thus be referred to as "Fadeev's" and the op. 117 as "UPA's."

46. RGASPI, f. 17, op. 125, d. 400, l. 34. The four deceased members were A. V. Aleksandrov, I. M. Moskvin, N. P. Khmelev, and A. N. Tolstoi. The musicians threatened with expulsion for poor participation were A. Maldybaev, and V. V. Sofronitskii. The conductor S. A. Samosud was one of two who no longer represented his old institution, and I. O. Dunaevskii was one of two who lacked creative authority. The nonmusicians were V. A. Vesin, I. Ia. Sudakov, and N. N. Aseev.

47. RGASPI, f. 17, op. 117, d. 689, l. 23. Of the musicians cut by Fadeev, UPA suggested keeping only Sofronitskii, whose poor attendance bothered Fadeev. The retained nonmusicians were Aseev and Vesin.

48. Minchenok, *Isaak Dunaevskii*, 468–69. In the excerpt from which the phrase is taken, a quoted but uncited Dunaevskii refers to a "shadow" that combined with anti-Semitism to have a negative influence on his "official, so to speak, position." He considered his removal from the KSP to be the first major sign of this fall. Minchenok suggests that this "shadow" was an active campaign led by Dunaevskii's friend and collaborator G. V. Aleksandrov, with whom Dunaevskii had a gradual cooling of relations in the first postwar years. In the materials pertaining to the immediate decision to remove Dunaevskii from the KSP, however, there is no evidence to suggest that Aleksandrov played any such role. There is some slight evidence that other changes were suggested apart from Fadeev's. In his letter to Zhdanov forwarding the KSP materials, the head of UPA, G. F. Alek-

plaint consistently attached to this popular and prolific songwriter emphasizes the highbrow pretensions and purposes of the Stalin Prize and its committee, but it also suggests that membership in the committee was meant to reflect authority with audiences within the member's broader cultural field. While there can be no doubt that membership on the committee augmented a composer's professional prestige, that membership itself was always intended to reflect authority already achieved. A clearer case of the simultaneous construction and reproduction of creative authority is hard to imagine.

The Committee on Stalin Prizes that emerged from the 1947 reorganization contained fifty-two members, including Dmitrii Shostakovich.[49] The replacement of the songwriters Dunaevskii and A. V. Aleksandrov (who had died) with Shostakovich reiterates the point suggested by the attack on Dunaevskii. Immediately after the war, the Committee on Stalin Prizes cemented its preference for large-scale symphonic music and serious musical theater at the expense of the popular song and operetta.

The reorganization also assured that composers would dominate the music subcommittee of the Stalin Prize Committee. Reinhold Glier was named first assistant chair of the entire committee, and he was joined by Shostakovich and three other prominent composers: Uzeir Gadzhibekov, Nikolai Miaskovskii, and Iurii Shaporin. The committee included only two performers: the pianist, conservatory professor, and Composers' Union member Gol'denveizer and the Kazakh coloratura Kuliash Baiseitova. In fact, composers formed the third largest group by occupation, trailing only literary figures and drama personalities, but leading those involved in film, the visual arts, architecture, and other artistic fields.[50]

When the Politburo signed off on the reorganization of this committee, which formed the most direct interface between political power and creative authority, it privileged music professionals' control over a field that was dominated in other ways by performers. In so doing, it endorsed the professional elite's musical preferences, giving the nod to serious symphonic music and large-scale choral works and to works by nationalities composers who strove to write music based on the traditions of Russian classical music. Of the five composers, at least one represented each creative viewpoint: Glier and Gadzhibekov represented nationalities and the Russian tradition; Glier and Miaskovskii, sym-

sandrov (Georgii Fedorovich, not to be confused with Grigorii Vasil'evich), asked to be permitted to remain on the committee after the reorganization so that he could continue to keep a close eye on KSP deliberations: RGASPI, f. 17, op. 117, d. 689, l. 23 (G. F. Aleksandrov to A. A. Zhdanov, 6 Jan 1947). It would be only a few months before Aleksandrov was disciplined and demoted during the Central Committee's philosophy discussion.

49. RGASPI, f. 17, op. 117, d. 698, ll. 27–30.

50. Ibid., l. 31 (report on specialities). There were seventeen drama directors, actors, and actresses; thirteen writers, poets, and playwrights; five composers; three film directors; three sculptors; two each performers, painters, architects, and arts oversight figures (including G. F. Aleksandrov); and one each conductor, historian, and graphic artist. For the final list, see RGASPI, f. 17, op. 3, d. 1064, l. 7, pt. 27 (Politburo Protokol #57, 22 Feb 1947).

phonic music firmly rooted in the Russian classics; Shaporin (whose *Kulikovo pol'e* was a recent success), large-scale oratorios and cantatas; and finally Shostakovich, who was still carrying the heroic wartime mantle of all that was right with Soviet music. Rousing popular songs, catchy tunes, and dance numbers (associated with Aleksandrov and Dunaevskii) were out.

This reorganization did not last long. In just a year's time, the Politburo ordered the drastic expansion and reorganization of the Stalin Prize Committee's music subcommittee and removed three of its five members. Gol'denveizer and Shaporin were immediately joined by nine new members and awaited representatives from five national republics to fill out the ranks. This reorganization almost completely excised the symphonic element of the committee, replacing it with representatives of every strain of choral music. Shaporin remained, and he was joined by two other proponents of traditional choral music (Aleksandr Sveshnikov and Andrei Shtogarenko), by a folk music devotee (Zakharov), and even by a popular song composer (Anatolii Novikov). Gol'denveizer was joined by respected performers Ksenia Derzhinskaia and Nikolai Golovanov, both noted for their contributions to opera. Though symphonic composers were eliminated from the committee, the Russian classical tradition remained well represented, as did the professional organization. Two music theorists, Asaf'ev and Tamara Livanova, also joined the committee, and Asaf'ev was named the subcommittee chair, replacing Glier. His assistant chair, Khrennikov completed the mix.[51] When the nationalities representatives filled in, Baiseitova returned, and she was joined by the Uzbek soprano Khalima Nasyrova. Though both were removed again in 1951, at the same time that Shostakovich was reappointed to officialize his return from disgrace, the basic contours of the music subcommittee remained relatively set until almost the end of the Stalin period.[52]

Simultaneously named general secretary of the Composers' Union, Tikhon Khrennikov was a sort of jack-of-all-populist-music, a proficient composer of popular songs, successful operas, and film music. However, his appointment as assistant to the chair of the subcommittee was an example of the Central Committee's attempt to use the Stalin Prize Committee as a vehicle to shape authority, to intervene in the profession and promote a composer's creative authority by naming him to powerful posts. In retrospect, Khrennikov seems to have recognized this aspect of his appointment. In his post-Soviet memoirs, he relates the shock he felt at suddenly being propelled to the front of the professional organization and the Stalin Prize Committee, for which he seriously doubted his qualifications.[53]

51. Ibid., d. 1069, ll. 3–4, pt. 4.7 (Politburo Protokol #62, 26 Jan 1948).
52. Ibid., d. 1087, l. 14, pt. 71 (Politburo Protokol #80, 20 Jan 1951); l. 112 (appendix). Shostakovich was joined by the following additional musical appointees: Kara Karaev (an Armenian composer), M. I. Litvinenko-Vol'gemut (a Ukrainian soprano), and L. P. Aleksandrovskaia (a Belorussian soprano).
53. Khrennikov, *Tak eto bylo,* 126. Khrennikov reiterated this point in a personal conversation with the author, 30 Aug 1999.

After Asaf'ev died a few months later, Khrennikov became the head of the Stalin Prize Committee's music subsection. From this post he was able to observe how Stalin himself sought to use the committee to shape his own image within the creative intelligentsia, especially in Moscow. Khrennikov described this conscious manipulation by proclaiming Stalin to have been a "marvelous actor."[54] His exemplary anecdote is extremely revealing for what it says about the understanding—Khrennikov's and Stalin's—of how information traveled among Moscow's intelligentsia, what role Stalin Prize Committee representatives could play in that spread of information, and how Stalin could manipulate those two mechanisms to try to shape public opinion. This effect is another crucial aspect of the Stalin Prize Committee's role as an interface between politicians and intellectuals.

Khrennikov explained that he became fully aware of what he considered Stalin's phenomenal acting abilities during their last meeting. The occasion was the Politburo meeting of December 1952, in which representatives from the Stalin Prize Committee met with the Politburo to discuss the year's Stalin Prize awards. In the course of the meeting, Stalin suddenly lost his temper and shouted at Malenkov in terms that Khrennikov remembered as follows: "What! There is anti-Semitism in the Central Committee?! Shame! That is an absolute disgrace for the party, and it must be *immediately* eliminated! Outrage!" The outburst continued so convincingly that a relieved and excited Khrennikov raced home after the meeting to his wife, Klara Vaks, to tell her that Stalin had just found out about the pervasive anti-Semitism and that it was finally sure to cease.

Of course, the anti-Semitism did not stop, and it was then that Khrennikov understood the purpose of Stalin's outburst. The key representatives of the entire intelligentsia had been in the room. Stalin knew that news about an outburst would travel throughout Moscow within twenty-four hours because of the Stalin Prize representatives, so he chose that moment to put on a "brilliant act" to shift the blame for systemic anti-Semitism from himself to the Central Committee and his immediate circle, especially Malenkov. Brilliant though he repeatedly called Stalin's performance, Khrennikov noted that it backfired in the end precisely because anti-Semitism continued to worsen until Stalin died, when it suddenly stopped.[55]

This anecdote is remarkable for what it reveals about creative authority, the Stalin Prize Committee, and elite authority-granting audiences. The Stalin Prize Committee was a vehicle for recognizing the authority accumulated in a broader public and attempting to influence the further accumulation of authority with that audience. Khrennikov and Stalin both conceptualized the Stalin Prize Committee as representative of a group or system of social networks. It could transform authority recognized by that group into hierarchies

---

54. T. N. Khrennikov, personal communication, 30 Aug 1999.
55. Ibid.

of prestige and privilege, and manipulating its hierarchies could shape the group's tastes and expectations. Finally, it could serve as an interface between politicians and the population for other issues as well. The awarding of a Stalin Prize was a complex process of recognizing and seeking to transform creative authority within the creative intelligentsia as a whole. Composers who sought such a prize would have to garner authority from their professional peers in the creative intelligentsia, from the artistic bureaucracy, and from top party leaders.

Though the committee became an interface between the Soviet Union's political leaders and its creative intellectuals, its primary responsibility was negotiating the awards process. In practice, the Stalin Prize decision-making process was much like the awarding of honorary titles, though with some crucial distinctions that reflect the different valence that the authority-granting audience provided in each case. Whereas the crucial audiences for titles were leaders of the relevant arts institution (especially the VKI), for Stalin Prizes it was the Stalin Prize Committee.

When it reviewed the membership of the Stalin Prize Committee in January 1947, the Central Committee apparatus sought to codify the ad hoc decision-making process that had arisen before the war.[56] True to their intent, the codifiers established a unified set of regulations that corresponded closely to practices observed during the preceding six years.[57] In fact, decrees pertaining to the Stalin Prize Committee were regularly reactive, codifying existing practices the committee had developed.[58] The new regulations also detailed the nominations and decision-making procedure. Candidates could be considered if they had been nominated by one of the creative unions, government ministries, agencies, artistic and scholarly research institutions, trade unions ("social organizations"), or individual members of the Stalin Prize Committee.[59]

In practice, some nominating bodies enjoyed greater success than others, since the collected experts favored certain opinions over others. For composers, a nomination from the Composers' Union or from a colleague on the Stalin Prize Committee was almost essential for moving on. Of the fifty-two eligible nominations it considered in 1946, the subcommittee suggested awarding twenty-one Stalin Prizes, nine first-class prizes and twelve second-class, includ-

56. RGASPI, f. 17, op. 125, d. 400, ll. 72–73 (Aleksandrov and Suvorov to Stalin [draft], 31 Dec 1946); ibid., op. 117, d. 689, ll. 36–37 (same, copy to Zhdanov, Kuznetsov, Patolichev and Popov). For the date and authorship, see l. 34 (Aleksandrov and Suvorov to Zhdanov, Kuznetsov, Patolichev, and Popov, 31 Dec 1946), attached to materials suggesting the codification (ll. 32–59).

57. For a few examples of this practice, see each year's UPA deliberations: RGASPI, f. 17, op. 125, d. 78 (1942); d. 233 (1944); d. 234 (1945); dd. 399–400 (1945–46). For the new regulations, see RGASPI, f. 17, op. 117, d. 689, ll. 42–43; and op. 125, d. 400, l. 79. In most cases, the Secretariat and UPA materials are nearly identical. The set of regulations circulated among members of the Stalin Prize Committee earlier: RGALI, f. 2085, op. 1, d. 1210, ll. 3–9.

58. RGALI, f. 2085, op. 1, d. 1210, ll. 1–2ob. (KSP booklet, 23 Jun 1940); l. 21 (SNK SSSR Post. #1066, 29 Nov 1943). The latter alters the membership of the KSP "to improve the work of the KSP and to take note of changes in the composition thereof."

59. RGASPI, f. 17, op. 117, d. 689, l. 43.

ing fifteen composers (six first-class, nine second-class). Of the fifteen composers who advanced, all but *one* were nominated by the Orgkom of the Composers' Union, by a local Composers' Union chapter, or by members of the music subcommittee. The sole remaining successful candidate was nominated by a local governmental body, the only successful one of seven such nominees. Likewise, only one subcommittee nominee and two Orgkom nominees failed to advance. Though local Composers' Union chapters placed three nominees, another fourteen were unsuccessful; still, even this rate (18 percent) is better than the 14 percent achieved by the nominees of local government and party organizations.[60]

The new set of regulations clarified eligibility, setting the date of first public performance to an open audience as the "date of publication." This clarification underscored the importance of public exhibition as the simultaneous recognition and production of authority within a broader audience. The regulations also reiterated earlier instructions about the internal operations of the Stalin Prize Committee and its deliberations. The Committee was permitted to organize subcommittees, invite outside experts, and organize special concerts and exhibits for members to evaluate nominated works. Final decisions were to be recorded after secret balloting.[61] In each of these cases, the new regulations simply restated older rules or codified existing practice, though some of these regulations were designed to fix earlier problems. For example, an official requirement of a two-thirds quorum sought to counter what seems to have been systematic absenteeism.[62]

In 1950 the Secretariat defined a new twenty-five-thousand-ruble Stalin Prize, third-class, to provide a category in which the Stalin Prize Committee could recognize outstanding young talent and developing artists who had not yet reached the level of mastery required by a Stalin Prize.[63] Again, musicians were perhaps disproportionately rewarded: prizes for eight to twelve composers and concert

---

60. RGALI, f. 2085, op. 1, d. 1210, ll. 23–25ob. (Glier's notes about music section deliberations, 1946). This distribution seems to have been typical.

61. RGASPI, f. 17, op. 117, d. 689, ll. 43–46. For earlier confusion, see RGALI, f. 2085, op. 1, d. 1210, ll. 29–34 (1946), especially "Levitin Iu. A.," "Popov G. N." both of whom were nominated for works either completed or first performed in 1947. Both were withheld for consideration the following year.

62. RGALI, f. 2085, op. 1, d. 1210, ll. 1–2ob. (1940). For an example of the Stalin Prize Committee's special concert going, see l. 16 (1940), a calendar that describes three long days of hopping from theater to concert hall to museum to movie theater and back again. Performances started as early as 9:45 a.m. and as late as 10:00 p.m. In at least one case, the committee intended to meet at a common location and shuttle around together. RGASPI, f. 17, op. 117, d. 689, l. 46. For clarifications about who was supposed to attend what meetings, see RGALI, f. 2085, op. 1, d. 1210, l. 13 (memo to Glier, 20 Sep 1949); and l. 22 (Moskvin to Moscow-based KSP members, 4 Feb 1945), in which the KSP chair complained about members' lack of preparation and poor attendance.

63. RGASPI, f. 17, op. 118, d. 729, l. 6 (Fadeev to Stalin, 31 Jan 1950). Fadeev noted that this overarching reform was actually just an extension of three earlier decisions (SM SSSR, 17 Aug 1947, 20 Apr 1948, and 8 Apr 1949), in which the Stalin Prize, third class, was created to apply only to literary prose and then extended to painting, but not to other areas of the arts.

performers and an additional three to five opera and ballet productions were allotted, compared to five to eight in drama theater and in prose, four to seven in the visual arts, four to six in film, three to five in poetry and in drama, three in literary criticism and art history combined, and two to four in architecture.[64]

After examining this new set of regulations, the Politburo apparently decided to watch the deliberations process even more closely than usual. It instructed Zhdanov to form an ad hoc committee of the Politburo to look into the decisions for 1947.[65] It did so and drastically reduced the number of prizes suggested by the Stalin Prize Committee, thus temporarily squelching Fadeev's effort to award more each year. In composition and concert performance, only eleven of the suggested twenty-one prizes were awarded. Beyond that, however, the ad hoc committee basically followed the Stalin Prize Committee's recommendations.[66]

Usually, there were many more steps before decisions reached the Politburo. Typically, Stalin Prize Committee decisions were passed on to the head of the Committee on Artistic Affairs, who forwarded them along with his remarks to the Central Committee's culture department for more detailed analysis. The Central Committee department then sent the whole lot, with its report, to the Secretariat and Politburo for final consideration.[67] During this process, a prospective Stalin Prize laureate's authority-granting audience shifted from professional colleagues and fellow members of the creative intelligentsia's elite to party bureaucrats. During this shift, the prize-granting process shifted from the recognition of creative authority within the creative intelligentsia to the shaping of opinion in the same group.

The effects of this shift can be demonstrated by examples culled from different years. In some cases, government or party bureaucrats claimed to correct Stalin Prize Committee experts' representation of broader opinion. For ex-

64. Ibid., l. 1 (materials to Secretariat Protocol #487, 10 Feb 1950, pt. 1s). The final decision is RGASPI, f. 17, op. 3, d. 1080, pt. 2 (Politburo Protokol #73, 11 Feb 1950).

65. RGASPI, f. 17, op. 3, d. 1065, l. 6, pt. 16 (Politburo Protokol #58, 30 Apr 1947). The ad hoc committee consisted of the following members: Zhdanov, G. F. Aleksandrov (UPA), A. A. Fadeev (KSP), M. B. Khrapchenko (VKI), and I. G. Bol'shakov (Ministry of Film). In fact, the Council of Ministers may never have found it necessary to pass this set of regulations, instead passing another set of additions to the 1939 and 1940 resolutions; RGASPI, f. 17, op. 118, d. 729, l. 3 (1950), which amends Postanovlenie SM SSSR #3006, 27 Aug 1947, as well as the 1939 and 1940 decisions. Regardless of whether the regulations were finally passed, they provide an accurate description of the existing practice before 1947 and that which continued thereafter.

66. The ad hoc committee's detailed findings were not available; their conclusions have been assumed from the later published list of Stalin Prize recipients. This list corresponds to the nomination sample detailed above. Of the twelve prizes, nine were given to composers, all of whom had been recommended by the KSP. Of those nine, the Orgkom had nominated four, local SSK chapters had nominated three (two from Georgia), and KSP members had nominated two. The lone local government nominee was one of the six KSP recommendations that did not make the cut.

67. For examples of this consistent procedure, see the files from the Central Committee's oversight department for each year: RGASPI, f. 17, op. 125, d. 78 (1942), d. 233 (1944), d. 234 (1945), dd. 399–400 (1945–46); op. 132, d. 234 (1949); op. 133, d. 307 (1951), etc. For oversight plans, see op. 133, d. 305, ll. 10, 12, 13 (1951); d. 343, l. 6 (plan for first half of 1952).

ample, in 1944, the head of the Committee on Artistic Affairs (Khrapchenko) suggested cutting Shostakovich's Eighth Symphony from the Stalin Prize Committee's recommendations because "the deliberate complexity, the absence of clear melodies makes Symphony no. 8 incomprehensible to the broadest strata of listeners. In this piece, D. D. Shostakovich repeats those formalistic mistakes that were apparent in a number of his earlier works."[68] Posing as the representative of "the broadest strata of listeners," Khrapchenko argued that the symphony's complexity disqualified it from consideration for a prize that was supposed to represent acclaim within such an audience. Translating that criticism into one of the catchwords (formalism) regularly directed against "bad" art solidified his point.

No Stalin Prizes were awarded in 1944. When Shostakovich's Eighth was up for consideration again a year later, Central Committee bureaucrats reflected on their earlier judgment. They had leveled a different criticism as they struck the symphony from the lists: "This symphony represents a step back when compared to the Seventh Symphony and contains remnants of Shostakovich's old formalistic mistakes."[69] This "step back" criterion was one that the Stalin Prize Committee members often used themselves. For example, in 1947 the committee justified its rejection of S. A. Balasanian's Armenian Rhapsody in very similar terms: "This piece produces a very good impression, both in its use of material and in its general form and artistic merits, but it is a rhapsodic piece and consequently uses somewhat variegated materials. Considering that Balasanian is a talented composer who writes successfully in large-scale genres, the Section finds the rhapsody significantly lower than Balasanian's capabilities and holds out against its promotion."[70] A composer who specialized in smaller musical forms, or a younger composer, might have received the support of the music subcommittee for an identical piece.

On the other hand, another candidate could receive support for a small piece precisely because of his status within the profession as "a talented composer." Such was apparently the case in the following request made by the Stalin Prize Committee in 1944:

> The Musical Section requests to include in the list of Stalin Prize laureates for 1943 the composer S. S. Prokofiev for his Sonata for Piano and Flute. Prokofiev is one of the most outstanding Russian composers. His sonata is a superb composition. One musical line does not stand up to the orchestration of pieces of larger-scale genres. In the small musical forms division, there were only two candidates mentioned. We request to transfer Prokofiev's sonata into this division and award it a prize.[71]

68. RGASPI, f. 17, op. 125, d. 233, ll. 28–33, here l. 28 (Khrapchenko to Stalin and Molotov, 1 Apr 1944).

69. Ibid., d. 234, ll. 34–37, here l. 34 (G. F. Aleksandrov and T. Zueva to Malenkov and Shcherbakov, 13 Apr 1944).

70. RGALI, f. 2085, op. 1, d. 1210, l. 33 (Music Section's evaluation, 1947).

71. RGASPI, f. 17, op. 125, d. 233, l. 27 (Moskvin to SNK SSSR, 31 Mar 1944). The quote is signed by Miaskovskii, Shaporin, Samosud, and Glier, reproduced here by Moskvin, who "whole-

This switch was the opposite of the position the bureaucrats took later regarding Balasanian's Armenian Rhapsody. The application of these relative criteria at the beginning and concluding stages of the awards process reveals how subjective, even personalistic, evaluation for the Stalin Prize often could be.

Still, there were serious limits to how far individualized, particularistic networks like patronage could change the findings of the Stalin Prize Committee. Fellow professionals and political leaders alike considered the members of the committee authoritative, so outside interference in their decision making was very rare. That is not to say that people did not try to alter Stalin Prize Committee decisions by mobilizing a patronage network. Very occasionally, if the patronage apparatus began to operate *before* the Committee began its deliberations, that intervention could work.

Such was the case for D. I. Arakishvili. Before the Stalin Prize Committee began its annual discussions in 1953, a party secretary in the Georgian Central Committee, A. Mgelidze, wrote to Malenkov to submit a special recommendation for Arakishvili, a nearly eighty-year-old composer of highly artistic romances. Malenkov forwarded it to the head of the Central Committee oversight department with a hand-scrawled instruction that the memo required consideration during Stalin Prize Committee deliberations. Though Malenkov did not order the Stalin Prize Committee to give a prize to Arakishvili, Malenkov's remark was much stronger than a more typical and more neutral "look into this."[72] Within the Central Committee apparatus, it was determined that Arakishvili's work was extremely popular, and the department supported Mgelidze's request. A month later, Kruzhkov noted that Arakishvili had been "included in the list."[73] No doubt, Mgelidze's intervention was crucial to attracting the Central Committee bureaucrats' attention to Arakishvili's work, but the bureaucrats still referred to the crucial popularity of the composer's romances with Georgian audiences.

Arakishvili's case was an extraordinary one. In the vast majority of such situations, attempts to intervene into the process merely caused the case to be referred to the Stalin Prize Committee without comment. If the decision had already been made, the Central Committee members or bureaucrats who received the requests almost always backed up the Stalin Prize Committee's initial decision.[74] This marked lack of success even characterized personalistic efforts that included attacks on the Stalin Prize Committee itself. For example,

heartedly" supported their request. In 1946, when Stalin Prizes were finally awarded for 1943, Prokofiev did not receive one for this piece. However, he did win two other separate prizes for his efforts in 1943–45.

72. RGASPI, f. 17, op. 133, d. 387, l. 65 (Mgeladze [the Georgian party secretary] to Malenkov, 7 Feb 1953), and marginal notation (Malenkov's response, 18 Feb 1953).

73. Ibid., l. 66 (Kruzhkov and Iarustovskii to Mikhailov, 26 Feb 1953), and marginal notation (Kruzhkov, 16 Mar 1953).

74. Ibid., ll. 49–64, 74–76, one year's example of six special appeals accompanying Stalin Prize deliberations, none of which were successful. The previous year's deliberations produced a similar result; RGASPI, f. 17, op. 133, d. 307, ll. 29–34, 55–58, 303–8. Almost all of these cases preceded KSP deliberations, emphasizing how rare Arakishvili's case was.

in 1941 the party member and longtime music administrator M. A. Grinberg wrote to Molotov to complain about the Stalin Prize Committee's decisions as a whole.[75] After first acknowledging that he was not an educated musician, Grinberg explained that he was risking an opinion on the matter because he had been deeply involved in music for a long time. Grinberg's attack would perhaps not have been possible years later, when the Stalin Prize and its selection committee were more established, but in 1941 Grinberg subjected selection procedure to thorough criticism.

Grinberg sought to overturn the stylistic priorities by which the Stalin Prize was awarded by suggesting that a number of pieces by the Composers' Union elite should be replaced by more tuneful works and popular songs. He attacked Shostakovich's Eighth Symphony and Piano Quintet, arguing that the latter was "deeply Western" in orientation and not worthy of *Pravda*'s laudatory characterization as "undoubtedly the best musical work of 1940." Grinberg's preferences were revealed in a positive description of the talented young Khrennikov's opera *V buriu*.[76] Grinberg also anticipated later developments in the Stalin Prize awards process when he suggested that one of the many good efforts by composers from the national republics be chosen (either U. Gadzhibekov or one of Glier's three most recent operas and ballets).[77]

Grinberg's striking analysis of the Committee on Stalin Prizes repeats many of the conclusions about the nature, purpose, and practice of the Stalin Prize Committee reached in this chapter. Grinberg notes that the committee oriented itself around the opinions of the musical members of the Stalin Prize Committee—the Soviet Union's most "authoritative composers" and favored pieces that had been nominated by the Composers' Union. Grinberg thus accurately identified how the Stalin Prize Committee was going to work for the next decade and more. But he was not happy about that state of affairs:

> But it is a shame that these composers who also direct the Composers' Union are extremely limited in their tastes. Their tastes and narrow professionalism, which were forged under the influence of the stormy traditions of Western music of the last few decades, compel them to look at the mastery of form as the self-contained beginning of a musical piece; they consider innovation the intentional complexity of form; the music of young composers who are standing on a broader democratic path is completely foreign to them. Sincerely believing themselves to be So-

75. RGASPI, f. 82, op. 2, d. 950, ll. 104–7 (Grinberg to Molotov, 7 Jan 1941). A copy of Grinberg's memo filed in the presidential archive has recently been published: "Proizvedenie Shostakovicha—gluboko zapadnoi orientatsii," *Staraia ploshchad': Vestnik Arkhiva Prezidenta Rossiiskoi Federatsii,* 1995, no. 5:156–59.

76. RGASPI, f. 82, op. 2, d. 950, ll. 104–6. Grinberg cited the 25 Nov 1940 issue of *Pravda.*

77. For evidence of the Stalin Prize Committee's efforts to expand its geographic reach (and consequently reward composers from the periphery who may not otherwise have become known in Moscow), see RGASPI, f. 17, op. 132, d. 234, ll. 203–4 (Kruzhkov and Tarasov to Suslov, archived 8 Dec 1949); l. 205 (Kruzhkov and Tarasov to Suslov, 28 Dec 1949). Both of these documents discuss significantly expanded efforts to visit performances in provincial cities in the Russian Republic and in the capitals of national republics.

viet composers, they still cannot, at the same time, overcome their deeply seated tastes.[78]

Grinberg wrote his denunciation to Stalin about the prize "issued in [his] name" because he was intimidated by professional opinion. The opinion that he articulated was a clear statement of one of the two poles of the debate (popular opinion versus professional evaluation) that would permeate professional discourse until Stalin's death; however, the form in which the Stalin Prize Committee would contribute to that debate would never change. Stalin Prize Committee members and the Composers' Union leadership would always dominate the selection process. Grinberg's thorough attack on the Stalin Prize Committee went ignored.

The point suggested by Grinberg's skepticism is made even clearer by one final case from the end of the Stalin period, that of the oratorio *Aleksandr Matrosov*. In a veritable barrage of letters in 1952, a host of characters attacked the veracity of professional opinions in determining a prize that was understood to acknowledge accomplishment in a larger audience. The eventual victory of professional opinion in this case, as in almost all others, underscores that the Stalin Prize Committee and the award that it issued reflected—and constructed—opinion within the creative intelligentsia, not usually within the general listening audience. Though the Stalin Prize Committee's decisions increasingly accommodated popular forms over time, those decisions were still governed by the tastes of the professional elite and the intelligentsia opinion that they represented.

Composed by V. K. Sorokin in 1951 on a text by V. Gur'ian, the oratorio *Aleksandr Matrosov* celebrated the bravery and sacrifice of a popular hero who had saved his military unit by throwing himself across a machine gun emplacement in 1943. The oratorio enjoyed a wide hearing and remarkable popular success before audiences in the armed forces, in factories, and on the radio. It was nominated for a Stalin Prize but did not win. In February 1952 a group of artists from the Radio Committee's Song Ensemble, one of the institutions that had nominated *Matrosov*, complained to Malenkov in terms similar to those used by Grinberg more than a decade earlier. They argued that "democratic forms," especially songs, had been a great accomplishment of Soviet composers. They greeted the Central Committee resolution of 1948 warmly because of its support for such forms, but they argued that the Composers' Union leadership installed after the resolution continued to push large-scale symphonic pieces, both in their programming selections and in their support for awards.[79]

The singers gave a nod to the well-established authority of the Composers' Union, claiming that three Union subcommittees and four Union officials had

78. Ibid., ll. 106–7.
79. RGASPI, f. 17, op. 133, d. 345, ll. 96–99 (seven VRK Song Ensemble members to Malenkov, 9 Feb 1952).

supported it.[80] The radio musicians sought to deploy professional opinion in support of their own, a fact that demonstrates how successfully the Composers' Union had established itself as the repository of musical expertise. In fact, the radio musicians' complaint concluded by claiming that the Stalin Prize nomination had been supported by both the Leningrad chapter of the Composers' Union and by the Composers' Union Secretariat. The nomination was derailed when it reached the Stalin Prize Committee by the efforts of Khrennikov and Shaporin, with Shostakovich's silent consent. The two allegedly used their musical authority and high positions to remove Sorokin's oratorio from the voting lists.[81]

It may seem that the radio musicians were repeating a familiar position in an intra-professional squabble about generic preferences and stylistic prejudice, but their appeal drew a larger distinction between professional creative authority and the popular opinion of mass audiences. Included with their introductory memo were letters from military commanders of Matrosov's old unit, factory directors and political workers, a head of the political department of the Dzerzhinskii Artillery Academy, the rector of the Central Committee's own Upper Party School, a student who identified himself simply as a "radio listener," and even the organizer of a military song and dance troupe who offered to pay for the transcription and postage if the Radio Committee could provide parts for his choir to sing.[82] It is safe to say that Sorokin's oratorio enjoyed an impressive degree of popular success with an audience ranging from rank-and-file military personnel to workers, students, and amateur musicians. This impressively demonstrated popular success made the radio musicians' case well enough to prompt Malenkov to ask Central Committee bureaucrats to investigate the complaint more thoroughly.[83]

Unfortunately for Sorokin and his supporters, popular success with a mass audience was not enough to overturn the opinion of the collected experts of the Stalin Prize Committee. Party bureaucrats unequivocally supported the decision not to award Sorokin the prize and reaffirmed the authority of the Stalin Prize Committee. They implicitly reasserted that the relevant audience for Stalin Prize awards was the creative intelligentsia—the Soviet cultural elite.

That said, the Central Committee *apparatchiki* did not just take the Stalin Prize Committee's decision on faith. Key to their decision was the finding that

80. Ibid. The subcommittees were for mass music, choral music, and musicology. The Composers' Union officials were M. I. Chulaki (a member of the SSK Sekretariat), V. F. Kukharskii, Danilevich, and Ikonnikov.

81. Ibid., l. 99.

82. RGASPI, f. 17, op. 133, d. 345, ll. 100–106 (Naumenko and Rodnev, 19 Jan 1952; Manvelov [director of "Kauchuk" factory], Iashkina [factory partorg], and Fedorova [head of factory zavkom] to A. A. Puzin [head of VRK], 18 Jan 1952; Andreev to director of music broadcasts, VRK, 18 Jan 1952; Mitronov to Puzin, 17 Jan 1952; M. M. Babushkin to editor of musical programming, VRK, 10 Dec 1951; and Laserson to VRK, undated). See also the similar opinions of another group of officers; l. 107.

83. Ibid., l. 96, marginal notation.

the supposed professional support for *Matrosov* had been exaggerated. In fact, opinion in the Stalin Prize Committee's music section was divided. After two separate performances and discussions, the section could not reach a consensus. A third performance was arranged for the majority of the full Stalin Prize Committee. At this last discussion, several positive characteristics of the piece were mentioned, but the committee decided that the piece was insufficiently perfected. The *apparatchiki* could find no reason to question the Stalin Prize Committee's decision, especially after their own evaluation of the piece found it to be "decidedly average."[84] Elite professional opinion of the Stalin Prize Committee won out over broad popular support.

The case of Sorokin's oratorio demonstrates that there were varying understandings of the purpose and meaning of a Stalin Prize right down to the last year it was awarded during Stalin's lifetime. Everyone agreed that the prize ought to acknowledge accomplishment that was recognized by some sort of audience. By the end of the Stalin period, almost everyone agreed that the relevant audience included professional opinion. What remained in some doubt was the extent to which an expert audience was the *only* relevant audience other than the party leadership. The *Matrosov* case suggests that when a general, popular opinion conflicted with a considered elite professional one, the elite opinion would prevail. Repeatedly, that opinion was considered representative of the broader creative intelligentsia, if not popular audiences in general.[85]

There were some years in which nonprofessional factors played a more prominent role in decisions about certain nominees. An example from the height of the anticosmopolitanism campaign demonstrates this point. In March 1949 the head of the Committee on Artistic Affairs, P. I. Lebedev, submitted his annual review of the Stalin Prize Committee's deliberations. Besides suggesting a few promotions from second- to first-class status to reward ideological soundness, Lebedev suggested striking the pianist G. R. Ginzburg from the list of laureates. A Jew, Ginzburg was criticized in the shrouded terms of anticosmopolitanism: "The performance culture of the pianist Ginzburg G. R. is based on an external display of virtuosity in the light of which the ideological content of the performed musical composition does not receive sufficient attention. The works of Russian composers are almost completely absent from his repertoire."[86] External flare masking internal ideology and a suspiciously antipatriotic paucity of attention to Russian classics—these were the alleged signs of a cosmopolitan orientation. Couple them with Jewish nationality, and Ginzburg barely had a chance. In his place, Lebedev suggested substituting a Russian violinist with impeccably patriotic credentials: "G. B. Barinova is one of the best

---

84. Ibid., l. 108 (Kruzhkov and Tarasov to Malenkov, 1 Mar 1952).

85. For a few explicit references to the importance of the opinion of this broader, yet still circumscribed audience, see RGASPI, f. 17, op. 133, d. 307, ll. 94, 97 (OKhLI TsK VKP(b) report, undated 1951), which contains three references to the opinion of *muzykal'naia obshchestvennost'*, generally supporting the KSP; and ll. 61, 64 ([16 Feb 1951]).

86. RGASPI, f. 17, op. 132, d. 234, ll. 2–8, here l. 2 (Lebedev to Malenkov, 8 Mar 1949).

representatives of the Russian violin school, a wonderful interpreter of Russian classics and Soviet music. In the twenty years of her creative activity, Barinova has performed a large number of solo concerts in various cities of the Soviet Union and abroad." Lebedev also noted that Barinova had toured the front during the war.[87] In the heated environment of anticosmopolitanism, Russian nationality lined up with a patriotic repertoire and service to the military to produce a much more ideologically attractive laureate. Lebedev emphasized this otherwise soft-pedaled agenda by suggesting that the artistic director of the Voronezh Russian Folk Choir, K. I. Massalitinov, receive a Stalin Prize, first-class, instead of the second-class prize suggested by the Stalin Prize Committee.[88] However, even in such an ideologically charged atmosphere, the Stalin Prize Committee's authority was unshakable—both Ginzburg and Barinova received Stalin Prizes, second-class, as did Massalitinov.[89]

Still, political intervention and ideological rigor were not insignificant considerations during the Stalin Prize deliberations process. After a number of close calls in the forties, the Stalin Prize Committee was publicly and dramatically overruled in 1951 in an event that demonstrates the last and rarest of the purposes that the Stalin Prize could fulfill—censoring professional authority. In February 1951 the Stalin Prize Committee suggested awarding German Zhukovskii a Stalin Prize, third-class, for his opera *Ot vsego serdtsa* and giving a second prize to the Saratov Opera Theater for staging it.[90] Both the Committee on Artistic Affairs and the Central Committee Department of Literature and the Arts supported the proposal, and the former even suggested elevating Zhukovskii's award to Stalin Prize, second-class. P. I. Lebedev described the opera in glowing terms: "[The opera] is a remarkable work of Soviet opera music which portrays our *kolkhoz* countryside in the period of postwar construction. The opera's author found expressive musical characteristics for the opera's heroes—the foremost people of socialist agriculture."[91] Similarly, the Central Committee *apparatchik* V. S. Kruzhkov praised the opera for its modern Soviet topic, Zhukovskii's use of folk themes, and especially for the opera's rousing chorus scenes.[92] Consistent with the normal practice of supporting the Stalin Prize Committee over the Committee on Artistic Affairs, Zhukovskii was awarded a Stalin Prize, third-class.

87. Ibid., l. 3.
88. Ibid., l. 2. It should also be noted that Lebedev suggested other changes to the opera and ballet awards that were not apparently related to anti-cosmopolitanism; ll. 6–7.
89. *Sobranie postanovlenii i rasporiazhenii Pravitelz'stva SSSR*, 1949, no. 6 (24 Jun), st. 52. For the Central Committee apparatus's rejection of Lebedev's materials, see RGASPI, f. 17, op. 132, d. 234, l. 18 (Tarasov to Malenkov, 22 Apr 1949). Tarasov noted that he was archiving Lebedev's materials because the Council of Ministers had already issued its decree. That decree was issued on 8 April, exactly a month *after* Lebedev submitted his report.
90. RGASPI, f. 17, op. 133, d. 307, ll. 35–43, here ll. 35, 41 (Lebedev to Malenkov, 14 Feb 1951).
91. Ibid., l. 35.
92. Ibid., ll. 85–112, here l. 91 (appendix to Kruzhkov to Stalin, [16 Feb 1951]). The report that accompanied it is ll. 60–65.

After the prize was awarded, the arts press issued several articles praising and critiquing the opera.[93] Despite significantly different scope and choice of topic, the evaluation of the opera was strikingly consistent from article to article. With varying degrees of detail, each critic praised the work as an accomplishment for Soviet opera because of its choice of a contemporary theme. They all noted that the choral scenes were the most successful, some observing this in passing and others providing musical examples of that success. And all of them noted that the least successful element of the opera was the musical characterization of individual characters.[94] Even after Zhukovskii had won a Stalin Prize, one of these authors gave the following almost scathing evaluation:

> The composer obviously ran short of mastery, a fact which is made evident both in the weakness of the vocal characterizations and in the melodic poverty of the recitatives, the absolutely identical sounding [*odinakovykh v ustakh*] individual heroes who are little connected to the intonations of living speech and the development of the action; the insufficiency of mastery in the solo parts is also revealed in the impoverishment of the harmonic language, which is sharply inferior to the simple but fresh and well-formed harmonies of the choral scenes.[95]

Though this critic's overall evaluation of *Ot vsego serdtsa* was positive, he could hardly be accused of whitewashing the opera's shortcomings.

In mid-April, the official evaluation of Zhukovskii's opera changed dramatically with the publication of an unsigned editorial in *Pravda* that blasted the libretto, the music, and the Bol'shoi's staging of the piece.[96] Most of the attack on the music related to its support of an ideologically faulty libretto. It was monotonous, so the characters were deprived of individual human (libretto) and musical (score) characteristics. Likewise, the change of setting from Siberia to Ukraine was not reflected in the music, and musical styles often contradicted what little dramatic tension there might have been in the libretto. A concluding attack on the positive professional evaluation repeated in less detail the main professional criticism of the piece: "Zhukovskii's music, weak in and of itself in professional terms, further underscored the ideological falseness of the

---

93. T. Livanova, "Neoplachennyi dolg (Ob obraze sovetskogo geroia v opere)," *Sovetskaia muzyka*, 1950, no. 12:13–17; T. Tsytovich, "Tema sotsialisticheskogo truda v sovetskoi muzyke," *Sovetskaia muzyka* 1951, no. 1: 19–28; K. Sakva, "'Ot vsego serdtsa': Novoe v opernom zhanre," *Sovetskoe iskusstvo*, 31 Mar 1951, 2; and V. Kukharskii, "Opera 'Ot vsego serdtsa,'" *Sovetskaia muzyka*, 1951, no. 3:25–34.

94. Livanova, "Neoplachennyi dolg," 14–16; Tsytovich, "Tema sotsialisticheskogo truda," 25–27 (Tsytovich makes this last point most gently); Sakva, "'Ot vsego serdtsa,'" 2; Kukharskii, "Opera," 25–28, 30–32 (Kukharskii alone of the critics provides a few examples of well-written arias, but this barely blunts his critique).

95. Kukharskii, "Opera," 32.

96. "Neudachnaia opera: O postanovke opery 'Ot vsego serdtsa' v Bol'shom teatre," *Pravda*, 19 Apr 1951, 2–3. The article contained a one-column introduction, 2⅔ columns on the libretto, two columns on the music, and 2¼ columns on the staging. It concluded with a paragraph on the earlier positive press. Though still mostly concerned with the libretto and staging, this editorial devoted more attention to the music than most official proclamations about music. Still, the comments about the music are almost entirely derived from criticism of the libretto.

libretto, further depersonalized and impoverished the images of the Soviet people, and further revealed the absence of living truth in the piece."[97] In almost all of the particulars, the *Pravda* editorial clumsily repeated earlier criticisms of the opera. What was new was the radical change in overall evaluation from praise despite some shortcomings to rebuke despite some accomplishments.

This evaluation was a far cry from Kruzhkov's praise (which Stalin had endorsed) just two months earlier, close though it was to the criticisms leveled at the piece in the press over the preceding months. In any case, the Composers' Union, the Committee on Artistic Affairs, and the Bol'shoi Theater were all to be held accountable, and even those who wrote critically positive evaluations were criticized for "disorienting listeners."[98]

The Stalin Prize Committee was also forced to take an unprecedented step. On 8 May it passed a special resolution admitting its mistake of awarding Zhukovskii a Stalin Prize, asked the Council of Ministers to revoke the award, and chastised the music subcommittee for not studying nominees carefully. The committee's reasoning demonstrates once again that its awards were supposed to reflect accomplishment acknowledged by a larger audience. The resolution's preamble notes that the opera was being reconsidered "in the face of serious critical remarks of Soviet society."[99] In this case, however, the representatives of broader opinion were not the professional experts of the Stalin Prize Committee, whose criticisms had long been on record, but the party leaders writing in *Pravda* who repeated those criticisms while reversing the evaluation of the opera.

The Stalin Prize Committee immediately submitted their revocation to Stalin and Malenkov. The Council of Ministers chimed in, and the Secretariat resolved to print a retraction signed by the Council of Ministers.[100] The Secretariat resolution required Politburo confirmation, which the Politburo provided the same day, but with one significant change. Rather than just publishing the Council of Ministers' resolution, the Politburo ordered the publication of the Stalin Prize Committee communication, which would be followed by a two-day wait before publishing the Council of Ministers' resolution.[101] Publicizing the Stalin Prize Committee's self-critical remarks emphasized that it was deeply implicated in the disciplinary action.

---

97. Ibid., 2.

98. The *Pravda* editorial singled out Sakva and Kukharskii. These two critics had written the two most recent of the articles praising the opera, and Kukharskii's was the single most critical of all of them. Its author mockingly quoted Sakva's evaluation, which Sakva had used to frame his analysis of the opera. Though *Pravda* quoted directly from his conclusion, Sakva's first sentence, which began with a reference to Zhukovskii's Stalin Prize, was nearly identical.

99. RGASPI, f. 17, op. 119, d. 336, ll. 181–82 (KSP Post., 8 May 1951).

100. Ibid., l. 179 (Fadeev and Kemenov to Malenkov, 8 May 1951). This note accompanied Malenkov's copies of the materials; originals were sent to Stalin; l. 175, pt. 223s (materials to Secretariat Protokol #563, 11 May 1951).

101. RGASPI, f. 17, op. 3, d. 1088, l. 88, pt. 399 (Politburo Protocol #81, 10 May 1951); op. 119, d. 336, l. 176 (excerpt sent to Malenkov, Pomaznev, and Orgbiuro).

In the year that followed, the Stalin Prize Committee was threatened with more serious action than any of the organizations mentioned in the *Pravda* editorial, with the possible exception of the Committee on Artistic Affairs. After having to call members to task for dragging their heels in January 1952, in May the Central Committee Department of Literature and Arts suggested liquidating the Stalin Prize Committee. Instead, the department would accept nominations directly from the Committee on Artistic Affairs, the Ministry of Film, and the creative unions and then make its final decisions.[102]

Fadeev, still head of the Stalin Prize Committee, submitted a counterproposal in July.[103] He reiterated what all players considered the essential characteristic of the Stalin Prize: its reflection of some form of public opinion. Eliminating the Stalin Prize Committee, Fadeev argued, would change the awards process into a "bureaucratic rather than a social path of preparation for granting prizes."[104] On the other hand, Fadeev agreed with Kruzhkov that the Stalin Prize Committee was failing in this task, and he offered statistics about "mistakes" made by the Stalin Prize Committee the previous year. Despite the high-profile reversal of the *Ot vsego serdtsa* decision, neither music nor opera made Fadeev's list of problematic categories. He focused on painting and literature, fields within his own area of expertise and ones that politicians felt much more competent to evaluate. He noted that for 1951 the Committee recommended issuing 133 prizes, 50 of which had been denied (23 in literature and 15 in the visual arts), while three outstanding works of literature were ignored.[105]

Fadeev offered several explanations for that lack of reliability and then suggested a remedy. He had been on creative leave during part of the year and was unable to keep watch over early deliberations, but that was a one-year aberration. There were several more serious structural problems. First, the committee worked actively only in December and January. In two months, it was unreasonable to expect the members to evaluate as many works as they needed to.[106] More troublesome, Fadeev thought, was that several members of the committee did not behave fairly during preliminary deliberations. The head of the visual arts subcommittee actively campaigned for formalistic and schematic works regardless of quality, and members who were up for nominations continued to participate in discussions rendering principled evaluation nearly impossible. The situation was particularly bad in the music subcommittee, seven of whose eleven members had been nominated in 1951. Fadeev also complained

102. RGASPI, f. 17, op. 133, d. 345, ll. 3–5 (Kruzhkov and Tarasov to Malenkov, 5 Jan 1952); l. 1 (Malenkov to Ponomarenko, Suslov, Khrushchev, 7 Jan 1945); l. 2 (Malenkov, 6 Jan 1952). RGASPI, f. 17, op. 133, d. 387, l. 20 (Kruzhkov to Mikhailov, 3 Dec 1952), which summarizes the course of events from May to Aug 1952.

103. RGASPI, f. 17, op. 133, d. 345, ll. 6–8 (Fadeev to Stalin, 18 Jul 1952); ll. 165–81 (Fadeev to Stalin, [before 25 Jul] 1952). Fadeev also forwarded all of these materials to OKhLI; l. 182 (Fadeev to Kruzhkov, 25 Jul 1952).

104. Ibid., l. 6.

105. Ibid., l. 165 (Fadeev to Stalin, Aug 1952).

106. Ibid., ll. 165–66.

about some members' passivity and the tendency of others to vote on the basis of local loyalties above all else.[107]

In his critique of the music subcommittee's modus operandi, Fadeev revealed the potential dangers of assembling a committee like the Stalin Prize Committee to represent more general opinion. Chosen on the basis of their authority within a broader audience, the members then utilized that authority to support their own candidates. Though he recognized the importance of the representative function, Fadeev sought to fight the exercise of authority within the committee itself. According to Fadeev, even a single skeptical pronouncement from one of the most active members resulted in a piece's elimination without discussion and without taking "public opinion" into consideration. On the other hand, a committee member might mention a student, and if out of respect for that committee member no one objected, the student would advance. After providing examples from the theater and literature subcommittees, Fadeev noted that the film subcommittee was worst of all. It simply approved nominations dictated by its chair, I. G. Bol'shakov, minister of film.[108]

These problems, Fadeev argued, prevented "the correct reflection of public opinion and [did] not facilitate objective evaluation of the works of literature and the arts nominated to receive a Stalin Prize."[109] To remedy the situation, Fadeev proposed reducing the Committee's seventy-one members to thirty-five experts who were capable of "principled and objective evaluation." Though Fadeev did not suggest principled or objective criteria for determining that capability, he did suggest a list of those members to be retained and those to be cut, with reasons for cutting each.[110] He also suggested making the Stalin Prize Committee a yearlong commitment with correspondingly increased financial and bureaucratic support.[111]

---

107. Ibid., ll. 166–67, 169–71.

108. Ibid., ll. 167–69. Fadeev's examples in the music field are Shaporin and Gol'denveizer. He noted that Gol'denveizer used his authority to get Stalin Prizes for his students Ginzburg and Lamm. Fadeev's more detailed analyses of the subcommittees of theater and literature no doubt resulted from greater familiarity; he must have sat on both.

109. Ibid., l. 172.

110. Ibid., ll. 174–75 (recommended list), which includes five musicians (Khrennikov [chair], Kabalevskii, Zakharov, Livanova, and Shostakovich); ll. 176–78 (current list), which includes twelve musicians (including K. G. Dzerzhinskaia, who had recently died); and ll. 179–81 (list of proposed cuts), which included eight musicians (Golovanov, Gol'denveizer, Dzerzhinskaia [deceased], Kara Karaev, Sveshnikov, Shaporin, Shtogarenko); and RGASPI, f. 17, op. 133, d. 387, ll. 36–37 (reasons to cut), which eliminated members for subjective evaluation (nine, including L. P. Aleksandrovskaia, Gol'denveizer, Golovanov, Sveshnikov, and Shaporin), local prejudice (six), unprincipled approach to evaluation (thirteen, including Kara Karaev, A. G. Novikov, and A. Ia. Shtogarenko), passivity (sixteen), too much work at other institutions (four), and death (two).

111. RGASPI, f. 17, op. 133, d. 345, ll. 172–73. For example, Fadeev called on OKhLI to help the KSP decide on a list of paid consultants to help the subcommittees with *quarterly* rather than annual evaluations, and he asked that the Ministry of Finance and Moscow government provide funds for travel and meeting spaces in Moscow. Also, Fadeev suggested that those who had been nominated for a prize be prohibited from attending meetings in which their nomination was discussed.

In the Central Committee apparatus, Suslov and Kruzhkov suggested forming a commission to draft a Council of Ministers resolution based largely on those proposals. The next day, that commission reported to the Council of Ministers, which did not act until long after Stalin's death in March 1953. In the meantime, the Stalin Prize Committee proceeded with its established operations.[112]

Despite increasingly stringent oversight and repeated threats of disciplinary action against the Stalin Prize Committee, the Stalin Prize remained exactly as intended when it was first introduced: simultaneously a prize that sought to acknowledge accomplishment recognized by the broader audience of the creative intelligentsia and a tool that political leaders hoped could shape opinion within that audience. Whether the opinion the leadership hoped to shape was about the content and structure of Soviet art or about the responsibility within the leadership regarding potentially unpopular policies, the Stalin Prize Committee was a crucial interface between the Soviet leadership and the society's cultural elite. The committee enjoyed enough authority to resist challenges to its decisions even from powerful patronage networks. A repository of creative authority recognized by intellectuals and politicians alike, the Stalin Prize Committee was also a crucial audience for music professionals to accumulate creative authority of their own, and to translate that authority into material privilege. The Stalin Prize was thus a powerful force that legitimated material privilege based on accomplishments recognized by elite audiences.

Honorary titles, orders, medals, and Stalin Prizes were all extraordinary honors that came with substantial material rewards. As this study of prize winners reveals, a preference for highbrow Russian traditionalism in music ensured that awards frequently went to prominent performers, especially opera conductors and singers, and that Soviet composers of operas, ballets, oratorios, and cantatas received most of the Soviet Union's highest honors and the resulting status, prestige, and material privilege.

Demonstrating creative authority to governmental and party arts oversight institutions was essential to winning a title. Most title nominations referred to musical talent, service to the state or society, and popular recognition of musical ability. These three criteria demonstrate the simultaneously reflective and constitutive relationship between the creative authority conveyed by audiences and official markers of status and privilege. The importance of creative authority within a broader public was even more obvious and important in the Stalin Prize process.

Creative authority within the Soviet cultural elite was critical in almost every

---

112. Ibid., d. 387, ll. 40–41 (Suslov and Kruzhkov to Malenkov, 14 Aug 1952); ll. 42–46 (Aug 1952); l. 20; RGANI, f. 5, op. 17, d. 404, ll. 206–15 (Apr–May 1953), ll. 100–198 (KSP materials and OKhLI reviews); RGANI, f. 5, op. 17, d. 406, ll. 12–156 (same, but with a different set of changes proposed by OKhLI, now ONK).

step of the Stalin Prize process, from the constitution of the actual Stalin Prize Committee to the rare occasions in which its decisions were overturned. The Stalin Prize Committee was an important interface between the Soviet Union's political leadership and its creative intelligentsia. Membership on the Stalin Prize Committee was supposed to reflect authority within the cultural elite, but the party leadership also sought to mold opinions within a broader public through its appointments to the committee and through the committee's decisions. The Stalin Prize Committee thus provided an arena for the recognition of creative authority among the intelligentsia, the conversion of that authority into legitimate material privilege, the manipulation of elite opinion about matters artistic and political, and the very occasional censorship of professional judgments.

Hierarchies of legitimate privilege differ strikingly from the seemingly illegitimate privilege conveyed by astronomical royalties earnings. If authority within an elite audience gained a "serious" composer prestige and material comfort, tremendous popularity within a much more general audience could lead to suspicion. Taken in combination, the legitimate privilege of titles and prizes and the suspect privilege of extreme royalties demonstrate that the party leadership was more comfortable recognizing and legitimizing the artistic opinion of the Soviet cultural elite than it was acknowledging and promoting composers who appealed to popular taste.

This distinction had profound implications. It at least partly undermined one of the most ingenious organizational elements embodied in the Composers' Union, the combination in one professional body of composers of popular songs, highbrow chamber music, and virtually everything in between. The functional separation of extraordinary rewards available to members of each group undoubtedly fostered resentment on both sides. This resentment was often already latent because of creative tensions between the two loosely defined groups. The structural elision of the distinction between "high" and "low" culture that was expressed in the Composers' Union was thus fundamentally undermined by the fact that political leaders and Soviet society consciously and unconsciously maintained the distinction between the two modes of artistic production. Ultimately, efforts of both highbrow composers of "art music" and lowbrow composers of "pop music" to appeal to a common audience may have been more successful in the Soviet Union than anywhere in the West. Those successes were no doubt partly the product of the professional organization of Soviet composers, but they also came in the context of this bipartite system of extraordinary rewards. Perhaps some of that success should be attributed to the efforts of Tikhon Khrennikov, virtually the only figure common to these debates who sought to legitimize both paths to material privilege.

The distinction between legitimate and illegitimate privilege also has an implication on a much larger scale. It suggests that at least in the field of artistic production, party leaders shared more underlying assumptions with the cultural elite than they did with the most general audience in whose name they often spoke. This contention may seem to be undermined by the tremendous popularity of folk music and the clear support that the leadership gave it. However, the system of extraordinary material rewards and the operative distinctions between legitimate and suspicious privilege uncovered here and in chapter 8 do not indicate that sort of support. Talent and skills acquired through education and mastered through professional practice—not popular success with a mass audience—were considered the legitimate path to privilege. In a spiral of multiple reinforcement, that path also augmented professional agency and the power to determine the criteria by which music would be judged in the Soviet Union.

CHAPTER 10

"Most Respected Comrade . . ."

*Informal Networks in the
Stalinist Music World*

In the 1930s and 1940s, an elaborate bureaucratic apparatus emerged to administer the production and performance of music in the Soviet Union. Aspiring musicians were trained in music schools, academies, and prestigious conservatories that were overseen by one government institution. Opera singers and some orchestral musicians were channeled into state opera and ballet theaters that were overseen by another government institution. Instrumental soloists, orchestral musicians, choral singers, and touring variety show musicians were steered into a system of philharmonics, radio music ensembles, and a concert tour association where they were overseen by yet another government institution. And composers and musicologists were concentrated in a progressively more prestigious and powerful professional organization, the Composers' Union. The task of trying to coordinate the activities of all these groups fell to an ever evolving cultural oversight department in the Central Committee of the Communist Party.[1]

This elaborate bureaucracy was intended to administer the production of Soviet music and provide for the material well-being of the musicians who produced and performed that music. For the second of these tasks, a subsidiary system of material support grew up within the bureaucracy. The professional music organization oversaw Muzfond; performers were housed, fed, supplied, and supported in their retirement by their theater or performance institution and its chapter of the arts trade union, Rabis; and yet another government com-

---

1. The government oversight body for the musical academies and conservatories was the Committee (later Ministry) of Higher Education. The government oversight body for musical theaters was the Chief Musical Theaters Administration (GUMT) of the Committee on Artistic Affairs (VKI). For the philharmonics and free-standing orchestras and choirs, it was the VKI's Chief Administration of Musical Institutions (GUMU). And for touring soloists, it was the Concert Tour Association (Gastrol'biuro). The party oversight department changed its name and configuration over time. Alternately, it was the Administration (or Department) of Propaganda and Agitation (UPA/OPA), the Department of Artistic Literature and the Arts (OKhLI), and the Department of Science and Arts (ONK).

mittee decided on the distribution of the most lucrative material rewards offered to artists during this period, the Stalin Prize.[2]

Taken together, the government bureaucracy and these material support bodies formed an official institutional system that has been the primary focus of this study. However, this official system never adequately accomplished its tasks. To explain how music was actually produced in the Soviet Union and how musicians met their material needs, we must examine a range of informal but endemic personalized practices and relationships. Such an exploration reveals a cast of characters who played unofficial roles within and around the official music bureaucracy. Patrons, clients, and brokers engaged in a range of informal activities while they negotiated the elaborate bureaucratic system. These informal practices and the personalized relationships on which they were based formed another crucial interface between the music world's most prominent members and the Soviet Union's elite politicians. Isolated relationships and entire unofficial networks facilitated individual musicians' attempts to work their way through bureaucratic channels. The existence of unofficial networks was also a continual cause for concern and a source of suspicion among those outside each particular network. During periodic crackdowns on music institutions, the perception that some networks were controlled by suspect groups (formalists, cosmopolitans, or Jews, depending on the campaign) made them lightning rods for attacks. The unofficial network constituted an endemic informal component of the complex system of administering the production and performance of music. It was also a critical element of one of the most sinister aspects of the same system—campaigns designed to expunge the system of undesirable music and musicians. Unofficial networks thus contributed to the agency of professionals, but they could also put them at serious risk.

Evidence of unofficial activity is difficult to come by in archives organized according to an official bureaucracy and its administrative divisions, as those of Soviet institutions are. Luckily, the fact that requests spawned by individual, personal relationships found bureaucratic resolutions has left traces. Still, this chapter should be read with that caveat: it is not an attempt to catalogue all the informal behavior of musicians and politicians during the Stalin period. In fact, it leaves rather untouched a ubiquitous array of informal contacts within the profession and a system of connections, or *blat,* which are both extremely difficult to document.[3] Instead it describes the specific unofficial activities—patronage and brokerage—that most clearly formed an interface between music and high politics. It also analyzes the significance of such personalized, individual interactions in the context of the bureaucratic system with which they were intertwined.

2. Rabis was overseen by the VTsSPS, the All-USSR Central Council of Trade Unions—a government body. The work of the Committee on Stalin Prizes was also thoroughly checked by the Central Committee apparatus.

3. Alena Ledeneva, *Russia's Economy of Favors: Blat, Networking and Informal Exchange* (Cambridge: Cambridge University Press, 1998).

From an earlier focus on patronage in Soviet politics, scholars have more recently begun to examine patronage as one element of a more pervasive phenomenon: the proliferation of individualized, personal relationships within a formally but inefficiently bureaucratized society. Patronage has come to be seen as part of a neotraditional paradigm, an unofficial cultural value system, or a means of settling professional conflicts, especially in academic circles.[4] These studies all define patronage as an ongoing, hierarchical relationship in which patrons occupy a more powerful position in the society and exchange their assistance for loyalty and feelings of noblesse oblige. This chapter examines the role of patronage and brokerage within a specific group, tying together its crucial role in both the professional, productive realm and the allocative, material realm. It seeks to synthesize earlier viewpoints and provide a key to understanding the underlying assumptions that allowed unofficial networks to function.

I refer to "unofficial networks" and "informal interactions" and juxtapose them to "official," bureaucratic procedures. However, the line between "official" and "unofficial" interventions is severely blurred by the fact that the party, officially and by design, always reserved the right to intervene in the normal functioning of the bureaucracy. This power to intervene at any moment encouraged people to appeal to party figures as clients, supplicants, and fellow party members. This confusion renders my distinction between official and unofficial somewhat artificial. In some cases the "unofficial" surely helped to constitute the "official," since personalized relationships profoundly affected how bureaucratic institutions were formed.[5] In fact, the crucial figure of the broker literally straddled the line, officializing the unofficial while linking the fields of politics and musical production. Despite these reservations, the terms provide a useful shorthand for differentiating between the regular, orderly, impersonal operation of established bureaucratic procedures and the personalized, individual interventions that helped certain musicians navigate that bureaucracy more successfully.

4. See *Contemporary European History* 11, no. 2 (2002), in which an earlier version of this chapter first appeared; T. H. Rigby et al., eds., *Leadership Selection and Patron-Client Relations in the USSR and Yugoslavia* (London: George Allen and Unwin, 1983); John Willerton, *Patronage and Politics in the USSR* (Cambridge: Cambridge University Press, 1992); Ken Jowitt, *New World Disorder: The Leninist Extinction* (Berkeley: University of California Press, 1992), esp. 121–58; Andrew G. Walder, *Communist Neo-traditionalism: Work and Authority in Chinese Industry* (Berkeley: University of California Press, 1988); Sheila Fitzpatrick, "Intelligentsia and Power: Client-Patron Relations in Stalin's Russia," in *Stalinismus vor dem Zweiten Weltkrieg. Neue Wege der Forschung / Stalinism before the Second World War. New Avenues of Research*, ed. M. Hildermeier and E. Müller-Luckner (Munich: Oldenbourg, 1998); Krementsov, *Stalinist Science;* and D. A. Aleksandrov, "The Historical Anthropology of Science in Russia," *Russian Studies in History* 34, no. 2 (1995): 62–91.

5. Barbara Walker, "*Kruzhok* Culture: The Meaning of Patronage in the Early Soviet Literary World," *Contemporary European History* 11, no. 1 (Feb 2002): 107–24.

Patrons and Clients in Professional Disputes

Professional disputes were one of the most important areas in which composers and other musicians attempted to bend or subvert established rules and regulations. Though much less common than other types of unofficial activity, the use of networks to decide professional disputes had the most profound effect on the production of music in the Soviet Union. The following case demonstrates how patronage could influence who decided how music would be composed.

In early 1936 Sergei Prokofiev decided to write a cantata based on quotations from the works of Lenin. He approached the newly formed Committee on Artistic Affairs (VKI) to get approval for his text before continuing with the composition. In his meetings with VKI bureaucrats and its leader, P. M. Kerzhentsev, a professional conflict arose. In two personal meetings with Kerzhentsev, Prokofiev insisted on using a text comprised exclusively of Lenin quotes. Kerzhentsev was dead set against the idea, arguing that it was unacceptable to use quotations that would inevitably be "gathered accidentally and not at all organically connected." In the opinion of the VKI, such a use of Lenin's words, especially in a vocal composition, "cannot be justified either politically or artistically."

However, Kerzhentsev did not want to discourage the talented Prokofiev from writing a cantata on such an exalted theme. Consequently, he did not forbid Prokofiev from using certain selected quotations but suggested that he also use material written by Soviet poets. Prokofiev was categorically opposed to that suggestion, and he left the meeting agreeing only to think about it and return with a new plan. Kerzhentsev called the head of music programming at the Radio Committee and told him not to sign a contract with Prokofiev for the cantata until a text had been approved.[6]

After his two meetings with Kerzhentsev, Prokofiev turned to a patron, Marshall M. N. Tukhachevskii, to ask him to intervene and settle the dispute in his favor.[7] Though the specific nature and wording of Prokofiev's request remain a mystery, Tukhachevskii assented and took the issue to Molotov, essentially fighting Kerzhentsev tooth and nail the whole way. When Kerzhentsev learned that Tukhachevskii planned to intervene on behalf of Prokofiev, he sent a preemptive memo of his own to Molotov, explaining the VKI position, forwarding him a copy of Prokofiev's composition plan, and asking Molotov not to give in to Tukhachevskii.[8]

Kerzhentsev's preemptive tactic failed. Almost two weeks later, Molotov returned both Kerzhentsev's memo and Prokofiev's composition plan with the fol-

---

6. RGALI, f. 962, op. 10s, d. 9, l. 4 (Kerzhentsev to Molotov, 4 May 1936).

7. Tukhachevskii was a military leader with many contacts in the music world. He was arrested, tried, and executed for treason during the infamous purge of the military during the Great Terror of 1937.

8. Ibid. For the composition plan, see RGALI, f. 962, op. 10s, d. 9, ll. 6–7.

lowing instruction: "I order you to withdraw your objection to the draft of the composer Prokofiev and to permit *him* to decide the question of the Lenin cantata."[9] Here we see that Prokofiev successfully utilized his personal connection with Tukhachevskii, and Tukhachevskii's access to Molotov, to override the VKI's opposition to his professional plans.

What does this example suggest about composers' utilization of patronage in professional disputes? First, it outlines the parameters of the dynamic structure in which this sort of patronage operated. In this dispute, as in virtually all other professional interventions in the music realm, there were three basic actors: (1) a client (Prokofiev) with a complaint directed against (2) a bureaucratic institution (the VKI) whose administrative practices interfered with the client's professional desires, and (3) a patron (Molotov through Tukhachevskii) to whom the client could appeal to intervene on his behalf. The operative, but deeply underlying, cultural constructs that governed the interaction were political power and professional creative authority. In this case, the crucial audience that granted authority was a potential patron, a powerful politician.

Clarifying this process requires understanding the dynamic relationship between political power and creative authority that was implicit in professional patronage. In the Soviet Union, the distribution of power was extremely hierarchical, and all the actors in a typical patronage transaction occupied distinct locations in a hierarchy of power. At the top stood the patron, a politician whose power derived from proximity to the apex of political power. The middle of the hierarchy was occupied by the bureaucratic institution's representatives, whose administrative power derived both from the power vested in them by more powerful political figures or institutions and from the rules and regulations of their institution. At the bottom of the hierarchy lay the client, usually divested of any power, whether institutional or political. Clients had to convince their patrons that they (the clients) had more creative authority than the institution whose regulations stood in their way. By soliciting a patron's intervention, the client called for the imposition of political power on the sphere of artistic production in hopes that the patron would see fit to invert the relative power of clients and government bodies.

The Prokofiev example illustrates a clear-cut case in which that inversion was not in doubt. The world-famous Prokofiev was a composer of universally acknowledged talent who had recently been courted back to the Soviet Union from emigration. His adversary, Kerzhentsev, was an administrator currently in favor, but his success in the political arena failed to translate into creative authority that surpassed Prokofiev's. Neither Molotov (the operative patron) nor Tukhachevskii (a military leader) had pretensions to artistic authority, but their political power enabled them to draw and enforce distinctions in the creative authority of those below them. They acknowledged and reproduced their

9. Ibid., l. 4, pencil notation in the margin (Molotov, 17 May 1936), Molotov's emphasis.

client's authority in the professional realm. This example shows how the currency of cultural authority was both minted and tendered at the border between the political and musical fields.

An unsuccessful attempt to use patronage for intervention in a quasi-professional dispute illustrates this point just as clearly as Prokofiev's successful effort. In April 1944 one of the most popular jazz musicians in the Soviet Union, Leonid Utesov, challenged the Committee on Stalin Prizes. Utesov was rumored to have been a favorite entertainer at Stalin's legendary parties, and he attempted to utilize that personal connection to advance his professional status. He wrote Stalin a letter.[10]

Utesov framed his request as a personal matter that had "social and political significance," arguing that the highest honor in the arts was being awarded the title "Stalin Prize Laureate," something for which all artists strived. In fact, the possibility of receiving a Stalin Prize was a continual stimulus to scholars and artists in their creative work. Unfortunately, popular entertainers were not included on the list of those eligible for consideration, and though Utesov did not presume to suggest that any such stars were yet worthy of the high honor, he argued that the possibility would spur them to greater heights.

As an example of the great possibilities that *estrada* (variety music) stars embodied, Utesov cited their contribution to the war effort, noting that they were the main constituents of concert brigades. In fact, of the 460,000 concert performances before the Red Army and Navy up to that point in the war, nearly 300,000 had been given by *estrada* performers. The "wide masses love *estrada,* the Red Army loves it," Utesov wrote, and he could no longer put up with the "insulting" treatment of the genre at the hands of the arts administration. Before he got any more carried away, Utesov caught himself, apologized for not being able to explain fully the complexities of the issue in such a short letter, and explained that he did not want to presume to waste Stalin's valuable time. "Just please help Soviet *estrada,*" he closed.

This appeal contains the elements of the beginning of a professional intervention, though of course it was more complicated when Stalin was involved. Certainly the power hierarchy described above was intact. Stalin, the potential patron, was the apex of political power in the Soviet Union. Utesov had none. The institution in the middle, this time, was the Committee on Stalin Prizes. Though popular, Utesov did not have anywhere near the professional authority that Prokofiev enjoyed. On the other hand, the Committee on Stalin Prizes was the most professionally authoritative government institution in the arts and a crucial interface between the political leadership and the Soviet creative intelligentsia. In the committee, otherwise dispersed artistic experts were enshrined in power. Each of its individual members had great professional au-

10. RGASPI, f. 17, op. 125, d. 234, l. 37 (Utesov to Stalin, 18 Apr 1944) and GARF, f. 5446, op. 46, d. 2421, l. 146 (same).

thority although no power (outside their institutional position), but the institution itself possessed both authority and power. Still, if Stalin wished it, Utesov's demand could have been fulfilled. Stalin did not intervene.

Apparently he let others look into the situation, without giving even a hint of support for Utesov. It is possible that the appeal never actually reached Stalin. The notation on the memo is from Molotov, who sent it to M. B. Khrapchenko, then head of the Committee on Artistic Affairs, for further information.[11] Khrapchenko's response indicated that *estrada* performers were not excluded from consideration in the deliberations of the Committee on Stalin Prizes. In fact, they were considered in a new category that had been created only a year earlier—concert performance.[12] Unfortunately for the *estrada* performers, only one of them, S. V. Obraztsov, was even considered, and his candidacy lost out to others. Khrapchenko agreed that *estrada* was a powerful musical genre, popular and important to the war effort, and he suggested awarding the best performers with orders and medals to stimulate continued creative efforts. Molotov placed great emphasis on the information about *estrada*'s eligibility, suggesting that he considered the original issue settled. He also emphasized the paragraph recommending orders and medals, suggesting that he thought the idea was worth pursuing. In fact, he passed the memo on to the Central Committee's cultural oversight body for further review.[13]

A month later, the issue was still being tossed around from one high-level committee to another. In the last remaining memo associated with Utesov's original request, the government apparatus declared that the matter required no further action on their part. The Central Committee apparatus would make the final decision during its review of the Stalin Prize Committee's final recommendations. When the Stalin Prize recipients were named, *estrada* performers were not in their number.[14] Utesov's appeal was dead. He had failed to convince either Stalin or Molotov that his own creative opinion was more authoritative than the collected opinion of the Committee on Stalin Prizes.[15]

The fluid, interdependent relationship of power and authority suggested by these examples is significant in two ways. First, it underlines the importance to music professionals of establishing their authority in the eyes of politically pow-

11. Ibid., marginal notation dated 18 Apr 1944.

12. RGASPI, f. 17, op. 125, d. 234, l. 38 (Khrapchenko to Molotov, 21 Apr 1944) and GARF, f. 5446, op. 46, d. 2421, l. 147 (same). The concert performance category was created by a SNK SSSR resolution dated 13 Mar 1943.

13. RGASPI, f. 17, op. 125, d. 234, l. 38, marginal notation.

14. GARF, f. 5446, op. 46, d. 2421, l. 148 (Tepferov to Vyshinskii, 15 May 1944). The final decision was not announced until after the war, on 26 January 1946, when prizes were given for both 1943 and 1944: *Sobranie postanovlenii i rasporiazhenii Pravitel'stva SSSR* 1946, no. 3 (15 Mar): 50–51.

15. For another unsuccessful appeal in the popular music realm, see RGASPI, f. 17, op. 133, d. 368, ll. 91–98 (Aug–Sep 1952), materials relating to an unsuccessful patronage request from the composer Muradeli and the poet Mikhalkov to Poskrebyshev, in which the unofficial channel simply fed the request back into the bureaucratic mill.

erful potential patrons. High officials were a crucial unofficial audience. In fact, patrons necessarily had to be able to wear both unofficial and official hats in order for the process to function.

Second, it explains the relatively rare occurrence of this sort of professional patronage in the music realm. High-level professional patronage in music was quite unlike the thoroughly competitive and politicized patron-client ties that Nikolai Krementsov discovered in biology, where two competing professional groups found highly placed political patrons to whom they could systematically turn for support and whose political struggles profoundly influenced appointments to editorial boards and professional research positions.[16] The operative element in determining the success of a patronage intervention in music was not political wrangling but a lower-level combination of professional authority and political power. In music, the phenomenon was probably limited to prominent performers and composers like Prokofiev, Shostakovich (who was also patronized by Tukhachevskii until the latter's execution), Dunaevskii, and just a few others.[17] The VKI and especially the Stalin Prize Committee were vested with enough creative authority that only the rare individual could convince politicians that their individual creative judgment trumped that of the relevant bureaucratic administration's leadership.

These two cases, one successful and one unsuccessful, reveal the underlying operative relationship between authority and power that governed musicians' use of patronage for intervention in professional disputes, but they certainly do not demonstrate the range of professional conflicts in which patronage intervention played an important role. Performers, artistic directors of performance ensembles, and opera singers used patrons to increase their press coverage and land better roles.[18]

In these examples, it is not always clear that the relationship between the musician and the politician fits a formal definition of patronage as an ongoing personal relationship. Scattered data about informal networks makes it difficult to know if an incident is not an isolated, one-time interaction. This uncertainty could undermine an argument that isolates patronage from other sorts of informal relationships, so it is important to think of patronage, strictly defined, as merely one type of relationship on a continuum of personalized interactions. The following example illustrates just how amorphous were the boundaries between these types of relationships.

Four days after the Central Committee issued its resolution attacking formalism in music in February 1948, the theater censorship organization, Glavrepertkom, released a decree that officially suppressed the performance of

16. Krementsov, *Stalinist Science*, esp. 80–82.

17. For Shostakovich's link to Tukhachevskii, see Fay, *Shostakovich*, 27, 92.

18. RGASPI, f. 17, op. 132, d. 238, ll. 37–38 (Moiseev to Stalin, complaining about lack of press coverage, Mar–Apr 1949); and op. 133, d. 328, ll. 173–76 (Gaidai to Stalin asking for help landing a role in the opera *Bogdan Khmel'nitskii*, Jun 1951). To Stalin, Gaidai was a supplicant, not a client, but she appealed to Stalin only after her regular patron abandoned her.

several works by the composers mentioned in the Central Committee resolution.[19] This singular decree remained in force for just over a year until it was revoked by order of the Council of Ministers in March 1949. The Council of Ministers even issued a reprimand to Glavrepertkom for what was described as an "illegal decree."[20]

The circumstances surrounding the decision to revoke the Glavrepertkom decree do not fit easily into the continuum of informal relationships. In early 1949 two American conductors (Arturo Toscanini and the Russian émigré Sergei Kusevitsky) invited Shostakovich to the United States for a series of concerts in which he would appear as a piano soloist in connection with the Congress for Peace in New York. The organization that administered international cultural ties (VOKS) saw the invitation as a great propaganda opportunity and a chance to raise money and the prestige of the Council of American-Soviet Friendship. Soviet decision makers agreed.[21] However, Shostakovich had foreseen a problem with his participation, so he approached the Central Committee apparatus with his concern. Since most of the works in the repertoire of the American conductors had been suppressed by Glavrepertkom, he asked that his participation as a performer be limited to chamber music and made a couple personal requests: that his wife be allowed to accompany him and that he be fitted for a tuxedo with tails for his American appearances.[22]

When he turned to the Central Committee, Shostakovich basically activated a mechanism that blurs the boundaries between the official and unofficial. He approached a member of the Central Committee's cultural administration apparatus, L. F. Il'ichev. Though Il'ichev was certainly ranked high enough to be a potential patron, there was nothing in either the language of Shostakovich's appeal nor the lore surrounding his relationship with Soviet power to suggest that he had an ongoing personal relationship with the party bureaucrat. Consequently, his appeal can hardly be described as patronage. On the other hand, he did not approach the Central Committee through official channels like VOKS or the Committee on Artistic Affairs. He did not even utilize semiofficial channels by, for example, having the head of the Composers' Union bring his concern to the Central Committee's attention. His request, therefore, must be considered primarily personal.

What happened next demonstrates how intimately connected bureaucratic and personalized operations sometimes were. Il'ichev sent the memo to Molotov, who apparently requested more information from VOKS and the Com-

19. RGALI, f. 2077, op. 1, d. 335, ll. 14–15 (Glavrepertkom Prikaz #17, 14 Feb 1948). Overall 42 works by 13 composers were suppressed, a number which did not include the actual object of the attack, V. I. Muradeli's opera *Great Friendship*.

20. Ibid., l. 13 (SM SSSR Rasp. #3179r, 16 Mar 1949).

21. RGASPI, f. 82, op. 2, d. 1019, l. 6 (A. Denisov to Molotov, 18 Mar 1949).

22. Ibid., ll. 4–5 (Shostakovich to L. F. Il'ichev, 7 Mar 1949). Il'ichev was a bureaucrat in the Central Committee's cultural administration apparatus.

mittee on Artistic Affairs.[23] The day after receiving confirmation that Glav-repertkom had indeed suppressed a number of Shostakovich's pieces, Molotov sent Shostakovich's letter (but not the VKI confirmation) to Stalin to familiarize him with the situation. He also sent copies to virtually all other top politicians: Beria, Malenkov, Mikoian, Kaganovich, Bulganin, and Kosygin.[24]

The denouement of this interaction has long been part of the lore surrounding Shostakovich and his relationship with Soviet power. In his memoir, the composer G. S. Frid relates his version of the event, recounted to him by Shostakovich while the two were traveling to the composers' working resort sometime later. Shostakovich first received a telephone call from A. N. Poskrebyshev, Stalin's secretary. He was out when the call arrived, but Poskrebyshev called again. As soon as he contacted Shostakovich, Poskrebyshev transferred the call to Stalin, who asked Shostakovich to explain his refusal to go to the United States and perform, for example, his Eighth Symphony. Shostakovich explained that the Eighth Symphony had been suppressed, and Stalin thundered, "By whom?"[25] Within days, so goes the lore, the "blacklist" of suppressed pieces disappeared. As we now know, the Glavrepertkom decision was revoked the same day that Molotov forwarded Shostakovich's letter to Stalin, probably initiating the phone calls. The road was clear for Shostakovich to perform in the United States.

This was an unusual circumstance, one in which politicians saw an important propaganda opportunity on the international stage. Though the individuals were all certainly acquainted with one another and had long-term relationships, their interactions were more sporadic and antagonistic than regular and supportive. The actual interactions straddle the boundaries between official and unofficial. Still, this whole slippery incident can be reduced to the same parameters as more clear-cut professional patronage examples. Here too, in a conflict between an individual musician and a government bureaucracy with at least a claim to jurisdiction over one aspect of the production of music, the decisive underlying factor was the relationship between hierarchical power and creative

---

23. Ibid., l. 6 (VOKS); and RGASPI, f. 82, op. 2, d. 950, l. 113 (Bespalov to Molotov, 15 Mar 1949).

24. RGASPI, f. 82, op. 2, d. 1019, l. 3 (Molotov to Stalin, 16 Mar 1949). The whole circle of top politicians was probably kept informed—and Stalin may even have been involved—primarily because the issue involved high-profile international travel and contact, decisions about which were always at least confirmed by the Politburo throughout the postwar period.

25. G. S. Frid, *Dorogoi ranenoi pamiati* (Moscow: Prosveshchenie, 1994), 274–75. Frid reports that everyone had assumed that the list of repressed works had been drawn up by Stalin himself, though he acknowledges that that might not have been the case, as it most probably was not. Frid tentatively dates the exchange in 1951 (ibid., 276), but the conversation must have been related to the events documented here. For other versions of the story, see Fay, *Shostakovich*, 171–72; Wilson, *Shostakovich*, 212–13; Khrennikov, *Tak eto bylo*, 133; and Volkov, *Testimony*, 147–48. Note also that the lore speaks of Shostakovich refusing to travel to the United States rather than suggesting that he only perform in concerts of his chamber music.

authority. Shostakovich's cultural authority derived from his international prestige and the propaganda advantage that the Soviet Union could achieve by exhibiting him abroad. The crucial authority-granting audience was a powerful decision maker (Stalin), but his decision reflected the implicit authority bestowed by an altogether different audience: the international music-following public. In the end, whether the authority derived from professional accomplishment or from potential international prestige, Stalin decided that Shostakovich had greater professional authority than the bureaucratic institution, Glavrepertkom. Stalin's decision also significantly increased Shostakovich's own prestige, as the multiple retellings of the story and its subsequent heroic coloration so eloquently demonstrate.

The authority of the artist and the power of the politician were taken very seriously, and those who abused their connections by promoting themselves beyond socially supportable levels or using them to bully subordinates could find themselves officially reprimanded and cut off from the unofficial network. Such was the case with the ballet librettist A. P. Abolimov, who was disciplined for abusing his official position and personal connections in late 1949. At the time, Abolimov was the head of the Council of Ministers Group on the Arts. He was accused of flooding Moscow's ballet theaters with productions based on his poorly written librettos, creating artificial excitement before the openings of his ballets, and cowing anyone who opposed him by flaunting his personal contacts and threatening to call for Politburo member Kliment Voroshilov's intervention. A joint investigative commission of the Central Committee's culture department and Party Control Commission consulted experts from the Composers' Union and opera and ballet theaters, all of whom testified that Abolimov was incompetent. His librettos were based on existing literature, often coauthored, and always completely reworked by composers and choreographers. Abolimov did not enjoy any professional authority. The accusation that he abused his power and flaunted his unofficial connections was confirmed, and the investigators concluded that he had violated the norms of proper conduct for a party member and government official, characterizing his conduct in strong language as "anti-party behavior."[26] This condemnation implicitly reaffirmed the ideal relationship between creative authority and political power. Political power was supposed to promote superior creative authority, so if that creative authority was considered insufficient in professional circles, it tarnished the patron's reputation.

The Broker, Patronage and Material Support

Musicians more frequently used unofficial networks to navigate the bureaucratic channels through which they secured their material needs. Providing ma-

---

26. RGASPI, f. 17, op. 132, d. 234, ll. 92–101 (Tarasov and Byshov to Suslov and Shkiriatov, archived 31 Oct 1949).

terial support for creative work was one of the bureaucracy's basic tasks, but goods were always too scarce to supply everyone who was entitled to receive them. Consequently, some sort of unofficial assistance was often needed before individuals could obtain what they sought. Though not as directly related to the production of music as professional disputes, patronage appeals for material support played an extremely important role in the lives of composers, musicologists, and other musicians.

The character who was most prominent in material support patronage was the broker, a middleman in an interaction that was both official and unofficial.[27] Brokers straddled the cultural and political fields because they had relevant authority in both. Often, a crucial source of this dual authority was the key institutional post that a broker held. Brokers were members of the Orgkom or Secretariat of the Composers' Union, directors of conservatories and higher middle schools, or artistic directors of opera and ballet theaters. Their institutional appointments gave them access to potentially powerful politicians, and they used that access to pass along—and endorse—requests from individual members of their respective institutions, or from friends and colleagues. But their brokerage did not follow patterns of impersonal bureaucratic practice. One of the essential characteristics of the brokerage interaction was its exceptional, often individualistic nature. By giving a personalized transaction an institutional stamp of approval, brokers dissolved the already illusory border between the official and unofficial, rendering official otherwise unofficial activities.

The most prominent broker in the postwar Stalinist music world was Tikhon Khrennikov, general secretary of the Composers' Union from 1948 until the end of the Soviet period. Almost immediately upon assuming his official post, Khrennikov had to act as broker for his predecessors and colleagues. From preserving their right to keep a car to saving them from expulsion from the Composers' Union, Khrennikov's brokerage was a significant point of articulation between the fields of resource allocation, party politics, and music production.[28]

Before World War II, Khrennikov was primarily known as a young and talented composer, primarily of popular songs, film music, and opera.[29] During the war he traveled with the Soviet army during its final push to Berlin, thus gaining important association with soldiers at the front.[30] After the war Khrennikov gradually came to represent a loosely defined populist artistic position

27. I borrow the term "broker" from Sheila Fitzpatrick; for her patronage typology, see Fitzpatrick, "Intelligentsia and Power."

28. For Khrennikov's intervention to save Glier's car, see RGALI, f. 2085, op. 1, d. 1209, l. 71 (Khrennikov to E. D. Sagerashvili, 19 Mar 1948).

29. Before the war, Khrennikov's opera *V buriu* (Into the Storm) was the subject of heated debate about the future of Soviet opera after 1936: Khrennikov, *Tak eto bylo*, 65–78. His "March of the Artillerymen," written for the 1944 film *Shest' chasov vechera posle voiny* (Six O'clock in the Evening after the War) was a huge success at home and in the rear.

30. Khrennikov, *Tak eto bylo*, 79–91.

within the professional organization, and he was named to the Orgkom in the spring of 1946.[31] Young, talented, with experience at the front and a penchant to write popular, accessible music, Khrennikov was an understandable choice to head the Composers' Union after the brouhaha that shook the professional organization in February 1948.

Once he was chosen to head the Composers' Union, Khrennikov was propelled into the realm of high politics, with a host of new associates in the Central Committee apparatus, figures that included everyone from Andrei Zhdanov and Dmitrii Shepilov (head of the Central Committee's culture department) to Boris Iarustovskii (the ranking music expert in that department).[32] He was also suddenly the chief spokesperson for the Composers' Union, supported by composers and musicologists who had more experience negotiating the overlap between music and politics. Most prominent among these supporters was Viktor Belyi, whom Khrennikov credits with helping him negotiate the tricky line between public discipline and private protection of professional colleagues during the early days of his tenure atop the Composers' Union.[33]

As Khrennikov gained experience in his new position, however, he discovered that there were definite limits to his authority. Two anecdotes from Khrennikov's memoirs serve to illustrate this point. The first demonstrates that in the Central Committee apparatus (the realm of party politics), Khrennikov's authority in the music realm was relatively secure from external attack, even when that attack was vitriolic and politically literate. One day at the height of the anticosmopolitanism campaign in 1949, the Central Committee secretary, M. A. Suslov, summoned Khrennikov and showed him a denunciation that the committee had received. The denunciation adroitly used the anti-Semitic attack language of anticosmopolitanism and fingered Khrennikov as the linchpin of a Jewish conspiracy that manipulated the Composers' Union administration through his Jewish wife. Rather than acting on the denunciation, Suslov merely passed it on to Khrennikov with the droll remark, "Here you go, read it and see how the people you interact with write about you."[34]

The second anecdote demonstrates that once Khrennikov strayed outside the circumscribed realm of cultural production, he was on shaky ground. Sometime in the early 1950s Khrennikov invited a previous head of the Park of Culture, Betty Glan, to serve in the Composers' Union's administrative apparatus. Glan had been married to a Yugoslav communist, and after the Soviet split with Yugoslavia she had been denied permission to live in Moscow. In order to hire her, Khrennikov had to intervene and personally obtain permission for her to return to Moscow. He did so. Shortly thereafter, he was summoned by the head

---

31. RGALI, f. 2077, op. 1, d. 139, ll. 13–13ob. (Protokol #5, 11 Mar 1946), pts. 3–4; l. 14 (Protokol #6, 5 Apr 1946), pt. 1.

32. Khrennikov, *Tak eto bylo,* 126–27, 130.

33. Ibid., 126, 134–35.

34. Ibid., 136. Though Khrennikov self-consciously refrains from mentioning the author of the denunciation, it was probably penned by A. S. Ogolevets.

of the arts department in the Central Committee apparatus, B. S. Riurikov. Riurikov reprimanded him and informed him in threatening terms that he was not to petition for "such people" in the future. Khrennikov was presently untouchable, he was told, only because Stalin had recently shown him favor.[35] These two episodes demonstrate that Khrennikov's authority in the political realm was limited to the field of his professional expertise (music) and to the professionals who populated that field (musicians).[36] Still, it was his limited connection with both realms that allowed Khrennikov to serve as a broker for his clients and colleagues.

Although brokerage authority in the music realm was probably most concentrated in the person of Khrennikov after 1948, other members of the Orgkom or Secretariat both before and after 1948 could act quite effectively as brokers, opening as they did personalized channels for musicians to negotiate requests relating to their material world. For instance, musicians used patrons and brokers to help them acquire or recover pianos and cars.[37] Because of an endemic and acute housing shortage, the most common and significant type of request was for assistance in acquiring an apartment, as in the following case where a group of conservatory professors used an unofficial network to broker a deal in order to get better housing for a gifted young student.

In April 1939 Glier, Gol'denveizer, and Miaskovskii wrote to Molotov about the living conditions of Lenia Brumberg, a promising student in the piano and composition departments of the Moscow State Conservatory's ten-year music school. They complained that Brumberg lived with his family in a damp basement, which disturbed his work and endangered his health, and asked Molotov to help the Brumbergs acquire a small, three-room apartment and establish "normal" living conditions for the gifted boy.[38] They also included a report, which appears to have been submitted to them by the boy's parents, describing the family's miserable accommodation and its detrimental effect on their son. The family occupied a seventeen-square-meter room in a collective apartment that housed a total of sixteen people. The apartment was dark, dirty, smelly,

35. Ibid., 137–38. B. S. Riurikov was trained as a literary scholar and had been climbing the ranks of the Central Committee apparatus since 1946, but he was fired in 1949 during the anti-cosmopolitanism campaigns.

36. At least in the Stalin period, therefore, Khrennikov can only be seen as a limited analog of the patron who is at the center of György Peteri's study of patronage in Hungarian economics, Istvan Friss. Friss operated more or less freely in the political realm, jockeying among his colleagues to protect (even during a purge) the economists who were his clients, from whom he maintained a professional distance. On the other hand, Khrennikov operated more or less freely in the professional realm, but his ability to maneuver in the political sphere was significantly curtailed. György Peteri, "Purge and Patronage: Kádár's Counter-revolution and the Field of Economic Research in Hungary, 1957–58," *Contemporary European History* 11, no. 1 (2002): 125–52.

37. On pianos, see GARF, f. 5446, op. 48, d. 2176, ll. 109–13, 120–23 (Mar–Apr 1946); op. 49, d. 2829, ll. 156–59 (Nov–Dec 1947). On cars, see GARF, f. 5446, op. 47, d. 2168, ll. 35–38, 78 (May–Jun 1945), one of which is a supplicant appeal with the same result.

38. GARF, f. 5446, op. 23, d. 1808, l. 139 (Glier, Gol'denveizer, and Miaskovskii to Molotov, 14 Apr 1939).

damp, loud, and infested with vermin. The only possible place to put a piano was too close to the stove for safety, so they were refused an instrument. The boy simply could not study normally and often suffered from headaches and nervousness, which his parents attributed to the living conditions.[39]

The Brumbergs also reported that they had turned to both the editorial board of the government's newspaper (*Izvestiia*) and the Committee on Artistic Affairs for help acquiring more reasonable living conditions. Both of these institutions, probably the parents' employers, had supported their request and advanced their case before the Moscow City Government (Mossovet), which was in charge of distributing housing. Unfortunately, their request had been denied by Mossovet in early April.[40] The parents had exhausted all the official channels available to them before turning to the conservatory professors as brokers.

Though it took the better part of a year, the unofficial channel seems to have worked. In early May 1939, the administrative department of the top government institution sent two memos to Mossovet asking for improvement in Lenia Brumberg's living conditions.[41] These requests seem to have met with passive resistance (Mossovet ignored them), but in November, the administrative department followed up with a concluding memo instructing the Committee on Artistic Affairs to follow through with appropriate measures, thus presumably empowering them to push the request through Mossovet or to implement a different Mossovet decree that granted the Brumberg family housing.[42] Little Lenia's health problems associated with life in a Moscow basement did not permanently hinder his career. In the years that followed, he matured into a prominent pianist, studying with Goldenveizer, G. G. Neigauz, and Shostakovich and eventually assuming a professorship in piano at the prestigious Gnesin Institute. He emigrated to Austria in 1981 and assumed a position on the piano faculty of the Conservatory of the City of Vienna.[43]

Students were not the only ones who used brokers to help them negotiate official channels. Even very prominent musicians sometimes turned to brokers, though in such cases the brokers often spoke more as representatives of collective opinion than as individuals exploiting their personal ties to politicians. The following example illustrates how a group of brokers helped a piano professor at the Moscow Conservatory improve his housing allotment by presenting a request implicitly on behalf of musical public opinion.

In October 1946 a group of brokers, eleven prominent musicians, including

39. Ibid., l. 138 (housing description, undated, signed by E. Brumberg).

40. Ibid.

41. Ibid., l. 140 (Vypiska to Mossovet, 7 May 1939); l. 141 (Bol'shakov to Pronin, 10 May 1939).

42. Ibid., l. 142 (M. Khlomov to Khrapchenko, 22 Nov 1939). The final resolution is not documented in these sources, but it is most likely that the VKI finally managed to resettle the Brumbergs.

43. "Leonid Brumberg," http://www.musikseminar.music.at/pers/brumberg_l.html (accessed March 2000); my thanks to Alison Smith for pointing me to this site.

the de facto head of the Composers' Union, the director of the Moscow Conservatory, and several acclaimed performers and music professors, sent a letter to Voroshilov on behalf of G. G. Neigauz, the head of a piano department at the conservatory. The brokers described the genesis and nature of Neigauz's housing problem. In 1936 he had been given his own three-room apartment in which his family of five could live and he could maintain a separate room for musical studies. When Neigauz was evacuated during the war and employed by the Sverdlovsk Conservatory, one of the rooms of his apartment was allocated to someone else. When he returned from evacuation in July 1944, Neigauz found himself in intolerable circumstances and unable to work. Before providing the outrageous details, the brokers sketched the importance of Neigauz's scholarly, creative, and pedagogical activity and pointed out his success training world-class pianists, including Emil Gilels, Sviatoslav Richter, and several others. Then, they provided the details of his housing woes: "The difficulty of Professor G. G. Neigauz's situation is aggravated by the fact that the individual who has been settled into the indicated room not only disturbs his peace but even disrupts his work in insulting and incomprehensible ways. Suffice it to say that during the preparation for a concert on 1 November of this year, the piano playing was cut off by pounding on the door and the screeches of the inhabitant: 'Stop that drumming immediately!'"

After painting this brief but clearly unacceptable picture, the brokers also described Neigauz's efforts to resolve his problem through bureaucratic channels. After all, he had been allocated the entire apartment and should have been able to have the insulting neighbor evicted. In fact, he had received some form of official success: on July 1 Mossovet had issued an order to resettle the encroacher. Unfortunately three and a half months had passed, and the character was still there.[44]

The brokers implicitly cast themselves as representatives of an even broader public, suggesting that honoring their request was necessary for the continued advancement of Soviet music performance:

> In the interests of the further development of our country's musical arts and the preparation of musical performers, we consider ourselves obligated to ask you to take measures to return to Professor G. G. Neigauz the room that was seized from him, or to resettle him into a different individual apartment. If you consider it necessary to receive more complete information about this matter, we would like to ask you to invite Professor G. G. Neigauz in for a personal conversation. We are sure that our request will not be put aside without proper attention.

As though to emphasize further their unified but unofficial opinion, the brokers signed the letter with their titles but without the typically obligatory institutional affiliations.[45]

44. GARF, f. 5446, op. 48, d. 2181, l. 43 (to Voroshilov, 17 Oct 1946).
45. Ibid., l. 42 (this file is paginated backward). The letter was signed by Shebalin, Khacha-

Not surprisingly, the brokers' appeal was successful. Almost a week after they received the original letter, bureaucrats in Voroshilov's office reported back to him on the case, summarizing the appeal and recommending that the collective letter be sent to Mossovet with instructions to restore Neigauz's rights to the occupied room. Voroshilov agreed, a curt note was dispatched to Mossovet along with a copy of the brokers' letter, and the brokers were informed of the positive decision.[46]

This incident suggests the role that this type of noninstitutional collective brokerage played in the arts administration system. It also illustrates how blurry the boundaries between hierarchical and more collegial unofficial support networks were and demonstrates how they often overlapped. This was a personal request about a specific individual's problems. In that sense, the whole incident was fundamentally particularized just like the other examples of unofficial networks provided so far. The locus of the particularized interaction, however, was primarily within the musical community—a nonhierarchical network of mutual support. Still, the final appeal activated a relationship that was just as hierarchical as other examples because it again brought the powerful Voroshilov into the negotiation.

The language of this appeal also suggest another important feature of these hierarchical unofficial networks. The brokers' statement of the stakes in their request and their noninstitutional self-identifications cast them as representatives of a wider opinion within the musical community. In that sense, the brokers were a collected manifestation of difficult-to-assess public opinion. By conceding to their request, the party could cast itself as the arbiter of taste and the official representative, the very embodiment, of public opinion.

A growing historical literature on letter writing in the Soviet Union suggests that letters, supplicant appeals to politicians, and complaints to newspaper editors were important sources of information about the popular reception of party policies.[47] Though clearly related to these more anonymous sources, the information that clients, or in this case brokers, provided characteristically differed in two ways. First, the brokers were experts, qualified representatives of a select group whose opinions were authoritative. Since they themselves were not random letter writers but known personalities, politicians could much more easily convert the information that brokers provided into information about sentiments in the group that they represented.

Second, clients could provide patrons with accurate information about the

---

turian, Raiskii, Gedike, Nechaev, Feinberg, Knushevitskii, Erdeli, Mostras, Gol'denveizer, and Nemenova-Lunts.

46. Ibid., l. 44 (Tepferov and Abolimov to Voroshilov, 23 Oct 1946). A handwritten note dated 31 October 1946 indicates that Shebalin was informed of Voroshilov's decision.

47. Sheila Fitzpatrick, "Supplicants and Citizens: Public Letter-Writing in Soviet Russia in the 1930s," *Slavic Review* 55, no. 1 (Spring 1996): 78–105; Golfo Alexopoulos, *Stalin's Outcasts: Aliens, Citizens, and the Soviet State, 1926–1936* (Ithaca: Cornell University Press, 2003); and Sarah Davies, *Popular Opinion in Stalin's Russia: Terror, Propaganda, and Dissent, 1934–1941* (Cambridge: Cambridge University Press, 1997).

clients' institutional surroundings. Accurate information was hard to come by in an environment in which subordinates often concealed crucial information from decision makers, especially if it was not good news. This exchange of information for support was an important element of the reciprocity required of a patronage relationship. Though this exchange was undoubtedly more important in spheres other than music, patronage requests in the arts offer information often enough to suggest that it is an important, widespread phenomenon.[48] Because of their institutional leadership positions, brokers were often an important conduit of information from the meek to the mighty as well as distributors of favors and goods from the political elite to the musician, composer, and musicologist. Furthermore, the need to protect the sources of information, combined with the overall conditions of scarcity, helped patrons justify their personalized interventions into bureaucratic processes.

Recourse to a broker was not the only unofficial channel that musicians used in their pursuit of improved living conditions. Some skipped the broker and appealed directly to the politician, sometimes as a patron, sometimes simply with a supplicant appeal. One spectacular case of such a direct patronage appeal suggests that prominent performers often did not need to use brokers. The world-renowned pianist Emil Gilels was such a musician.

In November 1947 Gilels sent a short request worded in a familiar tone to Voroshilov. He emphasized that his living conditions were seriously inhibiting his continued creative activity. For the last several years, he and his wife (a composer) had been living in one room of a three-room communal apartment with a woman who occupied the other two. These living conditions denied his wife a minimal work environment and disturbed the daily regimen that Gilels considered necessary for his own work as a concert pianist and teacher at the Moscow Conservatory. Since the other woman had just received her own apartment, Gilels asked that Voroshilov help him obtain the whole communal apartment.[49]

The response to this first letter remains a mystery, but five days later, Gilels sent another one. In the second letter, he was slightly more formal in tone and related more details about his regimen and creative responsibilities. Rather than describing the details of his living conditions, he simply noted that living in a communal apartment precluded the minimal living conditions: the quiet and calm required to support his and his wife's creative activities. Rather than asking again for the whole communal apartment, Gilels asked Voroshilov to help them acquire their own individual apartment.[50]

Explanations of what happened in the five days between these two requests are necessarily speculative. Perhaps Gilels learned that the rooms in their com-

---

48. RGASPI, f. 17, op. 114, d. 305, ll. 118–19 (Kirshon to Kaganovich and Stalin, archived 31 May 1932); op. 133, d. 396, ll. 87–91 (Solov'eva to Mikhailov, 13 Feb 1953).

49. GARF, f. 5446, op. 49, d. 2835, l. 164 (Gilels to Voroshilov, 18 Nov 1947).

50. Ibid., l. 165 (Gilels to Voroshilov, 23 Nov 1947).

munal apartment had already been reallocated. More likely, a member of Voroshilov's staff—or even Voroshilov himself—may have communicated directly with Gilels and explained how he could make his request more useful when it reentered bureaucratic channels. The latter scenario would explain the more formal tone, the lengthier list of Gilels's musical activities, and the change to a request for an individual apartment. (Presumably it was much easier to assign him a new apartment than to change the status of his apartment in a communal building.) That the two letters followed one after the other in such short order strongly suggests that much of this interaction occurred in face-to-face conversation or on the telephone.[51]

Gilels's second request was more successful than his aborted first one. Three days after Voroshilov received the letter, his secretary reported back to him about a quick further investigation of Gilels's living conditions. The secretary noted that the Committee on Artistic Affairs also supported the request, and he included a draft letter from Voroshilov to Mossovet.[52] The draft memo to Mossovet called Gilels "our most outstanding pianist," listed his titles and international triumphs, and politely asked the head of Mossovet to look into the situation and give him an individual apartment in one of the new housing buildings. It concluded with all but an order: "I support this request very much." Voroshilov approved the draft memo, and the issue was transferred to Mossovet.[53]

The range of unofficial networks that musicians used for material support was much broader than that of unofficial professional support networks, which depended on the relationship between power and professional authority. One last housing example, besides demonstrating yet another type of collective brokerage interaction, is suggestive of that broader logic.

In April 1947 the Orgkom of the Composers' Union acted as broker for a Composers' Union administrative worker. They wrote to Voroshilov on behalf of A. K. Shchepalin, the director of Muzfond's service center for music publishing and production institutions. Shchepalin and his family of four (two of whom were students at the Moscow Conservatory) had been evicted from their temporary housing because of fire hazards associated with construction on a new theater building. Since losing their temporary housing, the Shchepalins had fallen into extremely tenuous living conditions and literally ended up on the street. Since Shchepalin was a valued and experienced worker, the Composers' Union did not want to lose his services, which they would do if his family was not given housing in Moscow soon.[54]

---

51. With the increasingly broad distribution of telephones in elite circles, the details of personalized interactions become increasingly difficult to document. However, they were so intertwined with the bureaucracy that some document trail often remains, as in this case.

52. GARF, f. 5446, op. 49, d. 2835, l. 166 (Abolimov to Voroshilov, 26 Nov 1947). The VKI support was attributed to Surin.

53. Ibid., l. 167 (draft, Voroshilov to Popov, 26 Nov 1947), actually sent 27 November.

54. GARF, f. 5446, op. 54, d. 41, l. 191 (Orgkom to Voroshilov, 8 Apr 1947). The letter was signed by Glier, Shostakovich, Muradeli, Novikov, and Shaporin.

Voroshilov's response, a note to G. M. Popov, head of Mossovet, was so succinctly eloquent about the logic underlying brokerage that it is worth quoting in full: "When the best people from the musical-artistic world sign an appeal, it is somehow not good not to honor their request, especially since it touches on a third individual and one who isn't all that mighty. But at the same time, what can I do, how can I not turn to you, knowing that you really might not be able to do very much to help. All the same, what can be done, G. M.?"[55] What could be done was for the Shchepalins to be assigned new housing, which they officially were, ten days later.[56] Of course, in the face of such a request from Voroshilov, Popov had little choice but to find housing for the Shchepalins.

The successful resolution in this case, however, is not the point. The point is the set of assumptions that undergird Voroshilov's informal note to Popov. First, he referred to the brokers as "the best people from the musical-artistic world," alluding to the authority that the Orgkom embodied. Second, he noted that it was "somehow not good not to honor their request," as though such personages inherently deserved the best Soviet society could offer. That Voroshilov assumed that musicians should be so privileged was an implicit acknowledgment of the authority of culture in Soviet society. Third, Voroshilov implicitly endorsed others acting like he did—using his superior power to help the deserving, but less fortunate. The brokers' appeal was particularly convincing precisely because they were looking out for someone who was less prestigious and powerful than they, just as Voroshilov was in his appeal to Popov. In this sense, Voroshilov endorsed the whole notion of an unofficial *network,* which included not just patrons and clients but middlemen. Finally, Voroshilov acknowledged that these unofficial networks disrupted the bureaucratic distribution of scarce commodities, in this case apartments. He knew that assigning housing to Shchepalin would mean not assigning it to someone else, but he still asked Popov to do what he could.

On one level, the unofficial network for material support was governed by the same rough scheme as patronage interventions in professional conflicts: individuals with cultural authority appealed to other individuals with power, who disrupted a bureaucratic procedure or overturned a bureaucratic decision. Aside from this general similarity, however, these two types of processes diverge. The authority in this case is not relevant to the situation under consideration. Members of the Orgkom certainly knew less about housing distribution than Popov, if they knew anything at all. Furthermore, the individual and the government institution were rarely in direct conflict in cases where patrons intervened to provide material support. In each of the examples noted here, the clients (or supplicants) were legally entitled to what they requested. There was no antagonism between the bureaucracy and the individual; rather, the patron instructed a relatively uninterested bureaucracy to reach a solution

55. Ibid., marginal notation, dated 9 April 1947 and signed by Voroshilov. "G. M." is short for "Georgii Mikhailovich," Popov's name and patronymic. Popov was head of Mossovet, 1944–50, and first secretary of the Moscow oblast' and city party committees, 1945–49.

56. Ibid., marginal notation. Shchepalin was assigned housing by Mossovet, 19 April 1947.

that favored the individual more quickly than would have happened if the regular bureaucratic process had been allowed to run its course. These sorts of unofficial networks were born of pervasive conditions of shortage.

That there was little conflict between the bureaucracy and the individual does not, of course, mean that the process was entirely divested of antagonism. Those whose voices we do not hear in these stories (unless they were pounding on the door) were undoubtedly very angry about these interventions. After all, for everyone who had a squatter evicted, there was someone who lost their home because their neighbor pulled strings, and for everyone who jumped the housing queue, there was someone who lost their place in that queue. Unofficial networking undoubtedly contributed to the Stalinist system's reputation for arbitrariness and capriciousness.

The Dark Side: Real and Imagined Networks under Attack

The successful operation of unofficial networks helped the bureaucratic system fulfill its two primary tasks: administering the production of music and supplying musicians with the material support they needed to continue to produce music. Though inseparably and even constitutively intertwined with the bureaucracy, informal networks were just unofficial enough to be a continuing source of suspicion and resentment. Understanding the corollaries of this suspicion and resentment is crucial to explaining how the successive campaigns against perceived formalists, cosmopolitans, and Jews unfolded in the music realm. Political elites worried that scarce resources were being swallowed uncontrollably by shadowy groupings within the music profession, and musicians without access to unofficial networks resented those who received the special treatment that being plugged into a network provided. This suspicion by the political elites and resentment by colleagues and peers combined to make unofficial networks—real and imagined—lightning rods for attack during successive campaigns in the postwar Stalinist period.

In the broad sweep of Soviet history, the most infamous attacks on hidden unofficial networks took place during the Great Terror. Undoubtedly many of those attacks were groundless, paranoid, and motivated by fear. However, they did take a specific form. Rhetorically, they were attempts to uncover, or unmask, corrupt and counterrevolutionary underground rings of spies, wreckers, and other "enemies of the people." That the paranoia took this specific form indicates that unofficial networks were a source of suspicion and resentment long before the war. In fact, some historians have carefully illustrated how local elites formed circles that were destroyed—and their members executed—during the Terror.[57] Zhdanovshchina and anticosmopolitanism may not have

57. James Harris, *Great Urals: Regionalism and the Evolution of the Soviet System* (Ithaca: Cornell University Press, 1999), 146–90.

been the Terror, but they still provided excuses for attacks against unofficial networks both from political elites and from within the institutions under attack.

Political elites' suspicion of unofficial networks within the music profession was most clearly reflected during the aftermath of the brouhaha in 1948. In June of that year the Council of Ministers empowered the Ministry of Finance to conduct a review of the financial practices of Muzfond. Aleksei Kosygin submitted a report that reflects deep suspicion about a "small group of composers, the majority of whom are formalists," who controlled the distribution of Muzfond's resources and received more than 40 percent of Muzfond's loans in 1947. Kosygin could have explained this lopsided distribution in any number of ways. The most straightforward would have been to label it corruption. The people controlling the purse strings reached into the purse more frequently than anyone else. A more generous explanation may have tied inequitable distribution to honest evaluation of musical products. Those in power not surprisingly liked their own music and that of their close colleagues better than others', and they funded it accordingly. Such a reading would have been overly generous of course, for after 1944 the self-proclaimed purpose of Muzfond loans was to provide material assistance to the needy, not to reward artistic merit. However, Kosygin offered an explanation based on neither straightforward corruption nor in the generous terms of creative agreement.

Instead, he saw an illegal conspiracy in which formalists sought to undermine the health of Soviet music and get rich on the government's money. To demonstrate this conspiracy, Kosygin provided data about large loans that were drawn by a few composers mentioned in the Central Committee resolution. He singled out a few prominent composers as beneficiaries of particularly large loans and then suggested that allocating such loans to famous composers undermined Muzfond's basic task: "facilitating the creative activities of the broad masses of composers."

But there was more. Kosygin considered the distribution of Muzfond moneys not just inequitable. It was downright illegal. He noted that Muzfond leaders illegally published works of a group of formalist composers, paying them inflated royalties and allowing the published materials to sit unsold in Muzfond's music stores. Worse, they violated long-standing laws about publishing contracts, paying advances for works that were never completed and never published. After providing details about specific instances of various composers signing multiple agreements with different organizations for the same piece, Kosygin intimated that Muzfond leaders even illegally subsidized privileged composers' personal automobiles. The resulting picture was one of a corrupt group of formalists conspiring to undermine Muzfond's fundamental task of promoting Soviet music and using it instead to steal government money.[58]

58. RGALI, f. 2077, op. 1, d. 233, ll. 39–41 (A. Kosygin to Biuro SM SSSR, 14 Jun 1948). The letter was forwarded to the Composers' Union, and the new leadership was given five days to respond (l. 38 [Chadaev to Lebedev and Asaf'ev, 20 Jun 1948]), which they failed to do (l. 52 [Chadaev to Asaf'ev, 30 Jun 1948]).

On the basis of his report, Kosygin submitted a draft resolution to the Council of Ministers. The language of the resolution concisely summarizes his findings and emphasizes the suspicion of the concealed unofficial network, in this case, of formalists:

> On the basis of the investigation conducted by the Ministry of Finance, the Council of Ministers notes that Muzfond did not ensure the fulfillment of the basic tasks required of it—support of the creative activity of the broad masses of composers and the service of their everyday needs. The leadership of Muzfond paid attention primarily to servicing a small group of composers with formalist proclivities which were condemned in the 10 February 1948 Central Committee resolution on V. Muradeli's opera *Velikaia druzhba*. Funds which were received by Muzfond were squandered on concealed extra-budgetary and illegal expenditures both by the Muzfond leaders themselves and by the Orgkom of the Composers' Union, on payments to individual composers in illegal amounts, on payments of inflated royalties and the formation of huge debts for individual members of Muzfond, mainly the leadership workers of Muzfond and the Composers' Union themselves. . . . The Orgkom of the All-USSR Composers' Union did not direct or correct the work of Muzfond, instead using it only as an additional source for concealment of their unplanned expenditures.[59]

It is crucial to notice the draft resolution's repeated insistence that the financial impropriety was perpetrated by Muzfond leaders to benefit themselves and their fellow formalists at the expense of "the broad masses" of other composers. Even more important, Kosygin insisted on calling the financial impropriety "illegal." He sought to expand the attack on formalists from the already accomplished disciplinary action to a new level in which formalists would be liable to arrest and prosecution. This is not simply a condemnation of discredited leadership, it is an attempt to implicate that leadership in the concealment of a subversive unofficial network.

The Ministry of Finance suggested remedies: limit Muzfond's resources by adjusting the levels and distribution of royalties collected from musical performances, reexamine Muzfond's primary responsibilities, and entreat the new Composers' Union leadership to keep a more careful eye on its activities.[60] With very few changes, Kosygin's draft resolution was enacted by the Council of Ministers in early August. By accepting Kosygin's draft, the top governmental body endorsed Kosygin's vision.

That endorsement was not unqualified, however. One of the two changes introduced in the final version was actually a meaningful relaxation of the rhetoric: the characterization of the amount of money that was loaned to individual composers was changed from "illegal" to "significant."[61] This retreat allowed the Council of Ministers to break up the unofficial circle that it thought

59. Ibid., ll. 42–43 (Kosygin's draft resolution).
60. Ibid., l. 43.
61. Ibid., ll. 61–61ob. (SM SSSR Post. #2917, 2 Aug 1948).

controlled Muzfond without prosecuting the country's leading, and recently disciplined, composers. The change in leadership that had happened earlier in the year was implicitly deemed sufficient. The political elites may have been suspicious of unofficial networks, and they may have tried to shut down those that they did not oversee, but at least in this case they saw no need to destroy the individual members of those networks or to escalate the campaign against formalists from disciplining them to arresting them.

During the anticosmopolitanism campaign that followed within the year, rank-and-file musicians were not so merciful. In arts institution after arts institution, disgruntled musicians wrote to the Central Committee reporting on the sinister networks—invariably run by Jews—that they thought were controlling their institution and excluding them personally. Though these networks were either completely imaginary or described in a way that was profoundly distorted by anti-Semitism, they illustrate the pervasiveness of the belief in unofficial networks, and they express resentment about the advantages that they conferred.

One of the best examples of these anti-Semitic attacks on unofficial networks was provided by one Sokolov, a Russian song composer from Sverdlovsk who wrote to the Central Committee and to the All-USSR Radio Committee to denounce a network of Jews who he thought controlled the content and distribution of Soviet popular music. Sokolov explicitly condemned the unofficial, nationality-based network that connected various individuals in official positions. His letter was phrased as an addition to the transcript of a discussion on mass songs that the Composers' Union held in April 1949.[62] Sokolov argued that Soviet popular music was written by two groups of composers, those who used Russian musical materials, and those who used Jewish musical materials, which Sokolov conflated with Western popular music, including jazz. In Sokolov's imagination, the popular songs based on these "Jewish intonations" had long dominated the Soviet popular music scene and even infected healthy Russian songs with Western intonations "because all channels of popularization are controlled by Jewish representatives."

Sokolov then carefully surveyed the radio, the publishing house, and the Composers' Union's Mass Music Section to try to demonstrate that each was controlled by Jews. Thus the "leadership of musical programming of the Radio Committee was entirely in Jewish hands, under the leadership of M. A. Grinberg."[63] And who did Grinberg popularize? Blanter and Dunaevskii, two Jews (who also happened to have been two of the most popular song composers since the 1930s). Sokolov complained further that even after Grinberg was fired, radio programming remained in the hands of a Jew (Ia. S. Solodukho) who had been defended by the Composers' Union on the initiative of none other than

62. For the a transcripts, see RGALI, f. 2077, op. 1, dd. 381, 383 (stenogram, days 1–2, 12, 14 Apr 1949).

63. M. A. Grinberg had long been the head of the musical programming section on the VRK; in fact, he was fired during this campaign.

Blanter. Sokolov thought that the roots of this "mutual assistance" were clear. His solution: "It is essential that Solodukho—be committed to the earth."

This bloodthirsty vindictiveness was not extended to other figures in the network that Sokolov described, but he did emphasize that he was struggling against a whole informal but effective network. Dunaevskii was thus accused of using his influence in the publishing apparatus to promote the "doubtful" work of a young composer named Ostrovskii, "the young hope of the Jews," because a song written by Ostrovskii was published by Muzgiz despite receiving a negative evaluation from the Composers' Union. Not that the Composers' Union itself was any better. Blanter had recently begun "exerting his influence" on B. M. Terent'ev, the head of the Mass Music Section of the Composers' Union, by driving him around in his car and in general showing him a good time. As a result, the Composers' Union had defended Solodukho at the Radio Committee and "preserved a Jewish platform on the radio." Even Khrennikov was suspect because of his Jewish wife, whom Sokolov imagined exerting influence behind the scenes. And the orchestra conductor V. N. Knushevitskii had been roped into the network by Dunaevskii and Blanter through "the pleasures of money and spirits." And under Terent'ev's traitorous influence, a "synagogue" had taken over the Mass Music Section.[64]

The most striking thing about this letter is its virulent anti-Semitism, but it also provides insight into a possible unofficial network, the behaviors associated with it, and the resentment that it engendered. Though Jewish composers were particularly prominent in the popular music realm, the actual ethnic makeup of unofficial networks is not at issue here, and the control that Sokolov thought the network exerted over the production of popular music was obviously exaggerated. Still, the more sober features of the network that Sokolov described are worth noting. It was further ranging than most of those discussed so far, extending as it did from the Composers' Union to the Radio Committee to the Soviet Union's main music publisher. Though Sokolov ignored or did not see the hierarchical element of this network, it was clearly present. Composers' personal contacts with various officials (including Terent'ev) or more influential composers (like Dunaevskii) helped get their songs played and published. The success that those contacts provided was a clear source of resentment to those left out of the network. But the resentment did not stop at the professional problems that were ostensibly the reason for Sokolov's complaint. The social network that Sokolov described—the cars, the money, the booze, even the Jewish wife—were crucial to maintaining and expanding the network. They also further marginalized this anti-Semite from Sverdlovsk, who used the campaign against cosmopolitans as an opportunity to attack the network.

Sokolov was not the only one whose anti-Semitism overlapped with attacks on unofficial networks during the anticosmopolitanism campaign.[65] However,

64. GARF, f. 6903, op. 1, d. 284, ll. 70a–75 (Sokolov to Puzin and addition to mass song transcript, 25 Apr 1949).

65. RGASPI, f. 17, op. 133, d. 396, ll. 53–56 (anonymous letter to TsK VKP(b), early 1953,

not all such attacks had anti-Semitic content.[66] One final example both demonstrates the ubiquity of unofficial networks and offers a glimpse of how complicated their interaction could be, especially when one was under attack. In February 1953, Z. G. Solov'eva, a soloist at the Stanislavskii and Nemirovich-Danchenko Musical Theater in Moscow, wrote a personal letter to the powerful politician N. A. Mikhailov, a member of the Secretariat. After twice indicating that she was turning to Mikhailov for support in a personal capacity, Solov'eva ran through a list of official and unofficial channels that she had already exhausted before appealing to him. She had sought to argue the matter with the party organization in her theater, with the Moscow Committee on Artistic Affairs, with her local trade union and its regional governing body (Rabis), with the All-USSR Committee on Artistic Affairs (VKI), and finally with the Central Committee cultural apparatus. Not having received the desired result, and still convinced that her personal troubles reflected broader problems in the development of opera in the Soviet Union, she finally appealed to Mikhailov.

Her problem: "Recently in the Stanislavskii and Nemirovich-Danchenko Musical Theater, where I work, top management has formed a dismal atmosphere of despotism, the suppression of criticism, rotten mutual protection circles, sycophancy." Rather than training young talent according to Stanislavskii's traditional methods, Solov'eva complained, young singers were being promoted by these unofficial networks and their associated arbitrariness and toadyism based on "commercial rather than artistic goals."[67] The complaint about a policy problem with personal implications thus started as a typical attack on sinister unofficial networks.

Once she began to relate the more personal aspects of the problem, however, Solov'eva also provided a glimpse of the unofficial network of which she was a part, a network about which she obviously expected Mikhailov to approve. After three years of fighting for Stanislavskii's traditional training methods, Solov'eva had been fired from her position at the theater during the summer of 1952. In order to have herself reinstated, she activated her own unofficial net-

---

and Iarustovskii to Obshchii otdel Sekretariata, 27 Feb 1953). This anonymous attack on supposedly Jewish-controlled networks at the Leningrad Philharmonic drew limited attention in the Central Committee apparatus not explicitly for its attack on Jews but because of the unofficial network. See also ibid., ll. 117–18 (V. Antonov to Khrushchev, 6 Mar 1953; Kruzhkov and Tarasov to Khrushchev, 11 Mar 1953). This attack on the Jewish domination of the State Symphony Orchestra of the USSR was precipitated by its performance at Stalin's funeral, which Antonov (actually probably a pseudonym) thought was profoundly inappropriate. It was completely rebuffed by the Central Committee apparatus as simply wrong: while Antonov claimed that the orchestra was comprised of 95 percent Jews, OKhLI reported that composition by nationality was actually 59 percent Russian and only 36 percent Jewish.

66. For another example of an attack on an unofficial network that is not connected with anti-Semitism during the anticosmopolitanism campaign, see RGASPI, f. 17, op. 133, d. 328, ll. 177–88 (Jul 1951–Mar 1952), materials relating to an anonymous letter about corruption in Ukrainian arts institutions that accuses leaders of dividing creative workers into "theirs" and "others," promoting the "theirs" and repeatedly slighting the "others," of whom the writer was one.

67. Ibid., d. 396, ll. 87–91, here ll. 87–88 (Z. G. Solov'eva to Mikhailov, 13 Feb 1953).

work, which she labeled "the intervention of society." That intervention was actually a combination of patronage and brokerage. She turned to party members who were old workers at the Dinamo factory in Moscow, where she had worked before entering the opera world. These old contacts then took her case to M. F. Shkiriatov (a highly situated politician), through whose intervention she was returned to her position in the creative troupe of the musical theater. After a lengthy discussion of the continued importance of Stanislavskii's training method, she asked Mikhailov for a personal meeting, thus attempting to extend her own unofficial network to further heights of power—and have her dispute with the music theater's administration resolved in her favor.[68] In the end, Solov'eva won the battle for the support of Stanislavskii's training method but lost the struggle for her own position at the theater. The Central Committee apparatus endorsed the theater management's policy of promoting young talent and supported a plan to transfer Solov'eva to a different opera theater.[69]

This affair provides useful information about the interaction of various unofficial networks during a professional struggle. Even if we treat skeptically Solov'eva's characterization of the "despotic mutual protection circle" that was headed by the music theater's management, it is extremely likely that some unofficial groupings and personal relationships were in fact governing the theater's creative and personnel decisions, including who would sing what roles in which new productions. Excluded by this unofficial network, Solov'eva turned to other devices: official local channels (the party cell and her trade union chapters); official government channels (the VKI and Moscow Committee on Artistic Affairs); relatively official extra-governmental channels (Rabis and the Central Committee cultural apparatus); and finally, her own very unofficial channel comprised of powerful friends that she had made twenty years earlier while working at the Dinamo factory. This rich example provides a glimpse into the pervasiveness and complexity of unofficial networks in the arts.

Protection

Informal networks and patronage connections drew the suspicion of political elites and resentment of colleagues, but they could also provide a measure of security. It is well celebrated that strikingly few musicians, compared to writers or poets, for example, were arrested or excluded from their professional organization during the postwar ideological campaigns and associated attacks on sinister networks. Patrons could provide protection to clients who were under attack, even during the most heated campaigns. In the Composers' Union, very effective protection was provided most frequently by the head of the Union,

68. Ibid., ll. 88–91.
69. Ibid., ll. 96–97 (Kruzhkov and Tarasov to Mikhailov, 2 Mar 1953). Her good service duly noted, Solov'eva was transferred to another musical theater, scarcely the result she desired.

Tikhon Khrennikov, whose emergence and status as a broker were described above.

The most fully documented example of this protection occurred during the early stages of the anticosmopolitanism campaign in 1949. Since the pronouncement that initiated the campaign was directed against theater critics, the obvious targets for analogous attack in the Composers' Union were musicologists and music critics. In fact, those attacks did happen, both in print and in internal discussions. But no musicologist was actually kicked out of the Composers' Union in 1949, a surprising fact considering the havoc that the anticosmopolitanism campaign wreaked in other fields. As the following example demonstrates, musicologists remained in the Composers' Union simply because Khrennikov acted as a broker who interceded on their behalf and convinced the Central Committee apparatus that they should remain members of the professional organization.

Planning to exclude two musicologists, Semyon Shlifshtein and Aleksei Ogolevets, from the Composers' Union began as early as February 1949.[70] Ogolevets immediately began seeking personal ways to preempt that plan. In February, he wrote a letter to Malenkov in which he mentioned hearing about plans to throw him out of the Composers' Union and then launched into a counterattack against both an old nemesis (fellow musicologist A. I. Shaverdian) and the broker who would soon save his career (Khrennikov). There is no evidence that Malenkov reacted to this letter at all, but Ogolevets shortly thereafter asked the editors of the arts newspaper *Sovetskoe iskusstvo* to publish a letter in which he argued that his orientation toward music theory had always been correct but that he had made serious mistakes. He once again admitted to the ideological shortcomings revealed in 1947 and recommitted himself to the fight for Soviet music.[71] There is no evidence that this second letter elicited any response either. As for Shlifshtein, unlike the prolific letter writer Ogolevets he appears to have been silent between February and May.

Then, on 18 May 1949, the Composers' Union secretary Mikhail Chulaki wrote to Malenkov with an official request to exclude Shlifshtein and Ogolevets from the Composers' Union. In his lengthy letter, Chulaki accused the two of cosmopolitanism and formalism, and he noted that Shlifshtein was trained as a pianist so his musicological writings had a dilettantish quality. He also referred to the 1947 discussion about Ogolevets and the latter's problematic professional conduct, and concluded that both had been sufficiently discredited to warrant removal from the Composers' Union.[72]

The same day, Shlifshtein sent his own two pleas to remain in the Union. In a short letter to Malenkov, he admitted the mistake of supporting Shostakovich

---

70. RGASPI, f. 17, op. 132, d. 243, ll. 29–30 (Ogolevets to Malenkov, 27 Feb 1949).

71. Ibid., ll. 31–33 (Ogolevets to *Sovetskoe iskusstvo* editors, 6 Apr 1949). Shaverdian had been a major critic of Ogolevets during the affair of 1947.

72. Ibid., ll. 22–28 (Chulaki to Malenkov, 18 May 1949).

and Prokofiev (the basis of the charge that he was a formalist) and noted that he had already suffered—he and his family had been without any means of material support for half a year, since the first rumblings of his possible removal from the Composers' Union. The letter was a straightforward plea to be allowed to pursue his one desire: putting his strength and knowledge at the disposal of Soviet national musical culture.[73] As with the earlier Ogolevets appeals, there is no evidence that this request evoked any response. The same was true of Shlifshtein's second letter, a much longer appeal to Shepilov, the head of the Central Committee's cultural oversight department. Though longer and with many more details about his creative life, the gist of this second letter was the same: he had made mistakes but earnestly wanted to remain within the professional community.[74]

None of these appeals in and of themselves would likely have been sufficient to save the professional lives of Shlifshtein or Ogolevets from utter ruin. They were saved, however, when Khrennikov intervened with his own letter to Malenkov a few months later. In September, Khrennikov explained that the two musicologists had been alienated from the life of the Composers' Union, thus suggesting that they no longer posed a threat, and were busily reconstructing themselves. In short, it would be best and most productive to allow them to stay in the Union. Consequently, he requested that Chulaki's earlier memo calling for their exclusion be withdrawn.[75] This brokerage intervention was critical. Two weeks later, a bureaucrat in the Central Committee apparatus summarized the whole affair for Malenkov. The culture department agreed with Khrennikov's assessment, and their careers were saved.[76]

Khrennikov's role as a broker in this example is worthy of particular attention. Since these documents have been preserved in the Central Committee's archives, they do not include traces of communication between Khrennikov and the two musicologists. It is extremely unlikely that both did not discuss their cases with Khrennikov in the four months between the Chulaki memo and Khrennikov's intervention retracting it. On the other hand, Ogolevets in particular did not have a congenial personal relationship with Khrennikov, as his aggressive April letter made abundantly clear. It is just as likely that Khrennikov intervened on principle, to save threatened Composers' Union members, as it is that he acted because of personal relationships with the two individuals in question. His intervention exemplifies the combination of personalized action and institutional position that characterizes virtually all brokerage activity.

Of course, not all unofficial appeals for protection were successful. During the aftermath of the anticosmopolitanism campaign in the early 1950s, the prominent conductor N. S. Golovanov and the operatic tenor I. S. Kozlovskii

73. Ibid., l. 20 (Shlifshtein to Malenkov, 18 May 1949).

74. Ibid., ll. 21–21ob. (Shlifshtein to Shepilov, 18 May 1949).

75. Ibid., l. 34 (Khrennikov to Malenkov, 13 Sep 1949).

76. Ibid., l. 36 (Kruzhkov to Malenkov, 26 Sep 1949). The memo was archived the same day, suggesting that Malenkov considered the issue settled.

attempted to intervene on behalf of the former head of musical broadcasting at the Radio Committee, M. A. Grinberg. They considered him a valued leader in musical and theatrical circles and thought that the attacks on him were unhealthy and should be stopped in order to facilitate a return to more normal and productive work.[77] Unfortunately for Grinberg, his case may have been caught up with a more general attack on his patron in the Central Committee apparatus, B. M. Iarustovskii, and presumably after speaking to someone in the Central Committee apparatus, the two performers quietly withdrew their request. Grinberg was thrown out of the Composers' Union shortly thereafter.[78] In some cases, the attacks went too far to be overturned.[79]

During the Stalin period, Soviet composers, musicologists, and other musicians lived and worked in a world that was organized by bureaucratic institutions and organizations. From their student years to retirement, their professional lives were governed by creative unions and governmental arts institutions, and their material existence was ensured by the financial organizations that those institutions controlled. However, this system was profoundly inefficient, incapable of successfully accomplishing its two fundamental tasks: administering the production of music and guaranteeing the material well-being of the musicians who created it. When musicians encountered extreme difficulties while negotiating these bureaucratic institutions, they looked for special individual assistance from those who were more powerful—former teachers, friends, or highly situated acquaintances—either trumping the bureaucracy with their own creative authority or trading information, loyalty, or reflected creative success for that help. Born of inefficiency and encouraged by the party's long-standing self-proclaimed right to intervene to correct any bureaucratic shortcoming, unofficial networks permeated the bureaucratic system.

Pervasive though they were, unofficial networks did not operate according to regular rules or procedures. Rather, virtually every interaction was an independent, individual, often personalized event. Still, it is possible to discern a series of patterns within these unofficial networks, a set of categories of interactions, each with its underlying sets of governing principles and cultural assumptions or agreements. The most professionally significant and spectacular

77. RGASPI, f. 17, op. 133, d. 323, l. 216 (Golovanov and Kozlovskii to Malenkov, undated).
78. Ibid., marginal notations dated 8 Aug 1951 (request withdrawn) and 3 Nov 1951 ("remove from Composers' Union"). For the attack on Iarustovskii, which was mostly concerned with financial impropriety but overlapped with anticosmopolitanism, see RGALI, f. 962, op. 10s, d. 136, ll. 22–26 (F. Kaloshin to Suslov, 5 Nov 1950); ll. 49–50 (P. Lebedev to M. F. Shkiriatov, 5 Aug 1950); and ll. 63–64 (Lebedev to Malenkov, 26 Apr 1950). Nevertheless, Iarustovskii retained his position in the TsK apparatus.
79. For another example of an unsuccessful appeal, see RGASPI, f. 17, op. 132, d. 244, ll. 33–35 (L. [A.] Mazel' to Voroshilov, 6 Mar 1949; Shepilov to Voroshilov, 26 Mar 1949). Mazel' sought to avoid being fired from his teaching positions at the Moscow Conservatory and the Gnesin Institute after being denounced for evaluating Shostakovich's music too positively. Shepilov reported that he had already been fired and his appeal should go unanswered.

unofficial category was the intervention of highly placed patrons during a professional conflict. The success of patronage in a professional dispute was determined by the interaction of hierarchical power and creative authority. To succeed, musicians needed to demonstrate to a powerful potential ally that their bureaucratic antagonist's creative authority was dwarfed by their own, whether it derived from professional or international acclaim. This option was available only to a few extremely authoritative musicians.

Much more pervasive but less spectacular were the personal connections that musicians used to acquire material support, most frequently an apartment. Musicians appealed directly to patrons or used brokers, that is, patronage middlemen who straddled the official and unofficial systems and who used their institutional posts, or their authority to speak on behalf of a respected segment of society, to shape bureaucratic fiat. Musicians relied on powerful politicians' sense that music was an important cultural product, and that those who produced it should be kept in a material state that ensured their ability to focus on their creative work. They should have an apartment, a piano, and perhaps some other reasonable comforts, and if unofficial interventions were necessary to provide that material state, so be it.

Because they subverted or manipulated bureaucratic procedures, unofficial networks were targets of suspicion and resentment. They and those who comprised them became lightning rods for attack during the succession of disciplinary campaigns against formalists, cosmopolitans, and Jews. Attacks against real or imagined sinister networks demonstrated how ubiquitous and powerful people thought unofficial networks were, both at the apex of power and within an institution. An understanding of how unofficial networks became objects of attack, therefore, is critical to identifying a salient feature of the Stalinist system—the cyclical campaigns to purge Soviet arts and organizations of undesired characteristics and characters. But it was sometimes just the protection provided by an unofficial network that could save a potential victim from professional ruin.

Stalin's Soviet Union was a fundamentally hierarchical place, from the extreme concentration of political power in a tiny ruling clique to the system of closed stores and workplace provisions. Composers and musicologists occupied an elite position in that hierarchy as their monopoly over the creation and interpretation of Soviet music earned them, as a professional group, access to a whole network of resources administered by Muzfond and unavailable to the rest of the Soviet population. But even within that elite group, there were further significant hierarchical gradations, hierarchies of material well-being, privilege, and status. Finding a position in that hierarchical elite depended on the complex interplay of professional or creative authority and the various audiences that granted, acknowledged, and reproduced it. In this serious game of musical chairs, there were multiple routes to extreme privilege and high status, most of which were determined by particularly authoritative members of the profession who formed multiple interfaces between the Stalinist music profession and its political elite. Whether members of the Stalin Prize Committee or brokers who lubricated informal networks interwoven with the official bureaucratic state, these professional leaders used their creative visions, notions of professional value, prejudices, and preoccupations to structure the cultural elite. At the same time, they were always liable to political intervention and censure. Such was the professionals' dance of expertise, authority, and agency.

Conclusion

By the end of the Stalin period, Soviet music production was dominated by a professional organization. Neither a government agency run by career bureaucrats nor a trade union responsible only for its members' material well-being, the Composers' Union was founded on the principle of gathering musical expertise into a single institution, directed by composers and musicologists and focusing on the production of new Soviet music. That focus was so pronounced that two different leadership groups quietly asserted a separation between the fields of politics and artistic production in the decade before Stalin's death. Though always operating within the rubric of tasks set by the government and the party, this muted insistence on a professional sphere governed by professional norms opened up real possibilities of agency for composers and musicologists.

This is not to say that composers and musicologists operated autonomously from the political sphere. The party always reserved the right to intervene in musical life and occasionally did so, to traumatic effect. There were real structural, organizational, social, and intellectual shifts during the postwar cycles of ideological pressure and upheaval, but some of these shifts were unintended and the overall trend was toward professional consolidation. A rebuke from the party could increase a composer's prestige within the professional sphere, and the professional organization could use its discipline to excise music that it—and the party leadership—considered retrograde or inadequate.

In addition to the party's direct interventions and ideological campaigns, other social forces helped to integrate the music profession with the rest of the Stalinist system. Informal networks greased the wheels of a slow, inefficient, and overburdened bureaucracy and in the process tied composers and musicologists to one another and the political elite. As members of the Stalin Prize Committee, some professional leaders and elite performers were another crucial interface between the political elite and the intelligentsia, speaking for broader opinion even as they helped party leaders shape that opinion. They helped to create a common set of cultural evaluations and translated professional authority into the prestige and privilege associated with the Soviet Union's highest cultural honors and awards.

The Composers' Union dominated a profession some of whose defining characteristics were common to professions the world over while others were particular to the Stalinist system. As elsewhere in the modern world, expertise was vitally important, and acquiring it usually meant completing conservatory education or a special training program in the Composers' Union's creative apparatus. This expertise was essential to the production of the socially valuable work that the Composers' Union oversaw. Officially, the Union worked to unleash the creative potential of the Soviet people and to harness it to tasks of ideological education and enlightenment. In practice, experts—the Union's professional leadership—determined the specific content of those abstract goals. As in other modern societies, expert work was amply rewarded. The Composers' Union was ensconced in the ranks of Stalinist society's materially privileged; its rank-and-file members were provisioned at levels far greater than the norm, and the elite approached the pinnacle of privilege.

Other defining characteristics of the music profession were distinctly Stalinist in nature. Thus, the Composers' Union was an incredibly centralized organization with authority concentrated in a small, dominant leadership body, the Orgkom or Secretariat. This central leadership controlled the leadership of Muzfond, the Composers' Union chapters, and even Muzfond chapters. Extreme institutional centralization was reinforced by informal ties between members of the leading clique, formed through official interactions, unofficial socialization, creative affinity and friendship, and substantially overlapping personnel. Union leaders included conservatory professors, government consultants, and members of the Stalin Prize Committee. As a result, a few elite professionals had extraordinary agency to determine the criteria of musical value and hierarchies of status, prestige, and privilege.

On occasion, this domination by a concentrated elite afforded benefits to rank-and-file members. When the leadership maintained a separation between professional and political spheres, professional mistakes could be divested of political meaning or at least criminal ramifications. Even when that separation collapsed, the leadership's prerogative to interpret the meaning of ideological constructs in professional life enabled it to shield even those Union members who were disciplined from the most dangerous consequences, as vividly demonstrated in the minimization of the most egregious anti-Semitism of the anticosmopolitanism campaigns.

At the same time, extreme centralization and the prevalence of personalized decision making opened the door to arbitrariness and the possibility of corruption. For example, the financial investigation of Muzfond in 1948 found that the ruling clique had appropriated nearly 40 percent of its loan funds. In 1951 seven of the eleven members of the Stalin Prize music subcommittee were nominated for this most prestigious award. In this world of reinforcing authority, prominent composers assumed professional leadership posts and then they, or their colleagues, used those posts to extend their authority. It is no accident that the most famous composers often sat in leadership positions. Khachaturian, Shostakovich, Miaskovskii, Glier, Kabalevskii, Shebalin, Shaporin, and Khrennikov were all considered talented before they assumed leadership positions. Only Khrennikov's artistic reputation suffered as a result of his leadership activities, and that because he publicly presided over the traumatic party intervention that alienated even many critics of the old leadership. These leading talents used their domination of a centralized official and unofficial system to promote their own creative visions.

There can be little doubt that rank-and-file members of the professional organization sometimes resented this elite domination, much as they may have appreciated the leadership's efforts to preserve a professional sphere. Within the creative apparatus, they could level sometimes scathing critiques of their leaders' works. They unleashed vitriolic public attacks when larger cultural policies changed, and at other times they denounced colleagues and professional leaders to the Central Committee apparatus. These actions speak to ongoing tensions within the Composers' Union. M. A. Grinberg's denunciation of the Stalin Prize Committee in 1941 for following its own proclivities instead of more popular taste provides one such example.

This highly centralized professional body organized composers and musicologists but not performers. Performers were professional musicians in the sense that they made their living—often an extremely privileged one by the Soviet Union's living standards—by playing music. They received advanced musical education in the same conservatories that trained composers and musicologists, and they developed world-renowned skills that exhibited the excellence of the Soviet music system on domestic and international stages. But they were not admitted to the professional organization. The Stalinist music world thus institutionalized early on a typically modern division of labor into intellectual and technical work. Both shared in the privileges of the cultural elite, but they did not share a professional organization.

In combining within one institution the composers who created new Soviet music and the musicologists who explained what it meant to lay audiences, the Composers' Union followed the example of the Writers' Union, in which critics played a centrally important role. The unavoidably antagonistic relationship between critics and composers was another component of the institutionalized tension in the professional organization, something that could flare up whenever the profession came under fire. Critics attacked leading composers in 1948 and came under attack themselves during the anticosmopolitanism campaigns.

Another distinct feature of the Composers' Union was its elision of the age-old division between high and low culture. The concert violinists and piano virtuosi who helped construct highbrow musical culture were excluded from the professional organization, while the *melodisty* who crafted catchy tunes to patriotic lyrics and constructed popular culture were included. Though the academically rigorous upholders of the Russian classical traditions and these *melodisty* were mutually suspicious and potentially antagonistic, the creative apparatus and leadership body of the Composers' Union provided institutional venues and supports for both. The elision of high and low can be seen even in the work of the system's most prominent composers. Though he may have been more invested in his Twenty-four Preludes and Fugues, Shostakovich nevertheless wrote successful popular film scores. Prokofiev's *Peter and the Wolf* is perhaps the most popular piece of twentieth-century children's music, and his score for the film *Aleksandr Nevskii* in its cantata form has become a staple of the international repertoire. Though there were real limits, fiercely guarded, this Stalinist professional organization thus maintained a striking diversity of creative opinion. Its symphonic composers managed to develop older national traditions and a modern symphonic idiom that have proved very successful with international orchestral audiences. Its popular songwriters created a popular musical culture that lives on in post-Soviet Russia. Though self-conscious modernist experimentation was not viable at any time during the Stalinist period, this was nevertheless a strikingly diverse musical output.

Among creative unions, the Composers' Union appears to have been virtually unique in its ability to avoid the sometimes deadly consequences of political intervention. Just how exceptional the Composers' Union was in this respect awaits detailed studies of the Artists' Union and Architects' Union. But the infamous oppression of renowned Soviet poets makes it clear that the Writers' Union presents a somewhat different picture of the agency that artistic expertise afforded Soviet artists. Film also presents a very different picture from the one described here. It was much more closely monitored by party leaders, who could easily ban films (like *Ivan the Terrible, Part II*) or halt their production (like *Bezhin Meadow*). When Zhdanov upbraided those associated with the Bol'shoi Theater's production of *Velikaia druzhba* in 1948, he noted that the Central Committee (and it turns out, Stalin himself) screened all films before release. Stalin Prizes in film were dictated by the minister of film, a power that the head of the Committee on Artistic Affairs never enjoyed.

Mastery of a more abstract body of knowledge appears to have afforded music experts more maneuverability than their colleagues whose expertise was more easily grasped by politicians. It was much more difficult for party leaders to censure the music that they could not understand than it was for them to evaluate written texts. Even such political figures as Andrei Zhdanov recognized the limitations of their ability to speak intelligibly about music. Even if they had trouble understanding abstract poetry, party leaders had the language to talk about and censure literature, and they showed no reticence to discuss film or literature, including the opera librettos that were the main targets of their pronouncements in music. Music may thus be more analogous to abstract sciences such as mathematics and theoretical physics than to art forms such as literature and film, even though the music profession's structure resembled that of the other creative unions more closely than that of the universities, academies, and research institutes that organized scientific and scholarly life.

By ideological design and artistic proclivities, Soviet music was built in large part upon the successes of Russian classical music. But this tradition does not explain all of the success that Soviet composers enjoyed, from the triumphs of such song composers as Blanter and Solov'ev-Sedoi and musical film masters like Dunaevskii to the enduring symphonic works of Prokofiev and Shostakovich. The most distinctive characteristics of this musical culture, like the success of the professional organization itself, emerged during the war, when Soviet composers wrote the songs that remain today an indelible component of Russian musical culture and the symphonies that thrilled audiences and solidified their composers' international fame. Despite concerted efforts to develop Soviet opera both before and after the war, it was the introverted turn to chamber music beginning in the midst of the ideological campaigns of the late 1940s that led to some of the most remarkable contributions of Soviet music in the years immediately after Stalin's death. Until the end of the Stalin period, the Union of Soviet Composers would continue to provide the most important institutional forum in which this musical production took place, earning both criticism for the constraints it put on that production and praise for the support and material comforts it provided the composers who produced it.

Bibliography

Archival Collections

GARF—Gosudarstvennyi arkhiv Rossiiskoi Federatsii
  f. 5446 (Council of Ministers)
    op. 23, 44, 46, 47, 48, 49 (Upravlenie delami)
    op. 54 (K. E. Voroshilov)
    op. 75 (Cultural bureau)
  f. 5508 (Rabis)
  f. 6903 (All-USSR Radio Committee)
RGALI—Rossiiskii gosudarstvennyi arkhiv literatury i iskusstv
  f. 656 (Glavrepertkom)
  f. 962 (Committee on Artistic Affairs, USSR)
    op. 3 (Secretariat)
    op. 5 (Chief Agency for Music Institutions)
    op. 10s (Secret Department)
  f. 2075 (Committee on Artistic Affairs, RSFSR)
  f. 2077 (All-USSR Composers' Union)
  f. 2085 (R. M. Glier)
  f. 2452 (Copyright Administration, VUOAP)
RGANI—Rossiiskii gosudarstvennyi arkhiv noveishei istorii
  f. 5, op. 17 (Central Committee Department of Artistic Literature and the Arts and Department of Science and Art)
RGASPI—Rossiiskii gosudarstvennyi arkhiv sotsial'no-politicheskoi istorii
  f. 17 (Central Committee)
    op. 3, 163 (Politburo)
    op. 114, 116, 117, 118, 119 (Orgbiuro/Secretariat)
    op. 121 (Orgbiuro Tekhsekretariat)
    op. 125 (Propaganda and Agitation Administration, OPA)
    op. 132 (Propaganda and Agitation Department, UPA)
    op. 133 (Department of Artistic Literature and the Arts, OKhLI, and Department of Science and the Arts, ONK)
  f. 77 (A. A. Zhdanov)
  f. 82 (V. M. Molotov)
TsMAM—Tsentral'nyi munitsipal'nyi arkhiv Moskvy
  f. 2433, op. 5 (Mosgorispolkom, Housing)

Periodicals

Bolshevik
Informatsionnyi sbornik, Moscow
Izvestiia, Moscow
Kul'tura i zhizn', Moscow
Pravda, Moscow
Sobranie postanovlenii i rasporiazhenii Pravitel'stva SSSR
Sovetskaia muzyka
Sovetskoe iskusstvo, Moscow
Vedomosti Verkhovnogo Soveta SSSR

Sound Recordings and Memorial Installation

Aleksandrov, A. V. "Sviashennaia voina." On *Sviashchennaia voina: K 50–letiiu Pobedy,* track 1. Performed by Krasnoznamennyi ansambl'. RDCD 00433. [Moscow]: Russkii disk, 1995.
Khvorostovsky, Dmitry, et al. *Pesni voennykh let.* Delos DE 3315. Hollywood: Delos International, 2003.
Memorial installation. Second floor, Dom kompozitorov, Moscow.
Verdi, Giuseppe. *Messa da Requiem,* disc 1, track 2. Performed by Chicago Symphony Orchestra, cond. Georg Solti et al. BMG 09026-61403-2. New York: BMG, 1993.

Books, Articles, Document Collections, and Dissertations

Abbott, Andrew. *The System of Professions: An Essay on the Division of Expert Labor.* Chicago: University of Chicago Press, 1988.
Afanas'eva, E. S., et al., eds. *Apparat TsK KPSS i Kul'tura, 1953–1957.* Moscow: ROSSPEN, 2001.
Aleksandrov, D. A. "The Historical Anthropology of Science in Russia," *Russian Studies in History* 34, no. 2 (1995): 62–91.
Alexopoulos, Golfo. *Stalin's Outcasts: Aliens, Citizens, and the Soviet State, 1926–1936.* Ithaca: Cornell University Press, 2003.
Asaf'ev, B. V. "Nemetskoe i 'Nemetskoe' v russkoi muzyke i muzykal'noi kul'ture." In *Sovetskaia muzyka: Sbornik stat'ei No. 1,* 8–14. Moscow: Muzgiz, 1943.
Azov, L. M., and S. A. Shatsillo, eds. *Avtorskoe pravo na literaturnye proizvedeniia: Sbornik ofitsial'nykh materialov.* Moscow: Gosizdat Iuridicheskoi literatury, 1953.
Babichenko, D. L., ed. *Schast'e literatury: Gosudarstvo i pisateli, 1925–1938. Dokumenty.* Moscow: ROSSPEN, 1997.
Barber, J., and M. Harrison. *The Soviet Home Front 1941–1945: A Social and Economic History of the USSR in World War II.* London: Longman, 1991.
Becker, Howard S. *Art Worlds.* Berkeley and Los Angeles: University of California Press, 1985.
Belza, Igor. "Ogolevets, Alexey Stepanovich." In *The New Grove Dictionary of Music and Musicians,* ed. S. Sadie, 13:519–20. New York: Macmillan, 1995.
Bogdanova, A. V., ed. *Pamiati pogibshikh kompozitorov i muzykovedov 1941–1945: Sbornik stat'ei.* Vol. 1. Moscow: Sovetskii kompozitor, 1985.
Brooke, Caroline. "Soviet Musicians and the Great Terror." *Europe-Asia Studies* 54, no. 3 (2002): 397–413.
Brown, Malcolm Hamrick, ed. *A Shostakovich Casebook.* Bloomington: Indiana University Press, 2004.
Brown, Royal S. "The Three Faces of Lady Macbeth." In *Russian and Soviet Music: Essays for Boris Schwartz,* ed. M. H. Brown, 245–52. Ann Arbor: UMI Research Press, 1984.

Clark, Katerina. *The Soviet Novel: History as Ritual.* Chicago: University of Chicago Press, 1985.

Davies, Sarah. *Popular Opinion in Stalin's Russia: Terror, Propaganda, and Dissent, 1934–1941.* Cambridge: Cambridge University Press, 1997.

Dubinsky, Rostislav. *Stormy Applause: Making Music in a Worker's State.* Boston: Northeastern University Press, 1992. First published 1989 by Hill and Wang.

Eastman, Max. *Artists in Uniform: A Study of Literature and Bureaucratism.* New York: Knopf, 1934.

Edele, Mark. "Strange Young Men in Stalin's Moscow: The Birth and Life of the Stiliagi, 1945–1953." *Jahrbücher für Geschichte Osteuropas* 50, no. 1 (2002): 37–61.

XVIII S'ezd Vsesoiuznoi kommunisticheskoi partii (b), Stenograficheskii otchet. Moscow: OGIZ, 1939.

"Ellochka i drugie liudoedki," *Nastoiashchee tainoe* [May 1999], 5–7.

Fay, Laurel. *Shostakovich: A Life.* Oxford: Oxford University Press, 2000.

———. "Shostakovich versus Volkov: Whose Testimony?" *Russian Review* 39, no. 4 (1980): 484–93.

———. "Volkov's Testimony Reconsidered." In *A Shostakovich Casebook,* ed. Malcolm Hamrick Brown, 22–66. Bloomington: Indiana University Press, 2004.

Filtzer, Donald. *Soviet Workers and Late Stalinism: Labour and the Restoration of the Stalinist System after World War II.* Cambridge: Cambridge University Press, 2002.

Fitzpatrick, Sheila. *The Cultural Front: Power and Culture in Revolutionary Russia.* Ithaca: Cornell University Press, 1992.

———. *Everyday Stalinism: Ordinary Life in Extraordinary Times: Soviet Russia in the 1930s.* Oxford: Oxford University Press, 1999.

———. "Intelligentsia and Power: Client-Patron Relations in Stalin's Russia." In *Stalinismus vor dem Zweiten Weltkrieg. Neue Wege der Forschung / Stalinism before the Second World War. New Avenues of Research,* ed. M. Hildermeier and E. Müller-Luckner. Munich: Oldenbourg, 1998.

———. "Supplicants and Citizens: Public Letter-Writing in Soviet Russia in the 1930s." *Slavic Review* 55, no. 1 (Spring 1996): 78–105.

Frid, Grigorii. *Dorogoi ranenoi pamiati.* Moscow: Prosveshchenie, 1994.

Gan, B. M., ed. *Avtorskoe pravo SSSR i RSFSR: Sbornik dekretov i rasporiazhenii i tipovoi izdatel'skii dogovor, utverzhdennyi NKProsom i NKTorgom RSFSR, s alfavitno-predmetnym ukazatelem.* Moscow: Gosizdat, 1929.

Glikman, I. D., ed. *Pis'ma k drugu: Dmitrii Shostakovich—Isaaku Glikmanu.* Moscow: DSCH and Kompozitor, 1993.

Gol'denveizer, A. B. "O Miaskovskom—cheloveke." In Shlifshtein, *N. Ia. Miaskovskii,* 1:254–55.

Gorlizki, Yoram, and Oleg Khlevniuk. *Cold Peace: Stalin and the Soviet Ruling Circle, 1945–1953.* Oxford: Oxford University Press, 2004.

Gozenpud, A. A. "Ideia zashchity Rodiny v russkom iskusstve." In *Sovetskaia muzyka: Vtoroi sbornik stat'ei.* Moscow: Muzgiz, 1944.

Grinberg, M., and N. Poliakova. *Sovetskaia opera: sbornik kriticheskikh statei.* Moscow: Gosudarstvennoe muzykal'noe izdatel'stvo, 1953.

Grüner, Frank. "Juden und Sowjetstaat, 1941–1953. Vom öffentlichen Verschweigen der nationalsozialistischen Verbrechen an den Juden bis zur politischen Instrumentalisierung des Antisemitismus durch die sowjetische Staats- und Parteiführung." Ph.D. diss., University of Heidelberg, 2002.

Harris, James. *Great Urals: Regionalism and the Evolution of the Soviet System.* Ithaca: Cornell University Press, 1999.

Hessler, Julie. *A Social History of Soviet Trade: Trade Policy, Retail Practices, and Consumption, 1917–1953.* Princeton: Princeton University Press, 2004.

Ho, Allan, and Dmitry Feofanov. *Biographical Dictionary of Russian/Soviet Composers.* New York: Greenwood, 1989.

Jelagin, Juri. *Taming of the Arts.* Trans. N. Wreden. New York: E. P. Dutton, 1951.

Joravsky, David. *The Lysenko Affair.* Cambridge: Harvard University Press, 1970.

Jowitt, Ken. *New World Disorder: The Leninist Extinction.* Berkeley and Los Angeles: University of California Press, 1992.

Kabalevskii, Dmitrii. "O N. Ia. Miaskovskom." In Shlifshtein, *N. Ia. Miaskovskii,* 1:307–33.

Kabalevskii, D. B., et al., eds. *S. S. Prokof'ev i N. Ia. Miaskovskii: Perepiska.* Moscow: Sovetskii kompozitor, 1977.

Keldysh, Iu. V. *Istoriia muzyki narodov SSSR, Tom II (1932–1941).* Moscow: Sovetskii kompozitor, 1970.

Khachaturian, A. I. "Iz vospominanii." In Shlifshtein, *N. Ia. Miaskovskii,* 1:301–2.

———. "Master—Grazhdanin—Chelovek." In *Aram Khachaturian: Stat'i i vospominaniia,* edited by I. E. Popova, 189. Moscow: Sovetskii kompozitor, 1980.

———. "Muzyka i narod." In *Aram Khachaturian: Stat'i i vospominaniia,* edited by I. E. Popova, 9–30. Moscow: Sovetskii kompozitor, 1980.

———. *Vtoraia simfoniia.* Partitura. Moscow: Muzgiz, 1962.

Khentova, Sofiia. *Shostakovich: Zhizn' i tvorchestvo.* Leningrad: Sovetskii kompozitor, 1986.

Khrennikov, Tikhon. *Tak eto bylo: Tikhon Khrennikov o vremeni i o sebe.* Moscow: Muzyka, 1994.

Kojevnikov, Alexei. "Games of Stalinist Democracy: Ideological Discussions in Soviet Sciences, 1947–52." In *Stalinism: New Directions,* edited by Sheila Fitzpatrick, 142–76. New York: Routledge, 2000.

Kornai, Janos. *Economics of Shortage.* Amsterdam: North Holland, 1980.

Kostyrchenko, Gennadi. *Out of the Red Shadows: Anti-Semitism in Stalin's Russia.* Amherst, NY: Prometheus, 1995.

———. *Tainaia politika Stalina: vlast' i antisemitism.* Moscow: Mezhdunarodnaia otnosheniia, 2001.

Krementsov, Nikolai. *The Cure: A Story of Cancer and Politics from the Annals of the Cold War.* Chicago: University of Chicago Press, 2002.

———. *Stalinist Science.* Princeton: Princeton University Press, 1997.

Ledeneva, Alena. *Russia's Economy of Favors: Blat, Networking and Informal Exchange.* Cambridge: Cambridge University Press, 1998.

"Leonid Brumberg," http://www.musikseminar.music.at/pers/brumberg_l.html (accessed March 2000).

MacDonald, Ian. *The New Shostakovich.* London: Fourth Estate, 1990.

Maksimenkov, Leonid. "Partiia—nash rulevoi," *Muzykal'naia zhizn',* no. 13–14 (1993): 6–8; no. 15–16 (1993): 8–10.

———. *Sumbur vmesto muzyki: Stalinskaia kul'turnaia revoliutsiia, 1936–1938.* Moscow: Iuridicheskaia kniga, 1997.

Martynov, I. "Novye kamernye sochineniia Shostakovicha." In *Sovetskaia muzyka: Sbornik stat'ei No. 5.* Moscow: Muzgiz, 1946.

———. "Rozhdennaia burei (O Sedmoi simfonii D. Shostakovicha)." In *Sovetskaia muzyka: Sbornik stat'ei No. 1,* 41–47. Moscow: Muzgiz, 1943.

Mendel'son-Prokof'eva, M. "O Sergee Sergeeviche Prokof'eve." In *S. S. Prokof'ev: Materialy, dokumenty, vospominaniia,* 2nd ed., edited by S. I. Shlifshtein. Moscow: Gosmuzizdat, 1961.

Minchenok, Dmitrii. *Isaak Dunaevskii: Bol'shoi kontsert.* Moscow: Olimp, 1998.

"Muzyka i muzykanty nashikh dnei." In *Sovetskaia muzyka: Sbornik stat'ei No. 1,* 3–4. Moscow: Muzgiz, 1943.

Muzykal'naia entsiklopediia. Moscow: Sovetskaia entsiklopediia, 1973–82.

Nelson, Amy. *Music for the Revolution: Musicians and Power in Early Soviet Russia.* University Park: Pennsylvania State University Press, 2004.

Ogolevets, A. S. *Vvedenie v sovremennoe muzykal'noe myshlenie.* Moscow: Muzgiz, 1946.

Olkhovsky, Andrey. *Music under the Soviets: The Agony of an Art.* New York: Praeger, 1955.

Osokina, Elena. *Za fasadom "Stalinskogo izobiliia": Raspredelenie i rynok v snabzhenii naseleniia v gody industrializatsii, 1937–1941.* Moscow: ROSSPEN, 1998.

Paperno, Dmitry. *Notes of a Moscow Pianist.* Portland, OR: Amadeus, 1998.

Pervyi vsesoiuznyi s'ezd sovetskiskh pisatelei, 1934: Stenograficheskii otchet. Moscow: Gosizdat Khudozhestvennaia literatura, 1934.

Peteri, György. "Purge and Patronage: Kádár's Counter-revolution and the Field of Economic Research in Hungary, 1957–58," *Contemporary European History* 11, no. 1 (2002): 125–52.

Polianovskii, G. A., ed. *Sovetskie kompozitory—frontu: Samootchety-vospominaniia.* Moscow: Sovetskii kompozitor, 1989.

Pollock, Ethan. "The Politics of Knowledge: Party Ideology and Soviet Science, 1945–1953." Ph.D. diss., University of California, Berkeley, 2000.

"Postanovlenie TsK VKP(b) ot 2 avgusta 1946 g., O podgotovke i perepodgotovke rukovodiashchikh partiinykh i sovetskikh rabotnikov." In *KPSS v rezoliutsiiakh i resheniiakh s'ezdov, konferentsii i plenumov TsK,* 3:476–84. Moscow: Gos. Izd. Politicheskoi literatury, 1954.

Potter, Pamela. *Most German of the Arts: Musicology and Society from the Weimar Republic to the End of Hitler's Reich.* New Haven: Yale University Press, 1998.

"Proizvedenie Shostakovicha—gluboko zapadnoi orientatsii," *Staraia ploshchad': Vestnik Arkhiva Prezidenta Rossiiskoi Federatsii* 1995, no. 5:156–59.

Prokof'ev, Sergei. *"1940–i god:" Simfonicheskaia siuita. Partitura.* Moscow: Muzgiz, 1973.

———. *Sobranie sochinenii.* Vol. 14b, *Piataia simfoniia, soch. 100.* Moscow: Muzgiz, 1963.

Prokofjew, Sergej. *Sinfonie Nr. 5, Op. 100.* Leipzig: Edition Peters, [1970?].

Riauzov, S. N. "Muzyka v plenu." In *Muzyka na frontakh Velikoi otechestvennoi voiny,* edited by G. Pozhidaev. Moscow: Muzyka, 1970.

Rigby, T. H. *Communist Party Membership in the U.S.S.R., 1917–1967.* Princeton: Princeton University Press, 1968.

Robinson, Harlow. *Sergei Prokofiev: A Biography.* New York: Viking, 1987.

Rothstein, Robert A. "Homeland, Home Town, and Battlefield: The Popular Song." In *Culture and Entertainment in Wartime Russia,* edited by Richard Stites, 77–94. Bloomington: Indiana University Press, 1995.

Rubin, V. I. *Bol'shoi Teatr: Pervye postanovki oper na russkoi stsene, 1825–1993.* Moscow: Izd. Ellis Lak, 1994.

Rubinstein, Joshua, and Vladimir P. Naumov, eds. *Stalin's Secret Pogrom: The Postwar Inquisition of the Jewish Anti-Fascist Committee.* Trans. L. E. Wolfson. New Haven: Yale University Press, 2001.

Salisbury, Harrison. *The 900 Days: The Siege of Leningrad.* New York: Harper and Row, 1969.

Sargeant, Lynn. "A New Class of People: The Conservatoire and Musical Professionalization in Russia, 1861–1917," *Music and Letters* 85, no. 1 (2004): 41–61.

———. "*Kashchei the Immortal: Liberal Politics, Cultural Memory, and the Rimsky-Korsakov Scandal of 1905,*" *Russian Review* 64, no. 1 (2005): 22–43.

Schostakowitsch, Dmitri. *9. Symphonie, op. 70. Taschenpartitur.* Hamburg: Musikverlage Hans Sikorski, [1991].

Schwarz, Boris. *Music and Musical Life in Soviet Russia, 1917–1970.* Bloomington: Indiana University Press, 1972.

———. *Music and Musical Life in Soviet Russia, 1917–1981,* enl. ed. Bloomington: Indiana University Press, 1983.

Sewell, William H., Jr. "A Theory of Structure: Duality, Agency, and Transformation," *American Journal of Sociology* 98, no. 1 (July 1992): 1–29.

Shakhnazarova, N. G. *Paradoksy sovetskoi muzykal'noi kul'tury 30–e gody.* Moscow: Gosudarstvennyi institut iskusstvoznaniia, Izdatel'stvo Indrik, 2001.

Shebalin, Vissarion. "Iz vospominanii o Nikolae Iakovleviche Miaskovskom." In Shlifshtein, *N. Ia. Miaskovskii,* 1:276–98.

Shlifshtein, S., ed. *N. Ia. Miaskovskii: Sobranie materialov v dvukh tomakh.* 2nd ed. Moscow: Muzyka, 1964.

Shostakovich, Dmitri. *Symphony No. 7, Op. 60.* Leipzig: Edition Peters, [1971].

Shostakovich, Dmitrii. *Sobranie sochinenii.* Vol. 4, *Simfoniia No. 7. Simfoniia No. 8. Partitura.* Moscow: Muzyka, 1981.

——. *Sobranie sochinenii.* Vol. 5, *Simfoniia No. 9. Simfoniia No. 10. Partitura.* Moscow: Muzyka, 1979.

Silina, Elena. "Veniamin Fleishman, Uchenik Shostakovicha." In *Shostakovich mezhdu mgnoveniem i vechnost'iu: Dokumenty, materialy, stat'i,* edited by L. G. Kovnatskaia. St. Petersburg: Kompozitor, 2000.

Simmons, Cynthia, and Nina Perlina, eds. *Writing the Siege of Leningrad: Women's Diaries, Memoirs, and Documentary Prose.* Pittsburgh: University of Pittsburgh Press, 2002.

Smith, Susannah Lockwood. "Soviet Arts Policy, Folk Music, and National Identity: The Piatnitskii State Russian Folk Choir, 1927–1945." Ph.D. diss., University of Minnesota, 1997.

Soveshchanie deiatelei sovetskoi muzyki v TsK VKP(b). Moscow: Pravda, 1948.

Spravochnik Soiuza sovetskikh kompozitorov SSSR na 1957 god. Moscow: Sovetskii kompozitor, 1957.

Stalin, I. V. *Sochineniia.* Vol. 13. Moscow: Gosizdat Politicheskoi literatury, 1951.

Starr, S. Frederick. *Red and Hot: The Fate of Jazz in the Soviet Union, 1917–1980.* New York: Oxford University Press, 1983.

Stites, Richard. "Frontline Entertainment." In *Culture and Entertainment in Wartime Russia,* edited by Richard Stites, 126–40. Bloomington: Indiana University Press, 1995.

Taruskin, Richard. *Defining Russia Musically: Historical and Hermeneutical Essays.* Princeton: Princeton University Press, 1997.

Tomoff, Kiril. "Creative Union: The Professional Organization of Soviet Composers, 1939–1953." Ph.D. diss., University of Chicago, 2001.

——. "The Illegitimacy of Popularity: Soviet Composers and the Royalties Administration, 1939–1953," *Russian History/Histoire Russe* 27, no. 3 (Fall 2000): 311–40.

——. "Uzbek Music's Separate Path: Interpreting 'Anti-Cosmopolitanism' in Stalinist Central Asia, 1949–52," *Russian Review* 63, no. 2 (April 2004): 212–40.

Verdery, Katherine. *National Ideology under Socialism: Identity and Cultural Politics in Ceausescu's Romania.* Berkeley and Los Angeles: University of California Press, 1991.

Vishnevskaia, Galina. *Galina: Istoriia zhizni.* Moscow: Gorizont, 1993.

Vlasov, Vladimir. "Nikolai Iakovlevich Miaskovskii slushaet muzyku." In Shlifshtein, *N. Ia. Miaskovskii,* 1:351–55.

Volkov, Solomon. *Shostakovich and Stalin: The Extraordinary Relationship between the Great Composer and the Brutal Dictator.* New York: Knopf, 2004.

——. *Testimony: The Memoirs of Dmitry Shostakovich as Related to and Edited by Solomon Volkov.* Trans. A. W. Bouis. New York: Harper and Row, 1979.

Vsesoiuznyi s'ezd sovetskikh kompozitorov: Stenograficheskii otchet. Moscow: Izvestiia, 1948.

Vucinich, Alexander. *Empire of Knowledge: The Academy of Sciences of the USSR (1917–1970).* Berkeley and Los Angeles: University of California Press, 1984.

Waddington, Ivan. "Professions." In *The Social Science Encyclopedia,* 2nd ed., edited by A. Kuper and J. Kuper, 677–78. London: Routledge, 1996.

Walder, Andrew G. *Communist Neo-traditionalism: Work and Authority in Chinese Industry.* Berkeley and Los Angeles: University of California Press, 1988.

Walker, Barbara. "*Kruzhok* Culture: The Meaning of Patronage in the Early Soviet Literary World," *Contemporary European History* 11, no. 1 (February 2002): 107–24.

Weiner, Amir. *Making Sense of War: The Second World War and the Fate of the Bolshevik Revolution.* Princeton: Princeton University Press, 2001.

Werth, Alexander. *Musical Uproar in Moscow.* London: Turnstile, 1949.

Willerton, John. *Patronage and Politics in the USSR.* Cambridge: Cambridge University Press, 1992.

Wilson, Elizabeth. *Shostakovich: A Life Remembered.* Princeton: Princeton University Press, 1994.

Index

Page numbers in italics refer to tables.